TITANIC LEGACY

THE CAPTAIN, THE DAUGHTER
AND THE SPY

TITANIC LEGACY

The Captain, the Daughter and the Spy

DAN E. PARKES

AMBERLEY

In memory of Tina and of Brian.
A dearest mother and a closest friend.

First published 2025

Amberley Publishing
The Hill, Stroud
Gloucestershire, GL5 4EP

www.amberley-books.com

Copyright © Dan E. Parkes, 2025

The right of Dan E. Parkes to be identified as the Author
of this work has been asserted in accordance with the
Copyright, Designs and Patents Act 1988.

All rights reserved. No part of this book may be reprinted
or reproduced or utilised in any form or by any electronic,
mechanical or other means, now known or hereafter invented,
including photocopying and recording, or in any information
storage or retrieval system, without the permission in writing
from the Publishers.

British Library Cataloguing in Publication Data.
A catalogue record for this book is available from the British Library.

ISBN 978 1 3981 2435 6 (hardback)
ISBN 978 1 3981 2436 3 (ebook)

1 2 3 4 5 6 7 8 9 10

Typeset in 10.5pt on 13.5pt Sabon.
Typesetting by SJmagic DESIGN SERVICES, India.
Printed in the UK.

Contents

Foreword by Gary Cooper — 7
Prologue: The Riddle — 10

Part One – The Captain
1 Cities of the Sea — 14
2 Playing on *Titanic*'s Bridge — 41
3 The Convergence of the Twain — 102
4 'In the Hands of the Evil One' — 166
5 'A Deathless Crown at Duty's Post' — 191

Part Two – The Spy
6 London Life — 234
7 Cookie — 241
8 'Ambitious and Adventurous' — 262
9 An 'Inexplicable' Shooting — 287

Part Three – The Daughter
10 A Penalty, a Fire and a Collision — 306
11 Aviatrix and a Twin Tragedy — 315
12 Leafield Life — 336
13 The 'Remarkable Lady' — 354

Epilogue: The Legacy of Captain Smith — 365
Recommended Reading — 367
Acknowledgements — 368
Endnotes — 371
Index — 408

Foreword
by Gary Cooper

It seems so very long ago now that I wrote what I genuinely thought were my final words on the life of Commander Edward John Smith, the erstwhile captain of RMS *Titanic*. As his biographer, mine had been an odyssey of research into his life that had lasted, on and off, for over two decades. The final result of my research was *Titanic Captain: The Life of Edward John Smith*, published in late 2011, just in time for the centenary of the sinking. The reviews of my book were pleasing, it earned me my 15 minutes of fame and I gave my fair share of interviews and talks in its wake, but after all the fuss had died down I gladly relaxed back into obscurity, left Smith and *Titanic* to be explored and argued over by others and moved on to new subjects.

That said, like any doting parent, I've often felt the need since to see how my offspring is faring and have occasionally revisited the *Titanic* world, writing up an article or two, answering questions when asked, or just popping in to see how the information is disseminating. I'm happy to say that a number of books and academic essays have drawn on my work, which makes the whole effort worthwhile, and though I take a much dimmer view of productions on the internet, I have found some websites that have used my research faithfully, one of these being Dan Parkes' 'Titanic's Officers'.

I first came across his site in early 2021 and was pleased to discover that it comprised a set of well written biographies exploring the lives and careers of the men on the bridge of that doomed vessel. Naturally, I read the biography of Smith and was pleased to find that it was not too long or speculative, was very well illustrated and peppered with some delightful snippets that I'd not encountered before – I had to laugh at a story of a mahogany toilet seat touted as having belonged to

Captain Smith – ah, the gems I missed! Anyhow, I liked what I saw and I wrote to Dan saying how much I enjoyed his site. He was good enough to reply and we began corresponding. At first, we chatted occasionally on matters relating to his website, but about a year in he mentioned that he had come across new information on the life of Smith's daughter, Melville, and her husband, which he hoped initially to turn into an article. This, however, snowballed into the book before you and when Dan and his wife Itsuka paid a visit to Stoke early in 2023, we met up and he filled me in on the details of his tale and I was honoured to be asked to write this foreword to it.

Dan's book focuses on the legacy of the *Titanic* disaster for Captain Smith and his family, a subject I only lightly touched upon in my work. He has described his book as 'a sequel of sorts' to mine, but that does it a great disservice, as in truth it is more a family portrait. His account begins with a short biography of Edward Smith, plus a study of the *Titanic* disaster and its fallout on the captain's reputation. This section adds further to our knowledge of the man. Indeed, I must admit to a certain envy over some of the stories Dan has unearthed, tales that would have fitted very nicely into my own work.

The rest of the book does though follow on pretty much where I left off and a fascinating saga it is too, much of it previously unknown, that nicely rounds out the story of the Smith family. While Captain Smith is the central character in the first part, the hero of the latter is undoubtedly his daughter, Melville, who would go on to enjoy a very full and adventurous life that in some ways equalled or outdid her father's. Central to her story is her marriage to Sidney Russell Cooke, a wealthy stockbroker with a shadowy past that Dan explores in great detail. Cooke's is a very involved tale and one has to wonder when reading the account just how much Mel knew about her husband's affairs, and what she thought of his curious, untimely death, which excited such a great deal of speculation at the time.

Further tragedies followed. The sad, accidental death of her mother, Eleanor, then the loss of both of her children to war and illness left Mel alone, the last survivor of the Smith line, but she did not retreat from the world, or let her life be measured by the sorrows she had endured. She downsized and plunged back in, hosting parties at her new home and indulging in her many and varied passions, while in the 1950s when interest in the *Titanic* was rekindled, she played her part in adding gloss to the story.

Indeed, Mel's tale brings the *Titanic*'s story full circle, from the sad days following the disaster, through the lean years when people just tried to forget and forgive, to that point in the 1950s when she put pen to

Foreword

paper and recalled what she could of her father for Walter Lord, author of *A Night to Remember*, the book that arguably heralded *Titanic*'s passage into popular culture. More books followed, films were made, but in the resulting mix of fact and fiction the story of Captain Smith was subsumed. I attempted to change that and tell the real tale of Smith and his family and Dan now greatly expands upon and concludes that history. And as befits a professional cameraman and film-maker, he does so not only in words, but in pictures, for if you add to his engrossing biographical research the wealth of images that Dan has collected together – many of them not previously published – then you have a family album for this Smith family history that is very impressive.

Gary Cooper
Stoke-on-Trent 2025

PROLOGUE

The Riddle

Shortly after 8 o'clock on the morning of Thursday, 3 July 1930, Miss Ada Fancy from West Kensington noted that it was unusually quiet at number 12 King's Bench Walk. Situated in the Temple area of central London, it was a leafy business district, the buildings primarily given over to the legal profession. Overheard conversations were almost always unintelligible, but today she heard no hushed talking, or any noise at all for that matter. Just the distant sounds of London as its population readied itself for another day of work.

The 21-year-old housemaid, Miss Fancy, had gone into the kitchenette and prepared a glass of orangeade, just as she had many times before, the refreshing summer drink made of freshly squeezed orange and lemon juice with some sugar, mixed to her employer's taste. She had worked there for just on a year. As she navigated the hallway, her footsteps were the only sound in the second-floor apartment. The stillness of the morning was not entirely surprising. There was no one else in the building; neighbours in the chambers above were away and below were just empty barrister offices. For the last year she had been the maid of a vibrant woman in her thirties who was presently away in a Paddington nursing home, resting after a minor operation. Her handsome and wealthy husband had only just visited his wife the night before and returned home to no.12 expressing no concern. So it was that Miss Fancy was alone on the second floor of the spacious and beautifully furnished flat, except for the husband to whom she was bringing his daily glass of orangeade.

As she approached his living quarters, she instantly realised something was amiss. His bedroom door was open and the bed – although showing signs of having been slept in – was empty. Growing increasingly concerned, she walked toward the sitting room. The door was shut.

The Riddle

Holding the glass in one hand she knocked on the door, announcing she had his usual morning drink. There was no response. She tried a little louder, but the result was the same. The door was unlocked so she slowly opened it. Through the doorway she caught sight of a protruding foot. She could see he was still in his pyjamas. This was not at all usual. She hurried into the room and found him on his back, on the floor, in his dressing gown. Her eyes snatched a glance at a double-barrelled hunting gun on the sofa, but not before she saw the blood. There was a massive wound to the left of his stomach and a large pool of blood had formed around his body. His face was transfixed upward, eyes devoid of life. She dropped the glass of orangeade and screamed.

For a moment Miss Fancy was frozen, unsure what to do next, overwhelmed with shock and nausea. Her deafening scream reverberated throughout the Bath Stone chambers of King's Bench Walk, but no one responded. She needed to get help. She stumbled out of the room and rushed down the stairs, almost tripping over her own feet, still screaming uncontrollably. She burst onto the street, her scream cutting through the crisp morning air. Still, no one responded. Then in the distance, her bleary eyes focused on the dark silhouette of a man walking briskly along the pavement. He had a black officer's cap and a navy-coloured uniform, but the white bag over his shoulder quickly revealed he was not a police officer. He was a Royal Mail postman, out delivering the Temple mail. Miss Fancy rushed up to him and blurted out that she needed immediate help. The stunned postman heard something about a gun and immediately found the nearest telephone and called the police.

Within minutes, police officers were running up the steps to the second floor and entered the sitting room to be greeted by the mysterious scene of horror. It was immediately established there was no need to call any emergency medical personnel. Police sergeant Bruty, presiding over the crime scene, requested the officers call for Dr Westerman, a police surgeon, to establish a cause of death.

The victim was 37-year-old Sidney Russell Cooke. A stockbroker and author, he was the husband of Captain Edward John Smith's only daughter, Helen Melville, commonly known to friends as 'Mel'. The *Titanic* connection was not the only remarkable thing about him. Unknown to many, he was also a British spy, described as a 'prototype James Bond' – and the lover of famous Cambridge economist John Maynard Keynes.

Mel, recovering in a nursing home in Paddington, did not immediately hear of her husband's death. It was the matron, Miss Sinclair, who had the unenviable task of breaking the news. For the next few days, newspaper headlines would cover the story of the 'Stockbroker Shot Dead' with photographs of a smiling Sidney on the front page, along with tag lines such as 'inexplicable' and the 'riddle of a rich man's fate'. Within days, the mysterious death quickly disappeared from public consciousness as the country became gripped by an economic contagion that would later be called The Great Depression.

The shocking death of her husband of eight years was the beginning of a series of tragedies for Mel. Less than a year later, her mother, Eleanor, the *Titanic* captain's partially blind widow, was struck by a taxicab outside her Kensington home. She was holding an umbrella in the rain at the time and only a couple of months shy of her seventieth birthday when she died. Then Mel's non-identical twins both died – Simon in action as an RAF pilot in 1944 (crashing into the sea) and Priscilla from polio in 1947 just a year after getting married. This meant that Mel's father, mother, husband, son, and daughter all died in tragic circumstances before she was 49. Mel herself died in 1973, aged 75.

Captain Smith's lineage ended on that day. But Mel's 75 years were not simply punctuated by tragedy; she led a full life, growing up with a loving and attentive father, becoming a private pilot, a driver of fast cars, an artist's muse and collector of fine art, and living within a 'family' of suffragettes, politicians, royalty, Russian spies, yachtsmen, gay lovers and the spectacularly wealthy.

This is the intriguing story of a legendary captain, who ironically once said he was 'not very good material for a story', and of a daughter who stepped out of the shadow of misfortune to carve her own path, who, until now, has been mostly a footnote in history. It is a legacy that is truly Titanic.

===== PART ONE =====

The Captain

Figure 1: Captain Edward John Smith (1850–1912) of the White Star Line in an undated photograph, likely during the 1890s. (Courtesy of the University Photograph Collection, RG 145, Robert S. Cox Special Collections and University Archives Research Center, UMass Amherst Libraries)

1

Cities of the Sea

For many years, the only known photograph of Eleanor and Mel was taken when they were very young, Mel a young fresh-faced child on the knee, with curly hair (Figure 3). Eleanor looks a little uncomfortable, eyes averted from the camera, a hint of a strained smile. It was taken during the time they were living in Liverpool. Mel was born eleven years into Eleanor's marriage to Edward Smith, who had become master of the White Star liner *Majestic* based in Liverpool and would captain her for seven years (1895–1902), his longest command. It was during this time that Helen Melville Smith was born at the family home, 20 Alexandra Road, in Waterloo, Liverpool, on Saturday, 2 April 1898.

There was a brief announcement in the local newspaper the following Saturday in the Births, Marriages and Deaths column of *The Liverpool Weekly Courier* on 9 April 1898: 'Smith – April 2, at 20, Alexandra-road, Waterloo, the wife of E. J. Smith, of a daughter.[1] Edward would later officially register the birth on 3 May 1898.

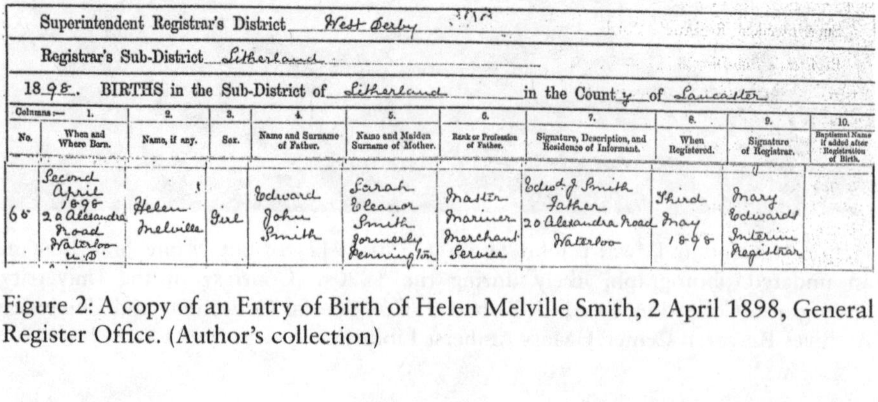

Superintendent Registrar's District West Derby

Registrar's Sub-District Litherland

1898. BIRTHS in the Sub-District of Litherland in the County of Lancaster

Columns:—	1.	2.	3.	4.	5.	6.	7.	8.	9.	10.
No.	When and Where Born.	Name, if any.	Sex.	Name and Surname of Father.	Name and Maiden Surname of Mother.	Rank or Profession of Father.	Signature, Description, and Residence of Informant.	When Registered.	Signature of Registrar.	Baptismal Name if added after Registration of Birth.
65	Second April 1898 20 Alexandra Road Waterloo U.D.	Helen Melville	Girl	Edward John Smith	Sarah Eleanor Smith formerly Pennington	Master Mariner Merchant Service	Edwd. J. Smith Father 20 Alexandra Road Waterloo	Third May 1898	Mary Edwards Interim Registrar	

Figure 2: A copy of an Entry of Birth of Helen Melville Smith, 2 April 1898, General Register Office. (Author's collection)

Figure 3: Sarah Eleanor Smith and daughter Helen Melville Smith, photographed in Liverpool *c.* 1900. Variations of this image were used in newspapers at the time of the *Titanic* disaster. (Author's collection)

Mel was a 'late' child. Her parents, Edward and Eleanor, had married eleven years prior and she would be their only one. Edward became a father at the age of 48 (born 27 January 1850) and Eleanor was 36 years old (born 17 June 1861).

Authors have varying views on the origin of the rather masculine name 'Melville'. Researcher John Pladdys claims it was due to her parent's love of Scotland, where the name of the Melville clan is popular.[2] Descendent Pat Lacey takes it a step further and writes in her dramatised novel that it derived from Melville House in Fife, where she believes the Smiths had holidayed in the past.[3] Others believe it was a tribute to one of Ted Smith's favourite authors, Herman Melville, author of *Moby Dick*. Nevertheless, as sometimes happened in those days, her middle name was used and henceforth her friends referred to her as Mel. Her mother Eleanor followed the same custom – her first name was Sarah. Edward would later use other names for his only daughter: he referred to her as his 'Gillie' (or girly) according to a letter written by Eleanor in 1912.[4] Or maybe his 'Babs', his baby.[5]

Labourer to 'Millionaires' Captain'

Edward Smith's was in many ways an inspiring rag-to-riches story. The legendary 'Millionaires' Captain', as he would later be known, was born to working class parents (his father a pottery presser and his mother a grocer) in a relatively poor area of Staffordshire, England, in a small town called Hanley, part of Stoke-on-Trent. Due to its local craft, the area is known as 'the Potteries' and young Edward – or Ted or as he was sometimes called – was destined to follow his father in the same career – were it not for some inspiration. He had an older half-brother from his mother's previous marriage named Joseph Hancock (1833–1893), who was then a captain, having already joined the Merchant Navy when Edward was born. Regaled by stories of life at sea, young Edward changed occupations from a labourer at age 15 to an ordinary sailor, aged 17, relocating to Liverpool, the seafaring centre of Great Britain. Mrs O'Donnell, who knew young Ted 'when he was a tyke who loved to wade barefoot into the combers on the beach', remembered that 'after that first voyage Ted returned home to thrill the youth of the town with his stories of having sailed to America, of his experience in California ... and with his mind firmly made up to spend the rest of his days on the ocean... From his boyhood days... he felt a strong attachment for the sailor's life.[6]

Nepotism had its place early in his career, quickly gaining promotion to Third Mate on his first voyage aboard the *Senator Weber* with his half-brother as master, after fourteen men deserted ship. This taste of rank likely prompted Smith to gain the requisite qualifications and within ten years he obtained his Second, First and Master Board of Trade certificates and gained first command of his own sailing ship, the *Lizzie Fennell*, at the tender age of 25. His age naturally subject to some ribbing by the older men under his command, Smith responded by saying that youth was something he would soon grow out of.[7]

Four years later, Smith saw the White Star Line's *Britannic* in Liverpool, a steamship that had broken transatlantic records, and he promptly arranged a tour that confirmed to him this was the future. He was willing to bet his career on it. On 1 March 1880, he joined the White Star Line. This resulted in an instant loss of rank; he had to drop from Captain all the way back to Fourth Officer aboard his first White Star Line steam vessel, the *Celtic*, an iron steamship with four masts and one funnel. It took another eight years before he returned to captain, when he was officially made the master of the aging *Baltic* on 27 March 1888, for two transatlantic runs.

During his time as an officer and chief officer, Ted established a fine reputation among his colleagues. A Mr G. A. Capen from California remembered Smith from when he was Second Officer on the *Coptic* on the San Francisco to Hong Kong run (1882–1884), calling him a credit to the company, 'for he was the ablest man on the *Coptic*'s payroll. He once wrote in my album the words 'Nil desperandum,"[8] 'never despair'.'

One fellow officer from 1885 to 1887 (while aboard the *Republic*), R. V. Wagner, remembered Smith as 'without exception one of the most charming men I ever met; he had a free-and-easy, at the same time gentlemanly manner, which immediately gave one the impression that he was superior to the average ship's officer.' Wagner gave an example of an occasion when he joined the ship 'in which Smith was chief ... we had never met before, but the moment he saw me, he came towards me with a few strides, a charming smile all over his face, and heartily shaking my hand, said, 'Hello, Wagner, pleased to meet you – heard a good deal about you – so glad you are joining this ship – come in and make yourself comfortable.' I there and then decided he was a splendid fellow, and I never had reason to change my opinion.' Another officer commented: 'Smith is a funny fellow – always praises up other people, but never has a word to say about himself.' Wagner considered this a 'rare quality, so seldom found in people, which I greatly admired in Smith'. This extended to Chief Officer Smith asking his brother officers in the mess-room 'not to criticise or ridicule the doings of the old man (the captain) – a rather favourite subject with some officers'. Wagner also remembered that Smith was the first into a lifeboat to rescue a vessel in heavy seas, and

Figure 4: A young E.J. Smith, as included in the article 'The Masters of the Sea' in *Town & Country*, 19 April 1902. (Courtesy of Gregg Jasper)

conscientiously ensuring everything of value was taken out of damaged lifeboats before they were thrown overboard.⁹

These admirable qualities were not only gaining the attention of his fellow officers. In April 1887, he had been temporarily promoted from Chief Officer to Captain aboard the SS *Republic*, hinting at things to come. Although that year bwas important for more than career progression. He had met a young woman named Eleanor.

On Thursday the 13th of January 1887, Smith married Sarah Eleanor Pennington at St Oswald's Church in Winwick, Lancashire. It was a logical location considering that Eleanor's family had owned a farm named Woodhead in Winwick for four generations, although by the time of their wedding her father, William Pennington, had passed away.

In the Gerard Chapel section of the church there is a photocopy of a parish register entry that records their marriage; sadly, the original was stolen some time ago. It contains some interesting details, such as that the wedding was attended by five witnesses (Thomas Jones, Joseph Hancock, Maria Annie Pennington, William Pennington and Mary Jowitt Rooke), rather than the required two, both the bride and groom's father are noted as deceased and that Edward was at the time residing at Tuebrook, Winwick. Smith had been living at 45 Osbourne Road, Tuebrook, a small house on the outskirts of Liverpool city, but that was soon to change.[10] Smith biographer Gary Cooper specifically places the newlyweds first

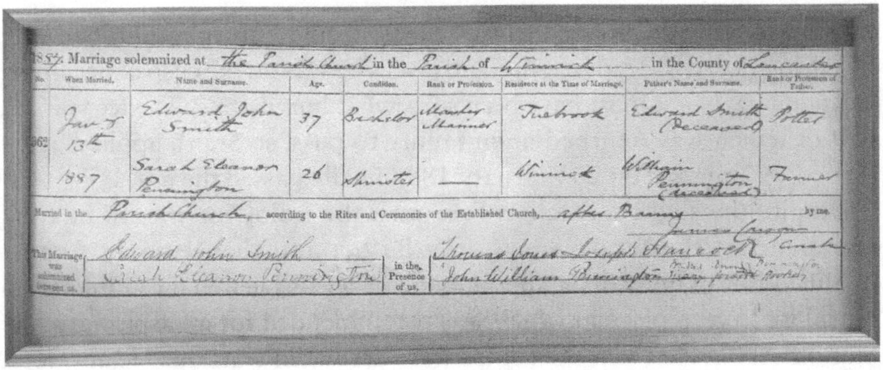

Figure 5: A photocopy of Ted and Eleanor's marriage certificate on display at the church of St Oswald, Winwick; the original was stolen. (Photograph by Paul Van Doodson)

at Spa Well Cottage, (Delph Lane, Houghton Green, Warrington), after which they moved to the more convenient location of Liverpool city.[11]

It was not all success for Edward, or Teddy, as Eleanor came to call him. On 14 February 1888, Smith decided to top his Master certification by sitting for the voluntary Extra Master's certificate, the highest and most difficult of mariner qualifications. Rather infamously, he failed in Navigation, a fact that would later haunt post-disaster appraisals of his abilities. It was a rare occasion that perhaps hinted at his landlocked heritage. The sea was not 'in his blood', as it was for some of his colleagues. William McMaster Murdoch, from Dalbeattie, Scotland, who would be his reliable First Officer for the large steam liners later in his career (the *Adriatic*, *Olympic* and *Titanic*) never once failed a Board of Trade exam – even skipping his Masters to sit for his Extra Masters and passing on first attempt. But then Murdoch came from a long and notable line of Scottish seafarers who sailed the world's oceans as early as the nineteenth century; William's father and grandfather were both sea captains, as were four of his grandfather's brothers.

It must be appreciated that the competency test was not an easy one. Dave Gittens, in an aptly named article entitled 'Could you make it to Extra Master?' noted that the exam took 26 hours spread over five days and included the solving of complex problems such as spherical trigonometry. The candidate also had to write essays on subjects such as tropical revolving storms and celestial navigation, along with associated diagrams. After a final oral examination, the candidate was immediately informed of his fate.[12]

Smith's failure in Navigation was not unique. Aboard *Titanic*, his Chief Officer Henry Wilde, Second Officer Charles Ligtholler and Fourth Officer Joseph Boxhall, had all failed on their first attempts at obtaining an Extra

Master's certificate. But as this was the first time Edward Smith had ever failed any Board of Trade exam – and just as he was on the cusp of becoming a captain again – it must have been somewhat humiliating. The fee was £2, half of which was returned upon failure to pass, so Smith applied again three days later and on 20 February 1888 finally passed the test.

Despite the slight setback in February, the following month he took command of the White Star Line's *Baltic*, and then later in August qualified for an immediate appointment as a full Lieutenant in the Royal Naval Reserve, a place in which was recommended for all aspiring White Star officers in the event their ships were needed in wartime. He also took command of the *Britannic* in 1888 – the ship that had inspired him to embark on a career at the White Star Line. One passenger, a Henry Martyn Hart, would later remember Smith commenting on his approach to ice:

> I sailed home in the *Britannic*, with Captain Edward Smith, with whom I became very friendly. One day standing on the bridge, we were in the neighborhood of ice and I asked him what his custom was in such water? He said, 'I go as fast as I can for by so doing I shorten the time of danger, and if we are so unfortunate as to strike a 'berg, it would only be a matter of three minutes difference in going down, between low speed and high speed.' He had evidently held to his custom when he Captained the *Titanic*, and went to the bottom with that palatial ship.[13]

In December, Smith had the honour of becoming captain for the maiden voyage of a new ship, the White Star's *Cufic*. It was a cattle transporter and a world apart from the glamorous transatlantic passenger liners he would soon command. But the privilege of being the master of a vessel on its maiden voyage would become something of a hallmark of Smith's career.

As Smith rose in stature in the White Star Line, so did his accommodation in Liverpool. Soon after their marriage in 1887, Edward and Eleanor moved to 39 Cambridge Road in Seaforth, just north of Liverpool and across from the docks, making it a convenient location for Smith's work. The two-storey red brick attached house exists today, and according to a 2012 *Liverpool Echo* newspaper article still boasts many features from the late 1800s, including a mahogany toilet seat in the hall that is believed to have belonged to the Captain.[14]

Seaforth, along with the neighbouring towns of Waterloo and Crosby, all sit just north of Liverpool's docks along the coast of the River Mersey and were home to many maritime crew, including captains and officers connected to *Titanic*. Senior surviving officer Charles Lightoller lived at 8 Cambridge Avenue, Waterloo, between 1905 and 1908. Captain Arthur Rostron, of the rescue ship the *Carpathia*, gave his address as 'Woodville,

Figure 6: A rare photograph of Ted and Eleanor together, *c.* 1895–1898. (© Henry Aldridge & Son Ltd. / Mary Evans)

Victoria Road, Crosby, Liverpool' during the 1912 United States Senate Inquiry into the disaster. His address of 52 Victoria Road, Crosby was on the same block as Lightoller's. Other notable residents from *Titanic*'s crew were Joseph Bell, the Chief Engineer (1 Belvidere Road, Crosby), and Andrew Latimer, the Chief Steward (4 Glenwyllin Road, Waterloo). So, it is not surprising to discover the Smith family living in several different locations in this area.

Smith's success at sea was in contrast to his sporting prowess, revealed in a curious newspaper extract from 1890 when he was captain of the *Coptic* on the Australasian run. On page 6 of the 20 February 1890 edition of *The Press*, the main newspaper of Christchurch city in the South Island of New Zealand, firstly established that the 'Shaw Savill and Albion Company's chartered White Star liner *Coptic*, Captain E. J. Smith, sails for London via Rio de Janeiro, Teneriffe, and Plymouth. She takes a large cargo from this port and is full in her passenger accommodation.' On the same page, under the headline 'Cricket. Lyttelton C.C. v R.M.S. Coptic', we catch a glimpse of Smith at play, when the officers of the *Coptic*, captained by the chief officer Mr H. Lindsay, faced the Lyttelton Cricket Club in a 'well contested' game. They played only one and a half innings in the time available, and Mr Cameron, the purser of the *Coptic*, acted as one of the umpires. Lyttleton won the short match, not helped by Captain Smith who was caught and bowled for no runs in his first at bat – a duck; and in the second he was bowled out for nought by a man named Hawkins. Smith regained face somewhat by catching a ball hit by batsman G. R. Webb at the end of Lyttleton's first innings. There were no hard feelings. 'In the evening the Lyttleton team dined with Captain E. J. Smith, R.N.R. upon his ship, and wished him and his officers bon voyage and success in the future.'[15]

Incidentally, Smith is often listed as the captain of the *Coptic* when it was involved in a grounding on Mai Island off Rio de Janeiro in 1890, but this was the voyage prior to Smith's visit to New Zealand, and the master during the grounding was Captain Burton. Smith could not be blamed for that particular misadventure.[16]

The port of Lyttleton in Christchurch, New Zealand, was quite possibly the most distant location to which Smith ever commanded a ship (or played cricket at), amplifying the separation from family in England. During the period of 1891 to 1895, the years leading up to the birth of their first daughter, there was much sorrow in the Smith household. Firstly, in March 1891, Smith learned that his first ship, the *Senator Weber*, had sunk, taking the lives of 14 sailors. Then on 1 November 1893, shortly after his ship the *Britannic* left Liverpool for New York, Smith's 86-year-old mother, Catherine, died. Later, his half-sister Thyrza's husband, William Harrington, died at the age of 57, on 1 March 1895, when Smith was home from the sea. Two months later to the day, Joseph Hancock, his half-brother who had inspired him to go to sea and was captain of his first ship, died from a heart attack on his way home from a local fish market.

According to Smith's White Star Line Service Record, the next address the couple lived at was 4 Marine Crescent, Waterloo. This is also corroborated by Kelly's Street Directory for 1891 that records Captain Smith as living there, as well as the 1891 census which has 29-year-old Eleanor Smith resident and listed as the 'head' of the household while her husband was at sea. The census also reveals that Eleanor was accompanied by two 19-year-old Scottish servants, Helen Thie and Emma Armstrong.[17]

At some point, however, Ted and Eleanor decided to move yet again. According to a local newspaper, the couple subsequently went back to the town where they were married and lived at 'The Poplars' on Liverpool Road, Great Sankey, Warrington, 50 yards from the Chapel House pub, and Smith was reportedly remembered by neighbours for his 'quiet sincerity and geniality'.[18] This is confirmed in the crew agreement for the *Majestic* dated 1897, in which Smith listed his address as 'The Poplars, Gr Sankey'.

Figure 7: A family photograph of the Smiths, with a small dog and an unidentified woman and child, *c.* 1895–98. (© Henry Aldridge & Son Ltd. / Mary Evans)

Titanic Legacy: The Captain, the Daughter and the Spy

The year 1898 would be one of great change for the Smiths. It was the same year a short novel was published by American author Morgan Robertson, a son of a sea captain, that would later take on greater significance. The book was entitled *Futility* and the plot has many similarities to the disaster that would completely change the world of the Smith family. In the story, the ship *Titan* was deemed unsinkable, carried insufficient lifeboats, and hit an iceberg in the North Atlantic in April, resulting in a large loss of life.[19]

It is unlikely Robertson's short novel even registered in Smith's life at that point, as a far more pivotal event undoubtedly took his attention: the birth of his one and only daughter, Melville. Although it was a busy time for Smith, with five return trips to the States in the latter half of 1897, indications are that he was there for Mel's delivery at the family home in Alexandra Road, Waterloo, Liverpool, on Saturday, 2 April 1898.[20]

It was almost within the same postcode as their previous house years earlier – two blocks away to be exact – so still convenient for the docks. As a semi-detached house, it was more spacious than previous residences (Figure 8). Modern real estate listings describe seven large bedrooms, an extensive garden and feature period fireplaces throughout, with servant quarters downstairs. North facing, weather damage forced a previous owner to render the exterior, so that it now no longer has the red brick appearance that it would have had when the Smiths were living there.

Figure 8: Alexandra Road, Waterloo, c. 1910. The second house on the left is number. 20, where Melville was born. (Formby Civic Society – Waterloo Alexandra Rd 1910c From Glass Plates Ref R11)

The Smiths never owned the property. The present owner in 2023, Timothy Cook, confirmed that the property deeds that date back to 1875 do not list an Edward Smith, indicating that it was most likely rented.[21] The Gores Directory of 1900 provides the Smith family address as 20 Alexandra Road ('Smith Edward J. master mariner') living next door to marine superintendent Captain George Davy. The street was also home to accountants, solicitors and merchants. They moved slightly further north to 17 Marine Crescent, Waterloo, Liverpool, sometime that year, during which Smith gave the White Star Line offices at 30 St James St, Liverpool as his temporary address, and then in a September 1900 voyage on the *Majestic* listed 17 Marine Crescent as the family home. Directory listings record their telephone number at the new address as WAT 271. The constant change of addresses is symptomatic of Smith's nomadic career at sea, away for weeks and sometimes months at a time.

One would have thought that with the birth of their new daughter, Ted's growing popularity and subsequent salary increase at the White Star Line, the Smiths were contemplating moving to a larger property. However, less than a mile from their previous houses in Seaforth, their new home, a five-bedroomed double-fronted property in Waterloo, was in many respects a downsizing, with less grandeur than Alexandra Road. The rooms and servant quarters are noticeably reduced in size. It could be speculated that as Smith spent most of his time at sea, Eleanor wanted a smaller, more comfortable property to raise her young daughter. Perhaps more likely, as the Smiths had lived at no. 4 Marine Crescent previously, is that they simply wanted to return to an area they had grown fond of, with its views of Crosby Park and the lake, and the seafaring traffic on the River Mersey. Maybe, during those long weeks while Ted Smith was away, it was comforting for Eleanor to see vessels coming and going on the Mersey, and even to take note when Ted's ship finally returned, if she was able to spot it.

Whatever the case, they would live there for the next seven years and it is where Mel spent her early years growing up, so the house must have held many childhood memories. It has been assumed that it was during her time there that the well-known photograph (Figure 1) of Mel and Eleanor was likely taken. Although there is not enough detail in the image to determine whether it was taken at the Marine Crescent residence or at Alexandra Road, or at a local studio. If Mel was younger than 24 months when photographed, then it is more likely it was taken while they were living in Alexandra Road.

Marine Crescent was a middle-class area. Their neighbour at 16 was a stockbroker by the name of Thomas K. Holden, while at number 18, an accountant by the name of Walker J. Lancaster resided.[22] There was one special neighbour. Just a five-minute walk down the road, at 13 Beach Lawn, Waterloo, on the beach front overlooking Crosby Coastal Park, there is a grand mansion owned by Thomas Henry Ismay, who founded the White Star Line. Allegedly, as it is placed at the mouth of the River Mersey, White Star vessels would offer a salute as they passed. His son Joseph Bruce Ismay lived there between 1865 and 1885 and would be closely connected with Smith in later years when he became the chairman and managing director of the White Star Line and survived the *Titanic* sinking. J. Bruce Ismay's father, Thomas, lived at the Waterloo property from 1837 to 1899 (according to the blue plaque on the house) so Smith and Ismay senior could well have crossed paths in the year 1899 in the area. It is unlikely, however, as that same year Thomas Ismay's health had dramatically deteriorated and he spent more time in his other house, Dawpool at Thurstaston, Cheshire, where he eventually died on 23 November 1899.

In 1972, the Smith's Marine Crescent house became a Grade II listed property followed by the Sefton Council installing a blue plaque noting that 'Captain Edward John Smith lived here 1898–1907'. Technically this should read 1900–1907. The British Listed Buildings website describes the house in some detail:

> House, forming part of terraced row; with attached verandah. c1826–30; altered. Painted stucco, slate roof with rendered chimneys to left and right. Double-depth double-fronted plan with back extension. 2 storeys and 3 windows, symmetrical; moulded gutter cornice. 3-bay verandah with elegant and unusually wide cast-iron standards of enriched geometrical open-work including capitals with Ionic volutes... The ground floor has a square-headed doorway with moulded architrave, panelled door and plain overlight, flanked by large canted bay windows with 4-pane sashed glazing.[23]

The current owner, Rose Gallagher, confirmed that despite some building work she had kept the double-fronted, five-bedroom house close to how it would have been in the early 1900s (Figure 9). She is particularly proud of the original elegantly tiled fireplaces.

Rose only learned that Captain Smith and his family lived in the house after researchers for director James Cameron's 1997 film *Titanic* visited the property to ask if they could film the opening scenes there, scenes which were later changed to Southampton.[24] She has written a self-published book entitled *The Captain, Titanic & Me* which details a 'weird connection' Gallagher has with the former resident via an 'amazing dream'. After having coachloads of tourists pulling up outside

Figure 9: 7 Marine Crescent, Waterloo, Liverpool, in 2022, with the front gate (Worrall & Co 26 Bryon St Liverpool) and the detail around one of the fireplaces. (Photographs: Dan Parkes)

her house during the height of *Titanic* fever, she has made plans to run tours of her home.

Regarding the plaque, she approached the Sefton Council in 2005 during Liverpool's 'Year of the Sea' with a 'heartfelt plea... The response was immediate, it should be recognised as part of our local heritage. The plaque was finally erected some two months later.'[25] By 2022, the plaque had fallen off the house and Gallagher was fighting a local council who lacked the enthusiasm of those in 2005 who originally installed it. At the time of writing, the plaque had finally been reinstalled.

There was one anomaly. The 1901 census, recorded on the night of 31 March 1901, did not record the Smiths at Marine Crescent. Instead, it lists Ted's mother-in-law, Sarah Pennington, her daughter Maria and two servants – the domestic cook, Kate Chambers (age 32), from Ireland and the housemaid, Annie Brett (age 17).[26] So where were Ted and Eleanor and the new baby Mel?

There is a clue in the 1901 Marine Crescent census record. In the column 'Profession or Occupation' for Sarah Pennington, a note is scrawled: 'Keeping house for son in law'. Smith had indeed been overseas aboard the *Majestic*, including two trips to South Africa, transporting troops to the Boer War, once in December 1899 and again in February 1900. Now he had rejoined the passenger service to New York. At the time of the census, he had returned to Britain to spend time with his family. The Smiths were recorded as visitors to 32 Leinster Gardens, Runcorn, 20 miles away from Waterloo at the other end of the River Mersey. Edward J. Smith is recorded as aged 50, married, and a Master Mariner and Lieutenant R.N.R., along with his wife, Sarah Eleanor, age 39, from Newton-le-Willows, and their 2-year-old daughter, Helen (Mel). They were staying with Thomas Jones, age 47, a Spirit Merchant, and his wife, Ada (age 37), and daughter, Nora (age 11), all born in Runcorn.[27] Thomas owned the Navigation Inn, 33 Canal Street, Runcorn, and it seems Edward was both a friend and a regular visitor to the inn (Thomas Jones was one of the witnesses at Ted's wedding).[28] In line with the fate of many local pubs it was converted and is now a pet food store, although the Navigation Inn signage remains. There were other Runcorn connections: Smith's mother Catherine and her daughter Thyrza and family lived at 30 Greenway Road, and it is where Catherine died, and she was buried at Runcorn Cemetery.[29]

In 1901, Eleanor suffered a bereavement of her own with the death of her mother, Sarah, on 8 October 1901. She was buried along with Eleanor's father at St Oswald's Church, Winwick. Less than ten years earlier, Edward had lost his mother, Catherine, and now with a young daughter and all their parents deceased, plus his rise in the White Star Line, it is not surprising that he started thinking about his financial legacy. There were other factors to consider.

When the Second Boer War started in 1899, Smith and the *Majestic* were called upon to transport troops to Cape Colony. Two trips were made to South Africa, one in December 1899 and one in February 1900, both without incident. He received the Transport Medal with the South Africa clasp from King Edward VII on 26 November 1903 for his efforts, and was even the subject of a patriotic 'Stevengraph' (a picture woven from silk) based on an earlier photograph from his career (Figure 10). Between December 1902 and May 1903, Smith was then master of the *Germanic*, while the *Majestic* was refitted with new passenger accommodation after its employment as a troop transporter. It was during his *Germanic* captaincy that he experienced a violent storm in February 1903 that continued for nine days. This hair-raising experience and the large loss of life in war that marked the beginning of

Figure 10: A patriotic silk 'Stevengraph,' circa 1900, possibly based on an early photograph of Smith in the 1880s or 1890s. (Courtesy of Donald J.A. Smith)

the twentieth century likely made him think with some renewed urgency about making provisions for Eleanor and Mel in case of his loss.

Thus, on 11 of May 1903, on his return ashore, Smith had his solicitor J. W. Thompson of Liverpool, draw up his last will and testament, signed and witnessed at the family home at Marine Crescent. Smith decided to leave everything to Eleanor, with a notable clause: only so long as she did not remarry, otherwise his estate would default to Mel. Two of his friends were listed as executors, David Cook of 6 Adelaide Terrace, Waterloo, and the Runcorn owner of the Navigation Inn, Thomas Jones. It was witnessed by Eleanor's sister Maria and Mr Thompson the solicitor.[30]

Baltic Letters

On 29 June 1904, Smith took the new RMS *Baltic* on its maiden voyage from Liverpool to New York, making the crossing in 7 days and 13 hours with 906 passengers. The Captain was very happy with how the ship performed: 'I tried to see how she would work coming around the tail of the Southwest Spit, and as the channel was clear, I sent her around at full speed. She behaved admirably. Pilot Johnson, who has brought up almost every one of the big vessels that come into this port, piloted us up.'[31]

Smith's new ship, or maybe news that he was the recipient of the Transport Medal, also impressed one of his schoolfriends, who wrote a letter to him in New York (Figure 11). In elegant copperplate, Smith's reply is addressed to Alvin Taylor, likely Thomas Alvin Taylor who was born in Hanley in 1852. It is lacking a response to any specific information, indicating that Alvin had sent a very simple letter of congratulations.

R.M.S. *Baltic*
21st July 1904

My dear Alvin Taylor
Many thanks for your letter of congratulation received in New York. I have not been to Hanley very often for some years but have never lost the recollection of many of my school friends. I have often thought about you and wondered how you made out. The next time I come down I shall most certainly look you up and have a crack about old times. I would like to hear about many of the boys who were at school when we were.

Thanking you again for your good wishes & hoping we may meet soon believe me with very kindest regards and all good wishes for you and yours

Very sincerely
Edw J Smith

While in command of the Baltic, Smith had a 'reputation of being a very careful commander' according to *On Board RMS Titanic – Memories of the Maiden Voyage* by George Behe, 'and was known to be on the Baltic's bridge for two days at a time during a foggy spell. Smith was always willing to hurry to the bridge whether he was on duty or off, and was known to leave his dinner table if he thought he was needed on the bridge.'

Smith was certainly intent on spending as much time as his work permitted with his daughter. A glimpse of this can be seen in the regular correspondence with his 43-year-old nephew Francis (Frank) Hancock (1862–1928, Figure 12), who lived in the United States. Frank was the youngest son of Joseph Hancock, Smith's older half-brother who had introduced him to the sea as captain of Smith's first vessel, the sailing ship the *Senator Weber* in 1867. The 1881 census showed that Smith had lodgings at 20 Berkley Street, Toxteth Park along with 19-year-old Frank, so it is likely a friendship had developed.[32] In 1895, after Joseph died from a heart attack, Frank subsequently emigrated to Savannah, Georgia, an area well-known to Ted Smith from his time in the States. What ensued was a series of letters between Uncle Edward and his nephew Frank from 1905 to 1912 that provide a unique insight into the family life of the famous White Star captain. The letters are now held in the G.W. Blunt White

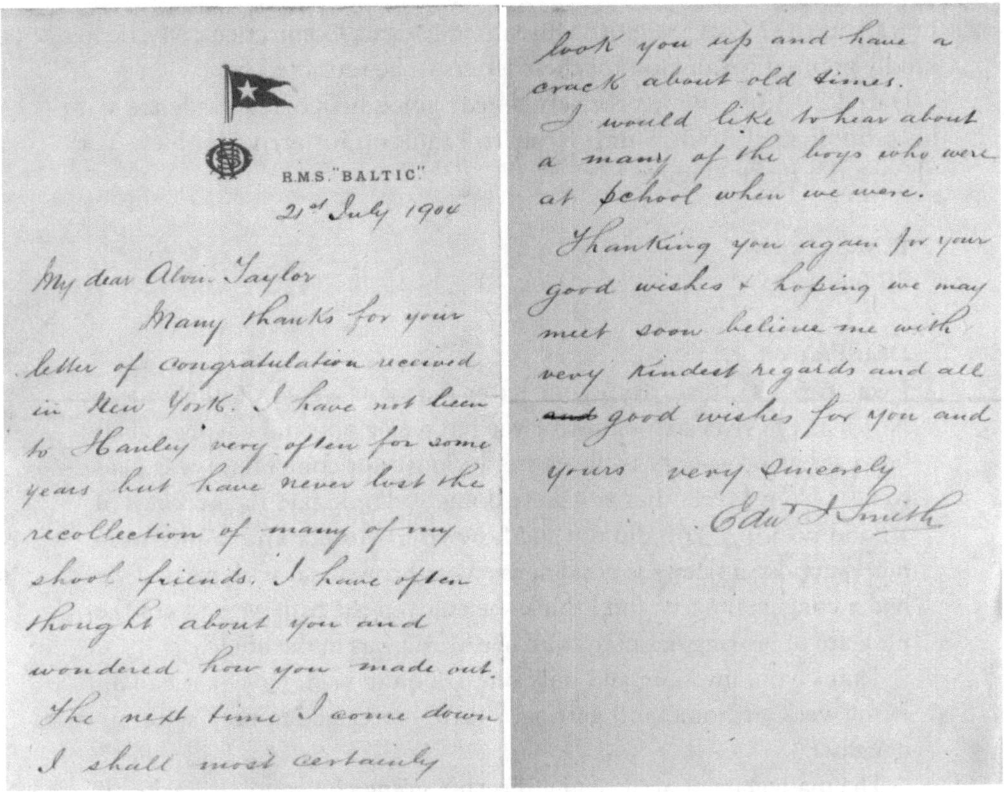

Figure 11: Captain Smith's 1904 letter to a Hanley school friend, Alvin Taylor. (Mary Evans Picture Library / Onslow Auctions Limited)

Figure 12: Frank Hancock (1862–1928) in an undated photograph with his wife and children. (Phil Gowan collection, courtesy of Phillip Hind / *Encyclopedia Titanica*)

Library at the Mystic Seaport Museum in Mystic, Connecticut. Mystic has kindly granted permission for these letters to be reprinted here.

Dated 20 July 1905, precisely a year since his correspondence with his schoolfriend Alvin, Smith wrote to Frank on his arrival in New York aboard the *Baltic* (Figure 13):

R.M.S. *Baltic*
20 July 1905

Dear Frank

I was sorry to learn from your letter that you were not likely to be North as I have been looking forward to seeing you and having a chat; however as prosperity is the cause we must not complain. I was glad to hear from Myers that you were doing well and had the makings of a good position. You did not say how your Mother and family were but I suppose no news is good news. Miss Browne sat with me and we had a congenial party and I think she enjoyed the trip; we had not the pleasure of hearing her play as all her Music was in the hold.

Thank you, my Wife and only one are quite well; have just had an extra week at home and getting a little better acquainted with my daughter.

The management are keeping this ship going constantly to make all they can while she is popular. If you ever have a journey north try and arrange it so as to be there when we are in port.

Give my regards to General Gordon, Churchill & Myers when you meet them. If you see George Walker you might mention me to him, he was very kind to me when I was in *Lizzie Fennell* though he may have forgotten me after so many years.

With kindest regards to all in your circle believe me
Your Affectionate Uncle Edw J. Smith

The letter implies that Frank was unable to travel north from Georgia to meet Smith in New York due to work constraints, and that Smith himself was busy as 'management are keeping this ship going constantly to make all they can while she is popular.'[33] There is talk of mutual friends – a musician named Miss Browne and Savannah acquaintances General Gordon, Churchill and Myers. Biographer Cooper has tentatively identified General Gordon as Colonel William Washington Gordon (1834–1912), a good friend of Smith's who was aboard the *Majestic* during a stormy crossing in September 1895. Gordon was a former lawyer and Confederate Army officer during the American Civil War and then became a cotton merchant,

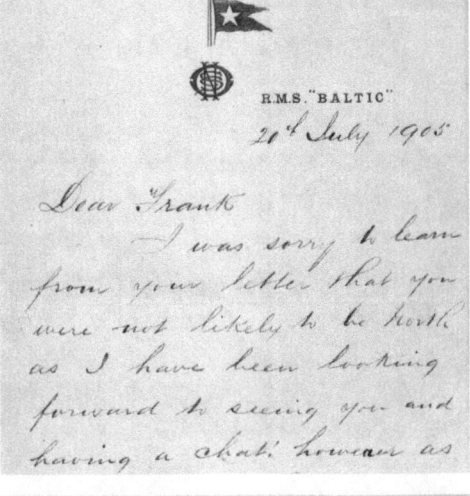

Figure 13: The first and last page in a four-page letter written by Captain Edward Smith to his nephew Frank Hancock from aboard the *Baltic* on 20 July 1905. He signs it 'Your Affectionate Uncle'. (Reprinted by kind permission of the Mystic Seaport Museum: VFM 194, Manuscripts Collection, G.W. Blunt White Library, Mystic Seaport Museum, Inc.)

which leads Cooper to surmise that Smith's friendship may have extended as far back as when he was transporting cotton aboard the *Lizzie Fennell* in the late 1870s.[34] As for Churchill, historical fiction author Pat Lacey has him as Winston Churchill, a graduate of the United States Naval Academy, who had given up the sea to write novels.[35] Smith concludes his letter by wondering if George Walker remembers him since their time together on his first command, the *Lizzie Fennell*, during which Walker did something 'very kind' for the young Captain. We do not know the nature of this kind act, although Cooper suggests it must have made a deep impression on Smith for him to recall it nearly 30 years later.[36]

What makes this friendly letter of particular note is his reference to Eleanor and Mel: '... have just had an extra week at home and getting a little better acquainted with my daughter'. Just as Frank had been unable to visit New York to catch up with his uncle, Smith himself was hinting that work was impinging on his family life, and that he had been missing out on time with his young daughter, then aged seven.

During this time at home, he may have discovered Mel's penchant for rabbits, which would explain an even more touching letter and growing bond between father and daughter the following year, while he was still master of the *Baltic* (1904–1907). Dated 29 November 1906, when Mel was 8 years old, Smith drew a picture of a little bird and apologised for

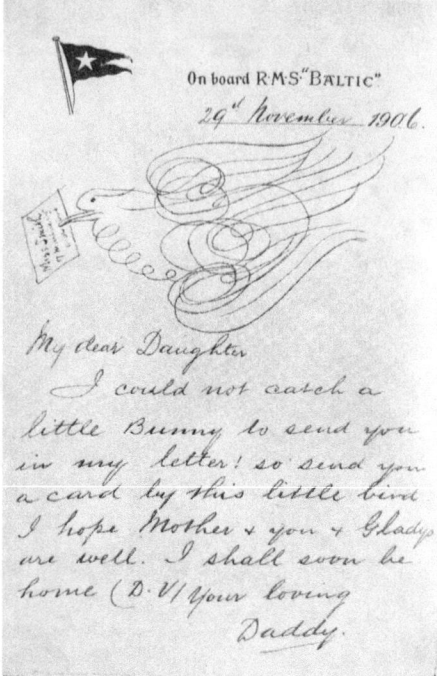

Figure 14: Smith's letter to his daughter in 1906. The letter includes a hand-drawn image of a bird and is signed 'Your loving Daddy'. (Photograph courtesy of John Pladdys)

not sending a bunny (Figure 14). Addressed to 'Miss H. M. Smith', he wrote: 'My dear Daughter, I could not catch a little bunny to send you in my letter so send you a card by this little bird. I hope Mother and you and Gladys are well. I shall soon be home. D.V. Your loving Daddy.' Smith made an extra effort with the detail; the letter in the bird's beak reads: 'Miss Smith 17 Marine Cr, Waterloo.' ('D.V.' for Deo Volente means God willing.) Mel's love of birds, and not just bunnies, is also seen in a family photograph taken some time later where a bird in a cage is visible behind her, although by that time dogs were her centre of attention (Figure 27).

The letter emerged in 2013 when it was auctioned at Henry Aldridge and Son of Devizes, Wiltshire, along with a description from the auctioneer that the letter shows a different side of the man, addressing his daughter in a 'loving and caring' manner.[37] The letter had been viewed during the 1990s when *Titanic* researcher John Pladdys discovered it among the items inherited by Anthony and Marietta Coleridge in Pratts House, Leafield.

That Smith was fond of buying gifts for his daughter was recalled in later years by J. E. Hodder Williams of Hodder and Stoughton Publishers, who wrote in 1914 that in addition to being the 'perfect sea captain' he was also 'a genial-warm-hearted family man; his face would light up as he recounted the little intimacies of his life ashore, as he told of his wife and the troubles she had with the dogs he loved, of his little girl and her delight with the presents he brought her and the parties he had planned for her.'[38]

Figure 15: An unidentified Smith family photograph. The girl looking at the camera strongly resembles photographs of Mel in later life, particularly her pilot's licence ID photograph. It could be her mother Eleanor sitting next to her and turning to camera. (© Henry Aldridge & Son Ltd. / Mary Evans)

It was also aboard the *Baltic* in 1906 that Smith was involved in a near miss due to fog – although to a steward it cemented his reputation of a 'careful' captain. With more than a thousand passengers onboard, they encountered dense fog off the coast of Ireland that suddenly lifted to reveal they were sailing headlong toward Daunt's Rock. There is no further information as to what Smith did to prevent disaster, but the account from 43-year-old steward John Martin, printed under the heading 'Smith a careful sailor', explained that Martin 'characterised Captain Smith as the most careful man he ever sailed under. He took deep interest in his crew and was exceedingly keen on fire and lifeboat drill.'[39] He was so adamant about Smith's careful nature that when Martin later heard of the *Titanic* sinking, he immediately put it down to 'loose rivets' that he believed existed in new ships, rather than condemn the commander of some malpractice.

Woodhead

In 1907, the Smith family moved yet again; this time a complete change of scenery and entirely driven by the demands of his profession. Leaving their circle of friends in Liverpool, the Smith family moved to

Southampton – not surprising since the White Star Line had moved its operations to the more convenient deep-water harbour there in 1907 to accommodate the increasing size of ships they were building, such as the *Adriatic*, and later the *Olympic* and *Titanic*, all of which would soon have Smith as their master on their maiden voyages. Smith must have seen the change coming, having taken command of RMS *Baltic* in 1904, then proclaimed the largest vessel afloat, one of what was dubbed 'The Big Four' (the others being RMS *Celtic*, *Cedric*, and *Adriatic*). At 23,876 gross tons, the *Baltic* was more than twice the size of the *Majestic* and remained the world's largest ship until 1905. The ships were fast outgrowing White Star facilities at the port of Liverpool. A southern port would also facilitate European connections to France.

The residence the Smith family chose to settle into was also in contrast to their previous Liverpool homes – almost as if to match the size of the vessels Smith was now commanding. The Smith family lived in Winn Road (Figure 17) in the Highfield area of Southampton, in a detached red brick, double-fronted house with twin-gables, named 'Woodhead' after Eleanor's family farm at Winwick.

Winn Road is situated next to Southampton Common, with the southern end of 'Lover's Walk' (sometime called 'Love Lane') starting where Winn Road adjoins The Avenue. It is easy to imagine Ted and Eleanor taking their dogs for a walk along the ancient pathway shaded by a canopy of trees.

Thanks to the 1911 census of England and Wales, we have a glimpse into the Smith household living in Southampton (Figure 18). Woodhead

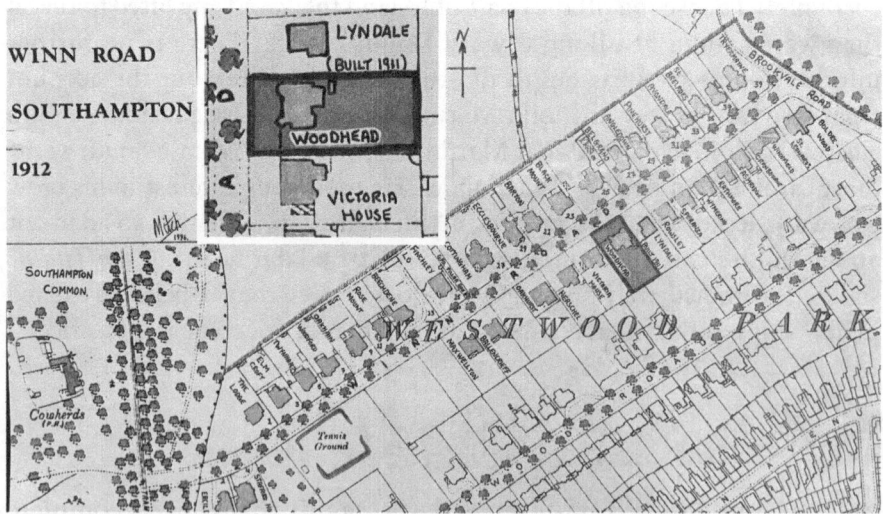

Figure 16: A map of Winn Road in 1912 with Woodhead indicated. (Adapted from the Ticehurst Collection held at Southampton Local History and Maritime Library).

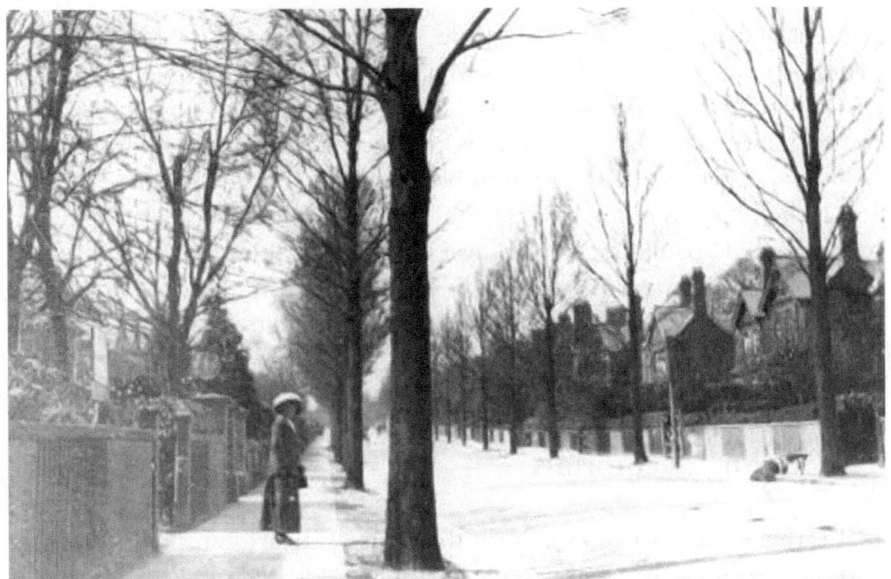

Figure 17: Winn Road *c.* 1910. From the incline of the street, it appears to be looking down the road, in which case the Smith family home of Woodhead would be on the left. (Courtesy of SEE Southampton)

is listed as having 18 rooms and accommodating seven people – 60-year-old Edward John Smith (who signed the document), his 47-year-old wife, Sarah Eleanor Smith (her age is heavily corrected – did Ted forget her age?), their 13-year-old daughter, Helen Melville Smith (with the word 'single' crossed out), and two servants – 22-year-old domestic cook, Mabel Lucy Inkpen, and 27-year-old domestic housemaid Ann Brett (the same servant listed as working at 17 Marine Crescent in 1901, then aged 17). At the time of the census, there were two visitors to the Smith residence: 22-year-old Thomas Martin, described as a medical student, and 12-year-old Florence May Curry. The document looks as if it was written by Edward Smith himself, while Martin's details are in a different handwriting, perhaps indicating that he was an unknown visitor, although Smith left a line free so was aware a person would be added.

1	Edward John Smith	head	60		married	Master Mariner R.D., R.N.R.	Hanley Staffs
2	Sarah Eleanor Smith	wife		47	"		
3	Helen Melville Smith	daughter		13	single		Waterloo Liverpool
4	Thomas Martin	visitor	22	–	Single	Medical Student	Lancs Walkden
5	Florence May Curry	visitor		12	—		Eltham Kent
6	Ann Brett	servant		27	single	housemaid domestic	
7	Mabel Lucy Inkpen	servant		22	single	cook domestic	

(To be filled up by the Enumerator.)

I certify that:— (1.) All the ages on this Schedule are entered in the proper sex columns. (2.) I have counted the males and females in Columns 3 and 4 separately, and have compared their sum with the total number of persons. (3.) After making the necessary enquiries I have completed all entries on the Schedule which appeared to be defective, and have corrected such as appeared to be erroneous.

Initials of Enumerator

Total		
Males.	Females.	Persons.
2	5	7

(To be filled up by, or on behalf of, the Head of Family or other person in occupation, or in charge, of this dwelling.)

Write below the Number of Rooms in this Dwelling (House, Tenement, or Apartment). Count the kitchen as a room but do not count scullery, landing, lobby, closet, bathroom; nor warehouse, office, shop.

13

I declare that this Schedule is correctly filled up to the best of my knowledge and belief.

Signature Edwd J Smith

Postal Address Woodhead Winn Rd Southampton

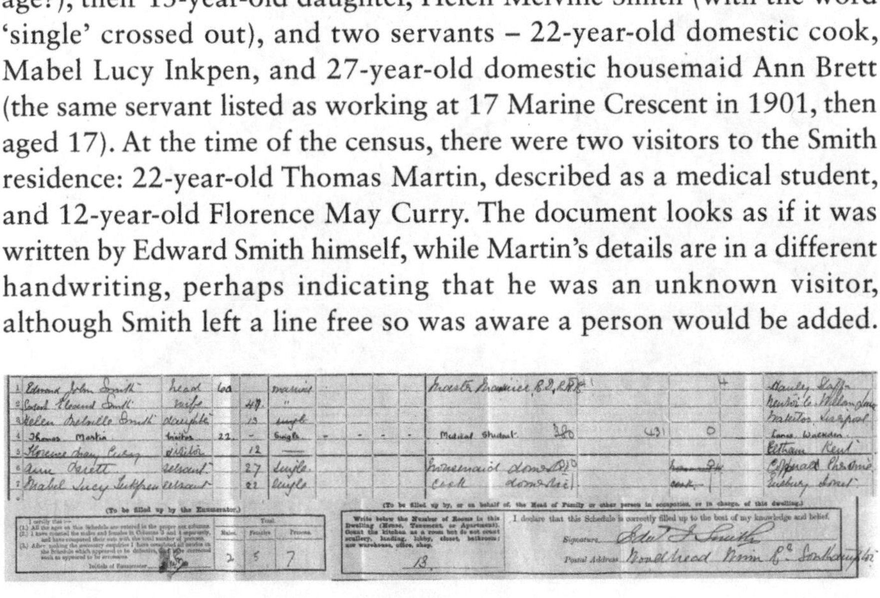

Figure 18: Excerpt from the 1911 census for Woodhead, likely written in Captain Smith's own hand. (Author's collection)

'Florence Curry' is in Smith's writing, so was known to the family, and it could be assumed was a friend of Mel's, at only a year her senior.

At the time the Smith family lived in Woodhead, it had no number – the south side of Winn Road was only fully numbered in 1918. However, it would have been what is now number 32. After Captain Smith's death in 1912, the house remained in the Smith family until 1915, after which it was renamed 'Coulhurst'. The house was bombed on 18 April 1942, and later a block of flats was built on the land.[40] The neighbouring houses do provide an indication of what Woodhead must have once looked like, as they are of a similar architectural design.

Two Wrong Memorials

In a rather odd twist of fate, both the house Edward Smith was born in and the last house he lived in have incorrectly located memorials.

It is often stated that Smith was born at no. 51 Well Street, Hanley, Stoke-on-Trent (Figure 19). There is a white plaque installed on the wall of the house to mark this, commissioned by the Titanic Brewery, a producer of local craft beers since 1985. Installed in 2012, during the centenary commemorations, it was made by local potter Kevin Milward to replace a previous plaque that had gone missing.[41]

Figure 19: 51 Well Street up for auction. Available documentation reveals that Smith was not born in this specific house. (Photograph: Dan Parkes)

The truth is that Edward Smith's birth certificate does not record a house number and more importantly the terraced houses were built in the 1880s or 1890s – long after Smith was born. The confusion is likely due to a misreading of the entry for the Smith family in the 1851 census (HO107 2004/139) when Smith was a one-year-old. No house number is indicated in the document, however, there is a number 51 written in the extreme left-hand column, likely as some kind of counting reference, that has been mistaken for a house number. Comparing other censuses shows that the Smiths lived at numbers 86, 17 (in 1861) and 30 (in 1871) which is probably the same house simply renumbered over the years. This can be deduced by the fact that despite the number changes, the names of the neighbours remained the same during this twenty-year period and confirmed by number 17 that is recorded in 1861 as a 'Grocer's Shop' (RG9 1932/7.) The actual house was likely demolished by construction of the ring road in Hanley and so no longer exists.

Similarly, while the Smith family lived at 32 Winn Road, Southampton, for reasons unknown, number 34 is frequently listed as their home. For example, the local Southampton newspaper, the *Southern Daily Echo*, in 2012, ran the headline 'Captain Edward J. Smith's home, 34 Winn Road, Highfield, Southampton' and noted that the Smiths lived in a large house named Woodhead. The house is no longer there, the site is now a block of flats called Cheltenham Court, inside of which is a memorial to the Captain.[42] In the foyer is a photograph of the *Titanic*, with the caption: 'Cheltenham Court stands on the site of the house once occupied by Commander Edward John Smith who was captain of the *Titanic* and went down with his ship. The house called 'Lyndale' was pulled down in 1977 to build these flats.' Without realising it, the caption assists in correctly identifying the location of Woodhead next door at no. 32. A 1912 map of Winn Road clearly shows 'Lyndale' was adjacent to Woodhead (Figure 16). Overlaying the 1912 map onto a modern satellite image of Winn Road also confirms that it was undoubtedly number 32, not 34.

Cross-checking with maps detailing bombing raids over the city during World War Two, there were two attacks that hit Winn Road, the first on 4 September 1940, and the second on 18 April 1942. In the first attack, the house next door to Woodhead was hit (where no. 30 is today). In the second, Woodhead suffered a direct hit (Figure 20). The rest of Winn Road was unaffected. It is unusual that such a small cluster of houses suffered such damage but may indicate the German Luftwaffe were specifically targeting the area. An account in the local *Daily Echo* detailing the bombing is cautiously lacking in specifics. Under the headline 'South Coast Town Again Raided' it confirms that it took place in the early hours of Saturday the eighteenth, that residential areas suffered the most and that 'nearly a dozen people were killed' with most of the casualties 'at a large house on the northern side of the town', which may refer to Woodhead. An air raid alert had sounded and most residents had taken refuge in shelters and cellars.[43]

In a series of dramatic photographs discovered in the Southampton City archives, what remains of the house can be seen in detail. As a large part of the roof is still intact, a rough outline of what the property would have looked like can be gained from the image, with the front taking most of the impact. In Figure 20, the man in a suit provides a sense of scale, dwarfed by the destruction behind him. Did any passer-by then know it was once the home of the captain of the *Titanic*?

Figure 20: The former Smith family house, Woodhead, suffered a direct hit on 18 April 1942 that destroyed most of the property. (Southampton Local History and Maritime Library Ref: SC/EN2/3/134f.).

Figure 21: The actual location of the Smith family house is 32 Winn Road, which is now the site of a block of flats. (Photograph: Dan Parkes).

2
Playing on *Titanic*'s Bridge

Figure 22: Original photograph of Captain Smith taken onboard *Olympic*. This famous image is the copy personally owned by Eleanor and, due to its clarity, appears to be a first-generation image. It was originally contained within a fine quality gilt leather frame. It was notably used in a full-page newspaper tribute in *The Sphere* on 27 April 1912, reprinted with Eleanor's permission as a memorial to Smith at his old school, and more recently as the basis of a large-scale mural in Hope Street in Hanley, Stoke-on-Trent. (© Henry Aldridge & Son Ltd. / Mary Evans)

Captain E. J. Smith, R.N.R., Commander of R.M.S. "Adriatic," 25,000 tons.

Figure 23: Captain Smith of the *Adriatic*. (*The Boys Own Paper*, 8 August 1908. (Author's collection)

When the *Adriatic* arrived in Southampton on 30 May 1907 with Captain Smith in command, it ushered in a new epoch in transatlantic service. While the new ship had departed on its maiden voyage from Liverpool on 8 May 1907, it was not to return there. Henceforth, the transatlantic service would depart on Wednesday from the new Southampton White Star terminal to New York, calling at Cherbourg and Queenstown on the westbound route, and Plymouth and Cherbourg on the eastbound return. The Liverpool-New York route still ran each Thursday but was serviced by older ships such as the *Baltic*, *Cedric*, *Celtic* and *Arabic*.[1]

After three years as captain of the *Baltic*, Smith had been given command of his second new 'big ship,' the *Adriatic*, the fourth of the 'The Big Four', which was never the world's largest but instead the fastest of the four, her two quadruple expansion steam engines capable of 17 knots, and with an impressive passenger capacity of 2,825. It was while captain of the *Adriatic* that Smith made comments that would later become legendary in hindsight. In an interview with a *New York Times* reporter in May 1907, he allegedly said:

> When anyone asks me how I can best describe my experience in nearly 40 years at sea, I merely say – uneventful. Of course there have been winter storms and gales and fog and the like, but in all my experience I have never been in an accident of any sort worth speaking about. I have seen but one vessel in distress in all my years at sea – a brig, the crew of which was taken off in a small boat in charge of my third

officer. I never saw a wreck and have never wrecked, nor was I ever in any predicament that threatened to end in disaster of any sort. You see, I am not very good material for a story.²

A rather dignified photograph of Smith (Figure 23) appeared in the 8 August 1908 issue of *The Boy's Own Paper* in an article entitled 'Captains of the crack liners, and the stories they have to tell'. In among many dramatic stories of mostly German liner captains and their adventures, there is only a brief mention of Smith as 'another famous Atlantic captain and a skilful seaman'. Perhaps he was correct – his career had so far been 'uneventful' and he was 'not very good material for a story'. Rather prophetically though, the same *Boy's Own* article contained a reported conversation with an unnamed captain who responded to a passenger's concern after passing a number of large icebergs. The lady passenger asked, 'Oh captain, what would happen if we struck that berg?' To which the captain replied cooly: 'Reckon we would go under.'³

The unnamed captain was unlikely to be Smith, as he made several statements expressing confidence in modern shipbuilding. *The Poverty Bay Herald* in New Zealand recorded him as saying, 'If there was a serious accident the vessel would not sink before ample time had been given to save the lives of all on board. This [the *Adriatic*] is the class of boat that pays; high speed eats up money mile by mile, and extreme high speed is suicidal.'⁴ In 1909, he was reported to have made similar remarks about the *Adriatic*, although the sentiments would later be used in a different context:

> I will not assert that she is unsinkable, but I can say confidently that, whatever the accident, this vessel would not go down before time had been given to save the life of every person on board. I will go a bit further. I will say that I cannot imagine any condition that would cause the *Adriatic* to founder. I cannot conceive of any fatal disaster happening to this ship. Modern shipbuilding has reduced that danger to a minimum.⁵

These quotations would of course later be reprinted with a sense of irony, but it should be understood that Smith's primary job when talking to the press was to promote the ships he was commanding – especially the sense of safety and continuity his presence brought. In the *Washington Times* 1912 quotation of this statement, there is an additional, thought-provoking comment. An officer of the *Adriatic*, who heard part of Captain Smith's remarks, added: 'Don't forget when you write of the captain's "uneventful" life to put in that it is the great captain who doesn't let things happen.'[6]

This same 1909 account aboard the *Adriatic* also contains Smith's attitude to life at sea:

> The love of the ocean that took me to sea as a boy has never left me. In a way, a certain amount of wonder never leaves me, especially as I observe from the bridge a vessel plunging up and down in the trough of the seas, fighting her way through and over great waves, tumbling, and yet keeping on her keel, and going on and on – I wonder how she does it, how she can keep afloat in such seas, and how she can go on and on safely to port. There is wild grandeur, too, that appeals to me in the sea. A man never outgrows that.

During this time, newspapers would give him the title 'Commodore' even though officially the White Star Line had let the rank lapse as far back as the 1880s when Commodore Hamilton Perry resigned after his ship the *Britannic* collided with the *Celtic*. The title was only reinstated in the 1920s when Captain Bertram Fox Hayes was conferred the rank of Commodore of the White Star fleet, along with an allowance of $1,000 a year in additional pay.[7]

With an unofficial honorific of Commodore, Smith was still well paid for his role. As a senior commander of the White Star Line, he received an annual salary of £1,250 per year plus a £200 bonus if no accidents occurred.[8] Such a salary was twice what most liner captains of the day would expect to earn. In accordance with his rank as Commander in the Royal Naval Reserve, Smith was entitled to fly the RNR Blue Ensign from the stern of whatever merchant ship he commanded instead of the normal Red Ensign of the merchant marine.[9]

On 8 September 1907, the day after a new Cunard ocean liner named the *Lusitania* began its maiden voyage, taking the crown as the largest ship and soon the Blue Riband as the fastest crossing the Atlantic, Smith was involved in another form of record-breaking transportation. Under the headline of a 'Wild Auto Dash,' the captain was returning from a visit to Pittsfield, Massachusetts, in between sailings of the *Adriatic*. He was travelling with none other than J. Pierpont Morgan and as a guest of millionaire Charles Lanier. They missed the New York train, arriving 'just in time to see the tail end of the New York Express whirl round a curve in the distance'. Morgan had to be back in New York that morning, so their host, Charles Lanier, sprang into action. He firstly sent a message ahead to Lee station twelve miles away for the train to be held for a couple of minutes. Then Lanier 'jumped into the auto and told the chauffeur to push it to the last limit of speed for Lee'. Once out of suburban streets, 'there the $15,000 car was let out to the last notch, and at sixty miles an hour or more it headed a trail of dust that stretched away two miles to the rear.' The newspaper account reported that this was 'the fastest run that has been seen in this vicinity up to date, and some folk in the Central Berkshires are still speculating as to the nature of the red streak that flashed down their beautiful roads.' Although the train had to wait more than a few minutes, the wild dash proved worthwhile: 'Everybody sat tight, and with horn-blowing and machinery rumbling the car dashed into Lee, whirled around to the station, and there found the delayed express train.' The account does not mention what Smith thought of this perilous exertion, but it did not seem to faze Morgan who simply boarded the train and 'waved a goodbye to his friends'.[10]

During 1909, we catch a rare glimpse of the man behind the uniform. The *Sunday Magazine* of the *New-York Tribune* noted: 'If gossip of the waterfront is true, Captain Ted Smith of the *Adriatic* has a small fortune in old prints. His collection at home in Southampton, and indeed the prints that adorn his cabin, include many of exceptional rarity.'[11] Later, his daughter Mel would become an avid art collector, perhaps inspired by her father, if this waterfront gossip was true.

His popularity with passengers allowed some to gain a rare insight into his private life with Eleanor and Mel. American writer Kate Douglas-Wiggin wrote that she crossed the Atlantic with Smith over twenty times, and on occasions visited his home: 'My knowledge of him was furthered from time to time by informal meetings at my own house in America, or at his home in England, where I saw him in his happy and delightful family life.'[12]

At sea, Douglas-Wiggin described Smith in glowing terms:

I can remember certain voyages when great inventors and scientists, earls and countesses, authors and musicians and statesmen made a 'Captain's table' as notable and distinguished as that of any London or New York dinner. At such times Captain Smith was an admirable host; modest, dignified, appreciative; his own contributions to the conversation showing not only the quality of his information but the high quality of his mind... His face, his manner, his voice, the grasp of his hand, showed simplicity, directness and strength. There was never any variableness about him 'neither shadow or turning.' He never flattered or curried favour with any one, or indulged in any small talk of policy, but his blunt, straightforward, seamanlike speech, his keen sense of humour, his essential kindness, his sunny smile – all these seemed to be just so many visible expression of a character intrinsically

Titanic Legacy: The Captain, the Daughter and the Spy

Figure 24: Edward John Smith in a rare photograph without his uniform, revealing a receding hairline. The studio photograph was taken in 1909 in New York. (© Henry Aldridge & Son Ltd. / Mary Evans Picture Library)

upright and trustworthy. A kind of steady loyalty, to his profession, his duty, his friends, and his own ideal, always seemed to me the compass by which his life was set.

Smith wrote a letter to his nephew Frank Hancock in the United States while onboard the RMS *Adriatic*, dated 28 April 1910. It is revealing about the strain caused by long absences from home: [13]

My dear Frank
It was a great pleasure to get your nice chatty letter. It is pleasant to get a cheery letter now and again, most of these I get from my folks are very blue. The last I had from Lill gave me very poor accounts of John but you have probably heard from her since then. I am glad to hear of your success & sincerely hope it may continue & that you may eventually get so placed as to enable you to have more leisure. I envy you your family, they are no doubt a care but certainly a great blessing.
   We have been very unfortunate, having only one girl, she is great company for her Mother in her lonely life. I see by the heading on your paper you have an Office in New York; is there no chance of your coming up on business some time, it would be great luck if you could do so when I am in port, I should enjoy a good long crack. I see by our list that Mrs. Malloch is crossing with us on Wednesday so I shall get the latest news of you. It is gratifying to know one has made friends, our position is a trying one at times, it takes all sorts of people to make a world and it seems to me people show the worst side of their natures on shipboard.

It was my intention to get to Savannah during our long stays in New York, but you know the saying 'the best laid schemes of mice & men gang aft agley' so it was with me, having two ships laid up the management took the opportunity of letting all the R.N.R. Officers get in their Drill so in three voyages I have had several changes in the staff, among them two Chiefs and while they were both able men they had never sailed with me before & I did not feel like being so far away; I am disappointed but it cannot be helped. During the last three months I have only had Monday & Tuesday at home, not very satisfactory: we are now on our regular sailings and should arrive Thursdays. It was good of Malloch to offer to put his car at our disposal, it would have been a treat to me to go over the old stamping grounds, though I have no doubt I would find things much changed.

We expect our new ship 'Olympic' out about July next year, she will be faster and should arrive early on Wednesday so if they keep to the present sailing arrangements I shall get to see you, if I don't see you before in New York.

Please give my kindest regards to your Wife, she probably remembers meeting me years ago, and with all good wishes to you believe me ever your affectionately

Edw J Smith

Biographer Cooper describes this particular letter as 'probably the most fascinating and yet most frustrating from a biographer's point of view'. Compared to newspaper reports, 'Smith in the raw is much more interesting.'[14] While there is a touch of envy – Smith even uses the very word itself – there is a glimpse into his family life with Eleanor and Mel and the frustration that work prevented him from spending more time with them. He describes Eleanor as 'lonely' and writes that having only 'one girl' – Mel – was 'unfortunate'. Reading between the lines it seems Smith wanted a larger family. Nevertheless, he adds a positive twist, that the 12-year-old was 'great company' for Eleanor while he was away at sea.

The letter also references a 'Lill' and 'John'. At this point their identify is unknown, but that Smith describes them as his 'folks' indicates they may have been family and as the nature of their news is 'blue' perhaps in ill health.

In private we also have the rare opportunity of hearing Smith complain about this work. Tellingly, he describes how aboard a ship 'people show the worst side of their natures'. The 'two chiefs' Cooper believes are E. J. English, replaced by Chief Officer Joseph Evans in early 1910.[15] 'I did not feel like being so far away' reveals how he was still keenly interested in engaging with his officers, and took his role seriously, rather than simply delegating duties.

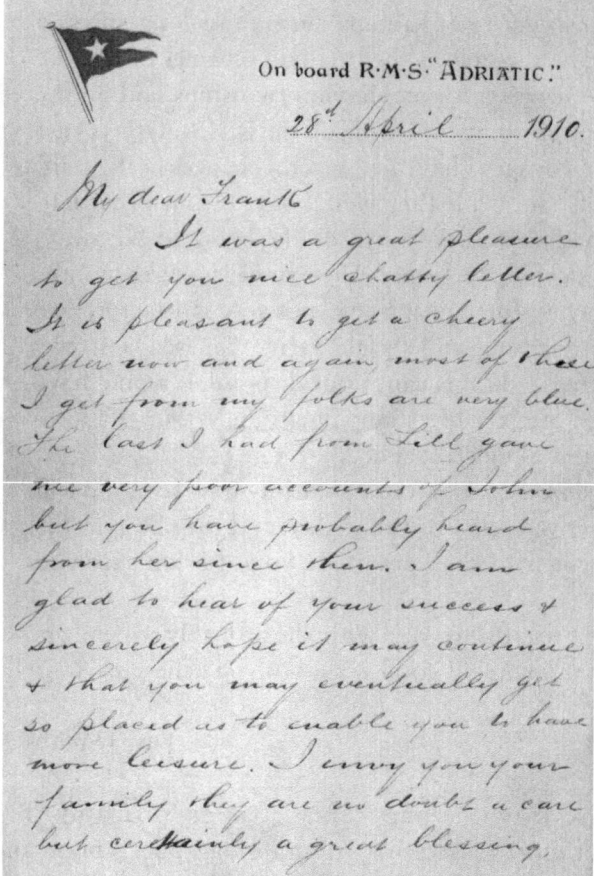

Figure 25: The first page in a four-page letter written by Captain Smith aboard the *Adriatic* in 1910 to his nephew in the United States. (Reprinted by kind permission of the Mystic Seaport Museum: VFM 194, Manuscripts Collection, G.W. Blunt White Library, Mystic Seaport Museum, Inc.)

Dogs and Cigars

One of the most popular photographs of Captain Smith has him holding tight the lead of dog, a large Russian Wolfhound, or 'Borzoi' (Figure 26). Books and websites insist that he was given the impressive canine by none other than the wealthy American businessman Benjamin Guggenheim, as a gift for Mel, the day before the *Titanic* sailed into maritime history. Mel took the gift home, so the story goes, and the dog survived – to the relief of dog lovers the world over. As a tribute to the wealthy benefactor, the dog was subsequently named 'Ben'.

On closer inspection, the photograph is almost certainly not taken aboard an Olympic-class ship, which means it was more likely either the *Baltic* or *Adriatic*, perhaps around 1907 after the family moved to Southampton. *Titanic* historian Bill Sauder identified the location as most likely the foredeck of the *Adriatic*.[16] Borzois live for approximately

Figure 26: The Borzoi was allegedly called Ben and a gift for Mel from the Captain – although this is likely a myth. (Author's collection)

seven to ten years, so it was likely still alive at the time of the *Titanic* tragedy – but the legend of the day-before escape does not stand scrutiny. In Russia the dogs were used by the aristocracy for hunting wolves. They were also known, despite their speed and hunting prowess, for a calm, sensitive temperament.[17]

The Guggenheim connection is possible. He likely knew the Captain and Guggenheim's daughter Peggy was only a few months younger than Mel, so if there was at least a talking point, even the possibility of friendship. Peggy, who became a great art collector, was also known for another passion – her love of dogs. She was buried with 14 of them.[18]

Truth be told, other than Mel's age matching Peggy's, and Peggy's interest in dogs, there is no other evidence to verify if Captain Smith really had a dog named Ben given to him by Guggenheim. The photograph seems to have first appeared in the 17 April 1912 edition of the *Illustrated Chronicle* that included a caption explaining it was 'a recent portrait' and it was 'his favourite dog'. A copy of the photograph now resides in the SeaCity Museum, in Southampton, where the exhibit label erroneously informs visitors that he 'was photographed on board *Olympic* with his Irish Wolfhound, Ben. Ben does not sail with his master on *Titanic*.' Smith biographer Gary Cooper simply notes that the photograph was probably taken aboard the *Baltic* or *Adriatic*.[19]

Titanic Legacy: The Captain, the Daughter and the Spy

With a complete absence of documentation, it is quite likely the 'Ben' story is another legend that has taken root due to its frequent retelling. Animals aboard *Titanic* are a popular source of myths, including fanciful stories of a cat mascot named 'Jenny' that foretold doom by removing her kittens just prior to sailing, providing superstitious crew with a bad omen (note the similarity to the 'Ben' story).[20] There is the story of First Officer William Murdoch's large black Newfoundland dog, Rigel, that survived the sinking while his master did not, and spent three hours in the freezing water searching for him to no avail. In seemingly typical Newfoundland-fashion, he ends up guiding the occupants of lifeboat no. 4 to the safety of the rescue ship the *Carpathia*. There were two key issues with the Rigel story. First, the crew member 'Jonas Briggs' who told the tale did not exist; and First Officer Murdoch never owned a dog, let alone a large black Newfoundland.[21]

Figure 27: Mel with a young dog on her lap, and a bird cage in the background, possibly photographed in the grounds of Woodhead in Winn Road, Southampton. (Photograph courtesy of John Pladdys)

Playing on Titanic's *Bridge*

There is an undated photograph of a young Mel in fancy dress with a large bow on her head. On her lap sits a small dog, and a bird in a cage is visible in the background (Figure 27). It is one of several family photographs in which a canine friend is present. Dogs were an integral part of the Smith's family life.

Of course, it is entirely feasible that Eleanor, from a farming family background, would have a country dog to keep her and Mel company while Ted was away. Edith Haisman (née Brown) would later recall Captain Smith telling her that he had a dog: 'Not on board the ship I hasten to add...When I get back to Southampton after this voyage, I shall have more time to spend with him.'[22]

Realistically though, in all probability the dog in the photograph is not Smith's at all and he simply posed with it for the photograph; the *Adriatic* was certainly known to have hosted dog shows during his tenure as master. And most of his ships – the *Titanic* included – had kennel facilities. Nevertheless, Smith is not in 'full company dress' nor is he wearing his medals, as he would have had this been a formal occasion. Instead, he is wearing his basic 'service dress' or 'undress' uniform, which indicates he was simply on duty.

Figure 28: Captain Smith on the foredeck of the RMS *Adriatic* in January 1908. (From the collection of Spencer Knarr)

In the photograph of Smith and the dog, in his left hand is a cigar in its holder. Smith was known for smoking cigars. On his final night aboard *Titanic*, he was seen smoking two cigars and enjoying an after-dinner coffee.[23] In 1909, at about the time the photograph of E.J. standing with the mystery dog was taken, while he was captain of the *Adriatic*, Smith had his cigars confiscated, according to a *New York Times* article entitled 'Hold-Up and Search of Steamship Captains' proving that even legendary captains could be subject to scrutiny by the law:

> Capt. Smith of the *Adriatic* of the same line and the ship's surgeon, Dr O'Loughlin, were invited to Marblehead to spend a few days. As they started ashore yesterday morning they went to the Customs Office on the pier and offered the valises they carried for inspection. Each officer was carrying a box of cigars, upon which the seals had been broken. In spite of their protests these cigars were confiscated. In the doctor's valise was a bottle of whisky. This suffered the same fate.[24]

'Two-Dollar Smith'

Smith's popularity with passengers was maybe galvanized due to a most unfortunate event that took place aboard the *Adriatic* during a westbound crossing on 14 June 1910. A black second class passenger by the name of Mrs Fanny Givens, widow of James Givens who had died two months prior, complained of mistreatment when she and four other 'dark Americans' were 'seated at a bad table in the corner' at dinner. Purser McElroy, usually known for his diplomacy, allegedly did not help the situation by responding that 'white folks were white folks and black folks were black folks and that the blacks would have to eat together.' In protest at being 'Jim Crowed' Mrs Givens embarked on a hunger strike for two days, until Captain Smith intervened on the third day. During an interview she recollected that the Captain 'wanted to know what terms would satisfy me, and I replied that all I wanted was to be assigned to a table with the rest of the passengers regardless of color. Orders were given that I be placed at any table in the dining room, which was done... I had no further trouble on board after the third day at sea.' McElroy's unfortunate handling of the situation meant it took an unnecessary three days to resolve and only after a 'heated discussion'. Mrs Givens received a 'ruling in writing' from the Captain and his measured response possibly mitigated the threat of lawsuits against the White Star Line.[25]

Racism was not the only awkward situation a ship's captain had to deal with. Early in 1910, as the *Adriatic* departed New York, a gunshot was heard in a locked second class cabin. Crew forced the door open to find a passenger 'lying on the deck with a bullet wound in the right temple'. Captain Smith wrote in the log: 'The revolver was found lying close to the man's right hand. The ship's surgeon was called and pronounced life extinct.' The entry was countersigned by Purser McElroy and Chief Surgeon William O'Loughlin. It transpired that the victim was an English music hall performer who had shot himself inadvertently in another passenger's stateroom, causing momentary confusion as to his identity. The *Adriatic* had not steamed far and so a tug was called to take the body off before recommencing the voyage.[26]

In an article entitled 'A Career of Continuous Advancement', it was explained that passengers liked Smith 'because of his breezy geniality, for he was the very personification of the typical liner "skipper". His employers trusted him because they knew him to be a good sailor and an able and careful navigator.' Such glowing terms could be disregarded as nothing more than generic publicity material, but the copy also highlighting his bad luck: 'To the veterans of the smoking-room Captain Smith of the *Titanic* is known by the nickname of "Two-Dollar Smith" for tradition has it that he loses every bill of that denomination which comes into his possession. If half the stories about him are true, it is not to be wondered at that Captain Smith is said to refuse bills of that currency whenever he can possibly get the money in some other form.'[27]

Olympic-class Records

Following closely on the heels of the successful *Adriatic*, the White Star Line launched a new class of ship, categorised with grandiosity as the 'Olympic-class'. It was no surprise that Smith was once again called upon to take command of the maiden voyage of the first in the fleet, the RMS *Olympic*, in June 1911. His White Star records officially list him as Commander from 15 May 1911.

Unlike the *Adriatic*, the *Olympic* was indeed the largest ship in the world, at 45,324 gross register tons, 882 ft 9 inches in length and 9 decks tall. White Star amplified the attention by timing the start of her first voyage to coincide with the launch of her sister ship *Titanic* that took place on 31 May 1911. Two weeks later, on Wednesday, 14 June, Smith took command of the *Olympic* as she entered service on her first crossing to New York. Only a short time before the maiden voyage, E.J. made a brief visit to his hometown of Hanley and visited his nephew James

Harrington, whose wife recalled a remark the Captain made to her 'to the effect that the *Olympic* was as firm as a church'.[28]

Not everything was smooth sailing. Initially, there was some doubt that the maiden voyage would even take place, with deckhands on strike demanding the same wages as those of rival Cunard's *Mauretania* and *Lusitania*. The *Olympic* outstripped the Cunard ships in size and the deckhands logically thought their pay should at least be equal. Fortunately, the situation was resolved the day before sailing, although a strike of coal porters also posed issues, relieved via imported labour.[29] Perhaps Smith heaved a sigh of relief that newspapers would run more positive headlines than delays due to strikes and instead described the *Olympic* as 'like a City' with its luxurious new features including a swimming pool, Turkish baths and a gymnasium.

Initially, the press also reported that the *Olympic* exceeded builders' expectations with an average speed of 21.89 knots.[30] Later calculations estimate an actual average speed of 21.43 knots.[31] On the Monday, they were slowed for four hours on account of fog, delaying their arrival by at least 90 minutes into New York, a fact that is often overlooked by those who would later point to Smith's adherence to speed no matter the weather conditions, especially on a maiden voyage.[32]

As the ship was docking at Pier 59 in New York Harbor on 21 June 1911, one of twelve tugs assisting, the *O.L. Hallenbach*, was caught in the *Olympic*'s backwash, spun around, collided with the maiden ship and was momentarily trapped. The press was thankfully lenient. *The New York Times* reported it as a 'playful touch given to the stern of a tugboat, drawn under the counter of the *Olympic* by the suction of the tide'.[33] Blame was later apportioned entirely to the tug in subsequent court hearings. A critical point was that the *Olympic* was under a harbour pilot, Julius Adler, at the time of the incident, not Captain Smith – a situation that would reoccur later that year in Southampton.

The docking took the better part of an hour to complete, with a photograph (Figure 30) showing Captain Smith in his summer whites on the starboard wing bridge observing its progress, along with an unidentified man in a bowler hat. Some have claimed it is White Star managing director J. Bruce Ismay, although he was technically not allowed on the bridge, especially during this critical moment. It is more likely Julius Adler, the New York harbour pilot, looking on aghast as the photograph shows signs of extensive damage to the paintwork on the starboard bow – evidence that these larger vessels were problematic to manoeuvre, something that both Smith and Ismay would keenly feel in the months to come.

The *Olympic* was well received in New York. On the day of its return voyage to England, 8,000 people toured the ship and an estimated

Playing on Titanic's Bridge

CAPTAIN SMITH AND OFFICERS S.S. TITANIC.
Lost on 15th April, 1912, after collision with Iceberg in North Atlantic.
PHOTO BY KENNEDY, 50 YORK ST.

Figure 29: A period postcard that is frequently labelled incorrectly as the officers of the *Titanic*. This is actually Smith with his *Olympic* officers. There are only two, in addition to Smith, who went on to serve aboard the *Titanic* – First Officer William Murdoch (seated, far right) and Purser Hugh McElroy (standing, far left). (Author's collection)

Figure 30: RMS *Olympic* arriving in New York Harbor on her maiden voyage, 21 June 1911, Captain Smith visible on the starboard wing bridge, the harbour pilot and another unidentified officer in the wing cab. (Library of Congress)

Titanic Legacy: The Captain, the Daughter and the Spy

10,000 watched it sail at 3 pm on the afternoon of 28 June 1911. A dozen tugs were required to move her into the North River, careful to avoid striking the new temporary pier extension work as the tide carried her downstream. With no further issues, 'the biggest ship in the world' disappeared down the bay and returned safely home.[34] Arriving back in Southampton on 5 July, her average speed had reached an impressive 22.5 knots.

Smith remained as *Olympic*'s captain, balancing his duties as its master with constant press scrutiny. During a voyage in August 1911, he was asked in New York by a reporter what the *Olympic*'s coal consumption was during her maiden voyage, but simply shook his head and said: 'That is a coal story I am not privileged to speak about. I'll tell you another coal story, though, if you'd care to hear it?' When the reporter responded positively, Smith told the tale of a poor sailor who was buried at sea along with lumps of coal to make him sink. The punchline is from a 'landlubber' who observes: 'Well, I've seen many a man go below, but this is the first one I've seen taking his own coal down with him.'[35]

We catch a glimpse here of the diplomacy of a man familiar with dodging difficult questions with a humorous diversion – no doubt a tactic frequently used at the Captain's table with an overly inquisitive

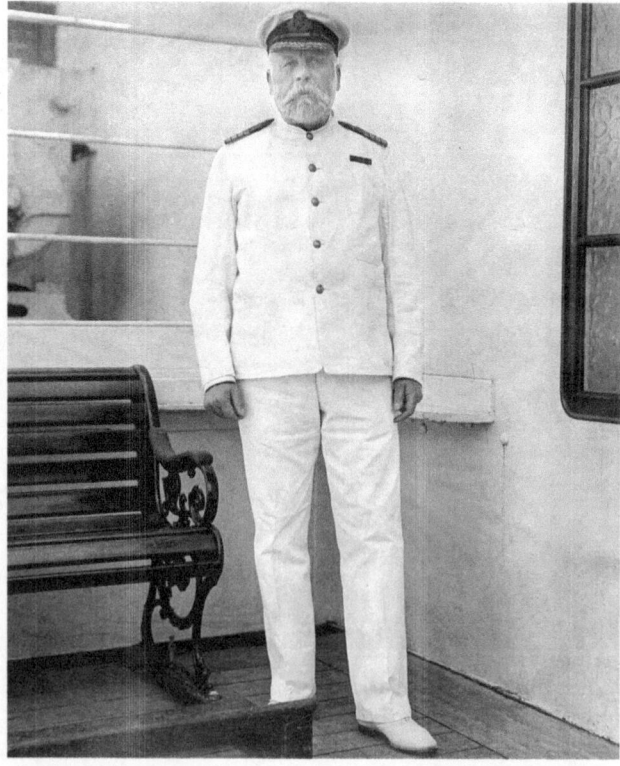

Figure 31: Captain Smith in his summer uniform, on the boat deck of the *Olympic* during summer 1911. (Kevin Saucier, Titanic Items Collection)

passenger. It would later become known that the daily coal consumption for the maiden crossing was 650 tons, with five of the single-ended boilers not used to reduce speed and save on fuel.[36]

The launch of a new class of ship came with the requisite publicity photographs and there were many taken of Smith and his officers in their summer white uniforms. There is even film footage of Smith pacing up and down the *Olympic*'s starboard wing bridge while they were docked in New York. He looks uncomfortable on camera, only smiling just before the shot ends – maybe relieved the ordeal is over. These shots would a year later be included in newsreels about the sinking, relabelled as if filmed aboard the *Titanic*, with names of tugs and pier signage scratched out to complete the illusion. It is also possible that Smith was filmed in colour, according to the 1912 edition of *The Moving Picture News*, under the heading 'Titanic's Captain in Kinemacolor':

> What is probably the last and best photograph ever taken of Captain E.J. Smith, the gallant commander of the ill-fated ocean leviathan, the steamship *Titanic*, was one posed by the veteran commodore of the White Star fleet especially for the Kinemacolor camera, just before his last voyage from America… This most lifelike Kinemacolor portrait in color-motion-photography shows the hale and hearty septuagenarian [sic] surrounded by his chief officers, a remarkable specimen of vigorous old age crowned with honors. The compact figure and broad shoulders, even the good-humored twinkle in the alert gray eyes, so familiar to thousands of ocean voyagers, are reproduced with perfect fidelity. This interesting group will be shown for the first time this evening (Wednesday, April 17th) at the Garden Theatre.[37]

The reference to his 'gray eyes' is interesting. Another source described him as 'bluff, blue-eyed, and bearded.'[38] This elaborate film synopsis is quite likely referring to a shoot before the *Olympic*'s departure from Southampton when a cameraman boarded the ship on 11 June 1911 and filmed Smith and his officers with a Kinemacolor camera, if a 1913 film catalogue is to be believed. The 4-minute reel thereafter disappeared but offers the tantalizing possibility that colour film of Smith and his officers exists somewhere.[39]

As was his routine while in New York during the summer, he would frequent the Glen Cove and the Nassau Country Club between voyages and was often spotted on the links where he 'played a good game'. In June 1911, during the coronation festivities for King George and Queen Mary, Henry W. J. Bucknall and his wife held a coronation dinner at their Glen Cove estate, with Captain Smith as the guest of honour.[40]

Figure 32: Captain Smith on the starboard boat deck of the *Olympic* in his summer uniform. This was likely taken at the same time as the more famous image of him, Figure 22. (Mary Evans Picture Library/ Onslow Auctions Limited)

Hawke Collision

The following month reporter's questions would take a serious turn, as Smith faced his most serious incident thus far. It occurred on the *Olympic*'s fifth voyage at 12:46 pm on 20 September 1911, when her hull was badly damaged in a collision with the Royal Navy cruiser the HMS *Hawke*, while leaving Southampton in the Solent, off the Isle of Wight. The warship, under the command of W. F. Blunt and with a bow designed to sink other vessels, lost her prow and the collision left two of *Olympic*'s compartments filled with seawater and one of her propeller shafts twisted. No one was killed or seriously injured and the *Olympic* was able to return to Southampton under her own steam.

It was an unusual situation. Both vessels were travelling in the same direction, on almost parallel courses. Suction was thought to be at play, explaining why the *Hawke* was inextricably drawn into the *Olympic*'s stern. What complicated things further, similar to the New York tug incident, is that the *Olympic* was technically under the control of Trinity House harbour pilot George W. Bowyer at the time of collision, while Captain Smith was still effectively in command. So, who was to blame?

The press reported that the White Star Line blamed the *Hawke* entirely for the collision, with experts saying the warship likely tried to cross the *Olympic*'s bow and then suddenly changed course. With an impending naval inquiry in Portsmouth, White Star refused to take any responsibility, alleging the cruiser was wholly at fault and heavy damages would be demanded of the government.[41] From a legal perspective, in 1911 shipowners were exempt from liability when under compulsory pilotage.[42]

During the Admiralty inquiry, it was established that Smith had been standing on the starboard wing and Bowyer was by the helmsman, Quartermaster Albert Haines, on the forward bridge. According to trial transcripts, Bowyer recalled Smith telling him that he did not believe the *Hawke* would go under their stern, and Bowyer requested Smith to tell him if she was going to strike so that he could put the helm hard-a-port. There was no immediate reply, so Bowyer followed up soon after with a direct question, asking if the *Hawke* was going to strike or not. It was only then that Smith told Bowyer in the affirmative, that the *Hawke* was indeed going to strike the *Olympic*'s stern, and Bowyer then ordered 'hard-a-port', but it was too late. By the time the wheel had been turned, the warship had collided with their stern. The implication is clear – that Bowyer felt Smith had not supplied the necessary information fast enough for him to take preventative action. However, in Smith's recollection, the two vessels were running at even speed and it was just as the *Olympic* accelerated and looked to outrun the *Hawke* that he noticed the warship suddenly start to 'fall in' and called out to Bowyer that he was 'starboarding' and was going to hit.[43]

The complex dance of authority between a captain and harbour pilot was something that Captain Arthur Rostron, of the *Titanic*'s rescue ship the *Carpathia*, commented on in his 1931 autobiography, *Home from the Sea*. Although Smith is not mentioned directly, Rostron makes a strong case for Smith being fundamentally to blame:

> Many people think, for instance, that when a pilot comes aboard the captain's authority and responsibility are superseded. Not at all. The captain is still the captain – even over the pilot. I have known a pilot run a ship aground because, poor fellow, he was on the verge of a seizure and was not responsible for what he was doing at the time. The captain of that vessel would have been blamed if he had not been at the man's side and was instantly ready to rectify the mistake he made.[44]

The impact of the *Hawke* collision would be far reaching. First, the voyage to New York had to be abandoned and the *Olympic* taken to Belfast for repairs, which took a good six weeks. This halted work on the *Titanic*, delaying construction, and her maiden voyage had to be rescheduled from 20 March to 10 April 1912. In another blow, in December the Admiralty inquiry found that the *Olympic* had indeed been responsible for the collision. There were several factors at play: the *Olympic* was allegedly sailing too fast for the conditions (16 knots) – although of course so was the *Hawke*. Eyewitness accounts indicated the *Hawke* appeared to be overtaking – Smith thought she had reached as far forward as the *Olympic*'s third funnel, while Bowyer believed she had reached the bridge. Notwithstanding, the rules at sea dictated that as the *Hawke* was to the starboard of the *Olympic*, it was for the *Olympic* to take avoiding action. That there were mitigating issues on both sides saw a judgment that decided the costs were to be equally shared by the two complainants. On a personal level, it absolved Smith specifically of blame, as his ship was under compulsory pilotage.

But the criticism was there, and it is interesting to see how both Bowyer and Smith handled it publicly and privately. For harbour pilot Bowyer, who came from a prestigious family of Southampton Trinity House pilots, it was a most embarrassing blip on an otherwise enviable career. A 1923 tribute in the form of a caricature described him as 'one of the world's greatest pilots'. A year after his retirement in 1929, he wrote a book entitled *Lively Ahoy*, reminiscing about his 58 years of harbour pilot service. The *Hawke* collision has only a brief mention and is clearly a painful memory:

> During the whole of my career I have met with two mishaps, namely, the 'St. Paul'–'Gladiator' collision on April 25th, 1908, and the 'Olympic'–'Hawke' collision on September 20th, 1911. Only those who have passed through an ordeal of this kind can appreciate the worry at the time... It is all very well for people who are not concerned in this case kindly to tell you not to worry; this is impossible, however much you feel that you are in the right. I had a clear conscience in both cases that I was right, and still hold a clear conscience, which nothing on earth can alter. Through the 'Olympic'–'Hawke' case, the late Capt. E.J. Smith, the officers, and I told the truth and nothing but the truth. It was taken to the House of Lords, but the verdict was not altered, the 'Olympic' losing the case. However, the company thought we were right, and I have piloted the 'Olympic,' the 'Homeric,' and the 'Majestic,' hundreds of times, up to my retirement on December 31st, 1929.[45]

We also have a rare insight into Smith's public response to the *Hawke* collision, albeit a newspaper article that was printed post-*Titanic* and hence emphasising the 'unsinkable' nature of the ships. The 16 April 1912 article in the *Washington Times* recalled a previous conversation a man had with Smith, in which an unidentified young officer interjected that 'the commander of the *Hawke* was entirely to blame. He was "showing off" his warship before a throng of passengers and made a miscalculation.' According to the newspaper article, 'Captain Smith smiled enigmatically at the theory advanced by his subordinate, but made no comment as to this view of the mishap. "Anyhow," declared Captain Smith, "the *Olympic* is unsinkable, and the *Titanic* will be the same when she is put in commission."'[46] Once again, Smith's famed diplomacy was on display. Smith even went further, according to the unnamed source, claiming 'either of these vessels could be cut in halves and each half would remain afloat indefinitely. The non-sinkable vessel has been reached in these two wonderful craft. I venture to add that even if the engines and boilers of these vessels were to fall through their bottoms the vessels would remain afloat.' The exaggeration was likely designed to deflect attention away from the ramifications and bad publicity of a collision to the design features in which a passenger should have confidence. And it is worth noting that claims of 'unsinkable' White Star ships were nothing new; reports using similar expressions went as far back as 1903.[47]

Privately, it was a different story. He was angry, as evidenced in a letter to his nephew Frank Hancock[48] The letter itself is also an insight into a man not only battling an unfair verdict, but also poor weather conditions, and considering the prospect of sailing aboard the *Titanic*:

On board R.M.S. 'OLYMPIC'
14th February 1912

My dear Frank
Yours of the 24th December and the one introducing Miss Brookfield came to hand and I owe you an apology for not answering promptly but I seemed to be kept in a perfect whirl and the days passed so quickly; when I thought of your letter it was somewhere it was not convenient to write and then it would slip from my memory, so there you are, it was not want of appreciation I assure you. I am pleased to hear you are hopeful of success in your undertakings, Sinclair is in Florida at present but when I meet him again will just mention you and sound him. You have no doubt heard we are appealing the case, I have not much hope as it is hard to upset a verdict in England; however it will let them see we are not going to take it lying down.

The Mallocks crossed with me last trip, we had a poor trip as far as weather was concerned but enjoy one or two chats at the Table. I did all I could for Miss Brookfield's comfort, I had her placed at my table but found she was in the Second Class, so could not have the pleasure of her company, however she was well looked after and I think was comfortable on the trip.

We had disagreeable weather and I had no opportunity of seeing her. We have not had pictures taken for years, you shall have one of the first.

I leave this ship after another voyage and bring out Titanic on April 10th from Southampton. Give my regards to the Gordons and Churchill if you see any of them. With Kindest and best wishes

Your Affectionate Uncle
Edw J. Smith

While brief and mostly in reply to the letter Frank sent in December, in addition to his distinct lack of hope in the *Hawke* court case, there is the tangible sense of a man leading a busy life – so busy as to neglect writing an immediate reply to Frank's letter, even too busy to have family photographs taken. His friendly disposition is on display – looking after the mutual friends the Mallocks and caring for a Miss Brookfield even if he could not enjoy the pleasure of her company as it turned out she was travelling second class. He certainly does not sound like a man in 'semi-retirement' and there is no mention of such a possibility when he notes

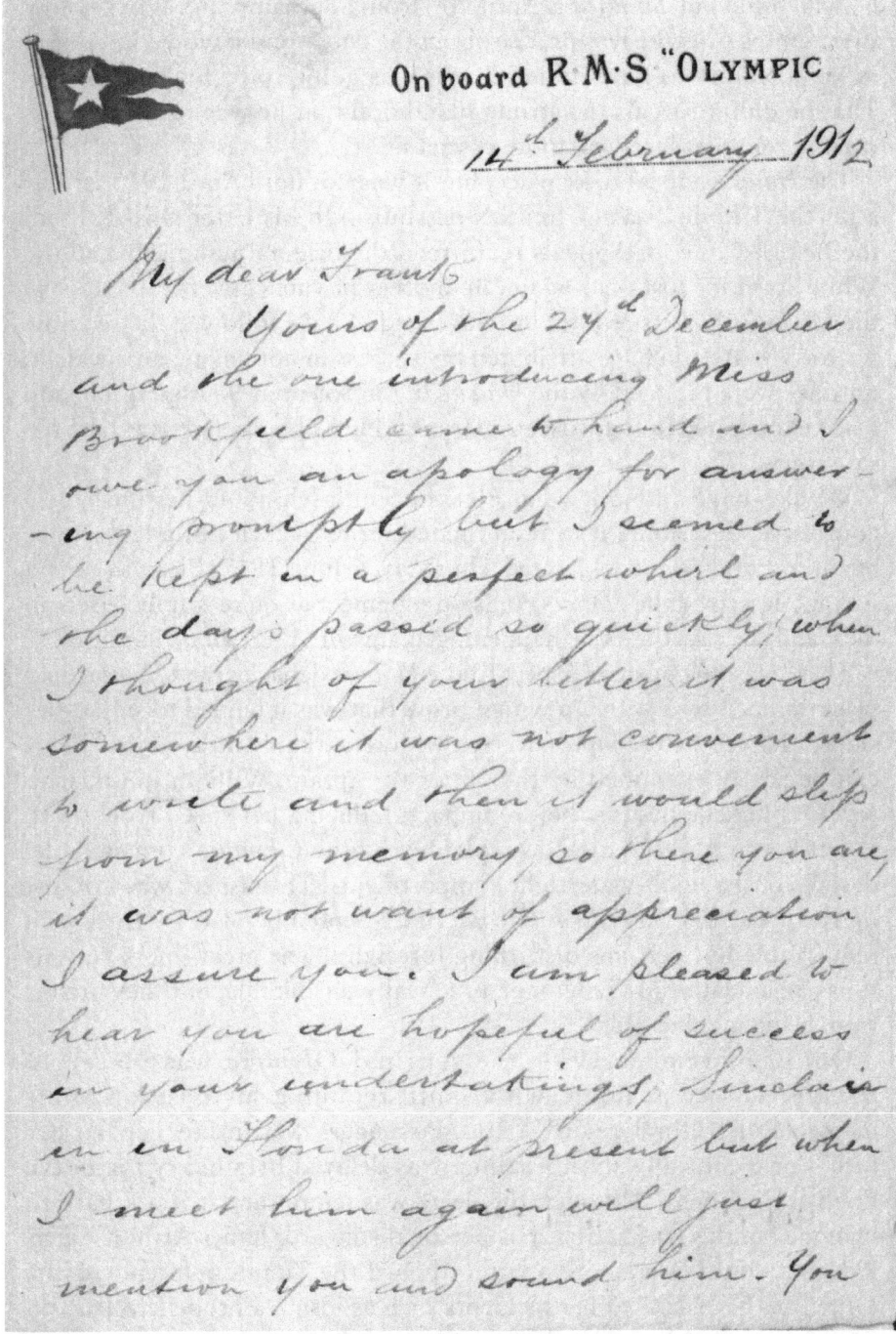

Figure 33: The first page in a three-page letter Captain Smith wrote in February 1912 while aboard the *Olympic*. (Reprinted by kind permission of the Mystic Seaport Museum: VFM 194, Manuscripts Collection, G.W. Blunt White Library, Mystic Seaport Museum, Inc.)

he will 'bring out *Titanic* on April 10th from Southampton'. Written only two months prior, he was precise about the date – and it would have been an opportunity to have added that it was going to be his last voyage. That he didn't reveals the strong likelihood that he was to continue as captain for at least several more voyages.

The *Hawke* appeal took place, but it was not until April 1913, a year after the *Titanic* disaster. Smith's pessimism in his letter was realised: the British Court of Appeals reaffirmed the original judgment and the White Star Line lost once again. In another private conversation aboard the *Olympic* he was reported to have said: 'I have followed the sea now for forty years and have attributed my success in not having an accident, until we were rammed by the *Hawke* in the Solent at Southampton, and I was exonerated in that case, to never taking a chance. I always take the safe course.'[49]

We also have a hint at what Eleanor Smith felt about her husband's court case, describing it in unmitigated terms as 'evil'. In a letter once again to Frank Hancock, dated Thursday, 6 June 1912, Eleanor, now a widow, described the *Hawke* collision judgment as quite simply based on 'lies' and she saw the same happening again with the *Titanic* inquiries.[50]

There was one positive aspect to the *Hawke* debacle: the *Olympic* had been rammed by a warship with a prow that was intended to sink other ships. And yet the *Olympic* survived with remarkably little damage. This can be partly explained by the *Hawke*'s captain, William Blunt, who reversed the engines just before impact, reducing her speed from 15 to about 8 knots. It can also be explained by the *Olympic*'s 'unsinkable' design consisting of watertight compartments. This aspect was not lost on the press. The *Aberdeen Journal* of 22 September 1911 wrote, with remarkable but perhaps disturbing foresight: 'The great liners may, as it has been claimed for them, be practically unsinkable, but they are far from being invulnerable.'[51]

On 30 November 1911, the repaired *Olympic* was poised to re-enter service at noon, with Smith retaining his position as its master. Frustratingly, with 1,200 passengers waiting to depart, her fifth – or technically sixth – sailing was delayed by a heavy fog in the English Channel.[52] Although the delay was temporary, it is not hard to imagine Smith's frustration. His personal steward, James Arthur 'Tiger' Paintin, would later write a letter aboard the Titanic referencing 'the *Olympic's* bad luck.' Other incidents such as losing a propeller blade on 24 February 1912 after striking a submerged object on a return voyage to Southampton would have only reaffirmed such feelings. Once again, the *Olympic* was in Belfast for repairs and the time spent on her was delaying efforts to ready the second in the fleet, the *Titanic*.

After the *Titanic* disaster, there would be retrospective claims that Captain Smith was the victim of 'the jealous power of Neptune'[53] or even 'Sea Kelpie' – that fate had turned against him causing him to experience 'bad luck' that began with the *Hawke* collision.[54] One American article, under the title of 'Bad Luck of Commander', said that the collision was the first of 'evil days' and there was 'amazement of officers in the service of the merchant marine of all countries, for the rule that the steam ship captain whose vessel suffers serious damage is ipso facto a captain out of employment.' The article referenced White Star Captain Inman Sealby, who in 1909 was dismissed from the company after the *Republic* was sunk by the *Florida*, despite no blame attached for faulty navigation or seamanship (it occurred during fog).

As for the White Star Line, they were still entirely confident in Smith's abilities. When company director Harold Sanderson was asked about Captain Smith's standing, he responded: 'He was our senior commander ... and a man in whom we had special confidence; otherwise, he would not have been in the position.'[55] At most, Edward Smith likely lost his £200 no-collision bonus in 1911.

The Dinner

On 19 December 1911, the Admiralty announced that the *Olympic* was solely to blame for the collision, although notably with negligent navigation on the part of harbour pilot George Bowyer. This was enough to signal the go-ahead of an event on 28 December 1911 in Captain Smith's honour, who 'had just been cleared of all blame in the accident which the ship he then commanded, the *Olympic*'. As a vote of confidence from Smith's wealthy admirers in the United States, this was no ordinary event. It was held at the Metropolitan Club in New York and was attended by 'millionaires ... some of the most notable men in New York's financial life' and 'kings of finance' who sat at tables in their finest tuxedos and 'raised $5000 as a testimonial to the seaman they all loved'.[56] J. P. Morgan was a member of what was aptly called the 'Millionaire's Club' and so was most likely in attendance. One attendee, Colonel William Hester, described the event:

> Last fall, on Captain Smith's return to New York after the collision with the Hawk, about one hundred of his friends gave him a dinner at the Metropolitan Club as an expression of their sympathy and confidence in him, at which Chauncey M. Depew spoke, as well as Controller Prendergast, Dr. St. Clair McKelway and Mr. Lawrence of the Lotos

Club and others. Captain Smith made a very modest speech thanking his friends for their esteem. Besides good wishes, a purse of several thousand dollars was presented to him.[57]

In an impressive photograph that accompanied the retrospective article, a blurry image of a balding Smith can be seen standing at the rear of a large room that is decorated with American and British flags, standing 'at the head of the table between two old friends, under the folds of the American flag'. This picture was a proud moment not only for Ted, but his family as well, as his wife Eleanor would later write in a letter to Smith's nephew Frank: 'I am more than proud of that picture, – I have a large one of 'the dinner' – it's a great souvenir to hand down to his Gillie [Mel] and her children.'[58] The widow Eleanor would later bring a copy of the photograph with her on trips to see family and friends.

Smith's fellow deck officers also saw this event as showing how New York felt Smith was free of blame for the *Hawke* collision. Officers of the White Star liner *Afric* later said: 'When Captain Smith arrived there on his next trip a huge banquet was tendered him by his admirers of the United States. At that dinner millionaires, senators, and leaders of society spoke to the toast of Captain Smith, and all recognised the guest of the evening as a navigator in whom they placed unbounded confidence.'[59]

Figure 34: Captain Smith, without a cap, can be seen on the far left at the rear of the room 'at the head of the table between two old friends, under the folds of the American flag'. This photograph was a proud moment for the Smith family and became a family heirloom. *The Hawaiian Gazette*, 23 April 1912. (Library of Congress)

Lifeboats

It was long after Smith's time aboard the *Olympic* that she would one day earn the title 'Old Reliable' after serving as a troop ship transporting thousands of Canadians during the First World War. There was evidence of her reliability during Smith's tenure, however, in an incident on 14 January 1912 on the west-bound crossing to New York when the *Olympic* encountered a storm so severe that Captain Smith remembered it as the worst of his career. Sixty-foot waves ripped away railing on the forecastle and tore the five-ton no. 1 hatch off, but her structure held sound; there was no sign of weakness in the hull.[60] During his command of the *Majestic*, he had garnered the impressive moniker of 'Storm King', hinting at his fortitude during inclement weather. He even had some input on the *Titanic*'s design after seeing room for improvement with the *Olympic* during stormy weather, suggesting the addition of protective windows with bull's eye lights to the square windows forward on the bridge, for protection against breakage in bad weather.[61]

Privately, Smith was not happy with the *Olympic*, nor with the prospect of commanding her younger sister *Titanic*, according to an account from a *Ship News* journalist, Jack Lawrence, who was familiar with several veteran White Star officers including Chief Officer Henry Wilde. Lawrence wrote:

> Captain Smith had not been happy in the Olympic and, according to what one of his staff officers told me later, the prospect of commanding the Titanic on her maiden voyage depressed him for many weeks before he ever saw that vessel's bridge. He was one of a great many of Britain's seafaring men who believed that naval architects had gone a little mad in their effort to produce new masterpieces in bulk, luxury and speed. He clung to the antiquated notion that a vessel of twenty-five thousand tons and seven hundred feet long was good enough to carry any man across the Atlantic in comfort. He did not believe that Ritz-Carleton restaurants, Roman baths and gold-encrusted ball-rooms were essential to the happiness of transatlantic travelers.[62]

Lawrence goes on to explain that part of the problem was because he had become a 'relic of the past' and that some of his contemporaries thought he was 'old fashioned. He certainly looked old fashioned with his rolling gait, his puckered eyes and white beard' – that was more evocative of the days of square-rigged sailing ships than modern steam liners.

Smith possibly had concerns over one design feature aboard the *Olympic*: the lifeboats. In a curious story by Glenn Marston who travelled to Europe aboard the *Olympic* and published his recollection after the *Titanic* disaster, Smith had noted in conversation the shortage of lifeboats and expressed his concerns. Marston claims Smith told him:

> We have not enough boats or rafts aboard to take care of more than one-third of the passengers. The *Titanic* too, is no better equipped. It ought to carry at least double the number of boats and rafts it does to afford any real protection to the passengers. Besides, there is always danger of some of the boats becoming damaged or swept away before they can be manned... I don't think it's from motives of economy as the additional equipment would cost only a trifle when compared to the cost of the ship, but the builders nowadays believe that their boats are practically indestructible as far as sinking goes, because of the watertight bulkheads, and that the only need of lifeboats at all is for purposes of rescue from other ships that are not so modernly constructed or to land passengers in case of the ship going ashore. They hardly regard them as life-saving equipment.[63]

If this conversation is accurate, Smith had a point. In the first decade of the twentieth century, as wireless technology and ship design advanced and sea routes became more popular, ships were equipped with lifeboats primarily for transferring people from one vessel to another in the event of a disaster, rather than holding a full complement of passengers and crew. Intercontinental ships operated by Cunard and White Star were almost always on busy routes where there were dozens of other vessels nearby at any given time, so the concept was that in the event of an evacuation all passengers and crew would eventually be ferried to another vessel. Despite their size, the lack of lifeboats was not unique to the *Olympic* and *Titanic* and was certainly not new to the industry. According to figures supplied by the Board of Trade at the time of the *Titanic* disaster, almost all other large passenger liners had a gross deficiency in lifeboat numbers compared to capacity. For example, Canadian Pacific Steamship's *Empress of Britain* (1906) had a capacity of 1,914, but only 21 boats for 1,045. Even more surprising, Cunard's *Mauretania* (1906) had a capacity of 2,972, but only 16 lifeboats for 976.[64] *Titanic* sinking survivor Lawrence Beesley pointed out the irony that the rescue ship, Cunard's *Carpathia*, had a 'lower [lifeboat] accommodation per head than the Titanic, and I don't think the Carpathia was built as an unsinkable boat'.[65] For what it's worth, the White Star Line's Olympic-class ships were originally equipped with more lifeboats than what was legally required by the British Board of Trade regulations. For example, *Titanic*'s lifeboat capacity was increased by almost one-fifth between the design stage in 1908 and final construction. The combination of increased lifeboat capacity and the reduced number of passengers and crew meant that *Titanic*'s lifeboat capacity as a proportion of the total number of passengers and crew she could carry rose by almost 39 per cent.[66]

Regardless, according to Martson, Smith believed a shipping line should take no chances and had an obligation to ensure a place for everyone in a lifeboat, although he admitted he had no say in the decision-making process. Smith allegedly told him:

> Personally, I believe that a ship ought to carry enough boats and rafts to carry every soul aboard it… While there is only one chance in a thousand that a ship like the *Olympic* or *Titanic* may meet with an accident that would injure it so severely that it would sink before aid would arrive, yet, if I had my way, both ships would be equipped with twice the number of lifeboats and rafts. In the old days it was different from to-day, with the mergers and Trusts in the steamship business. Now the captain has little to say regarding equipment. All of that has been taken out of his hands and is taken care of at the main office.[67]

The accuracy of Glenn Marston's recollection of his conversation with Captain Smith is impossible to verify, but we do know that Smith took lifeboats seriously. During the British Board of Trade *Titanic* Inquiry in 1912, it was revealed that Smith was progressively checking and testing the *Olympic*'s lifeboats. The Solicitor-General concluded, based on Smith's reports, that it would 'appear as though two boats were selected on each occasion, but they do not take the same two boats, and by taking different boats it does appear as though there was a gradual testing of different people.' The Solicitor-General read out a list of dates accompanied by the lifeboat number that was tested – each time a different lifeboat. The final entry was Tuesday, 22 March 1912, in which Smith noted: 'Nos. 13 and 15 swung out, lowered, and crews exercised. All davits and falls in good order.'[68]

March 1912 was Smith's final time aboard the *Olympic*. His next command was the *Titanic*. In contrast to his concerns expressed to Marston, those who dined with him just prior to taking command reported he was full of confidence in his new ship. In a newspaper report published post-disaster, a 'Mr. and Mrs. W.P. Willis of Flushing' recalled having dinner with Captain Smith the night before he left for Europe and that he was

> …enthusiastic over the prospects of his new command. He said he shared with the designers of the vessel the utmost confidence in its

seagoing qualities, and told Mr. and Mrs. Willis that it was impossible for it to sink. He looked forward then to the most successful days of his seafaring career, and especially dwelt upon the idea that the *Titanic*'s appearance on the Atlantic would mark a high point of safety and comfort in the evolution of ocean travel. He regarded that vessel as one that would keep above water in the face of the utmost unexpected trial. He said that even if a part of the ship should be seriously damaged there need be no doubt that she would reach port.'[69]

Smith could never have known how soon his faith in shipbuilding would be tested.

Titanic

Edward Smith was not *Titanic*'s first captain. As early as 1910, newspaper reports had indicated that Captain Herbert Haddock would take command of *Olympic*'s sister ship.[70] Haddock was not as popular as Smith but was a very much admired and capable captain in his own right. The two captains had been born on the same day – 27 January – Smith in 1850, Haddock in 1861, in Rugby, Warwickshire. Joining the White Star Line in 1888, as fourth officer, he very quickly climbed the ranks, reaching chief officer within four years and made commander in his fifth year at the line. Haddock spent the next twelve years establishing himself as the respected, multi-talented (painting, fencing, French, German and wireless operating are listed among his many hobbies) and reliable master of the *Britannic*, *Germanic*, *Cedric* and *Oceanic*.

He was a solid choice to become the new commander of the *Olympic*, allowing Smith to captain the maiden voyage of *Titanic*. So as Smith returned from New York aboard the *Olympic*, on 25 March 1912, 51-year-old Herbert Haddock took command of the newly built *Titanic* for six days. He would never take the ship out to sea; she remained moored at the Harland and Wolff dockyards in Belfast. His duties were just as critical – assisting with the mustering of the senior and junior officers and other crew and the rigorous Board of Trade safety inspections, all in preparation for the sea trials scheduled for when Smith arrived on 1 April and took over as master. One person who noted his arrival with interest was the youngest of the junior officers, Sixth officer James Moody, who wrote a letter to his sister shortly thereafter: 'Though I believe [Smith]'s an awful stickler for discipline, he's popular with everybody. "Daddy Haddock" is going to the Olympic until old "E.J." retires on his old age pension from the Titanic.'[71]

Figure 35: An impressive close-up of Captain E.J. Smith in his summer uniform, so probably in the summer of 1911 aboard the *Olympic*. (Kevin Saucier, Titanic Items Collection)

It is interesting that Moody referenced Smith's impending retirement, revealing that it was a common rumour among the officers, and one that would gain more traction after 'E.J.'s death. Although there was no legal requirement in 1910, rival line Cunard put an age limit of 60 years for captains of their new ships the *Mauretania* and *Lusitania*. Newspaper reports from 1911 indicate Smith was due for retirement. *The New York Times* of 6 June 1911 reported: 'Capt. E.J. Smith, R.N.R., the Commodore of the White Star Line, who is to command the new mammoth liner Olympic, will retire at the end of the present year, it is understood, as he will have reached his age limit. He will be relieved by Capt. H.J. Haddock of the Oceanic.'[72] To allay any concerns for passengers who planned their voyages around Smith's schedule, on 10 April – *Titanic*'s sailing day – several newspapers printed a statement from the White Star Line that Smith would remain in command of the *Titanic* until 'a larger and finer vessel' was commissioned, which would have been the *Britannic*, still under construction and likely a year away from entering service. The *Halifax Morning Chronicle* of 9 April 1912 carried the same story.[73]

While it is certain that Smith was on the verge of retirement for at least a year prior to *Titanic*, he was not necessarily going to retire immediately after *Titanic*'s voyage to New York as is frequently claimed, in an attempt to heighten the sense of cruel fate taking a hand. There is no documented evidence it was to be his last voyage. Notably, his wife Eleanor, when writing soon after his death, never mentioned it. Author Gary Cooper has suggested that the White Star Line might even have encouraged rumours of retirement, not denying them until the last moment, in order to benefit from bookings by passengers not wanting to miss out on the famous E.J.'s 'last' voyage.[74] Another author, Simon Angel, theorises that the confusion was partly caused by his recent retirement from the Royal Navy Reserve, with whom he held the rank of Commander. Angel also recounts an unverified and unlikely story that prior to departure, Smith visited the father of stewardess Sarah Stap, himself a master mariner, and told him that this would be his last crossing, and he would be returning as a passenger.[75]

You can detect a sensitivity surrounding his age from the man himself. When Smith signed the *Titanic*'s crew agreement document on the 6 April 1912, he put his age down as 59, while he was in reality 62 (Figure 36). The average life expectancy for a male in England in 1912 was 51 years, so Smith may well have felt his age and did not want to depart from his cherished job too soon.[76]

The constant changing of ships was becoming tiresome for Dr William O'Loughlin. The same age as Smith, he met with E.J. and a fellow doctor, J. C. H. Beaumont, in the months leading up to their impending transfer from the *Olympic* to *Titanic*. They were in the South Western Hotel in Southampton when O'Loughlin admitted he was 'tired at this time of life to be changing from one ship to another. When he mentioned this to Captain Smith the latter chided him for being lazy and told him to pack up and come with him.'[77] While Beaumont stayed aboard the *Olympic*, O'Loughlin followed Smith's advice and was later lost in the disaster.

There was no denying that Smith's appointment as commander of another maiden voyage was also due to his popularity among passengers – including those sailing eastward. New York journalist Jack Lawrence noted:

He had his own following in the North Atlantic passenger trade. He had his loyal customers who would have sailed with him even

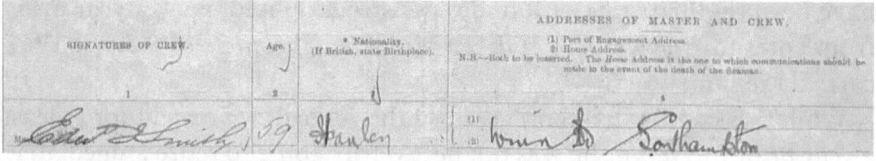

Figure 36: An excerpt from *Titanic*'s Agreement and Crew List. 62-year-old Smith signed on as aged 59. (National Archives, BT/100/259)

though his command had been only a leaky and wallowing cattle ship. He had the complete confidence of those solid, conservative travelers to whom crossing the Atlantic is a regular item on each year's schedule... Clerks in the White Star offices on lower Broadway used to say that many customers, coming in to book passage, would begin operations by asking for the ship commanded by Captain E.J. Smith. The identity of the ship didn't seem to matter at all so long as Captain Smith was on the bridge.[78]

An example of this popularity is first class passenger Frederick Hoyt who acknowledged that he decided to sail aboard *Titanic*, not because of her maiden voyage, but 'because Captain Smith was a personal acquaintance, as was also Dr William F.N. O'Loughlin.'[79] Author Walter Lord was also aware of Smith's magnetic character. He later told Smith's daughter: 'My grandfather would never travel with any other Captain, always insisted on going on the *Baltic*, and later the *Adriatic*, because Captain Smith was there.'[80]

In a frustrating delay after much anticipation, *Titanic*'s sea trials were postponed on 1 April to the following day due to unfavourable sea conditions. On Tuesday, 2 April, the weather eased, and Smith was finally able to take *Titanic* along Belfast Lough and out into the Irish Sea. Manned by a skeleton crew, the ship was put through a series of speed and turning tests over the course of twelve hours, under the watchful eyes of Board of Trade surveyors. By 7 pm that evening, the *Titanic* had been declared seaworthy, valid for twelve months, and without any further delay Smith immediately ordered *Titanic* for Southampton, as much remained to be done in preparation for the maiden voyage in just over a week's time. On the short 'delivery trip' Smith allegedly had his first paying passenger, a Wyckoff Van Derhoef, travelling from Belfast to the States, who, if true, would have had first class all to himself. Recent research has cast doubt on this story.[81]

On the same day *Titanic* passed her sea trials, Melville turned 14. No doubt Smith was eager to return to give his only daughter belated birthday wishes. In the early hours of Thursday, 4 April, the *Titanic* arrived in Southampton and docked at berth 44. While he still had to oversee the huge amount of work required to ready *Titanic* for sailing day, Smith could once again spend precious family time back home in Woodhead with Eleanor and Mel, maybe walking their dog along Lover's Walk in the nearby Southampton Common. Not only that, but it also meant Mel could visit him aboard *Titanic*. 45 years after the disaster, Mel recalled in a newspaper interview her memories of *Titanic*: 'My father came out of retirement to take the ship across the Atlantic as a special favour to the company. He had completed eight million miles at sea before retiring. Many of the crew were about to retire but decided to make the trip to serve under him just once more. Passengers would often wait for his ship before making a trip.' [82]

The details are not entirely accurate but the sentiment is clear. Most poignantly, she remembered that 'while he was fitting out the ship before sailing, she often went with him and played on the bridge.'

As a teenager, it is hard to imagine Mel skipping around the bridge playing hide and seek with imaginary friends – she was likely too old for such games. But this quote does reveal time spent with her father in his workplace, possibly aboard his earlier ships when she was young enough to consider a bridge a playground. The bridge was strictly off limits to passengers when a ship was in service; allowances were made for press and dignitaries when a ship was docked. That Smith was comfortable to have his daughter in such an environment is testament to their relationship and perhaps the guilt he felt for not being there for her while at sea. Mel also recalled she 'often' visited him on the bridge, so it was not a one-off occurrence.

It was certainly not unusual for White Star officers to have family aboard *Titanic* and in the Officers' Quarters during this busy time. Chief Officer William Murdoch wrote a letter to his younger sister Peg on 8 April, two days before sailing, in which he told her his wife Ada 'is on board just now, having a look through; one of the officers is taking her around.'[83]

There was not much time for rest – in the same letter, Murdoch explained that 'the holidays are on down here & it takes me all my time to get men to work even at overtime rates, but we are nearly ready for the road.' Henry Wilde also wrote a letter on 7 April expressing how much work needed to be done. 'I have been kept very busy on board all day on Good Friday and again today Sunday with the crew getting the ship ready. She is very far behind to sail on Wednesday. Working on her night and day.'[84]

The letters Wilde and Murdoch wrote to family hinted at a disturbance that occurred among the officers on 9 April – the day before sailing. At 2:30 pm Henry Wilde was officially confirmed as *Titanic*'s Chief Officer – 'bumping' William Murdoch from that rank down to First Officer, Charles Herbert Lightoller down to Second Officer, and the original, David Blair, lost his rank altogether and had to leave ship. This last-minute reshuffle also meant that officers Murdoch and Lightoller did not have enough time to change their uniforms – as the jacket sleeves contained rank insignia in the form of golden lace cuff braids, with an executive curl: three stripes for chief officer and two for first officer. In the last known photograph of William Murdoch, taken in Queenstown, Ireland, *Titanic*'s last port of call, on 11 April, he is seen working beside Lightoller as they prepare to close the gangway door. On Lightoller's sleeve there are two stripes, indicating the rank of First Officer, when he was Second. This would suggest that Murdoch was still wearing his Chief Officer's stripes (that is, three stripes and would explain later confusion among eyewitnesses who incorrectly described Murdoch as the 'Chief Officer').

Murdoch and Lightoller were not happy. Dropping down a rank meant a decrease in salary – from £25 to £17 in Murdoch's case. He wrote to his sister Peg on 8 April: 'I am still Chief Offr [Officer] until sailing day & then it looks as though I will have to step back, [to First Officer] so I am hoping that it will not be for long.'[85] Lightoller wrote that 'this doubtful policy threw both Murdoch and me out of our stride; and, apart from the disappointment of having to step back in our rank, caused quite a little confusion.'[86]

The 'doubtful' officer reshuffle has often been attributed to Captain Smith preferring to have Wilde, rather than Murdoch, as his Chief Officer. Was Smith really to blame for this unfortunate situation? The reality is that Smith likely had little say in the matter. As early as 30 March, before Smith had arrived to assume command of *Titanic* and while Wilde was still aboard the *Olympic,* Wilde wrote that he was 'not sailing in this ship on Wednesday but going to join the *Titani*'. He gave a specific reason: 'All arrangements are upset just now owing to the coal strikes.' On the following day, 31 March, Wilde elaborated in a letter to his sister-in-law Annie, telling her, 'I am awfully disappointed to find that all arrangements for my taking command of the 'Cymric' this time are altered, due to this coal strike and having to cancel so many of the ships and sailings... I am now going to join the 'Titanic' for a time until some other ship turns up for me. How long that will be I cannot tell.'[87]

Wilde's disappointment at not taking command of the *Cymric* created an opportunity for White Star to exploit his availability to assist with preparing the *Titanic* for her departure. By the seventh at the latest, Wilde was aboard helping Smith and his officers. Then on 9 April, Wilde described receiving a telegram from Liverpool informing him of his appointment.

Lightoller described the instruction as coming from 'the ruling lights of the White Star Line' while Murdoch, in his letter, also clearly lays the blame for his demotion, not with Smith, but at the feet of White Star headquarters in Liverpool: 'The head Marine Supt. [Superintendent] from L'pool seemed to be very favourably impressed & satisfied that everything went on A.1 & as much as promised that when Wilde goes I am to go up again.'[88] Whatever the case, Smith would have seven deck officers under his authority who were all technically captains in their own right; they all – even the junior officers – held Master's certificates, a qualification that enabled an officer to take command of a ship.

Titanic Legacy: The Captain, the Daughter and the Spy

The night before the ship sailed from Southampton, Smith was said to have been asked by a friend over dinner: 'What wind or weather would you fear supposing your ship were in danger?' The Captain was said to have responded: 'I fear no winds or weather. I fear only icebergs!'[89]

Thanks to the efforts of Smith and his officers, come sailing day, Wednesday, 10 April 1912, *Titanic* was ready. Both Eleanor and Mel would later recall their last moments with the Captain before he departed Woodhead for his new ship.

Eleanor later wrote to Frank Hancock about wanting to leave Woodhead and 'what a wrench to leave the sacred room of his, where one last said goodbye.'[90] Exactly which room was Smith's 'sacred room' is unknown, (Cooper suggests it was his study)[91] but the possessive tense of the phrase suggests he may well have had his own private room, an office, kept aside for work, where Eleanor wished him well for the maiden voyage and they said their last goodbyes.

Mel remembered her father 'wearing a high bowler hat and a long overcoat. It was before seven o'clock on April 10th, 1912... He got into a taxi and I can remember him leaning out to wave goodbye to my mother and myself.'[92]

Figure 37: Captain Smith on the port side of the bridge of the *Titanic*. His daughter Mel recalled playing in this bridge area. It is also the only image of *Titanic*'s bridge known to exist. The port engine telegraph is visible through the window. (Author's collection)

Playing on Titanic's *Bridge*

The time of seven o'clock is corroborated by Albert 'Ben' Benham, an eleven-year-old boy who had a paper round that included Winn Road. He remembered giving Smith his paper on that very morning:

> I used to do that round before I went to school in the week. When I got up to the last house before where Captain Smith lived, he was just coming out. And I always remember him saying to me, 'Alright son, I'll take my paper.' And I gave him his newspaper. He was going down to the docks to join the *Titanic*. It was about 7 am in the morning. He was going down there for the Board of Trade muster at 8 am when all the members of the crew had to be there, from the captain right down to the bellboy.[93]

Travelling south by taxi, it is a three-mile downhill route to the White Star Line dock at berth 44 – no more than a ten-to-twelve-minute journey in normal traffic. Smith would have arrived aboard *Titanic* no later than 7.30 am and received the day's sailing report from Chief Officer Wilde to prepare for the Board of Trade muster at 8. By that time, the 15-foot long R.N.R. Blue Ensign flag would have been raised on *Titanic*'s stern.

Figure 38: A computer-generated visualisation of Captain Smith's sitting room, with a doorway through to his bedroom and bathroom. (Courtesy of Christopher Walker @rmstitanicdesign, rmstitanicdesign.com)

Once aboard, Smith would have proceeded to his cabin and changed into his uniform. His private quarters were situated on the forward starboard side of the Officers' Quarters and consisted of three rooms – a sitting room, a bedroom and a bathroom (Figure 39). The largest of the three rooms was the sitting room accessed directly through the Navigating Room which in turn was connected to the Wheelhouse, which meant that Smith could be on the bridge within seconds if need be. The sitting room had a table, settee, wardrobes and a desk and could possibly be used for entertaining guests or private meetings (see Figure 38). The bedroom was very simple, consisting of a bed and desk. The Captain's lavatory was fitted with a porcelain bathtub with intricate plumbing for both fresh water and sea water. Famously, this bath can still be seen in the wreck – although as the wreck deteriorates it is disappearing slowly from view. Another prominent feature was a large bookcase. Cooper notes that 'one of his great passions was reading and he kept a small collection of books in his cabin.'[94]

Smith's usual uniform was, as with the other officers, the 'service dress' or 'undress' uniform, the most basic White Star Line uniform the officers would wear when on duty. The waist-long reefer jacket was double breasted (sometimes referred to as a 'monkey jacket') with eight raised White Star Line brass buttons, four on each side, all bearing the White Star emblem. The material was 'Navy blue' almost black in colour and most often of the 'Melton' variety or 'naval doeskin', a smooth, finely woven wool. Under the jacket he would wear a white dress shirt with separate collars and cuffs, with the collar turned down, and a black silk tie. The Captain's rank insignia (four stripes) was on both sleeves using black lace with an executive curl. The cap was worn with or without a white 'topper' (depending on the season – a white version of the uniform was used during the summer months).

On more formal occasions, Smith's uniform would change to 'Full Company Dress.' The reefer/monkey jacket would be replaced with the double-breasted, knee-long jacket (frock jacket), with a stand and fall collar, and ten brass buttons featuring the White Star emblem. A noticeable part of this 'Mess Dress' were the ceremonial gloves, most often white, to be held in the left hand whenever photographed.

So, on the day of *Titanic*'s maiden voyage, Smith put on his Full Company Dress and held his black cloth gloves in his hands and was subsequently captured in two locations by press photographers. Firstly, he was photographed standing outside the port side Officers' Quarters on the boat deck. The First and Second Officers' cabin windows were behind him. The rush to prepare *Titanic* for her maiden voyage is visible

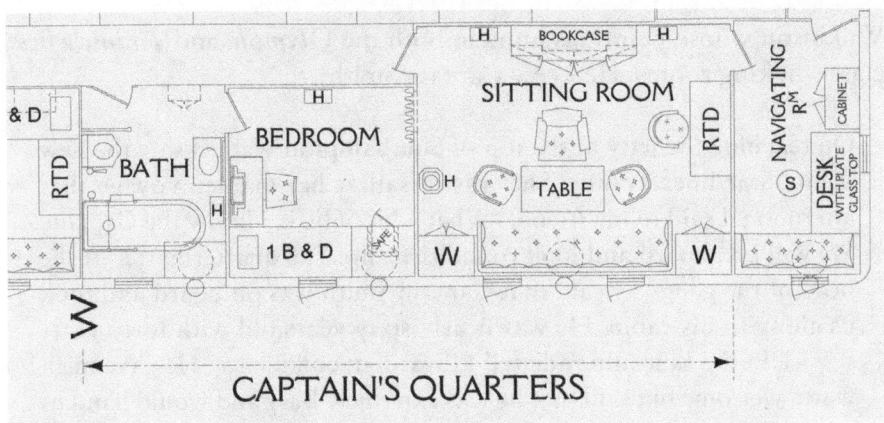

Figure 39: The layout of the Captain's Quarters aboard *Titanic*, comprising sitting room, the bedroom and bathroom. His quarters were directly connected to the Navigating Room, which was accessible via the bridge wheelhouse. (Courtesy of Matthew DeWinkeleer, 'Titanic: Honor and Glory', titanicdeckplan.com)

in the debris (with plant trimmings from the night before) on the deck at his feet. He was photographed by three different agencies from three slightly different angles – the Newspaper Illustrations Ltd, Illustrations Bureau and Central News.[95]

The second and more impressive location was the bridge, Smith seen standing somewhat pensively on the port side of the wooden navigational structure, allowing us one of the only tantalizing glimpses into *Titanic*'s interior bridge, with a large telegraph visible through the window behind his shoulder (Figure 37). The photograph was taken by the Newspaper Illustrations Ltd agency.

There was other pressing work to be done aside from posing for the press. In the series of photographs, one can detect a sense of unease on the Captain's face, with knowledge that his time was limited – they were just over an hour away from departure and he was eager to get back to work. The crew muster, in which First officer William Murdoch called out the names, finished at around 9 am and at 9.30 am the first class passengers began arriving. A boat drill was also performed for the Board of Trade inspector. At 11 am, Trinity House harbour pilot George Bowyer arrived and readied the ship for departure. It was now many months since the frustrations of the *Hawke* collision and although the legal wranglings were still in process, no doubt Bowyer (the officers referred to him as 'Uncle George') and Smith were determined to ensure a smooth and trouble-free sailing.

During this time, passengers continued to board, along with some inquisitive visitors. One such visitor was the maritime artist Norman

Wilkinson whose paintings hung in both the *Olympic* and *Titanic*'s first class smoking rooms. He knew Captain Smith:

> On reaching the jetty at the top of Southampton Water I saw the new White Star liner Titanic. She was to sail as her maiden voyage that afternoon. I said to my friend, "What a bit of luck. I know the Captain. We will go aboard and look round the ship. The quartermaster at the head of the gangway said that Captain Smith was on board and took us along to his cabin. He was nearly sixty years old with forty years service in the Line and radiated Edwardian confidence. He gave me a warm welcome but said that he was extremely busy and would hand us over to the Purser, who would show us round.[96]

Another Southampton visitor also observed how busy the *Titanic*'s master was. Roy Diaper's father took him aboard to meet the captain:

> My father was a mariner, at one time he was in the Royal Mail Steam Packet Company… My father just simply said to me 'I'm taking you down to see the Titanic'… he thought it would be a good thing for me to see it and he knew Captain Smith… We went up a covered gangway into the ship, it was huge, I was very overawed… My other impression I got then was of a tall man completely bearded and wearing a frock coat, he had on a peaked cap and the thing that struck me was that it was not like the ones that are worn today, it had a small brim and small top. I remember my father speaking to him. Captain Smith didn't speak to me but he bent down and shook me by the hand, there was a tremendous bustle going on and Captain Smith was surrounded by people.[97]

Once the senior officers Wilde, Murdoch and Lightoller had submitted their reports to Smith, First Officer Murdoch reported the vessel ready to sail. One of the reports Smith signed was *Titanic*'s crew list that detailed numbers signed on to the Deck department (73, including two window cleaners), Engine department (325), Steward department (494, including two 'telegraphists') that came to a total of 892 (Figure 40). First and second class passenger lists were hurriedly completed, one copy sent to the ship's print shop, the other handed to Smith who likely scanned the names, recognising many from previous voyages and already anticipating those who would be at his table. There were other more pressing matters, such as a minor coal fire in the number 10 bunker of boiler room number 5. Chief Engineer Bell reassured the Captain the situation was under control. There was likely no damage, and it would

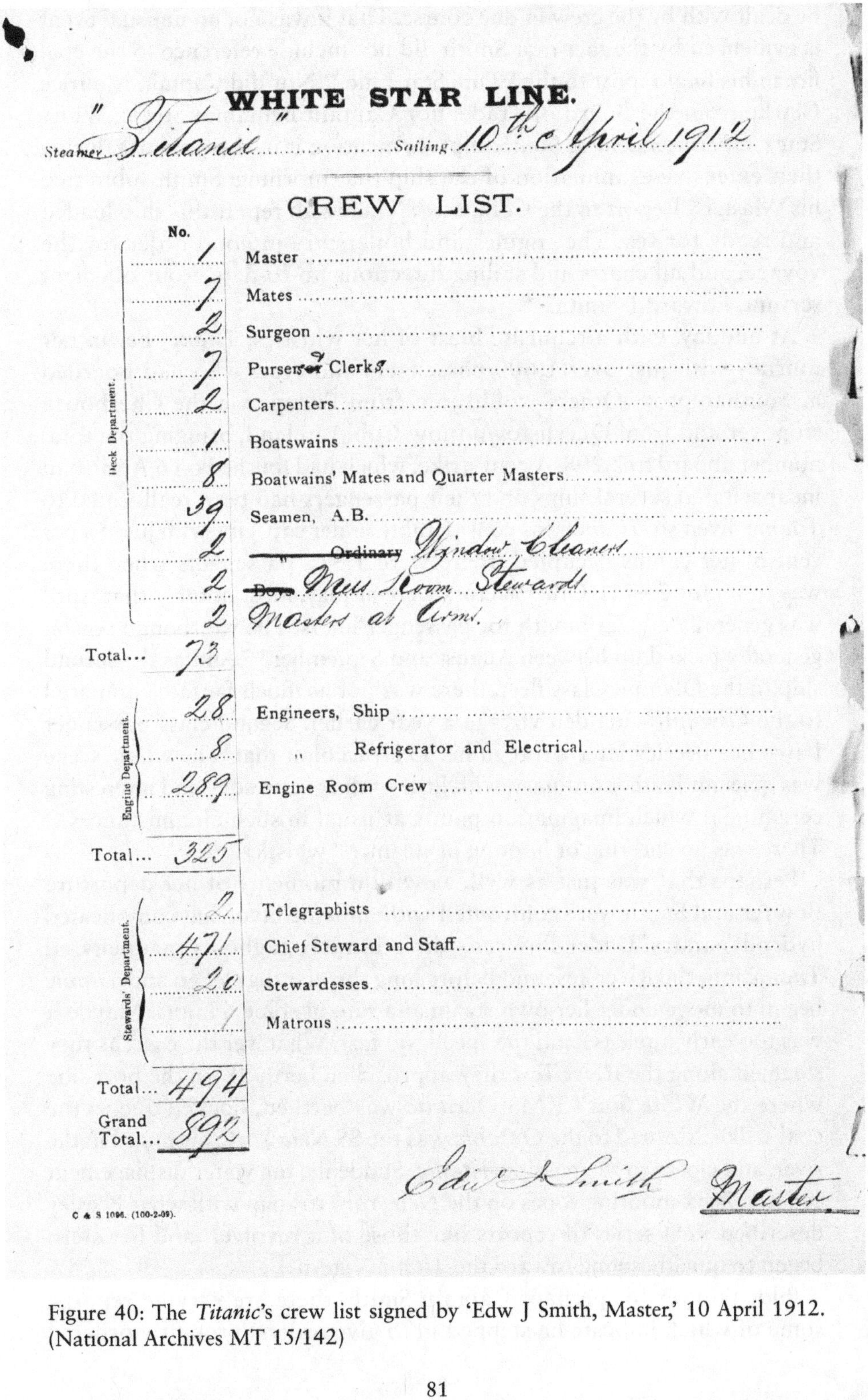

WHITE STAR LINE.

Steamer *Titanic* Sailing 10th April 1912

CREW LIST.

	No.	
Deck Department	1	Master
	7	Mates
	2	Surgeon
	7	Pursers & Clerks
	2	Carpenters
	1	Boatswains
	8	Boatwains' Mates and Quarter Masters
	39	Seamen, A.B.
	2	~~Ordinary~~ Window Cleaners
	2	~~Boys~~ Mess Room Stewards
	2	Masters at Arms
Total...	73	
Engine Department	28	Engineers, Ship
	8	" Refrigerator and Electrical
	289	Engine Room Crew
Total...	325	
Stewards' Department	2	Telegraphists
	471	Chief Steward and Staff
	20	Stewardesses
	1	Matrons
Total...	494	
Grand Total...	892	

Edw J Smith Master

Figure 40: The *Titanic*'s crew list signed by 'Edw J Smith, Master,' 10 April 1912. (National Archives MT 15/142)

be dealt with by the crew in due course. That it was not an unusual event is evidenced by the fact that Smith did not include reference to the coal fire in his final report to the White Star Line.[98] Nor did Captain Maurice Clarke from the Board of Trade, nor Captain Benjamin Steele, White Star's superintendent at Southampton, mention it in their reports during their extensive examination of the ship that morning. Smith submitted his 'Master's Report to the Company': 'I herewith report this ship loaded and ready for sea. The engines and boilers are in good order for the voyage, and all charts and sailing directions up-to-date. Your obedient servant, Edward J. Smith.'[99]

At midday, with a requisite blast of her whistles, *Titanic* began her journey with just over 1,600 passengers and crew who had boarded at Southampton. Others would join from Europe via the Cherbourg stopover and from Queenstown (now Cobh) Ireland, bringing the total number aboard to 2,208. A coal strike, which had finished on 6 April, had incapacitated several ships and their passengers had been reallocated to *Titanic*. Even so, *Titanic* was considerably under capacity, with just 53 per cent of her cabins occupied (there were 1,317 passengers when there was room for 2,471). Other factors were at play, most notably that April was generally a quiet month for passenger liners. The westbound season generally picked up between August and September.[100] And as the second ship in the Olympic-class fleet, there was not as much fanfare compared to the *Olympic*'s maiden voyage a year earlier. Second class passenger Lawrence Beesley later wrote in his 1912 account that 'The whole scene was quiet and rather ordinary, with little of the picturesque and interesting ceremonial which imagination paints as usual in such circumstances... There was no cheering or hooting of steamers' whistles.'[101]

Perhaps that was just as well, as within moments of her departure Bowyer and Smith were confronted with an issue involving complicated hydrodynamics. Under Bowyer's direction, six tugboats manoeuvred *Titanic* into the River Test and before long the first tugs let go and *Titanic* began to move under her own steam at a rate of some 6 knots. Maybe it was too early a release and the speed too fast. Whatever the case, as they steamed along the River Test they approached berth 38 on the port side where the White Star's RMS *Oceanic* was berthed, docked due to the coal strike. Moored to the *Oceanic* was the SS *New York*, outboard in the river, and closer to the passing *Titanic*. Suddenly, the water displacement caused all six mooring ropes on the *New York* to snap with what Beesley described as 'a series of reports like those of a revolver' and her stern began to quickly swing toward the *Titanic*'s stern.

Pilot Bowyer (or perhaps Captain Smith, there are varying reports, some of which indicate he stepped in to give orders) promptly ordered the *Titanic*'s engines stopped and then the port propeller full astern, which immediately averted a collision, but by only four feet. The tugboat *Vulcan* intervened by throwing a line to the *New York* to slow her drift and moved her to a berth a little beyond the *Oceanic*, on Dock Head.

Beesley mentioned how interesting it was 'to see on the *Titanic*'s docking-bridge (at the stern) an officer and seamen telephoning and ringing bells, hauling up and down little red and white flags, as danger of collision alternately threatened and diminished.'[102] Disaster had been prevented – but only just. Francis Browne photographed two tugs manoeuvring the starboard side of *Titanic*'s forecastle away from the *New York*, the stern of which can be seen swinging across *Titanic*'s bow. Steam from the tug *Neptune*'s engines is billowing out into the harbour as third class passengers eagerly gather at the railings to catch a glimpse of what was causing the commotion. According to Beesley, the event had also been recorded on film: 'A young American kinematograph photographer ... followed the whole scene with eager eyes, turning the handle of his camera with the most evident pleasure as he recorded the unexpected incident.'

It must have been a moment of some alarm to Bowyer – and yet he never mentioned the *Titanic* in his memoirs, the 1930 book *Lively Ahoy*, even though he owned several photographs of *Titanic*. The *Titanic* was still a taboo subject in the offices of its owner, the White Star Line, and was spoken of discreetly, if at all, on Southampton's streets, associated with the most infamous disaster in maritime history. It seems that Bowyer bowed to this pressure and simply did not include it, denying us a full account of what really happened on the bridge that day.

After an hour's delay and assistance from tugboats, the *Titanic* slowly departed Southampton through the Solent and into the English Channel. The near collision would not be soon forgotten, with parallels drawn with the *Olympic*. Beesley noted that 'The scene we had just witnessed was the topic of every conversation: the comparison with the *Olympic-Hawke* collision was drawn in every little group of passengers, and it seemed to be generally agreed that this would confirm the suction theory which was so successfully advanced by the cruiser *Hawke* in the law courts, but which many people scoffed at when the British Admiralty first suggested it as the explanation of the cruiser ramming the *Olympic*.'[103]

While docked in Cherbourg, and perhaps in an attempt to ensure there were no further issues, Captain Smith intervened when his First Officer refused a French Naval Commander's request to come aboard. Due to a lack of docking facilities, passengers were ferried by two tenders, the SS *Traffic* and the SS *Nomadic*, and it was aboard the *Traffic* that allegedly a French Naval Commander by the name of Leloup asked to visit the new ship but was refused by First Officer Murdoch – maybe due to the delays incurred in Southampton. The story was told by Jules Munsch, a young French man accompanying the commander, who noted that 'Lieutenant Murdock [sic] disobeyed a major maritime regulation' by prohibiting a French officer access to a foreign merchant ship in a French port. Leloup escalated the issue and Captain Smith was called. He immediately overrode his First Officer's refusal and took the Navy Commander on a personal tour of the ship.[104]

A 29-year-old man, only five months married and suffering from a bad cold, had also observed the events of the day, and concluded that 'The *Olympic*'s bad luck seems to have followed us.' His name was James Arthur Paintin and he was Captain Smith's personal steward, known as 'Tiger', who worked at Smith's proverbial beck and call, bringing meals and messages. Paintin had been at the White Star Line since 1907 and served Smith specifically since the *Adriatic*, so he arguably knew the Captain better than anybody else aboard. When the *Titanic* arrived in Queenstown (Cobh) on Thursday 11 April, Paintin posted a letter to his parents in Oxford, and although he describes *Titanic* as a 'fine ship... much better than the *Olympic* as far as passengers are concerned', his cabin left much to be desired: 'My room is nothing near so nice, no daylight, electric light on all day, but I suppose it's no use grumbling.'[105] It was the near collision on departure that caused him to believe there was some 'bad luck':

> We have now commenced the quick voyages all the summer (bar accidents). I say that because the *Olympic*'s bad luck seems to have followed us, for as we came out of dock this morning we passed quite close to the 'Oceanic' and 'New York' which were tied up in the 'Adriatic's' old berth, and whether it was suction or what it was I don't know, but the 'New York's' ropes snapped like a piece of cotton and she drifted against us. There was great excitement for some time, but I don't think there was any damage done bar one or two people knocked over by the ropes.

Titanic had departed Cherbourg at 8:10 pm and on Smith's orders the ship made a series of long 'S' turns on the way to Ireland, to test her performance and ready her for the open sea. This is evidenced in one of the photographs Browne took during his brief one-night stay aboard the ship, showing the stern on the morning of the 11th and revealing a wake that twists wide toward the horizon.

Francis Browne is often credited with two other famed photographs of Captain Smith – although neither are what they seem. In one image there is a striking silhouette of a man walking away from camera down the first class port promenade on A deck, looking aft. While the figure bears a resemblance to Smith in his frock jacket and officer's cap, the presence of the passing Portuguese vessel the RMSP *Tagus* places the photograph on the afternoon of 10 April, just after departure from Southampton and still under the control of the Trinity House pilot George Bowyer. That is a time that Smith would undoubtedly not have been taken a lonely stroll aft on the first class promenade, instead he would have been on duty on the bridge with the pilot – especially after what had just happened.[106] And if it was indeed the Captain, Browne would almost certainly have included it in his description of the photograph, but he did not.

The other image attributed to Browne is most definitely Smith. He is shown gazing down from the *Titanic*'s starboard wing cab as he watches a tender alongside. The height is impressive and the sombre mood of a final departure is palpable. The photograph is frequently attributed to Browne (appearing on the front cover of a book containing Browne images) and often accompanied by the moving description that it is the last image of Captain Smith seen alive. The photograph was actually taken by Dr William McLean, a Sanitary Surveyor of the Board of Trade at Queenstown who took the image from one of two tenders, the *America* and *Ireland*, transferring passengers and cargo to the *Titanic*.[107] Somehow a copy found its way into Browne's collection of photographs.

Figure 41: Chief Purser Hugh McElroy and Captain E.J. Smith – one of the last images of either seen alive – standing on *Titanic*'s forward starboard boat deck. The five windows behind Smith are for his private quarters. (Author's collection)

One of the last photographs of Captain Smith was taken by Cork Examiner photographer Thomas Barker, after the tender had started offloading its passengers. Smith is standing on the starboard side of the Officers' Quarters alongside Chief Purser Hugh McElroy (Figure 41). And it is just as poignant. These were arguably the two most important men aboard the ship. McElroy, born in Liverpool to an Irish father and Scottish mother, had settled in County Wexford, Ireland, so the port of Queenstown was close to home. As Chief Purser, he was responsible for all administration (including the ship's cargo and passenger manifests) and any other finance-related requirements, as well as the comfort and welfare of the passengers and crew. Like Smith, McElroy was very popular, so much so that passengers were known to time their voyages so as to sail on the same ship and were honoured to dine at his table.

Smith and McElroy knew each other well, having worked together aboard the *Baltic*, *Adriatic*, *Olympic* and now the *Titanic*. They stand, a little apprehensively, in front of the starboard side of the Officers' Quarters. Fourth Officer Boxhall's cabin is to the left of McElroy, the next four windows belong to the Captain's quarters – his bathroom, bedroom and sitting room. After the photograph was taken, Thomas Barker departed in a tender, taking with him one of the last known images of these two men.

At Sea

The next few days, as *Titanic* made its way across the North Atlantic, were largely uneventful. One routine that occurred every day except Sunday was an inspection of the ship. This started with a meeting in Smith's quarters, with reports from Chief Engineer Joseph Bell, Chief Purser Hugh McElroy, Assistant Purser Reginald Barker, Surgeon Dr William O'Loughlin, and Chief Steward Andrew Latimer. From 10:30 am, along with the deck officers, they would tour the ship, taking note of anything that was amiss or required attention. If a photograph of Smith leading an inspection aboard the *Adriatic* is an accurate reflection of the procedure, then the Captain would be in his full dress uniform, wearing his Transport and R.N.R. medals, followed by officers with notebooks jotting down observations. The imposing figure would prompt crew to attention, and provide photo opportunities from the passengers (Figure 42).

The Captain was known to be friendly and even joke with the crew. Seaman William Törnquist recalled how E.J. treated 19-year-old William

Playing on Titanic's *Bridge*

Figure 42: A rare image of Captain Smith at work, taking unidentified officers on a tour of the RMS *Adriatic* as he would aboard *Titanic*. He is in 'full company dress' and wearing medals on his chest. (Author's collection)

'Billy' Johnson, an American sailor working for the American Line, who was forced to return to the United States on a passenger ticket: 'On the Titanic the officers took to him right away, and especially the captain, who called him "Kid" and used to joke and talk with him.'[108]

Passenger interactions were just as essential, and Isaac Frauenthal, in first class, observed that 'Captain Smith and his officers seemed to be at pains to make everybody comfortable and gay.'[109] Lady Duff Gordon had a similar experience, later writing that everything aboard 'this lovely ship reassured me from the captain, with his kindly, bearded face and genial manner, and his twenty-five years of experience as a White Star commander'.[110]

Smith had a table in the first class restaurant and entertained guests, as was his custom, on the evenings of 12 through to 14 April (presumably eating in his own quarters on the first two days, 10 and 11). Contrary to popular depictions, his table was not an imposing status symbol. Befitting his background and character, it was an ordinary table that seated just six, located in the dining saloon's central section. Guests fortunate enough to dine with him described Smith as a charming host, attentive to their needs and to their safety.[111] An example of this was given by first class passenger Marion Kenyon who was travelling with her husband on their wedding anniversary and who formed a friendship with the Captain, who called them 'the bride and groom':

> On the 10th of April we embarked on the Titanic. The next day being our anniversary, when we came down to dinner, the captain's table was the first inside of the dining saloon and the next was the first mate's, Lightoller. Well, our table was bedecked with flowers and Captain Smith coming in a few moments later came over and asked, 'Is this a bride and groom?' And we explained to him it was just an anniversary. And he congratulated us. And in a short time, brought over a huge bottle of wine. Well, none of us imbibed. But we took a sip anyhow, and we sent the bottle back to his table so that they would have some too. That was our introduction to Captain Smith, and he seemed always to stop us and call us the bride and groom. It really was a lovely friendship. He was a middle-aged man with whiskers and was kind eyed and was very lovely, gentlemanly in every manner. I remember that so well.[112]

Smith could entertain even very young passengers. Seven-year-old Eva Hart in second class was accompanied on the voyage by a large teddy bear that was spotted by the Captain, who enquired where she had got it from. When Eva explained her father had bought it for her, he went a step further and playfully wondered as to their respective heights and upon measuring them both discovered the bear was marginally taller than its owner.[113] In an BBC radio interview with Eva in 1987, she described it this way:

> Captain Smith, he was on deck and when my father and I were on deck – I imagined he went all over the ship and he was very nice. He had a beard like my own grandfather, and he admired a doll I had. I had this beautifully dressed doll and I had a big teddy bear too which a lot of the children used to play with and he admired my doll. I remember talking to him and my father telling me that he was the captain.[114]

The issue with this particular memory is that it changed in its retelling. In another interview during 1987, she described the conversation with the captain as taking place along with Lawrence Beesley:

> I was aware he was the Captain and I spoke to him several times and he sort of patted me on the head so to speak and I knew he was the captain of this big ship, my father described that to me. And it was then that he said that 'God himself couldn't sink her' when they were commenting on what a beautiful ship it was. He said: 'She's a wonderful ship. God himself couldn't sink her.'[115]

When asked by the interviewer if she thought this 'epitomised the arrogance' she responded: 'It conveyed nothing to me at the time, but it did afterwards.' Statements that 'God could not sink the ship' became a common thread in Eva Hart's recollections, along with her phrase that it was 'flying in the face of God'. Neither description of her conversation was included in Eva's written autobiography. Nor did her mother include any mention of it in her personal account published in 1912. And Lawrence Beesley did not include it in his recollections.[116]

Another family in second class, and who were dinner companions with the Hart family, also had a pleasant conversation with the Captain. At around 10 am on Saturday 13 April, Smith visited the second class enclosed promenade deck and spoke with the Brown family, parents Thomas and Elizabeth and their 15-year-old daughter Edith. According to Edith's son, David Haisman, who wrote a book about his mother's experience (he worked for Cunard White Star from the 1960s, including as a lookout man) Smith's visit to second class was 'one of his public relations exercises for the White Star Line. It was company policy for the captain to visit all classes at least once on each voyage.' As with Eva Hart, Captain Smith spotted the Brown's young daughter, who was close in age to his own daughter Mel. David Haisman relates his mother's story:

> As he [Smith] continued his walk around the deck, he stopped and went over to the Browns sitting in deck chairs. Addressing them all he asked if they were enjoying the voyage. Thomas replied for all of them when he said they were enjoying it very much. Captain Smith then turned his attention to Edith and smiling asked, 'And how about you, young lady?' Edith, looking first at her mother and then back to the Captain, replied, 'It's the best ship we've ever been on.' Captain Smith, letting out a laugh, said he was glad to hear it. Edith asked whether it was true that there were dogs on the ship. The captain replied that the ship had what was known as a 'dog deck', which was situated up by the funnels. There were kennels there where the dogs were looked after by one of the ship's butchers. Edith then asked, 'Have you got a dog, Captain?' 'Yes,' came the reply and then he added with a laugh, 'Not on board the ship I hasten to add. He's back home in Southampton where he should be.'

Thomas, changing the subject, then asked the captain whether the ship was running to schedule. Captain Smith replied that the ship was making good time with the excellent weather. He said they would reach New York by the time advertised. He then added that it was 'a pity that it had got colder but it's what you could expect in those waters at that time of the year. With that, he gave them a half salute and wished them a pleasant day.'[117]

The accuracy of David Haisman's recollection of his mother's account is somewhat questionable as it was published in a book in 1999, three years after his mother Edith passed away. While it is quite possible the family conversed with the Captain about dogs and the ship's schedule, the precise wording may have been lost or influenced by other survivor tales. The reference to Smith spending more time with his dog on his return to Southampton, for example, seems an addition made to connect with the unfounded rumour it was Smith's last voyage.[118]

Nevertheless, such interactions with passengers, especially children, match the character reference given by a former passenger, Andrew Grieve, on the Australasian service:

> There was nothing that 'Cap.' Smith wouldn't do to make the long passage interesting for us. He was a big stout man, but he was full of fun, and his great consideration was for the welfare of his passengers. He would join them in all the deck sports, quoits, deck cricket and all the other pastimes that make the long voyage less tiresome… He was a thorough man, and he took a great interest in his passengers. Oftentimes he would come down from the bridge deck and have a talk with them. He was a man amongst a thousand. If a kid was sick Captain Smith would go on his knees and pick the little one up and do the best that he could for her or him. Nothing seemed to please him so much as to be at the call of his passengers, and he was always ready whenever he was wanted.[119]

Smith's reputation with children is reflected in an observation from New York reporter Jack Lawrence: 'When [Smith's] ship was ready to back out of her North River pier it was not unusual to see parents herding flocks of happy children aboard and leaving them there to make the crossing in care of governesses – and Captain Smith. They knew the youngsters would be safe with him.'[120]

The Captain was also allegedly seen by a Mrs Elizabeth Lines in the first class reception room, just after lunch, on both Friday and Saturday, talking with J. Bruce Ismay, chairman and managing director of the White Star Line. According to her deposition at the Limitation of Liability hearings on 27 October 1913, she was sitting four to six feet away and heard Ismay say: 'We made a better run to-day than we did yesterday, we will make a better run to-morrow. Things are working smoothly, the machinery is bearing the test, the boilers are working well.' They went on discussing it, and then she heard him make the statement: 'We will beat the *Olympic* and get in to New York on Tuesday.'[121]

Captain Smith apparently did not say anything in reply other than 'nod his head a few times' and Ismay was described by her as 'very positive, one might almost say dictatorial. He asked no questions.' It is this conversation that has often led to an inference that Ismay was driving Captain Smith to increase speed through dangerous waters, although Smith's actions of maintaining speed were nothing extraordinary for the time. And *Titanic* was built for luxury, not speed.

Ismay vehemently denied such accusations. On 21 April 1912, he stated that he was nothing more than a 'passenger' and 'was not consulted by the commander about the ship, her course, speed, navigation, or her conduct at sea. All these matters were under the exclusive control of the Captain. I saw Captain Smith only casually, as other passengers did. I was never in his room; I was never on the bridge until after the accident. I did not sit at his table ... it is absolutely and unqualifiedly false that I ever said that I wished that the Titanic should make a speed record or should increase her daily runs.'[122] During the Senate *Titanic* inquiry, Ismay admitted having dinner only once with the Captain on the Friday evening – which must have been at Ismay's table. Otherwise, communications with the Master was always in an unofficial capacity: 'I was never in the captain's room the whole voyage over, sir, and the captain was never in my room. I never had any conversation with the captain except casual conversation on the deck.'[123]

On the matter of speed, Colonel Archibald Gracie, in his 1913 account of the disaster, observed that 'The Captain had each day improved upon the previous day's speed, and prophesied that, with continued fair weather, we should make an early arrival record for this maiden trip.'[124] Making a timely voyage was always high on the agenda for a Royal Mail steamer – with or without Ismay's prompting.

This must be seen in the context of rumour circulating among the passengers of a record crossing. For example, second class passenger Ruth Becker noted that immediately on arrival she heard gossip of this nature: 'When we got on the Titanic, we heard people say we were going to get there in about 4 or 5 days, that Captain Smith was going to make his maiden voyage a record one.'[125]

It must also be considered that the White Star Line sent each of its captains a letter advocating safe practice including the warning to 'dismiss all idea of competitive passages with other vessels, and to concentrate your attention upon a cautious, prudent and ever watchful system of navigation which shall lose time or suffer any other temporary inconvenience rather than incur the slightest risk which can be avoided.'[126] Ismay was the White Star managing director and Smith had already followed these company guidelines on the *Olympic*'s maiden voyage – losing time due to fog.

It also has to be pointed out that Lines said she was 'told' this was the Captain – she did not recognise him and even admitted she was not sure he even had a beard. She remembered the two men had liqueurs and cigars – something which does not ring true for a Captain on duty. Additionally, she remembered the two men finishing the conversation by saying they would visit the squash courts – again an activity only a passenger, and not a working captain, would entertain. It is thus quite probable the gentleman she saw was a passenger who had the rank of captain, for example 70-year-old Captain Edward Crosby, simply discussing *Titanic*'s progress over lunch.

On Sunday 14 April, Captain Smith led the 10:30 am first class interdenominational worship service in the dining saloon. According to passenger Colonel Archibald Gracie, those assembled sang 'O God Our Help in Ages Past'. Notably, Gracie does not mention the service as specifically taken by the Captain.[127] And despite becoming something of a *Titanic* trope – a scene showing Smith taking a Sunday service appears in many films about the disaster – there was surprisingly no 1912 eyewitness account actually placing him there. It does seem quite likely he did – captains by tradition would take the service if they were available to do so. Even today, Cunard continues the tradition, stating on its website that if you are at sea on a Sunday, then they offer an interdenominational religious service and that it is usually hosted by either the Captain or in his absence the Staff Captain.[128]

Twenty years after the disaster, the question of identity was finally clarified in a May 1932 letter written by first class passenger Mrs Eleanor Genevieve Cassebeer to her son Lewis. Translated from the French by Charles Provost and published in *The Death of a Purser* by Frankie McElroy, it included the following passage: 'On Sunday morning (April 14) we assisted to a religious ceremony in the restaurant, which was presided over by our dear captain, a tall man, very polite, who sported a white beard. It was easy to say, by giving him a single look, that his life had been entirely devoted to the sea.'[129]

There is no indication that the 'Eternal Father' hymn was sung, with its unforgettable line, 'for those in peril on the sea', as portrayed in several films, such as James Cameron's 1997 epic. It was, however, sung later that day by second class passengers in a prayer service, as noted by Lawrence Beesley.[130]

There was also the cancellation of the 11 am lifeboat drill, possibly due to the fact Smith was preoccupied with taking the religious service. There could be an equally compelling reason. According to lookout Archie

Jewell, it was cancelled due to a 'strong wind'.[131] Not that it would have had much impact on that night's tragic proceedings; it was simply a crew muster and did not involve any passengers. There had already been several drills in Belfast and Southampton, and Smith mostly preferred to complete his lifeboat drills while in port.[132]

Ice Reports

One of the first ice reports the *Titanic* received was at 5:46 pm on 12 April from the French ocean liner *La Touraine*. This was subsequently followed by a marked increase in reports on Sunday 14 April from the *Caronia* (9:12 am), the *Amerika* (1:49 pm), the *Baltic* (1:54 pm), *Mesaba* (9:52 pm) and the *Californian* (11:07 pm).[133]

These wireless messages are often mislabelled as ice 'warnings' that were 'ignored'. The messages were in reality 'reports', and it was commonplace for ships to share relevant information, mostly weather conditions as well as the positions of derelicts and ice. These reports were never ignored. Once received by the wireless operators, in most cases they were taken to the bridge where the officers on watch would post them on the chartroom noticeboard and if necessary, the positions were marked on the ship's navigational chart.

First class passenger Helen Ostby was sitting on deck late on Sunday morning and observed what she thought might be the delivery of an ice report: 'Captain Edward Smith was talking nearby to a few passengers when a steward came out and handed him a message. Captain Smith looked at it, but then continued talking for a while with the passengers. I have always felt this might have been one of the several messages received that day warning of ice ahead.'[134]

Second Officer Lightoller remembered Captain Smith coming onto the bridge during lunch on 14 April and 'in his hands he had a wireless message, a Marconigram. He came across the bridge, and holding it in his hands told me to read it.' The message was about ice, likely from the *Noordam* via the *Caronia*, and Lightoller passed the information onto First Officer Murdoch who relieved him as Officer of the Watch.[135] As with most of the reports coming in, the *Noordam*'s 11:47 am message was a mix of information and felicitations, with Captain Krol expressing 'congratulations on new command'. And as he did with most of the reports, Smith personally responded with 'many thanks. Had moderate weather throughout. Compliments. Smith'.[136]

Around the same time, Captain Smith was also given an ice report from the *Baltic* which was relaying information from the Greek ship the *Athinai* that she had been 'passing icebergs and large quantities of field ice'. Shortly after, Smith happened to meet Ismay and showed him the message. Ismay put it in his pocket, presented it to some friends and returned it only when Smith requested at about 7:10 pm that evening. There has been speculation as to why Smith would have given Ismay the message. Ismay later made a statement clarifying what happened:

> The only information I ever received on the ship that other vessels had sighted ice was a wireless message received from the *Baltic* which I have already testified to. This was handed to me by Captain Smith without any remark as he was passing me on the passenger deck in the afternoon of Sunday, April 14th. I read the telegram casually and put it in my pocket. At about ten minutes past seven, while I was sitting in the smoke room, Captain Smith came in and asked me to give him the message received from the *Baltic* in order to post it for the information of the officers. I handed it to him and nothing further was said by either of us. I did not speak to any of the other officers on the subject.[137]

This message was not an ice 'warning' as often depicted. It was simply a message between two White Star Liners. This is in evidence when reading the entire message:

STEAMSHIP 'BALTIC,' April 14, 1912.
Capt. SMITH, *Titanic*:

Have had moderate variable winds and clear fine weather since leaving. Greek steamer *Athinai* reports passing icebergs and large quantity of field ice today in latitude 41.51 north, longitude 49.52 west. Last night we spoke German oil tank *Deutschland*, Stettin to Philadelphia, not under control; short of coal; latitude 40.42 north, longitude 55.11. Wishes to be reported to New York and other steamers. Wish you and Titanic all success.

COMMANDER.[138]

There has been some speculation that Smith was even considering a plan to rescue the *Deutschland* as a publicity stunt, and he was trying to obtain Ismay's approval, although this is highly unlikely as it would interrupt their maiden voyage and more pertinentlyy, the stricken vessel was already receiving assistance from the Leyland Line's ship, the *Asian*.[139] The nature of the message is clearer when reading Smith's response:

'Commander *Baltic*. Thanks for your message and good wishes. Had fine weather since leaving. Smith.'[140]

It was an exchange of recent information in the context of good wishes, of friendly communication between two White Star ships. Captain Smith was the *Baltic*'s first master, and he commanded her for three years (1904–1907). That Smith demanded the message back for posting in the bridge later in the evening is also evidence that it was not treated as trivial. The information was important, and maybe Smith was also ensuring Ismay was aware ice was ahead and that it may at some point impede their progress. The late author and maritime captain David Brown also believes there was more than meets the eye:

> The Ismay ice warning affair has been wrongly elevated to mythical proof of Captain Smith's cavalier attitude toward ice warnings. Not so. In the social context of 1912 the exact opposite was more likely true. Smith would not have bothered his employer with trivial matters. By sharing the Marconigram ice warning with Ismay, the captain emphasized the danger. Ismay indicated he understood the importance of the message by returning it at the captain's request. In the end, this warning was posted in the ship's chartroom by 7:30 pm.[141]

Mysteriously, officers Lightoller and Boxhall did not recall ever seeing the *Baltic* message.

Passengers were detecting a drop in temperature and there was talk of ice. Mrs Imanita Shelley, travelling second class, claimed 'there were rumors of wireless messages from other ships warning of icebergs close at hand. It was also reported that certain first class passengers had asked if the ship was to slow down whilst going through the ice belts and had been told by the captain that, on the contrary, the ship would be speeded through.'[142] Later that afternoon, Lady Duff Gordon was walking on the deck outside when she noted the 'cold increased' and when she suggested there 'must be icebergs around' to her husband, Sir Cosmo Duff Gordon, 'he made fun of my ignorance, and Captain Smith, who happened to be passing, assured me that we were right away from the ice zone.'[143]

On the bridge, the *Baltic* wireless was not the only message thought to have gone astray that day. At 9:52 pm, a message from the steamship *Mesaba* was sent to about ten ships including the *Titanic* reporting 'heavy pack ice and great number large icebergs, also field ice'. Unlike the other messages received, the report was prefixed 'S.G.' (Service Gram) rather than 'M.S.G.' or Master's Service Gram (intended for the Captain).[144] It is maybe why this message was – according to Lightoller –

never received by those on the bridge. The change in Officer of the Watch, when First Officer Murdoch relieved Lightoller, occurred eight minutes later at 10 pm. Lightoller wrote in his autobiography that since he did not receive the message, 'That delay proved fatal and was the main contributory cause to the loss of that magnificent ship and hundreds of lives.' He even went as far as to claim that he spoke to the senior wireless operator, Jack Phillips, on an upturned lifeboat before Phillips died, who admitted: 'I just put the message under a paper weight at my elbow, just until I squared up what I was doing before sending it to the Bridge.'[145] However, it is highly unlikely that it was Phillips who said this, as his evidence is contradicted by another eyewitness on the upturned lifeboat, Colonel Archibald Gracie. It may well have been the junior wireless operator, Harold Bride, who did survive on the upturned collapsible B, that Lightoller spoke with. Bride later defended Phillips against Lightoller's accusations, so it is difficult to imagine he was the source of the *Mesaba* story.[146]

Notwithstanding, Lightoller's emphasis on the *Mesaba* message is, all things considered, a moot point. Smith and his officers, including Lightoller himself who had made ice position calculations, knew there was ice ahead; the *Mesaba* information only confirmed what was already known. Based on previous plotted positions they had already calculated, they would reach the area of ice between 9:30 pm and 11 pm at the latest. Additionally, as the message arrived so close to the change in watch, it could well have been received by Captain Smith, First Officer Murdoch or Sixth Officer Moody. We simply cannot claim with any certainty it did not reach the bridge since the key players – Phillips, Smith, Murdoch and Moody – were all lost in the disaster.

The final ice report, sent from the *Californian* at 11:07 pm, was also lacking the 'M.S.G.' prefix and gave no position, only reporting that they were 'stopped and surrounded by ice'. Due to the proximity of the two ships, the *Californian*'s message would have come across Phillip's headphones as much louder than the faint transmissions from Cape Race he had been working on until then, so may well have given him a jolt. Infamously, his response was: 'Shut up, shut up, I am busy. I am working Cape Race.'

The 'shut up' message is often misconstrued as Phillips rudely insulting the *Californian*, when that is not entirely accurate. Phillips was busy 'working' Cape Race, trying to catch up on a backlog of messages that had accumulated after his wireless equipment broke down the day before. In his response, Phillips used the code 'DDD' which is literally translated 'shut up' but not with the same aggressive meaning that it has in conversational English. It was procedural code between operators meaning to 'give way', to ensure efficiency and was not an insult. And all messages could be heard by any radio in range.

There is also evidence that Smith was taking keen note of these ice reports. In later testimony, Boxhall remembered seeing the Captain on the bridge from 'time to time' during his evening watch and saw him 'in the navigation room with the chart before him. He was pricking out the ship's position at 7.30 pm on stellar observations made by him [Boxhall].'[147] Smith also included instructions in the night order book requesting a sharp lookout for ice. One order is often misconstrued: that he requested *Titanic* to travel a further 10 miles southwest before 'turning The Corner' at 5:50 pm that evening. 'The Corner' is a point on the journey west when the ship is turned slightly starboard to align her sights on New York. Claims that Captain Smith turned late are often made to suggest he was travelling further south to avoid ice. The evidence does not support this; in truth, Smith was aligning very closely to the southern track he had been asked to maintain by White Star.[148] And in doing so had unknowingly pointed the ship on a collision course with disaster.

The Last Dinner

That evening, a large dinner party was arranged by first class passengers George and Eleanor Widener, apparently in Captain Smith's honour, in the á la carte restaurant on B deck. Others at the table included John and Marian Thayer, William and Lucile Carter, and Major Archibald Butt. Smith's presence in the restaurant was witnessed by many people. According to first class passenger Sir Cosmo Duff Gordon, Smith was in his 'evening uniform'.[149]

When it came to food, Smith had a reputation for having a healthy appetite. A Mrs Frieda Sengstacke cooked for the rich and famous in New York and, while working for a Long Island family, met Captain Smith: 'He was such a fine man. And what a hearty eater! Every time the captain was in port we had all sorts of special dishes, and he would eat and eat. My how I cried when I heard he went down with his ship, for we all liked him so well.'[150]

As for conversation, first class passenger Marian Thayer, one of the guests at the table, later wrote in her affidavit that she did 'not remember hearing, during the dinner on Sunday night, any mention made by any person of ice being in the neighborhood, or that we might expect to see ice.'[151] In another account, Smith allegedly made bold claims about the ship during the dinner. Written in 1944, the privately published account by survivor Elmer Taylor describes how he and his friend

Fletcher Lambert Williams were close enough to Captain Smith's table to overhear a conversation on the night of the 14th in which Smith said the 'ship could be cut crosswise in three places and each piece would float.' For Taylor, that 'remark confirmed my belief in the safety of the ship.'[152]

When claims were made that Captain Smith was drinking, things took a more serious turn. Rumours of drinking had been festering among the discontented survivors soon after the disaster, most notably expressed by Luis Klein, a Hungarian man who spoke little English and claimed he was a surviving member of the crew with some sensational evidence involving officers and crew asleep 'drunk or drinking'. This resulted in *The New York Times* running stories with headlines such as 'Officer on Watch Accused' on 22 April 1912.[153] Shortly thereafter, Klein escaped before giving evidence and his reports were widely discredited as he was not to be found on any crew lists. Second Officer Lightoller testified he did not know him, and it was clear the evidence Klein supplied did not align with any other testimony.[154] Hence, Klein has been widely acknowledged as an imposter. A month after *The New York Times* ran the first story on Klein, on 22 May 1912, they followed it up with an article referencing evidence from the Widener family that 'exonerates Capt. Smith of the Titanic from any suspicion of drinking on the evening of the disaster'.[155] It came in the form of an affidavit in which Marian Thayer stated that she noticed that 'the captain never took any alcoholic liquor of any kind at any meal.'

Thayer's statement was confirmed by saloon steward Thomas Whiteley, who said that Captain Smith 'talked and joked with Mr. Astor' but he 'did not see the captain drink anything; I do not think he ever indulged.' First class passenger Harry Anderson said that Smith 'refused to drink that night. When I insisted, he had a small glass of port, sipped once and left it.'[156] Similarly, in her brief affidavit to the Senate Committee investigating the disaster, Eleanor Widener herself wrote: 'Capt. Smith drank absolutely no wine or intoxicating liquor of any kind whatever at the dinner.' At the same United States inquiry, passenger Charles Stengel was insistent that the captain 'smoked two cigars' that night but definitely did not drink.[157] As Lucian and Mary Smith departed the restaurant, they also saw that Captain Smith smoked two cigars that evening and enjoyed a cup of after-dinner coffee.[158]

The drinking rumours were not to die that easily. Even one hundred years after the sinking, during the 2012 centenary, a previously unseen letter was unearthed in which 24-year-old second class survivor Emily Richards claimed: 'The Captain was down in the saloon drinking and gave charge to some-one else to stare [sic] the ship. It was the Captan [sic] fault.' The letter was up for sale, with auctioneer Andrew Aldridge acknowledging that there were no other reports to corroborate such an account and that it was inconsistent with other eyewitness testimony that the Captain did not drink.[159] There is quite an obvious reason to doubt Richard's claim: she was in second class and would not have been able to see Captain Smith, let alone know what he was drinking.

Smith had a reputation to maintain regarding alcohol according to author George Behe: 'Captain Smith never drank (at least while at sea) and would not stand for any of his crew drinking, either; he would immediately discharge any crewman he heard of who took a drink on board his ship. (Smith's bedroom steward on the Baltic later said that he never found any kind of liquor in Smith's room.)'[160]

Another eyewitness to Smith's *Titanic* dinner party was 35-year-old first class passenger René Harris (also known as Irene or Renée) who had broken her right arm after a fall on the aft staircase in the late afternoon of the 14th. With her arm in a cast, she still managed to attend the evening dinner and briefly spoke to the Captain who admired her 'spirit':

> I had just sat down at our table when Captain Smith came into the room. I had not before met the captain. In passing our table, he stopped, complimented me on my spirit, and went to an unoccupied place at the Ismay table. He was not there five minutes, for on his passing me again I asked him if he wasn't going to stay to enjoy the festivities. He answered that he was going back to the bridge because of the presence of icebergs in the region where we were. Captain Smith had not indulged in any drinking bout, as has been the general impression. On the contrary, he was one hundred per cent on his job.[161]

Miss Ida Daisy Minahan wrote a letter to the Senate Inquiry saying that she went to the 'café for dinner at about 7:15 p.m. (ship's time). When we entered there was a dinner party already dining, consisting of perhaps a dozen men and three women. Capt. Smith was a guest, as also were Mr. and Mrs. Widener, Mr. and Mrs. Blair [Thayer] and Maj. Butt. Capt. Smith was continuously with his party from the time we entered until between 9:25 and 9:45, when he bid the women good night and left... [Smith] was having coffee with these people during this time. I was seated so close to them that I could hear bits of their conversation.'[162]

There was one snippet of conversation Miss Minahan heard – whether at the dinner party or elsewhere is unclear – that she did not include in her affidavit to the Senate Inquiry. It was about why Smith was not slowing down:

There is one thing I want to say about the way the Titanic was speeding. We had been cautioned that the icebergs were drifting in the waters and someone asked the captain if he meant to slow down. He said no; that if anything, the boat would be given more speed. A bulletin was posted just a short while before the accident saying that the boat was then making the fastest time of the whole trip and that if we kept up the speed we would land in New York ahead of record time.[163]

A Flat Calm

There is much justification for why Smith would not consider drinking at the dinner party: there was still work to be done. At about five minutes to nine (according to Lightoller – Miss Minahan was adamant it was at least thirty minutes later) Smith returned from his time with passengers and when he arrived on the bridge had a long conversation with the Second Officer. As the commander's eyes adjusted to the darkness, Lightoller recalled discussing the unusual weather conditions:

> He remarked that it was cold, and as far as I remember I said, 'Yes, it is very cold, Sir. In fact,' I said, 'it is only one degree above freezing. I have sent word down to the carpenter and rung up the engine room and told them that it is freezing or will be during the night.'... He said, 'There is not much wind.' I said, 'No, it is a flat calm as a matter of fact.' He repeated it; he said, 'A flat calm.' I said, 'Yes, quite flat, there is no wind.' I said something about it was rather a pity the breeze had not kept up whilst we were going through the ice region. Of course, My reason was obvious; he knew I meant the water ripples breaking on the base of the berg... I said, 'It is a pity there is not a breeze,' and we went on to discuss the weather. He was then getting his eyesight, you know, and he said, 'Yes, it seems quite clear,' and I said, 'Yes, it is perfectly clear.' It was a beautiful night, there was not a cloud in the sky. The sea was apparently smooth, and there was no wind, but at that time you could see the stars rising and setting with absolute distinctness ... on the horizon. We then discussed the indications of ice. I remember saying, 'In any case there will be a certain amount of reflected lights from the bergs.' He said, 'Oh, yes, there will be a certain amount of reflected light.'[164]

In a later account, Lightoller added that during this conversation they acknowledged that they were 'soon entering the reported area, and they agreed that they would be able to see ice three or four miles away'.[165]

Smith remained on the bridge until around 9:25 pm when he then decided to go to his quarters. His last instructions to Lightoller, which would also need to be passed onto Murdoch as 'night orders' when he relieved him, were simple: 'If it becomes at all doubtful let me know at once; I will be just inside.'[166] Just as Captain Smith turned to leave, he added, according to a later account by Lightoller: 'If it is going to be hazy, we shall have to go very slow.' And instead of 'just inside' Lightoller remembers he said he would be 'just inside his navigating room'.[167]

This aligns with the last known action of Smith prior to the collision. At 10 pm, just over an hour and a half prior to contact with ice, Smith was in the chartroom plotting the ship's course. Fourth Officer Boxhall recalled: 'The Captain put down the star position when I gave it to him, somewhere about 10 o'clock. He put the position on, and I was standing close to him, but I did not take that much notice whether any other positions were put on or not … we had three stars for latitude, and I think three or four for longitude.'[168] In another account, Boxhall remembered that he showed the Captain 'the position on the chart, she was just over twenty miles ahead of her Dead Reckoning.'[169]

What Captain Smith could not have seen on the chart was what awaited them, concealed in the darkness ahead.

3

The Convergence of the Twain

At 2.20 am on 15 April 1912, the stern of the *Titanic* disappeared into the icy waters of the North Atlantic. Of the 2,208 aboard, 712 managed to find a place aboard a lifeboat, resulting in the loss of 1,496 passengers and crew, including the 'Millionaires' Captain', E.J. Smith.

How soon Eleanor and Mel discovered the terrible news, we do not know. In the Monday 15 April edition of *The Southern Daily Echo*, the local Southampton newspaper, which Eleanor would likely have read (it was the only local daily paper), was the banner headline, 'Titanic Collides with Iceberg in Mid-Ocean', followed by a lead paragraph stating that 'fortunately more reassuring tidings reached us this afternoon, when all passengers were reported to be safe.' (Figure 43). It clarified that a 'wireless message to Halifax stated that all the passengers were safely taken off the Titanic at 5.30 am. The White Star Company emphasises their claim that the Titanic is unsinkable.' Sandwiched in-between this optimistic report and a long list of all the first and second class passengers spread across three columns, was a short passage under the heading 'The Titanic's Skipper,' outlining biographical information on Smith along with confidence in his abilities: 'Captain E.J. Smith has always been a conscientious worker in the interests of his profession… His connection with the White Star is a long and extensive one, and his abilities well fitted him for the command of the world's greatest ship.'[1] The implication was that the long list of passengers was in safe hands.

The following day, on Tuesday 16, the newspapers were publishing conflicting stories. *The Western Times* ran the headline 'Passengers Safe' with the subheading 'Don't Worry', stating that the ship was making slowly for Halifax. The article was based on an earlier report from Reuters that 'no lives were lost.' As more details emerged, optimism was quickly dissipated after a statement was received from White Star Line

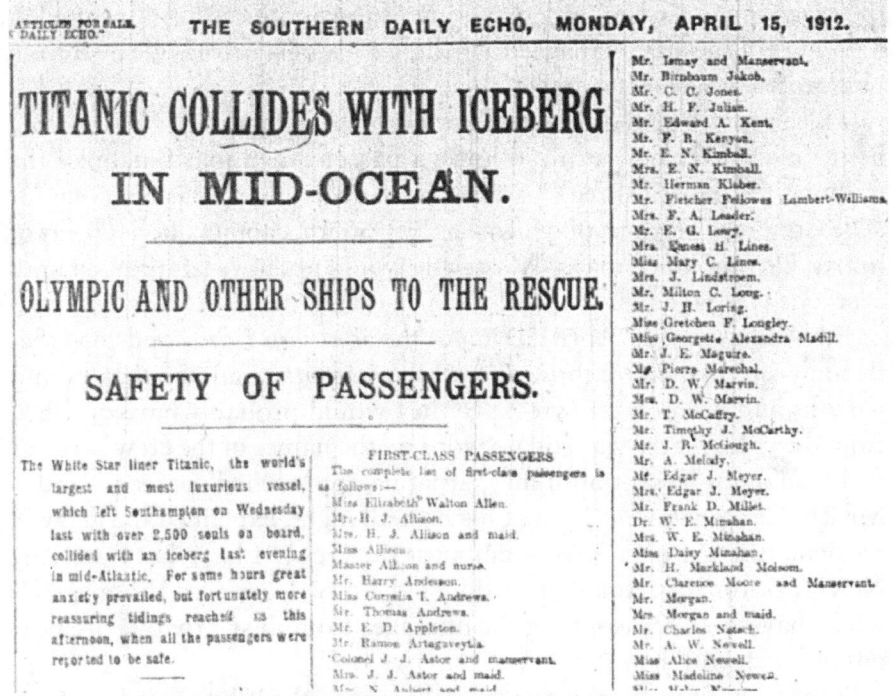

Figure 43: The headline that likely alerted Eleanor and Mel to what had befallen Captain Smith in the Monday 15 April 1912 edition of *The Southern Daily Echo*. (Courtesy of the Southampton Local History and Maritime Library)

officials later on that day that the *Titanic* had indeed sunk with a great loss of life.[2]

The local *Southern Echo* ran the headline 'Ocean Catastrophe' on the sixteenth with the more accurate subheading 'Many Passengers and Members of Crew Saved' and 'All Hope of Salvage Abandoned'. The number of 675 souls saved, of which 200 were crew, was included several times in the copy. It was based on a brief message that was posted outside the offices of the White Star Line in Canute Road, Southampton, that read: 'Titanic foundered about 2.30am, April 15th. About 675 crew and passengers picked up by ship's boats of Carpathia and California [sic]. Remaining and searching position of disaster. Names of those saved will be posted as soon as received'.[3]

The note was both ambiguous and highly inaccurate, but without an accompanying list of those saved it also offered hope. The police had to control the crowds gathering in Canute Road to read the message, eagerly awaiting further word on their loved ones. The manager of the White Star Line office in Southampton, Phillip Curry, sent an urgent message to New York specifically requesting clarification 'concerning the crew of the Titanic'. A late edition of the *Southern Echo*, printed at 6:45 pm on Tuesday, managed to include a list of survivors gleaned from intercepted wireless messages.

If Eleanor had read or heard of any of this, she knew what was coming next. In a corrected list of all known passengers aboard, naming the millionaires and all three classes of passengers, there was also one for 'The Crew' the very top of which was 'E.J. Smith, captain.' In her heart of hearts, Eleanor knew that as Master, he would not have left the ship until everyone was saved.

The Wednesday, 17 April edition of the *Southern Echo* confirmed that the only survivors were those aboard the *Carpathia*, adding that 'even if persons had been on the wreckage they would probably have perished from the cold.' There was still no word on the names of the crew saved as that 'could not be sent until the Carpathia approached nearer to land... Mr P.E. Curry, who has been at his post all night, explained the delay in receiving the list of survivors amongst the crew. "I have been pressing New York for the names," he said, "but I now learn that those vessels which have been transmitting the messages from the Carpathia are now out of touch with her."'[4]

In the meantime, there was a message sent to the White Star Line from King George at Sandringham: 'The Queen and I are horrified at the appalling disaster which has happened to the Titanic, and at the terrible loss of life. We deeply sympathise with the bereaved relations, and feel for them in their great sorrow with all our heart.'

Then at 9 am on Wednesday, an important message came through. An official posted the notice outside the White Star offices, the very first news of the surviving crew:

> New York office cables that the following from the Titanic are saved: – Second Officer C.H. Lightoller; Third Officer H.J. Pitman; Fourth Officer J.S.Boxall [sic]; Fifth Officer H.G. Lowe; Second Marconi Operator H.S. Bride. The Virginian and Tunisian report that they have no survivors on board. We are now shortly expecting further advices regarding other member of the crew saved.

To many in the crowd, these names were unfamiliar. Most of the officers were not locals. To the discerning reader, it had been listed in order of seniority and so when Eleanor read or heard this message it confirmed the inevitable: she was now a widow. As the shock registered in the Smith home, hundreds of other relatives who had gathered in Canute road watched as workmen erected a large black hoarding at the front of the office. Upon this make-shift noticeboard, the names of just over 200 of the surviving crew would be affixed out of a total of 900. Eleanor would not be alone in her sorrow.

According to the *Daily Sketch* of Wednesday, 17 April 1912, 'At Captain Smith's house the garden is full of spring flowers, but the blinds are half drawn as if to show that the fate of the captain is still in doubt. When I called this morning I was told by the maid that Mrs. Smith was prostrated with grief. No communication has been received from the captain since he sailed from Southampton.'[5]

Mel had just turned fourteen years old when her father was lost. The *Philadelphia Press* of 19 April 1912, under the headline 'Sympathy for Captain's Family' wrote: 'There is no more pathetic figure in Southampton than Mrs. Edward J. Smith, widow of the commander of the ill-fated *Titanic*. The Smiths and their one daughter, a golden-haired and hitherto vivacious girl of thirteen years [sic], reside in a suburban villa in Winn Road... She and her daughter are absolutely prostrated. They refuse to see any but intimate friends.'[6]

Shortly before three pm on Thursday on 18 April, the grief-stricken widow of Captain Smith posted a message outside the White Star Line offices in Southampton that was subsequently reprinted by local and national newspapers under the heading 'Touching Message from Captain's Wife':

TO MY POOR FELLOW SUFFERERS.
My heart overflows with grief for you all and is laden with sorrow that you are weighed down with this terrible burden that has been thrust upon us. May God be with us and comfort us all.

Yours in deepest sympathy,
(Signed) Eleanor Smith.[7]

Eleanor's short yet heartfelt message had been posted where anxious crowds gathered to see if their loved ones had survived or not. It was the scene of both despair and relief, as lists were constantly updated each day. Their response to Eleanor's note was conveyed in the *Southern Daily Echo*: 'As a clerk posted the message from Mrs. Smith ... the crowd pushed forward. There must be news at least. But if the news was not that which was sought, the poignant, human message from a fellow sufferer from the great disaster, united every woman in the crowd in a common bond of sympathy.'[8]

A large number of newspapers worldwide published Eleanor's message on 19 April 1912. The most insensitive was the London *Daily Mirror*, which printed it directly under a photograph of the Captain with the headline 'Captain Smith Shoots Himself on the Bridge' (Figure 47). There was an attempt at redemption when the same newspaper printed a large photograph of Eleanor and Mel on their front page (Figure 53) on 22 April, repeating her same message to fellow sufferers with the comment: 'The sympathy of the whole world goes out to Mrs. Smith... Though no woman could have lost her husband in more tragic circumstances, she has borne her overwhelming grief with a bravery which compels admiration. In the midst of her distress, her thoughts have been as much for others as for herself.'[9]

Author Julie Cook's great-grandfather was a stoker lost in the disaster and she believes her great-grandmother would have taken some consolation from the 'chief wife' of the mourning widows: 'Reading Captain Smith's wife's words at their kitchen table must have been a soothing balm; showing that even women at the elevated heights of Captain's wife were sharing the grief of the poorest widow.'[10]

Now equal in mourning with other 'poor fellow sufferers,' Eleanor and Mel were at the mercy of incomplete and frequently inaccurate information printed in the newspapers or reports from the inquiries that were to follow. It must have been a painful experience to be drip-fed clues as to what really happened to the father and husband in his final hours. Early reports focused on his sacrifice and heroism, while others spoke of him asleep at the time of collision, of being inactive during the evacuation, and even committing suicide.

'Just Inside'

While we cannot be sure exactly what Captain Smith was doing in his quarters at the moment of the iceberg collision, Gary Cooper is sure he was not asleep, noting that 'at both the American and British inquiries into the *Titanic* disaster Fourth Officer Boxhall testified quite specifically that he saw the captain on numerous occasions that evening from when he first arrived on the bridge during Lightoller's watch, up until the time of the accident.' Cooper surmises that the same would have occurred during First Officer Murdoch's watch from 10 pm onwards:

> Smith was not asleep in his cabin, he was in fact at work, either plotting their progress thus far, puzzling a route around the reported ice, planning out the next day's navigation, or perhaps even taking time to complete the mass of official documents and requisitions he would have to present on reaching New York.[11]

The Convergence of the Twain

Second Officer Lightoller confirmed this opinion during the British Board of Trade Inquiry. In answer to the question 'Was the Captain dressed?' he responded, 'I do not think there was any doubt about his being dressed, because in the ordinary conditions, as the Captain said, he would be just inside, he would not turn in under those conditions. He would just remain in his navigating room where his navigating instruments are, chart books, etc., where he would be handy to pop out on the bridge.'[12]

Smith also had a reputation for not sleeping at such critical times, according to Dr. Willam E. Peniz, a passenger aboard the *Majestic* in 1902. He remembered that 'for three days Captain Smith went without sleep, while we were among the ice and bergs.'[13] The three authors of the extensive *Titanic* volume *On a Sea of Glass* concluded after considering the evidence:

> There is also good circumstantial evidence that Captain Smith did not fully retire before the collision, as he was apparently dressed when he arrived on the Bridge very shortly after the impact. Perhaps he might have been involved in something in the Navigating Room adjacent his private quarters or was in his Sitting Room resting without retiring. It is possible that he intended to be close at hand during the night, in case there was any deterioration in visibility or if ice fields were spotted and he was needed on the Bridge.[14]

That Smith would not have immediately gone to sleep was also indicated in his final instructions to the Officer of the Watch: 'If it becomes at all doubtful let me know at once; I will be just inside.' According to the layout of the Officers' Quarters, 'just inside' would refer to the Navigating Room, as that is the door immediately off the wheelhouse, located in between the Captain's Sitting Room and the bridge. Equipped with a chart table, this room would undoubtedly be where Smith plotted their course and where ice reports were kept. The inference is clear: he wanted to know immediately if there were any changes in the conditions so as to adjust their course accordingly. He was still on duty.

A few moments before 11:40 pm, lookout Frederick Fleet saw an iceberg dead ahead about 500 yards away, towering some 60 feet above the water. First Officer Murdoch, responding to the lookout's alert as well as likely seeing the berg himself, ordered the helmsman 'hard-a-starboard' (effectively turning the ship hard to port) and later 'hard-a-port' in a futile effort to manoeuvre around the mass of ice that had unexpectedly appeared in their path. During the tense minute of initial response, Captain Smith was likely unaware, still in his cabin.

He maybe heard a disturbance and detected a change in speed and direction. Under normal circumstances, before any change to the ship's speed and direction, he would have been called by the Officer of the Watch to authorise such orders. Something was clearly wrong. As he burst out into the wheelhouse section of the bridge which was completely darkened (Quartermaster Hichens, at the wheel, said 'the skipper came rushing out of his room'),[15] he would have noted that the ship's wheel had been turned hard over, to hard-a-port. Exiting the wheelhouse into the open section of the navigational bridge, he would then have seen the engine telegraphs set to 'stop'. And standing there, First Officer William Murdoch would have been catching his breath.

Some have criticised the amount of time it took for Smith to appear on the bridge. In reality, it was only 20 or 30 seconds between the time of the collision and when Smith appeared there. It must be remembered that he had entrusted the care of the ship into the very experienced and safe hands of First Officer Murdoch – ostensibly the Chief Officer, if it was not for Wilde's presence. There would be no doubt in Smith's mind that whatever last-minute commands Murdoch had ordered without first consulting him had to be serious and calculated. Indeed, some researchers have concluded that Murdoch almost pulled off a miracle with his orders that night.[16] Smith would have considered it reckless to burst onto the bridge in a state of uninformed panic and instead allowed his First Officer to make the necessary orders without his interference or any added confusion. If Smith was in the middle of plotting a new course in the event of encountering ice, or some other paperwork, he would likely have taken his time to finish his calculations – expecting an officer or crew member to fetch him if necessary. It was most likely the vibration of the ship's brush with ice that prompted him to make his own way out to establish the cause. Within that context, 20 to 30 seconds is a reasonable response time.

What happens next is quite possibly the most analysed piece of history ever. From the moment of the collision at 11:40 pm, it took *Titanic* two hours and 40 minutes to sink, and every single minute of this tragic timeline has been painstakingly told and retold, researched, cross-examined, reviewed, and dramatised in infinite detail. The exact times each lifeboat was lowered has been minutely reconstructed, as well as the most likely occupants of each boat. It seems that we know as much as is humanly possible to know about an event extracted entirely through oral and written testimony and in the absence of any first-hand photographic, film or audio recordings of the event. With such minutiae of information, it is incredible to think that for many years the role of Captain Smith during this critical time has been somewhat indistinct.

The Convergence of the Twain

It must have been frustrating for Eleanor and Mel of 1912 to know so little about what he did on that fateful night. In letters written shortly afterward, Eleanor expressed her opinion that her husband had been nothing less than gallant in behaviour, and perhaps this was based on personal accounts or letters sent to her. She also referenced a published portrait photograph, so she was reading contemporary newspaper accounts about her husband.

The official public record was scant in detail as to his precise activities. For some, the conclusion is that he simply was not active. Descriptions such as that of Lightoller, who indicated Smith was reticent to initiate the loading of the lifeboats, has led to a cinematic portrayal of Smith as almost comatose, stunned by the enormous scope of the disaster unfolding before him.

The reality is quite different. Fourth Officer Boxhall appeared on the bridge shortly after Smith and witnessed his conversation with Murdoch. On day 13 of the British Wreck Commissioner's Inquiry, Boxhall reported:

> He asked him what we had struck… The First Officer said, 'An iceberg, Sir. I hard-a-starboarded and reversed the engines, and I was going to hard-a-port round it but she was too close. I could not do any more. I have closed the watertight doors.' The Commander asked him if he had rung the warning bell, and he said 'Yes.'[17]

After that, according to Boxhall, the Captain and the First Officer walked to the starboard side of the bridge, to the wing cab, to see if they could see the iceberg, with Murdoch pointing it out as it disappeared behind them (Figure 44). Boxhall's recollection was not entirely accurate. The engines had not been reversed – an erroneous conclusion possibly formed after seeing the engine telegraph set to 'astern' to slow the ship post-collision. At the British Inquiry, Boxhall admitted that he 'had just come out of the light, and my eyes were not accustomed to the darkness', so his observations may not be entirely reliable. There is also some confusion over what Boxhall had been doing at the time of the collision. He had testified at the inquiry in England that he had been 'coming out of the Officers quarters' but decades later confessed during a 1962 BBC radio broadcast that more specifically he 'was sitting in my cabin having a cup of tea', despite the fact he was still on duty.[18] There has been no explanation as to his absence, although a later illness has suggested he was not well and Murdoch may have allowed him to return to his cabin. These factors combined obfuscate his evidence. There were certainly no other witnesses – including those in the boiler and engine rooms – who reported a 'full astern' order, and the mechanics involved dictate that the engines could not be reversed in time to be of any effect – of which Murdoch was undoubtedly aware.

What we do gain from Boxhall's observation is that Smith was quickly assessing the situation. He had firstly confirmed the watertight doors were closed, and then made a personal observation of the condition of the ship from the vantage of the bridge, as well as an attempt to spot the cause of the situation they now faced. His primary task was to gather as much data about the ship's present condition to form an accurate picture from which to base his initial response.

First Orders

His first order though – within a minute or so of the collision – was perhaps surprising. He personally changed the engine room telegraph to 'Half-Ahead.' *Titanic* was underway. This was witnessed by 28-year-old Quartermaster Alfred Olliver who at the Senate Inquiry not only confirmed that the engines were not reversed at the time of the collision but that 'after she struck; she went half speed ahead. The captain telegraphed half speed ahead.'[19] Olliver, similar to Boxhall, arrived on the bridge just in time to hear Murdoch give his second order: 'Hard-a-port.'

It may not have been exactly 'half speed ahead' – as those in the boiler and engine rooms only remember receiving 'slow astern' and 'slow ahead' orders. Engine room trimmer Thomas Dillon remembered that after the

Figure 44: Captain Smith peering down from the *Olympic*'s starboard wing cab just as he would have done the night the *Titanic* struck the iceberg. (*The Sphere* 11 May 1912, courtesy of Paul Lee)

engines had been 'stopped' during the collision 'they went ahead again ... for about two minutes' before stopping again.[20]

That the *Titanic* started moving once more was witnessed by passengers including second class passenger Lawrence Beesley, who wrote that in his cabin he had 'felt the engines slow and stop'. Once on deck, he then noticed 'the ship had now resumed her course, moving very slowly through the water with a little white line of foam on each side. I think we were all glad to see this: it seemed better than standing still.' On discovering that an iceberg had caused the disturbance, Beesley overheard someone joke 'I expect the iceberg has scratched off some of her new paint and the captain doesn't like to go on until she is painted up again.' Beesley laughed at this 'estimate of the captain's care for the ship. Poor Captain Smith! – he knew by this time only too well what had happened.' When some lady passengers insisted the engines had stopped, Beesley even proved it was not the case when he 'took them along the corridor to a bathroom and made them put their hands on the side of the bath: they were much reassured to feel the engines throbbing down below and to know we were making some headway.'[21]

Some have misinterpreted Smith's 'half-ahead' or 'slow ahead' order – blaming it on J. Bruce Ismay, although Olliver is quite clear that Captain Smith personally telegraphed half-speed ahead well before Ismay appeared on the bridge. Others claim that Smith's order to keep *Titanic* underway doomed the ship. Second Officer Lightoller's granddaughter, Lady Louise Patten, went public in 2010 accusing Murdoch of making a fatal steering error and that her 'grandfather described the decision to try and keep *Titanic* moving forward as criminal. The nearest ship was four hours away. Had she remained at 'stop,' it's probable that *Titanic* would have floated until help arrived.'[22] The implication has been made that Smith even wanted to try for the nearest port – a concept partially substantiated by early press reports that the *Titanic* was steaming for Halifax.

There are several issues with Patten's claims. Lightoller was not on the bridge at the time the orders were given and by extension, Patten is repeating something she heard when she was only a child – and from her grandmother at that. It maybe explains why her claims are actually founded on what appears to be confusion over traditional tiller commands that were in place in 1912 and in which the 'hard-a-starboard' order actually turns a ship hard-to-port (just as turning a rudder in the rear of a rowing boat in one direction turns the vessel's head in the opposite direction). We know for sure that Murdoch's order was correctly relayed and enacted by Quartermaster Hichens, an order that would have been verified by Sixth Officer Moody, whose job was to oversee orders were correctly followed through and stood directly behind the quartermaster at the wheel. More importantly, Patten's claims were timed to coincide with the release of her book, *Good As Gold*, which rather tellingly is a work of fiction.

While the command is not in doubt, why would Smith order the *Titanic* slow ahead after a collision? There have been several theories postulated: that Smith may have based the decision on early reports that there was no damage below and wanted to clear the dangerous area of ice, test the propellers and shafts were still operational, and move north of their course to place them in a position more visible to other traffic, all of which are entirely feasible.

The consensus seems to be that it is unlikely that 'slow ahead' would have caused any substantial pressure to build up in the flooded compartments as the water ingress was through relatively small apertures. However, moving a damaged ship is not recommended; the forward motion can cause stress on damaged areas of the hull. Nonetheless, we do know that only minutes later, at 11:46 pm, Smith had changed the engine telegraphs to 'Stop'. So, any damage would be minimal and its effect on the loss of the ship marginal at most.

Smith's next order was to Quartermaster Olliver, to go and find the ship's carpenter and have him sound for damage. Olliver went to E deck, where the *Titanic*'s carpenter, likely 29-year-old John Maxwell, was already taking a draft. Water coming into the empty ballast tanks would have indicated damage to the hull. While Olliver was there, he did not personally see any damage.[23] Fourth Officer Boxhall also made a self-initiated trip forward as far down as F deck 'and inspected all the decks as I came up, in the vicinity of where I thought she had struck'. He then returned to the bridge shortly thereafter to report to Captain Smith that he had 'found no damage'. In response Smith said, just as he had told Olliver, 'Go down and find the carpenter and get him to sound the ship.'[24]

As Boxhall was fetching the carpenter, he met the man himself, Maxwell, coming in the opposite direction on the 'ladder leading from the bridge down to A deck, and he wanted to know where the Captain was. I told him he was on the bridge. [Maxwell] said the ship was making water fast, and he passed it on to the bridge.'[25]

At this time, Smith began receiving disturbing reports from multiple quarters. After Maxwell, postal clerk Jago Smith reported to the Captain – upon Boxhall's urging – that the mail hold, one deck below the post office on G deck, was filling with water. The RMS prefix in *Titanic*'s name referenced her commission as a Royal Mail Steamer under contract with the British Royal Mail for the transatlantic postal service. There were five postmen aboard with 3,364 bags in total, 200 of which they attempted to move to upper decks. Ultimately all the mail was lost – along with the five postal workers.[26]

The realisation this was serious was no doubt becoming apparent to Smith. Soon thereafter, Quartermaster Alfred Olliver, returning from his first errand, was immediately given a note by Smith to take down to the engine room and deliver to Chief Engineer Bell. Olliver said it was 'on a piece of paper and the paper was closed'. By the time he reached the engine room, he noted that the engines were stopped, indicating that Smith had changed the engine room telegraph to 'Stop'. As for Smith's note, we do not know what was contained in it. Olliver, who waited several minutes for a response, said the reply from Bell was 'to tell the captain that he would get it done as soon as possible.'[27] Bell had been given an order.

Other concerning reports were coming in. According to an account by 31-year-old Boatswain Mate Albert Haines, he discovered, along with Chief Officer Henry Wilde, that air was escaping from the forepeak tank, indicating that 'water was coming in… The chief officer then went on the bridge to report.' After Wilde had passed this disturbing news to Smith, Haines had further investigated to find that 'the tarpaulin was bellying up, raising, showing that the water was coming in… I went on the bridge and reported to the chief officer… I told him No. 1 hole was filling.' By now the orders had changed. Wilde told Haines to 'get the men up and get the boats out'.[28]

Smith's conclusion was obvious – the ship was seriously damaged. And he did not mince words when J. Bruce Ismay, appeared on the bridge soon after. Unlike modern portrayals, Ismay had not frequented the bridge area, as it was strictly off-limits to passengers. As something was clearly wrong, Ismay ignored protocol and left his room, putting on his coat, and went up on the bridge where he found Captain Smith. 'I asked him what had happened, and he said, "We have struck ice." I said, "Do you think the ship is seriously damaged?" He said, "I am afraid she is."' The Captain's appraisal was shortly after reaffirmed by Chief Engineer Bell who Ismay met as he went down below. Bell was coming up – perhaps responding to the earlier note from Smith – and when Ismay met him in the companionway he confirmed that 'the ship was seriously damaged… but was quite satisfied the pumps would keep her afloat.'[29] No doubt Bell also reported this to Smith. Just as with Haines' account, by the time Ismay returned to the bridge, the order was to prepare the lifeboats. The reports had been enough for Smith to start taking action – rousing crew and passengers and getting the lifeboats ready for a worst-case scenario.

When Boxhall returned to the bridge and reported to the Commander what he had seen in the flooded post office, with the sea only two feet from the top of the post office stairwell and heavy bags of mail floating, Boxhall told the British Inquiry that Smith did not say anything in reply and simply 'walked away and left me. He went off the bridge, as far as I remember.'[30] The Captain may have been stunned into silence. Although in Boxhall's Senate Inquiry testimony he does recall Smith responding with 'all right'.

While Smith may have momentarily left the bridge, he was not deserting command. At this point – it must have been around midnight – and in line with Haines' and Ismay's accounts, Boxhall remembered his next order from the Captain: 'And then the order came out for the boats … to clear the lifeboats.'[31]

Authors Tad Fitch, J. Kent Layton and Bill Wormstedt, in their well respected and detailed account of the sinking, *On a Sea of Glass* (2012), note that the order to clear the lifeboats came before he had received the dire prognosis to come, and that 'these were proactive acts that, in the end, wound up saving lives … the historical record tends to disprove the popularly held concept that Captain Smith was a weak leader in a time of crisis. In retrospect, it seems that Captains Smith's actions saved many lives.'[32]

Inspection

If we were to follow cinematic tropes, it would be at this point in the story where Captain Smith would address his officers lined up on the bridge, with the unthinkable news that the ship would soon sink. This never happened. While Fourth Officer Boxhall after his investigations below deck was ordered by Smith to rouse the off-duty officers 'approximately 20 minutes to half-an-hour [after impact]',[33] Wilde, Lightoller, Pitman and Lowe were not summoned for a meeting on the bridge. In any case, of the four off-duty officers, only Lowe was still asleep, later famously explaining that the harsh four-hours-on and four-hours-off shifts meant that 'when we sleep we die.'[34] The other officers were already in the process of dressing. Pitman was in his cabin smoking a pipe, waiting for his watch to begin at midnight as he 'thought that nothing had really happened, that perhaps it might have been a dream'.[35] Lightoller pointed out that it would break protocol for an off-duty officer to enter the bridge without being requested to do so, explaining, 'If I was wanted, naturally my cabin would be the first place where anyone sent for me would look,' and so he was cooling his heels until he was called.[36] Once requested on duty by the Captain, the surviving officers never reported a meeting in the bridge, and indeed their testimony reveals a distinct lack of communication and understanding of the seriousness of the situation during the initial stages of the sinking. As pointed out by the authors of *On a Sea of Glass*, Smith was 'confronted with a conundrum ... calling these men, even if it was only the officers, to the Bridge for a confab would have wasted precious time. It seems that he believed it was better to let them do their work without interruption.'[37] That there was no meeting did not mean Smith was not giving orders. Marian Thayer was on the boat deck and caught sight of the Captain giving orders on the port side of the bridge.[38]

About the time Boxhall was rousing the off-duty officers, Captain Smith was in the Marconi room, situated at the other end of the Officers' Quarters, where wireless operators John 'Jack' Phillips and his junior, Harold Bride, had been working tirelessly to catch up on a backlog of private messages. According to Bride, he was standing by Phillips, 'telling him to go to bed, when the captain put his head in the cabin, "We've struck an iceberg," the captain said, "and I'm having an inspection made to tell what it has done for us. You better get ready to send out a call for assistance. But don't send it until I tell you."'[39]

At that, the Captain left and indeed embarked on an inspection – with none other than the *Titanic*'s shipbuilder himself, Thomas Andrews, managing director at Harland & Wolff. The varying reports Smith had been receiving up to this point needed to be properly verified by someone who could determine the exact impact on the ship's condition – and there was no one more qualified than Andrews. So as Boxhall roused the officers and lifeboats began to be uncovered and the Marconi operators prepared a distress message, Smith and Andrews inspected the ship. The tour was witnessed by first class saloon steward James Johnstone from whom we can establish the main locations visited. During the British Inquiry, he testified that he saw 'Mr Andrews come down and go down to the engine room, and then I saw the Captain directly following him ... he came three or four minutes before the Captain... He had to come down through the stairs to get down to the engine room to get on to E deck.'[40] Afterwards, he saw Andrews visit the mail room and squash court area, where he also noticed water entering the ship.

Helen Ostby, in first class, was walking 'up to the boat deck by the main staircase. I remember seeing Captain Smith and one or two other officers coming down it to explore the ship and see what damage had been done. The officers looked very sober. They didn't stop to talk to the passengers at all.'[41]

Stewardess Annie Robinson was another eyewitness, spotting the 'mail man' pass along the crew's corridor and then return with

Captain Smith and someone she described as 'Mr. McElroy' although it may have been Thomas Andrews, 'and they went in the direction of the mail room, but that was before.'[42] In another account attributed to an unnamed stewardess, who was likely Robinson, she identified a 'bareheaded and insufficiently clad' Andrews as telling Smith while they were on the 'upper deck' that 'three have gone already, Captain,' that must be in reference to the first three watertight compartments – the only documented occasion of Andrew specifically reporting on damage.[43] There is one other account that also places Smith at the mailroom: first class passenger Norman Chambers and his wife were at the top of the stairs to see what the commotion was, and, according to Walter Lord's paraphrasing of his story, said that the Captain visited the mailroom during their time there.[44]

German steward Alfred Theissinger was on E deck when heard a fireman report flooding and then Captain Smith passed him, coming from what he thought was the dining saloon.[45] Bathroom steward Charles Mackay said he witnessed Smith coming down the staircase on E deck at about midnight and then return up the same stairs: 'I saw him come down the working staircase and go along, I presume, to the Chief Engineer's room. About 10 minutes after that I saw him come back up the same staircase.'[46] The Captain was also seen by Paul Maugé, secretary to the chef of the à la carte restaurant, who said he 'saw Captain Smith had been to the engine room. He came back two minutes after.'[47] First class bathroom steward Samuel Rule confirmed Smith had been to the engine-room: 'He [Smith] was walking back from the engine-room, where I heard he had been to consult Mr. Bell, the chief engineer. That, of course, would be the first thing he would do after the collision.'[48]

When the Captain returned, he was spotted by Charles Stengel and his wife on A deck. 'We came down to the next deck, and the captain came up. I supposed he had come up from investigating the damage. He had a very serious and a very grave face. I then said to my wife, "This is a very serious matter, I believe."'[49]

While this critical inspection took place, the off-duty officers had arrived and were quickly assessing the situation. Their presence was important, as around midnight the Captain had made the decision to ready the lifeboats – and most importantly the two emergency cutters. Quartermaster William 'Walter' Wynn, who had immediately made his way to the bridge to receive orders, recalled receiving an order from the Captain to 'get the two accident boats ready'.[50] The two emergency lifeboats, numbered 1 and 2, were situated on the forward sections of the starboard and port side boat deck, often swung out at key moments in a voyage in preparation for a possible emergency – someone falling overboard for example. Boxhall recalled Captain Smith previously giving the order to 'clear the lifeboats,' so Boxhall 'went around the decks and was clearing the lifeboats; helping take the covers off ... and clearing them generally ... and assisting generally around the decks.'[51] This order was not to load the lifeboats but simply to prepare them for the possibility of an evacuation. Second Officer Lightoller had put on 'a pair of pants, sweater and bridge coat' and was out on deck. Due to the deafening sound of steam exhausted via the funnels (as the engines had stopped), Lightoller could not even shout orders to his men and instead showed them 'with my hands that I wanted [them] to start stripping off the boat covers'.[52]

Another witness who saw Smith giving the lifeboat order at midnight was Quartermaster Robert Hichens who testified that he heard the Captain say '"Get all the boats out and serve out the belts." That was after 12.' Hichens noted there was another piece of information that added to the urgency: 'The Captain then looked at the commutator and he found that the ship was carrying a list to starboard.'[53] At the Senate hearings, Hichens said that Smith 'came back to the wheelhouse and looked at the commutator in front of the compass, which is a little instrument like a clock to tell you how the ship is listing. The ship had a list of 5° to the starboard.'[54] It was possibly at that point when Smith rang 'Stop' on the engine telegraph.

As for the results of the inspection that Smith and Andrews took, we do not know exactly what conversation took place between these two men except what Fourth Officer Boxhall later recalled in his testimony. After clearing the boats, Boxhall had a conversation with Captain Smith in which the commander related Thomas Andrew's assessment: 'The Captain did remark something to me in the earlier part of the evening after the order had been given to clear the boats ... he was inquiring about the men going on with the work, and I said, "Yes, they are carrying on all right." I said, "Is it really serious?" He said, "Mr. Andrews tells me he gives her from an hour to an hour and a half." That must have been some little time afterwards. Evidently Mr. Andrews had been down.'[55]

This was all the information that Smith needed to make a final decision – the ship was to be evacuated and a distress call sent. One of his first actions was to send Fourth Officer Boxhall to the chartroom to work out the ship's exact position.

There was another urgent reason to send the distress call: another vessel had been spotted. While Boxhall had been uncovering the lifeboats, he 'heard the look-out bell sound again, and went back on to the bridge. Through his telescope he verified the report as being another ship, and informed the captain. He was told to keep an eye on it.'[56] In another account, Boxhall stated that he 'went on the bridge right away, and I found this light with my own glasses but I wanted the telescope to define what it was and I realized then it was two masthead lights of a steamer below the horizon and the lights were very close and I went back and told the Captain, "There is a steamer insight very nearly ahead but slightly on the Starboard Bow and if she continues on her course she'll pass close to us down the Port Side."'[57] It must have been one of few glimmers of hope that was reported to Smith that night.

As Boxhall calculated their position, Smith quickly returned to the Marconi room. Bride estimated it was ten minutes between his first and second visit – and on the second occasion he was 'barely putting his head in the door' when he ordered the wireless men to 'send a call for assistance.' Smith had not said which call. '"What call should I send?" Phillips asked. "The regulation international call for help, just that." Then the captain was gone.'[58] It is not surprising that when Second Officer Lightoller saw Smith leaving the Marconi room 'his face [was] stern but haggard'.[59]

As Boxhall had not yet completed his calculations, Smith had given the operators a position based on Fifth Officer Lowe's earlier 8 pm calculation, at Latitude 41°44' North, Longitude 50°24' West. Boxhall explained to the Captain this was inaccurate:

> The Captain said, 'I've already sent a distress signal.' 'What, what position did you send it from?' He said, 'From the eight o'clock DR.' 'Well,' I said, 'that was about, she was about twenty miles ahead of that sir. If you like I will run the position up from the star position up to the time of the contact with the iceberg.'[60]

Meanwhile, Phillips decided to use 'C.Q.D.' which had been adopted in 1904 as an international distress call (CQ indicates a 'general call' and the D 'distress'). 'Five minutes later the captain returned again and asked, "What are you sending?" and Phillips replied it was "C.Q.D."' Bride found this a moment for light relief: 'The humour of the situation appealed to me, and I cut in with a little remark that made us all laugh, including the captain. "Send S.O.S., I said, "it's the new call, and it may be your last chance to send it." Phillips, with a laugh, changed the signal to S.O.S.' The captain told us we had been struck amidships, or just aft of amidships.'[61] It is strange to think of Captain Smith laughing at this crucial moment. Had Boxhall's report of a nearby vessel given him some hope? Or was he simply humouring the wireless operators to ensure they continued with their important task?

Boxhall had been calculating a new position that took into consideration their 7:30 pm reading and an estimation as to the speed of the ship,

The Convergence of the Twain

Figure 45: A 1912 illustration of Captain Smith giving wireless operator Jack Phillips the order to send out the S.O.S. that appeared in *The Wireless Man* by Francis A. Collins. (Author's collection)

allowing for 22 knots. This resulted in a position of 41°46′ N., 50°14′ W. Immediately, Boxhall submitted the *Titanic*'s position to the Captain. 'He said, "Take it to the Marconi room."... there was too much noise of the steam escaping, so I wrote the position down for them and left it.'[62]

With the discovery of the wreck in 1985, at 41°43′ N, 49°56′ W, we now know that Captain Smith's and Fourth Officer Boxhall's positions were respectively 20 miles and 13 miles too far to the west of *Titanic*'s actual sinking position. It was only by chance that Captain Rostron of the *Carpathia* stumbled upon a lifeboat en route to the incorrect location – a lifeboat ironically commanded by Boxhall himself.

Interestingly, if you take Captain Smith's original distress position and calculate 20 miles backward on the reverse course, it arrives at a position only a mile away from the where the *Titanic* wreckage is located. Perhaps Smith's position would have been more accurate than Boxhall's if he had been given the correct information.[63]

Evacuation Begins

Shortly afterward, at what must have been about twenty-five past midnight, Smith was outside on the boat deck, where he met Lightoller who had uncovered the boats and was wanting approval to begin loading. At the British Inquiry, the Second Officer described this moment: 'After I had swung out No. 4 boat I asked the Chief Officer should we put the women and children in, and he said "No." I left the men to go ahead with their work and found the Commander, or I met him and I asked him should we put the women and children in, and the Commander said "Yes, put the women and children in and lower away." That was the last order I received on the ship.'[64]

Lightoller's 1935 description of this conversation has often led to the erroneous perception that the Captain was shell-shocked, as frequently portrayed on film. In Lightoller's book, he described his meeting with Smith on the boat deck, likely the port side, during the time the venting steam was deafening: 'Drawing him into a corner, and cupping both my hands over my mouth and his ear, I yelled at the top of my voice, "Hadn't we better get the women and children into the boats, sir?" He heard me, and nodded reply.'[65] The non-vocal response to Lightoller's request was out of necessity; Lightoller had earlier described how he had directed the readying of the lifeboats using only gestures due to the volume of noise. And as we have already established, Smith had been busy investigating the precise condition of the ship. He may well have been experiencing some shock, but he was not idle, and certainly not comatose.

Lightoller was not the only officer to enquire of the Captain regarding the loading of the lifeboats. Third Officer Pitman, in the process of working on lifeboat no. 5 on the starboard side, had been dealing with a man 'dressed in a dressing gown, with slippers on', someone he did not recognise at first, who had been telling him 'there is no time to waste' and 'you had better go ahead and get the women and children.' Like Wilde and Lightoller, Pitman would not proceed with the loading without an order. He told the man: 'I await the commander's orders.' The man replied 'very well' or something similar and it was then that Pitman recognised the man as possibly Ismay, the managing director, likely stirred by the information from the Captain when he had met him on the bridge. Pitman then realised he needed to talk to the Captain directly. 'So I went along to the bridge and saw Captain Smith, and I told him that I thought it was Mr. Ismay that wished me to get the boat away, with women and children in it. So he said, "Go ahead; carry on." I came along and brought in my boat. I stood on it and said, "Come along, ladies." There was a big crowd. Mr. Ismay helped to get them along; assisted in every way.' Pitman explained his response to Ismay: 'We take no orders from anybody except the commander.' Ismay did not try again to pre-empt the Captain's orders. According to Pitman 'the next I saw of him was coming onto the *Carpathia*.'[66]

Pitman's conversation with Captain Smith on the bridge was the last he ever saw of the *Titanic*'s commander. Not that Smith disappeared

The Convergence of the Twain

from view from that point onward. Pitman left early, in lifeboat no. 5 as instructed by First Officer Murdoch. Henceforth, the number of accounts mentioning the Captain would start to dwindle as each lifeboat departed, winnowing down the number of survivors who could recall his activities and orders. But he was involved. Paul Maugé, from the à la carte restaurant, saw the Captain trying to encourage reluctant passengers to enter the lifeboats. 'I saw Captain Smith again at the first lifeboat. He said to a lady, "It is all right, lady." … because no lady or gentleman would like to go; everybody thought it would be quite safe.'[67]

Wireless operator Harold Bride was in frequent contact with the Captain, especially after receiving an answer from the *Carpathia* at 12:49 am, ensuring the commander was kept informed of their progress. 'Phillips told me to run and tell him what the *Carpathia* had answered. I did so, and I went through an awful mass of people to his cabin. The decks were full of scrambling men and women… Every few minutes Phillips would send me to the captain with little messages. They were merely telling how the *Carpathia* was coming our way, and giving her speed.' Not only did Bride make constant errands to the find the Captain, but Smith himself also made several visits to the wireless room to keep them updated.[68]

Bride also noted that when he reported communications to the Captain, he 'found him engaging in superintending the filling and lowering of the lifeboats'[69] – so it was clear that Smith was actively involved in the lifeboat evacuation. At the British Inquiry, Bride was more specific about the location, stating that when he reported to the Captain 'he was on the boat deck, the starboard side, if I remember… He was superintending the loading of the lifeboats.'[70] During one of these errands, Bride relayed Phillip's frustration that he was having difficulty hearing the replies to their distress calls, due to the noise of steam released above the Marconi room: 'This I also reported to Capt. Smith, who by some means managed to get it abated.'[71]

Lamp trimmer Samuel Hemming testified that he received a message from the Captain asking him to put lamps into each lifeboat, which were on the davits ready to be lowered when he did so. Hemming managed to bring up 14 lamps in total, full of oil, and lit them himself so that they were 'all brought up alight' and put in the boats.[72] Equipping the lifeboats with lamps was a practical piece of foresight.

Next was the loading order – and again this came from Captain Smith. Quartermaster Robert Hichens remembered that he heard the captain say, '"Women and children first", and the Officer [Lightoller] repeated the words from the captain.' The testimony and the final number of survivors from the port side strongly suggests Lightoller adhered to 'women and children *only*'. Hichens even remembered exactly where on the port side the Captain was when he gave the order: 'Just standing ... between the Officers' quarters and the collapsible boat'.[73] Able seaman John Poingdestre was making his way to his assigned lifeboat no. 12 when he 'heard the Captain pass the remark, "Start putting the women and children in the boats."'[74]

Smith was also personally involved in ensuring passengers were wearing their lifejackets. First class passenger Mrs Mary Eliza Compton recalled: 'When Captain Smith handed us life preservers, he said cheerily: "They will keep you warm if you do not have to use them."'[75]

Three French first class passengers – Paul Chevré, Pierre Maréchal and Alfred Fernand Omont – were playing bridge at the time of the collision and saw Captain Smith chewing on a toothpick, or at least it appeared that way. In a joint account they wrote: 'Captain Smith nevertheless appeared nervous; he came down on deck chewing a toothpick. "Let everyone," he said "put on a lifebelt, it is more prudent." He then ordered the boats to be got out.'[76]

Gladys Cherry was out on the first class deck with some other ladies and was contemplating returning to her cabin 'when suddenly the Captain appeared and said: "I don't want to frighten anyone, but will you all go quietly and put on your life belts and go up on the top deck?"' They followed the Captain's orders and dispersed calmly to fetch the life belts.[77] In contrast, another first class passenger, Marie Young, remembered the urgency: 'Suddenly Captain Smith ran downstairs, calling out "Put on your lifebelts!"'[78]

Some of the richest passengers were personally accorded an early warning from the Captain. First class passenger Isaac Frauenthal saw the Captain speak privately to Colonel John Jacob Astor, the richest passenger aboard the ship:

> Presently, I saw the Captain appear, apparently from the bridge, and several men approached him. One of these was Col. Astor and I heard him say to Capt. Smith: 'Captain, my wife is not in good health. She has gone to bed and I don't want to get her up unless it is absolutely necessary. What is the situation?' Capt. Smith replied quietly, 'Col. Astor you had better get your wife up at once. I fear we may have to take to the boats.'[79]

Astor thanked the Captain courteously and rapidly departed. Frauenthal noted that from the Captain's demeanour he 'got an inkling of the peril we were in'.[80]

Not long after, first class passenger Helen Bishop also saw Smith speaking with Astor: 'The captain told him [Astor] something in an undertone. He came back and told six of us, who were standing with his wife, that we had better put on our lifebelts. I had gotten down two flights of stairs to tell my husband, who had returned to the stateroom for a moment, before I heard the captain announce that the lifebelts should be put on.'[81]

Caroline Brown, of first class, also saw Smith with Astor and described the Captain as pale but 'perfectly calm' with a reassuring voice:

> It was some little time after midnight that Capt. Smith, followed by John Jacob Astor, went rapidly along our deck. As he passed, Capt. Smith was quite pale and I have since had a feeling that he realized the extent of our danger even at that time. But he seemed perfectly calm and his voice was quite natural as he ordered all on deck to put on lifebelts. His steady, quiet tones were reassuring.[82]

Algernon Barkworth, in first class, said: 'The last of Captain Smith I saw was when he was surrounded by a crowd of crying ladies asking him many questions, "Go back to your cabins, ladies, and put on your lifebelts, and come back to the boat deck. I assure you there is no danger." I thought that sounded rather bad myself.'[83] Yet it did prompt Barkworth to return to change into more suitable clothes – and he ended up surviving aboard upturned collapsible B.

Another first class passenger, Albert Dick, who left in lifeboat no. 3 from the port side, also noted that the Captain was attempting to keep the situation calm. 'As the minutes flew by we did not know what to do or which way to turn... Captain Smith was everywhere doing his best to calm the rising tide of fear.'[84] 20-year-old Vera Dick described Captain Smith as 'among the coolest men on board', at first encouraging her to take an early boat and then when she didn't, saying, ;'This is no place for a woman and you will have to go in the next boat.'[85] The Captain also enlisted help from passengers to ensure that women and children first was adhered to. First class passenger Robert Daniel remembered: 'We all stood near the captain and he told us that the way we could help best was to see that no men entered the boats. That's what we did.'[86]

Margaret Smith was involved in what she described as the loading of 'the second boat'. It was 'Captain Smith [who] insisted that we get into it, and as the sailors pulled away from the ship I heard him say, "Row for that light," and I saw him point to a dim glimmer that must have been three miles distant.'[87]

Just before the lowering of the same lifeboat no. 6, someone called out: 'Captain, we have no seaman.' First class passenger Mrs Helen Candee described his response: 'Captain Smith then seized a boy by the arm and said: "Here's one." The boy went into the boat as ordered by the captain, but afterwards he was found to be disabled.' When Gracie reprinted Candee's account, he clarified that 'the Italian boy who was in the boat was not a stowaway, he was ordered in by the captain as already related. Neither did he refuse to row. When he tried to do so, it was futile, because of an injury to his arm or wrist.'[88]

Another passenger in lifeboat 6 was Mrs Margaret Brown of Denver, Colorado (who would later become famous as the socialite and benefactress 'the Unsinkable Molly Brown'):

> When the sea was reached, smooth as glass, she looked up and saw the benign, resigned countenance, the venerable white hair and the Chesterfieldian bearing of the beloved Captain Smith with whom she had crossed twice before, and only three months previous on the *Olympic*. He peered down upon those in the boat, like a solicitous father, and directed them to row to the light in the distance – all boats keeping together.

Interestingly, Quartermaster Robert Hichens, who was put in charge of lifeboat no. 6, thought he heard the Captain call for them to 'come alongside' but was overruled by the passengers. The final orders were to 'keep boats together and row away from the ship'. [89] There may well have been a reason for a change in the Captain's order.

Mistakes in communication with the crew were frequent, especially on the port side, where the evacuation was overseen by Second Officer Lightoller. He did not realise the urgency of the situation. As a result, the lifeboats were not completely filled with passengers. They were built to take 65; Lightoller was loading as few as 40. He later admitted that if he had known how urgent it was 'I would have taken more risks. I should not have considered it wise to put more in, but I might have taken risks.'[90] He also made the unusual choice of lowering lifeboat no. 4 down to A deck, so that instead of loading the passengers from the boat deck they could enter from the promenade deck, until Lightoller realised that the *Titanic* was designed differently from the *Olympic* and the A deck had windows – that were closed. This resulted in the lifeboat being delayed by at least half an hour – during which time Murdoch on the starboard side had already launched three.

Bertha Chambers, in first class, happened to be on the port side boat deck when she heard Captain Smith say, 'Ladies, if you will go down to deck A I think you can get in more easily.'[91] Thus, some have attributed this mistake to Captain Smith who would have been in the vicinity when this bad decision was made. Smith should have been familiar with the

Olympic and the open A deck promenade configuration, while this was the first time Lightoller was aboard an Olympic-class ship, so he would not have necessarily known that *Titanic* was different from the *Olympic*; the forward section of the A deck promenade on the *Titanic* was actually enclosed. The blame is supported in testimony given at the United States Inquiry by first class passenger Hugh Woolner, who also overheard the Captain –who he 'knew by sight' – give the order while he was on the port side. According to Woolner, Smith said:

> 'I want all the passengers to go down on A deck, because I intend they shall go into the boats from A deck.' I remembered noticing as I came up that all those glass windows were raised to the very top; and I went up to the captain and saluted him and said: 'Haven't you forgotten, sir, that all those glass windows are closed?' He said: 'By God, you are right. Call those people back.' Very few people had moved, but the few that had gone down the companionway came up again, and everything went on all right.[92]

It is quite possible Woolner confused Smith with the Second Officer, as Lightoller had already taken the blame for the decision ten days earlier at the same Senate Inquiry: 'We had lowered a boat from A deck one deck down below. That was through my fault. It was the first boat I had lowered. I was intending to put the passengers in from A deck. On lowering it down I found the windows were closed. So I sent some one down to open the windows and carried on with the other boats.' It was doubtless a mistake that cost lives. Although Lightoller defended the decision by stating on record that it was for the safety of the passengers: 'My idea in filling the boats there was because there was a wire hawser running along the side of the ship for coaling purposes, and it was handy to tie the boat in to, to hold it so that nobody could drop between the side of the boat and the ship.'[93]

Lightoller was likely covering for Smith or Wilde, as they must have been aware of, or had even given, the order. It is one of several examples of miscommunication that took place in those fateful last hours. Another example was the use of the gangway doors. Lightoller was not loading the lifeboats fully, planning to load more passengers after the lifeboats had been launched via a rope ladder at sea level. He told the British Inquiry that he told the boatswain 'to go down below and take some men with him and open the gangway doors with the intention of sending the boats to the gangway doors to be filled up... We should probably lower the rope ladder; that was our idea.'[94]

Captain Smith was apparently unaware of this plan. When Smith noticed that the lifeboats leaving *Titanic* were not fully loaded, he had to resort to using a megaphone to call out for them to return, an order they did not obey. This was witnessed by first class passenger Peter Dennis Daly, who 'saw the veteran skipper rush to the railing after the boats had put out from the sinking ship, and call: "Bring those boats back, they are only half filled!" ... it is a fact that many boats did get away only half filled. I can relate merely the incident I witnessed. How many boats obeyed the Captain's order to return I am unable to tell.'[95]

Lightoller, the officer primarily responsible for the low numbers, also heard Smith calling out to the boats:

> I heard the Commander two or three times hail through the megaphone to bring the boats alongside, and I presumed he was alluding to the gangway doors, giving orders to the boats to go to the gangway doors... During the time I was launching the boats on the port side, I could not give you any definite time... He did not know about my order about the gangway doors... I had not discussed the matter with the Captain... It came to both our minds and naturally anyone familiar with the ship, any seaman, any one attached to the ship, would know at once that was the best means of putting the people into the boat – by the gangway doors.[96]

The key part of this testimony is that Lightoller admitted he 'had not discussed the matter with the Captain'. As valuable time passed, decisions were made in the commander's absence that would ultimately cost lives. The reality of course is that Smith could not be in all places at once. Although he was primarily seen on the port side with Wilde and Lightoller, there are accounts of him assisting on the starboard side, during which time Lightoller may have made those errors of judgement. For example, the Captain was observed by seaman Frank Evans during the lowering of lifeboat no. 1, the emergency cutter, on the starboard side. 'He [Smith] came to the starboard action boat that I was lowering... He passed some remark to a tall military gentleman there with white spats on, but what it was I could not say, as I was attending to the fall.'[97] Also at no. 1, dining room steward William Burke remembered Captain Smith giving the order 'to the sailors that were working with me to go aft and assist about the last boat which I thought was going to be launched on that side'.[98]

Morse Lamp, Rockets and Guns

As these early lifeboats were lowered, Smith also ordered Fourth Officer Boxhall to attempt to contact the mystery vessel that had been spotted on the horizon. The first stage was to gain their attention using distress rockets. Boxhall testified that he told the Captain he had sent for some rockets, and told him he would 'send them off, and told him when I saw this light. He said, "Yes, carry on with it." I was sending rockets off and watching this steamer.'[99]

Quartermaster George Rowe wrote to author Walter Lord: 'On reaching the bridge Capt. Smith asked if I had the rockets. I told him yes and [he] said fire one every five or six minutes.'[100]

Boxhall kept the Captain informed of his progress with the rockets. 'I never knew how many I had fired. I knew very well that there were some in the box. The box holds a dozen and when I told the Captain I said, "There are still some in there, sir, but I don't know how many I fired."'[101]

The firing of the rockets began at about the same time as the first lifeboat (no. 7 on the starboard side) reached the water. We know this as Boxhall received a telephone call in the wheelhouse when he was 'putting the firing lanyard inside the wheel-house after sending off a rocket ... that one of the starboard boats had left the ship, and I was rather surprised. I did not know the order had been given even to fill the boats. I reported it to the Commander.'[102] The telephone call came from Rowe, who then came to assist.

When the mystery ship appeared to be closer, Boxhall then used the Morse lamp located above the port side wing bridge cab, as that was the side facing in the direction of the mystery light. He explained at the Senate Inquiry that Captain Smith was with him: 'She got close enough, as I thought, to read our electric Morse signal, and I signalled to her; I told her to come at once, we were sinking; and the captain was standing... I told the captain about this ship, and he was with me most of the time when we were signalling... I went over and started the Morse signal. He said, "Tell him to come at once, we are sinking."... It was sent in the Morse key, the Morse code.'[103]

Smith was keenly observing this ship looking for an answer. Boxhall noted at the time: 'There were a lot of men on the bridge. I had a Quartermaster with me, and the Captain was standing by, at different times, watching this steamer.' Boxhall used his binoculars to check for an answer, as did Smith: 'Captain Smith also looked, and he could not see any answer.'[104]

The quartermaster with Boxhall, George Rowe, also remembered the Captain there and using the binoculars:

> Capt Smith asked me if I could Morse, I replied I could a little, he said call that ship up and when she answers, tell her that we are the Titanic sinking please have all your boats ready. I kept calling her up in

between the rocket firing but we never got a reply though we could see his white light quite plain. After a while I said to Capt Smith there is a light on the starboard quarter, he looked through the glasses and told me he thought it must be a planet, then he lent me his glasses to see for myself.[105]

In between checking in on the mystery lights and keeping up-to-date with the Marconi room, Smith was also helping with the loading and lowering of various lifeboats. A stewardess by the name of Mary Sloan was waiting for a lifeboat on the port side when she noticed the frequency of the rockets and 'Captain Smith getting excited.'[106] It was enough to make her take the next boat.

He was noted by several at lifeboat no. 8, including first class steward Alfred Crawford, who said Smith 'personally superintended the loading and the lowering' of that lifeboat: 'Capt. Smith and the steward lowered the forward falls of the boat I was in.' Afterwards Smith 'went to No. 10 boat. I could not see that being lowered into the water. He gave us instructions to pull to a light that he saw and then land the ladies and return back to the ship again. It was the light of a vessel in the distance. We pulled and pulled, but we could not reach it.'[107]

Crawford's account is supported by first class passenger Margaret Swift. Rescued in lifeboat no. 8, she recalled that when it was being filled 'Captain Smith insisted that we get into it, and as the sailors pulled away from the ship I heard him say, "Row for that light," and I saw him point to a dim glimmer that must have been three miles distant.'[108]

Able seaman Thomas Jones described Smith at lifeboat 8. The Captain first of all 'asked me was the plug in the boat, and I answered, "Yes, sir." "All right," he said, "Any more ladies?" There was one lady came there and left her husband. She wanted her husband to go with her, but he backed away, and the captain shouted again – in fact, twice again – "Any more ladies?" There were no more there, and he lowered away.' The Captain also told him to 'row for the light, and land the passengers and return to the ship.' Jones followed the order and pulled for the light for about 2 hours until they lost sight of it.[109]

Marie Young in lifeboat 8 similarly recalled: 'Capt. Smith called to us to pull for a green light seen in the distance to unload passengers and return to the boat at once.'[110] Smith personally assisted 'the bride and groom' anniversary couple he had befriended earlier in the voyage, helping her into lifeboat no. 8. Marion Kenyon later recalled:

We walked along the outer deck and leaned against the staircase that went up to the top deck where the Captain's cabin is, and Captain

Smith evidently saw us down this place and said, 'Is that you Kenyon?' and he says 'Yes,' he says 'We're just waiting around.'

'Well come on up deck,' on top with Captain Smith... Captain Smith didn't stay very long with us, he kept going into the little cabin and conversing and telephoning. But he came back and he said to Kenyon, 'I want to speak to you.' And my husband left me and went and spoke with Captain Smith and came back and said, Captain Smith said he'd feel a lot better if all the women would go on the little boats and stay around that he'd feel better if we did.

And I started my old song, 'I Won't Leave Ya.' And when Captain Smith went to the edge of the boat he whistled and the boat came up and he and my husband lifted, helped me over into it. And I sat in the middle of two men on the front of the boat. I don't know how many people were in the boat, but seemed terribly crowded to put me into it, it did.

And he [Captain Smith] said, 'Do you see that light in the northwest?' I said, 'Yes.' 'Well,' he said, 'You tell the men to keep rowing towards that light.' And my husband turned abruptly and he turned right and he wouldn't look at me. And the boat was lowered. And as I said, to the men, the young boy on this side was our table steward. And I said, 'You heard what the captain said.' And he said 'Yes.' Well, we went, they rowed towards the northwest.[111]

Another survivor from no. 8 was Emma Bucknell in first class who said she was personally placed in the lifeboat by Captain Smith, who said to her: 'It is only a matter of precaution and there is really no danger.' Mrs Bucknell also spotted some men growing desperate upon realising they would not be allowed a place. 'Captain Smith, who was standing by, cried out: "Behave yourselves like men! Look at all of these women. See how splendid they are. Can't you behave like men?"' Before lowering, 'Captain Smith himself picked up a big basket of bread and handed it across.'[112]

A notable occupant of lifeboat no. 8 also remembered Smith assisting and giving orders: Lucy Noël Martha, the Countess of Rothes:

Captain Smith stood shoulder to shoulder with me as I got into the lifeboat, and the last words were to the able seaman – Tom Jones – "Row straight for those ship lights over there; leave your passengers on board of her and return as soon as you can." Captain Smith's whole attitude was one of great calmness and courage, and I am sure he thought that the ship – whose lights we could plainly see – would pick us up and that our life boats would be able to do double duty in ferrying passengers to the help that gleamed so near.[113]

Some years later, the Countess of Rothes added: 'About Capt. Smith I think he really thought we might reach the other steamer – but he looked to be under a terrible strain.'[114]

There is a far more emotional portrait of Smith from the Countess of Rothes' personal maid, 20-year-old Roberta Maioni, who accompanied her employer into lifeboat no. 8. In a sometimes overly dramatic account published in the *Daily Express* of 1926, she wrote the following: 'An elderly officer, with tears streaming down his cheeks, helped us into one of the lifeboats. He was Captain Smith – the master of that ill-fated vessel. As the lifeboat began to descend, I heard him say, "Goodbye, remember you are British."'[115]

After the drama of lifeboat 8, Smith was again actively involved in the loading and lowering of lifeboat 6 that followed. Major Arthur Peuchen recalled:

> The captain said – I do not know whether it was the captain or the second officer said – 'We will have to get these masts out of these boats, and also the sail.' He said, 'You might give us a hand,' and I jumped in the boat, and we got a knife and cut the lashings of the mast, which is a very heavy mast, and also the sail, and moved it out of the boat, saying it would not be required. Then there was a cry, as soon as that part was done, that they were ready to put the women in; so the women came forward one by one. A great many women came with their husbands.

Martha Stone of first class was there and remembered that 'Captain Smith had said: "Women and children first," and then men put their wives and daughters and sisters in the boats and then stood back and helped other women in.'[116]

Once the boat began to be lowered, it was discovered that there was only one man aboard and so Peuchen, a yachtsman, offered his services.

> The captain was standing still by him at that time, and I think, although the officer ordered me to the boat, the captain said, 'You had better go down below and break a window and get in through a window, into the boat'… and I said I did not think it was feasible, and I said I could get in the boat if I could get hold of a rope … we got hold of a loose rope in some way that was hanging from the davit, near the block anyway, and by getting hold of it I swung myself off the ship, and lowered myself into the boat.[117]

Peuchen is one of the few adult male passengers Lightoller allowed into a boat that night, his dictum being 'women and children *only*'. According to Peuchen, the result was clear – there were only 24 in a lifeboat with a capacity for 65. Interestingly, another lifeboat 8 occupant, Mrs Tillie Taussig, a first class passenger, names Smith as directly responsible for the lack of men.

> Capt. Smith was preparing the eighth boat to be let down. There was only one seaman in sight, but a number of stewards had rushed up between the crowding men and women. The Captain turned to the stewards and asked them if they knew how to row. They answered 'Yes' hastily, and four of them were allowed to jump in... There was room for fourteen more after the last woman had found her place, and they all pleaded to let the men take the empty seats. But the Captain said that he would not allow it. I was frantic. There was that boat, ready to be lowered into the water and only half full... When we got to the water the four stewards who had told the Captain they could row couldn't row at all.[118]

In his Senate testimony, Peuchen wanted to clarify that he had been misquoted in the press: 'I wish to state that I have not said any personal or unkind thing about Captain Smith. I have been quoted as saying some very unkind things about the late captain, but I assure you I have never made any statement of that kind.'[119]

Another occupant of lifeboat no. 6, first class passenger Mrs Mary Eloise Smith, standing beside her husband, Lucian Smith, remembered Captain Smith using a megaphone to enforce the 'women and children' rule:

> Captain Smith was standing with a megaphone on deck. I approached him and told him I was alone, and asked if my husband might be allowed to go in the boat with me. He ignored me personally, but shouted again through his megaphone, 'Women and children first.' My husband said, 'Never mind, captain, about that; I will see that she gets in the boat.'... The captain looked over to see us, I suppose, or something of the kind, and noticed there was only one man in the boat. Maj. Peuchen, of Canada, was then swung out to us as an experienced seaman.[120]

In a separate newspaper account, she also added that the Captain specifically said no men were permitted in the lifeboats: 'I turned to Captain Smith, who was standing by the port rail, and asked him to allow my husband to go with me. He said: "No, madam; under no circumstances will any man be permitted to leave this boat."'[121]

At about the same time as the loading of lifeboat 6, another issue became apparent: *Titanic* was now listing to port instead of to starboard as Smith had observed on the commutator on the bridge earlier. This was noticed by Martha Stephenson and Elizabeth Eustis who were coming up the narrow iron stairs that led to the forward boat deck, close to the bridge. Martha recalled: 'At the top of the stairs we found Captain Smith looking much worried, and anxiously waiting to get down after we got up. The ship listed heavily to port just then. As we leaned against the walls of the officers' quarters rockets were being fired over our heads, which was most alarming.'[122]

Washington Dodge of first class explained that the list was perhaps caused by Captain Smith: 'In times of danger the captain always draws a crowd. The most notable men on board, who were known by sight to other passengers knew Captain Smith personally and remained near him. These men attracted others. In this way the crowd grew on the port side, while at no time was there anything like a crowd on the starboard side... Captain Smith took command of the port side and never left there.'[123]

Some time after 1 am, it was decided to counter the list by moving passengers from the port to starboard side of the ship. Fireman John Hagan says it was by the order of the Captain, as referenced in Gracie's *The Truth about the Titanic*: 'When we were loading the last boat, just a short time before it was fully loaded, a palpable list toward the port side began, and the officer called out, "All passengers to the starboard side," and Smith [his friend Clinch Smith] and myself went to the starboard side, still at the bow of the ship.'[124]

Lightoller remembered the list, but recalled it was an order from Chief Officer Wilde to move passengers from one side of the ship to the other – perhaps after Captain Smith initiated it. Lightoller said: 'I may say that my notice was called to this list – I perhaps might not have noticed it; it was not very great – by Mr. Wilde calling out "All passengers over to the starboard side."... it was then I noticed that the ship had a list. It would have been far more noticeable on the starboard side than on the port.'[125]

A shift of passengers to the starboard does tally with the lifeboat numbers launched on that side after 1 am, which increased from 12 occupants of no. 1 at 1:05 am, to 40 occupants in no. 9 at 1.30 am. All further boats departing from the starboard side would leave reasonably full. Would such a movement of people assist in stabilising the ship? Author and *Titanic* researcher Tim Maltin thinks it may have had a minimal effect:

Due to the ship now lying on her rounded bilge keel, and not the much flatter central keel on which she was designed to float, the shape of her hull made her 'tender', and thus it was possible to affect the list to some extent by moving people around ... one of the Titanic designers, Edward Wilding, estimated that moving 800 people 50 feet would only have corrected the list by about 2 degrees—not much when the ship was listing by as much as 10 degrees.[126]

Crew were also directed to the port side. Saloon steward William Ward remembered preparing lifeboat no. 9 for loading when 'a sailor came along with a bag and threw it in the boat. This man said he had been sent down to take charge of the boat by the captain.'[127] Even if Smith was not visible in person, he was still giving orders. Third class passenger Charles Dahl said he 'did not see Captain Smith after the ship struck, but I heard his voice on the bridge giving orders as I was going down to [lifeboat] No. 15'.[128]

About halfway through the lifeboat evacuation, at what must have been around a quarter past one, crowd control was on the Captain's mind, as the reducing number of remaining lifeboat spaces became more apparent and the crowds on the boat deck more numerous. He joined the senior officers when they entered the First Officer's cabin to arm themselves with company-issued firearms in case they were needed. Lightoller recalled that it was initiated by Chief Officer Wilde: 'Into the First Officer's cabin we went—the Chief, Murdoch, the Captain and myself—where I hauled them out, still in all their pristine newness and grease. I was going out when the Chief shoved one of the revolvers into my hands, with a handful of ammunition, and said, "Here you are, you may need it." On the impulse, I just slipped it into my pocket, along with the cartridges, and returned to the boats.' Not long after that Lightoller had occasion to use it to remove men from a lifeboat by 'vigorously flourishing my revolver... the revolver was not even loaded!'[129] Smith was also described as threatening use of his gun. Fireman Harry Senior remembered the Captain saying: 'All firemen keep down on the well deck. If a man comes up I'll shoot him.'[130]

Men in boats was becoming an increasing problem – with the most infamous case undoubtedly that of J. Bruce Ismay stepping into collapsible C on the starboard side, under First Officer Murdoch's supervision. It was a step into a life of severe criticism, especially in the eyes of the press, until the day he died. According to Lightoller's Senate testimony, it was Chief Officer Wilde who 'simply bundled [Ismay] into the boat'.[131] This was confirmed by Quartermaster George Rowe, who was rescued aboard collapsible C and had until that moment been firing rockets on the starboard side, right where the collapsible was situated. Captain Smith gave him orders to stop firing the rockets and to enter the lifeboat: 'The chief officer, Wilde, wanted a sailor. I asked Captain Smith if I should fire any more, and he said "No; get into that boat"... When Chief Officer Wilde asked if there was any more women and children there was no reply. So Mr. Ismay came aboard the boat.'[132]

Not everyone was taking the opportunity to leave, even on the Captain's orders. William 'Billy' Johnson, the 19-year-old sailor returning to the United States that the Captain had nicknamed the 'Kid,' was spotted working hard helping load the lifeboats – even though he was not a paid member of the crew. In an account from seaman William Törnquist, Captain Smith noticed this:

> The captain at the time was rushing past and he turned and, seeing Billy, placed his hand on his shoulder and said: 'Jump in, Kid, you might as well have a chance.'
>
> 'Nothing doing,' replied Johnson, 'I'll wait until the women and children are all off and the other officers go.'
>
> The captain turned away, saying, 'You're made of the right goods, Kid, but it is too bad to waste them.'[133]

Billy the 'Kid' was last seen working in the bridge area and was lost in the sinking.

Fourth Officer Boxhall had been working with Rowe firing distress rockets when he, too, was relieved by Smith on the port side. Captain Smith was standing near the wheelhouse door, supervising the loading of the port side lifeboats, when he ordered Boxhall to take command of lifeboat no. 2, the emergency cutter that was just being lowered by Chief Officer Wilde: 'The captain was standing by this emergency boat... He was standing by the wheelhouse door, just abreast of this boat... He told me I had to get into that boat and go away.' When Boxhall took command of lifeboat no. 2, he also followed through on the plan that had been initiated by Lightoller – to make for one of the gangway doors to load more passengers as despite a capacity of 40, they likely had no more than 18 onboard; Boxhall estimated 'about 25'.[134]

The idea of rowing to a gangway may have actually been Smith's, according to a later account by Boxhall:

> The Captain came across the bridge and said, 'Mr. Boxhall, you go away in that boat,' pointing to the Port Emergency Boat number two. And he said, 'Now hurry up, Mr. Wilde is waiting to lower it."... the Captain looked over the side from the bridge and sang out and said, told me to 'go round to the Starboard side to the gangway doors', which was practically at the opposite side to where I was lowered. I had great difficulty in getting the boat around there.[135]

The Convergence of the Twain

Despite the difficulty in rowing, Boxhall was indeed following the Captain's orders – but not completely. When he finally arrived at the aft starboard gangway doors, after rounding *Titanic*'s stern that was starting to rise into the night sky ('her propellers were out of water') he decided it was too risky as 'there was such a mob standing in the gangway doors, really, I daren't go alongside because if they'd jumped they'd swamp the boat.'[136]

Smith's actions at lifeboat 2 are supported by D. W. McMillan's recounting of his sister Elizabeth Robert's recollection of what occurred: 'My sister, Georgette and Miss Allen were taken off in one of the last boats with the fourth officer in charge, following his being commanded by Captain Smith to take charge of the boat. There was room for about two or three more persons in the boat and Captain Smith called for the boat to come back. The officer ordered the boat turned, but as they started back they saw the stern of the Titanic rising in the air, and didn't dare to go near for fear it was going to sink.'[137]

Boxhall's departure from the ship did not end the firing of the rockets. Chief Steward John Hardy was asked at the Senate Inquiry when he last saw Captain Smith and replied that he saw the Captain on the bridge 'superintending the rockets, calling out to the quartermaster about the rockets'.[138]

Mrs Mahala Douglas, in first class, was waiting to board lifeboat no. 2 when she noticed the captain request his megaphone and evict 'stowaways' who had crept into nearby collapsible D:

> As we stood by a collapsible boat lying on the deck and an emergency boat swinging from the davits was being filled, it was decided I should go. Mr. Boxhall was trying to get the boat off, and called to the captain on the bridge, 'There's a boat coming up over there.' The captain said 'I want a megaphone. Just before we got into the boat the captain called, 'How many of the crew are in that boat? Get out of there, every man of you'; and I can see a solid row of men, from bow to stern, crawl over on to the deck. We women then got in.[139]

At about 2 am, around the same time collapsible D was being loaded, first class passengers Henry B. (Harry) and René Harris, her arm in a cast, passed through the bridge from starboard to port. In a 1932 magazine article, René recalled seeing the Captain, who made a comment that likely saved her life:

> We crossed to the port side, passing through the bridge where the captain was standing with Major Archibald Butt and the little doctor

[William F. O'Loughlin]. I saw the clock, I can still see it with its hands pointing to two twenty.

The captain looked amazed when he saw me. 'My God, woman, why aren't you in a lifeboat?' I kept repeating: 'I won't leave my husband, I won't leave my husband.' The little doctor said, 'Isn't she a brick?' To which the captain replied: 'She's a little fool – she's handicapping her husband's chances to save himself.'

'Can he be saved,' I asked, 'if I go?'

'Yes,' he answered; 'there are plenty of rafts in the stern and the men can make for them if you women give them a chance.'[140]

The Captain's deception – that there were more lifeboats at the stern – worked, as René Harris allowed herself to be carried into collapsible D, the last lifeboat to be successfully lowered.

Smith's actions up until this point had been extensive and exhausting. The authors of the book *On a Sea of Glass* conclude: 'For a man of his age, his physical exertion during the disaster seems to have been great.'[141]

Every Man for Himself

Smith had just relieved two important crew members, Boxhall and Rowe, who had been instrumental in using the Morse lamp and firing distress rockets that had given them an opportunity for rescue – life now came before duty. *Titanic* had less than half an hour above sea level. From here, Smith was variously reported giving an order relieving men from duty, to give them a reasonable chance to save themselves. Smith was preparing the crew to 'abandon ship'.

At some point, he may have visited the engine room once again, according to 19-year-old third class passenger Edward Dorking, who allegedly saw Smith towards the end below decks in the engine room, giving orders. 'The perspiration was pouring down his face in streams but he was calm and collected, and as I recollect him now, he appeared like a marble statue after rain.'[142] A fireman by the name of Charles Judd described Captain Smith as looking 'very pale' during *Titanic*'s final moments.[143]

One of his last moves was to the Marconi room, where the two wireless operators had been working tirelessly. Despite the increasingly precarious situation he was in, senior wireless operator Phillips was not thinking of himself. Some minutes earlier, during one of the many visits the Captain made to the Marconi room that night, he had brought some frightful news. Bride recalled: 'The captain came and told us our engine

The Convergence of the Twain

rooms were taking water, and that the dynamos might not last much longer. We sent that word to the *Carpathia*.' In another account, Bride said: 'The captain also came in and told us she was sinking fast and could not last longer than half an hour.'[144]

A little later, as one of the last lifeboats had been lowered, the Captain returned to the wireless room. 'Then came the captain's voice: "Men, you have done your full duty. You can do no more. Abandon your cabin. Now it's every man for himself. You look out for yourselves. I release you. That's the way of it at this kind of time. Every man for himself."' Even after the Captain had released him, Phillips continued working for another ten or fifteen minutes, despite water coming into the cabin.[145] As long as there was power to keep the Marconi unit operational, Phillips would continue his work.

Other men remember similar releases from the Captain, such as 29-year-old fireman James McGann:

> I was helping to get off a collapsible boat. The last one launched when the water began to break over the bridge on which Captain Smith stood. When the water reached Captain Smith's knees and the last boat was at least 20 feet away from the ship, I was standing beside him. He gave one look all around, his face firm and his lips hard set. He looked as if he was trying to keep back the tears, as he thought of the doomed ship. I felt mightily like crying as I looked at him. Suddenly he shouted: 'Well boys, you've done your duty and done it well. I ask no more of you. I release you. You know the rule of the sea. It's every man for himself now, and God bless you.'[146]

Another fireman, who is unidentified but could quite likely be McGann described Smith's demeanour likewise: '[Smith] was in the supreme moment calmness itself. The fore part of the ship had disappeared from sight, the centre of the great vessel was slowly sinking down. With the water well above his knees, Captain Smith, addressing those who had stood by him to the last, said, "Well, boys, there is nothing more we can do; you must look after yourselves." Half-a-dozen of them made their way aft. They did not actually see the captain disappear, but some time afterwards they saw him swimming in the water without a lifebelt.'[147]

Engine room greaser Alfred White reported almost exactly the same parting words: 'I was told to go up and see how things were, and made my way up a dummy funnel to the bridge deck. By that time all the boats had left the ship, yet everyone in the engine-room was at his post. I was near the captain and heard him say, "Well boys, it's every man for himself now."'[148]

The same expression was repeated in first class passenger Washington Dodge's account: 'Captain Smith, so I was told by an eyewitness, called out: "Now it's every man for himself"' and sprang into the water.'[149]

Smith was surely giving orders to the very end. Lamp trimmer Samuel Hemming remembered Smith at the collapsible boat on the port side which was being brought down from the roof of the Officers' Quarters, giving an order: 'The captain was there, and he sung out: "Everyone over to the starboard side, to keep the ship up as long as possible."'[150] Leading fireman Thomas Threlfall said that 'the captain ordered all articles that would float to be thrown overboard and gave the command, "Every man for himself."'[151]

Robert Williams Daniel saw the Captain with a megaphone while he was on the forward half of the boat deck: 'Captain Smith was the biggest hero I ever saw. He stood on the bridge and shouted through a megaphone, trying to make himself heard.'[152] The Master was also heard giving advice through the megaphone, according to an unidentified greaser: 'Up to the last he walked up and down the deck, giving advice through a megaphone to those trying to save their lives.'[153] When steward Edward Brown testified at the British Inquiry, he remembered some of Smith's final words: 'The Captain came past us while we were trying to get this boat away with a megaphone in his hand, and he spoke to us... He said, "Well, boys, do your best for the women and children, and look out for yourselves."' Brown watched the Captain, megaphone in hand, walk slowly back into the bridge. A few seconds later, the ship took her last plunge.[154]

31-year-old fireman Harry Senior, who was preparing collapsible A (which was never successfully lowered in time) had this to say: 'While we were preparing to lower these, we heard the captain shout "Every man for himself". I had seen the captain on the bridge. When he shouted his last command the ship was sinking fast. I dived over the side.'[155] Another crew member working at collapsible A remembered similar words. Trimmer Eustace Snow claimed Smith said: 'Wait till the boat takes to the water, then every man for himself.'[156]

Smith would go down in history as exclaiming 'Be British!' with the phrase used in memorial services and inscribed on plaques. His final words were most likely as just described – releasing crew from their duties. An unidentified steward said that Smith did not put on a lifebelt and 'behaved splendidly. Captain Smith's last words were not "Be British" but "I'm finished. Look after yourselves."'[157] The detail that he refused a lifebelt is also confirmed by another survivor who, on arriving in England, told a reporter that he 'went to Captain Smith just before the ship sank and begged him to put on a lifebelt and swim to one of the boats. The captain shook his head, said "Nothing doing, my lad," and waved the man away.'[158]

Author Gary Cooper agrees that 'Be British' is an unlikely final statement and points out there is no eyewitness testimony *Titanic*'s commander ever uttered those words – not to mention that many of the passengers and crew were not British or even European. He concludes that it can 'be safely put down to sheer sensationalism'.[159] However, the sentiments of the expression, likely a posthumous reimagining, is clear: to maintain decorum in the face of death.

Suicide Rumours

The question of exactly how Captain Smith died has fascinated writers and filmmakers ever since his demise. Marie Young in first class wrote in October 1912: 'Who can imagine the earthly purgatory of anguish endured by Captain Smith, during the pitifully short time vouchsafed him to prepare for death – whose claim upon him, he, more than all others, must acknowledge?'[160] Many have imagined his death. Legends have developed from grisly rumours and speculation. Author Wyn Craig Wade wrote in his 1992 book *Titanic: End of a Dream*, that Captain Smith 'had a least five different deaths, from heroic to ignominious'.[161]

As soon as the bewildered survivors gathered on the decks of the *Carpathia*, there were stories of gun shots and a suicide, no doubt cross-pollinated with an appetite for blame as the incredible loss began to register. For example, Dr Árpád Lengyel, a Hungarian doctor aboard the *Carpathia* who treated survivors, later said that 'he had talked with a survivor of the *Titanic*, who told him that the survivors in his lifeboat had said that Capt. Smith of the *Titanic* had shot down two men who had tried to climb into a lifeboat, and that the Captain had also shot the man on the lookout in the crow's nest of the *Titanic*.'[162] Such unfounded rumours were rife. During the Victorian and Edwardian eras, it was not unusual for a commander to make the ultimate sacrifice by perishing along with his ship, and, in some cases, committing suicide.[163]

The local Southampton newspaper, *The Southern Daily Echo*, the most likely source of regular news for the Smith family, gave an indication of what lay ahead. On 19 April under the heading of 'Captain Smith's Last Moments', it reported: 'According to a story published by the 'Evening World' revolver shots were heard just before the Titanic went down, but the crew discredit the reports of the captain's and engineer's suicide.'[164] It is not surprising the *New York World* (with its morning and evening editions) was the source of the rumours. Carlos F. Hurd, a *St. Louis*

Post-Dispatch reporter and his wife happened to be passengers aboard the *Carpathia*. Despite Captain Roston's valiant attempts to keep the couple from contacting survivors, they succeeded in interviewing many, including a ship's officer who was allegedly at the helm during the iceberg collision (although the two officers on the bridge at the time, Murdoch and Moody, did not survive). As they steamed into New York Harbor, Hurd evaded the *Carpathia*'s crew and delivered his 5,000-word scoop of a lifetime by wrapping it in a waterproof package and throwing it overboard into a waiting tug.[165] Before the day was out, his report was already entering publication, including the following in the *New York Morning World* on 18 April: 'Revolver shots heard shortly before the Titanic went down caused many rumors, one that Captain Smith had shot himself, another that First Officer Murdoch had ended his life, but members of the crew discredit these rumours.'[166]

One of the first named accounts was from a Miss May Birkhead, a 30-year-old passenger aboard the *Carpathia*, who was recorded in the *New York Herald* on 19 April 1912 as saying, 'I also am told that Captain Smith of the *Titanic* shot himself with a pistol as the ship was going down.'[167] *The New York Times* had only the day before recorded a similar statement from Miss Birkhead – with a significant caveat: 'I was told that Captain Smith shot himself, but, on the other hand, I have heard this contradicted.'[168]

Miss Birkhead was not the only *Carpathia* passenger who heard the rumour. Dr J. F. Kemp, a physician on the last lap of a world tour, suddenly found himself in the midst of a terrible tragedy in which his skills were most valuable. His newspaper interview is persuasive:

'A boy and one of the last of the children to be taken from the *Titanic* told me that he saw Captain Smith put a pistol to his head then fall down'... 'Of course,' he said, 'I cannot tell whether the boy told me the truth, but it seems to me hard to believe that the little fellow would invent such a tale. I was talking with him on the deck of the *Carpathia* when he voluntarily told me.'

'Was there any other report to substantiate it?' he was asked. 'A number of passengers spoke of the use of pistols and the firing of shots,' he replied, 'but we were all too busy with the rescued and those who suffered from exposure to follow up any investigation of that sort.'[169]

The name of the boy was not mentioned, but of the long list of suicide accounts that have appeared in newspaper reports and private letters over the years, the youngest is third class passenger Johan Cervin Svensson, a 14-year-old boy from Knäred, Halland, Sweden. In an account in May

Figure 46: Captain Smith dramatically committing suicide as illustrated in the French newspaper *L'Excelsior*, 20 April 1912, in a drawing by Paul Thiriat, although the caption notes 'according to the accounts of some survivors'. (Author's collection)

1912, he declared that 'he saw a man, whom he thought to be one of the officers, shoot himself. "He put his gun right in his mouth and shot." He also says there was considerable shooting on deck. After they were in the boat they heard many shots.'[170] The rest of his account is not sensational but lacks enough detail to identify the officer he said he saw.

There is a third witness from the *Carpathia*, Harold H. Lee, a waiter, who passed on a tale he said he heard from one of *Titanic*'s quartermasters:

> Lee stated that he had taken in four members of the Titanic's crew in his bunk, and among them was a quartermaster who saw the captain calmly walk to the chart room, draw a revolver from his pocket and fire a shot through the right side of his head. This was done, Lee said, after the life boats had all left the doomed vessel and Smith was satisfied that he had performed his duty. The ship's printer ventured further to state that he had been told by the Titanic's survivors that twice previous to killing himself, the captain had been found on the act of taking his life. On the bridge of the Titanic, according to Lee, Chief Officer Wilde snatched the revolver from Smith's hand and blew his brains out.[171]

Lee's second-hand sensational account had further support according to the *Brooklyn Daily Eagle* newspaper that ran the story, adding that 'four stewards of the Carpathia, who were surrounded by half a hundred newspaper men, also stated that they had been given to understand that Captain Smith shot himself.'[172]

One of the candidates for the *Carpathia* sources could have been Paul Romaine Chevré, a 45-year-old French first class passenger who was quoted in a syndicated report from the *Montreal Herald*: 'A few minutes before the ship sank Captain Smith cried out, "My luck has turned," and then shot himself. I saw him fall against the canvas railing on the bridge and disappear.' Since Chevré was rescued in lifeboat no. 7, the first to depart, it is highly unlikely he could have seen this event 'a few minutes before the ship sank'. But there was a more critical issue with his account: he claimed it had been fabricated by a journalist who did not understand his French. Most importantly, he denied saying Captain Smith had committed suicide. In an article printed in the *Worcester Evening Gazette*, Chevré firstly admitted he 'was off the *Titanic* before there was any real panic' and praised the heroism of the crew lost: 'I will take my hat off to the English seamen who went down with their ship.'[173] That would have included Captain Smith.

In another dramatic account, first class passenger Miss Gretchen Longley stated emphatically that she 'knows Captain Smith sent a bullet into his brain'. Although she escaped aboard lifeboat no. 10, which departed from the port side at about 1:50 am – at least twenty minutes before the bridge was submerged – she was confident in her story, placing him in his library, struggling with his officers no less:

> Miss Longley's story relates that Captain Smith was alone in his library when his trained mind told him that hope was gone, and supplanted only by death and despair.
>
> 'Captain Smith made two attempts to kill himself,' said she, 'and at last he succeeded. He was in his library when the officers saw him with a revolver in his hand. They rushed their superior officer and tore the gun from him. The captain struggled with them desperately, broke away, and rushed to the bridge, where he killed himself, placing the revolver to his mouth and firing.'[174]

The *Washington Times* summarised this disturbing story by explaining that 'unable to bear the terrible strain of the disaster that overtook his mighty ship, Capt. E.J. Smith killed himself and gave to the seas a life spent in mastering her cunning and thwarting her designs.' To its credit, the article also balanced Longley's far-fetched account with an alternative description from a first class passenger, Mrs Ruth Dodge in lifeboat no. 5, who stated that Smith had drowned, but with no less drama:

> Then I saw a man who I am sure was Captain Smith. He was being pushed onto a life raft. He flung his arms about and struggled like a mad man. It was easy to see he did not want to go. But the men who pushed him (probably the remaining ship's officers) insisted and at length they got him onto the raft. He looked wildly about for a moment, waving his arms in despair and supplication. Then he leaped off the raft into the ice-caked sea which closed over his head forever. A woman in my boat moaned and fainted when she saw the captain take his life and I felt sick at heart for I thought of my absent husband.

Not surprisingly, Ruth Dodge's account was later discredited as a fabrication.[175] Lady Duff Gordon reportedly claimed, rather dramatically, that 'many men crowded for the boats and were shot down by Captain Smith. Several fell to the decks mortally wounded before there was a semblance of order or discipline... Captain Smith was on the bridge when the liner took her final plunge to the bottom.'[176] She was in lifeboat 1, which was launched earlier in the night and her autobiography never mentioned anything about Smith shooting men, indicating it was fabricated by a press hungry for more sordid news.[177]

If it was not Longley or Chevré, then the 21-year-old American tennis champion Richard Norris Williams is another possible source of the *Carpathia* rumours. His personal account was revealed in 1997:

> Presently we found ourselves on the Captain's bridge – only two other people were there, Captain Smith and a quartermaster... The ship seemed to give a slight lurch; I turned towards the bow. I saw nothing but water with just a mast sticking out of it. I don't remember the shock of the cold water, I only remember thinking 'suction' and my efforts to swim in the direction of the starboard rail to get away from the ship... I heard the crack of a revolver shot from the direction where I had left Captain Smith; I did not look around.[178]

What makes William's account more credible is that he was aboard the *Titanic* until the very end, when the first funnel collapsed, and survived

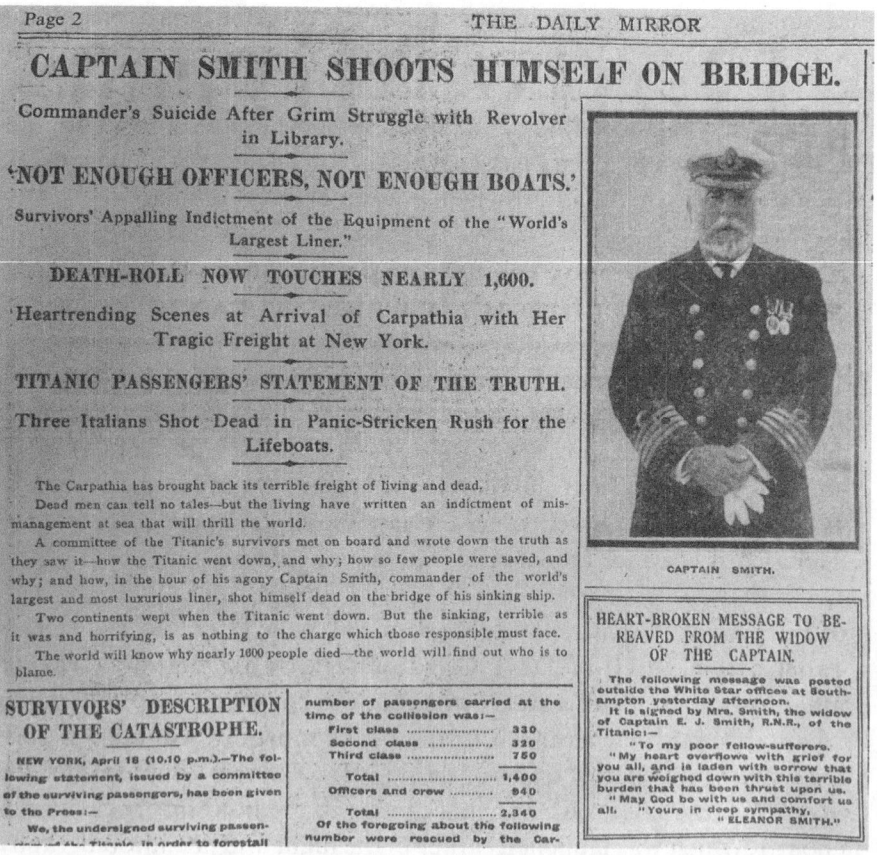

Figure 47: The 19 April 1912 edition of the *Daily Mirror*, page 2. Beneath the photograph is a 'heart-broken message' from his widow Eleanor. (Author's collection)

aboard collapsible A – along with several other eyewitnesses of an officer shooting and suicide. Yet it must be acknowledged he did not actually witness what happened to Smith, so his account is both tantalizing and inconclusive.

Other anonymous reports also surfaced in the 1912 newspapers. *The New York Times* published an account that Smith and the first engineer were 'reported to have shot themselves' and the *Daily Mirror* mentioned a committee of *Carpathia* passengers that said Smith 'shot himself on the bridge' and that the 'Commander's suicide' was after a 'grim struggle with revolver in the library'.[179] *The Mirror* article, published on 19 April (Figure 47), attributed the account to an unnamed *Carpathia* passenger:

> NEW YORK, April 19 (11 p.m.) It is asserted by one passenger of the Carpathia that Captain Smith committed suicide on the bridge of the Titanic before she went down and that the chief engineer also committed suicide. The same passenger states that three Italians were shot dead in the struggle for the lifeboats. According to this circumstantial account of the captain ... the revolver was wrested from his hands in the library, but he broke away to the bridge and shot himself through the mouth – Reuter.

There were further reports of Captain Smith shooting steerage passengers. Mrs Aasaf Mariana in third class said that 'Captain Smith shot down several of them.'[180] It was quite likely that those unfamiliar with Smith used his name as a blanket description of authority.

In the absence of detail, not one of these accounts is convincing. While Smith was one of the four who entered the First Officer's cabin to retrieve company-issued Webley revolvers, there is no firm evidence he ever used one. There is, however, a large body of eyewitness accounts, across the full spectrum of class, age and nationality, that did report an officer shooting and suicide, and so, in the eyes of an unprejudiced researcher, it cannot be completely discounted.[181] The identity of the officer concerned is frequently described as either an 'officer' or 'Murdoch' or sometimes the 'senior' or 'chief officer'. This has led researchers and historians to agree with author Tim Maltin, who surmised that although there is no evidence that is 'proof positive that it was Murdoch who shot himself, it does seem that an officer did shoot himself and Murdoch seems the most likely candidate.'[182] An additional factor to consider is that Captain Smith had a distinctive look – a white beard and the Captain's uniform – that would have clearly distinguished him from a deck officer.

In response to the suicide rumours, *The Daily Sketch* of Saturday 20 April 1912 ran a front-page tribute to the Captain: 'It is evident

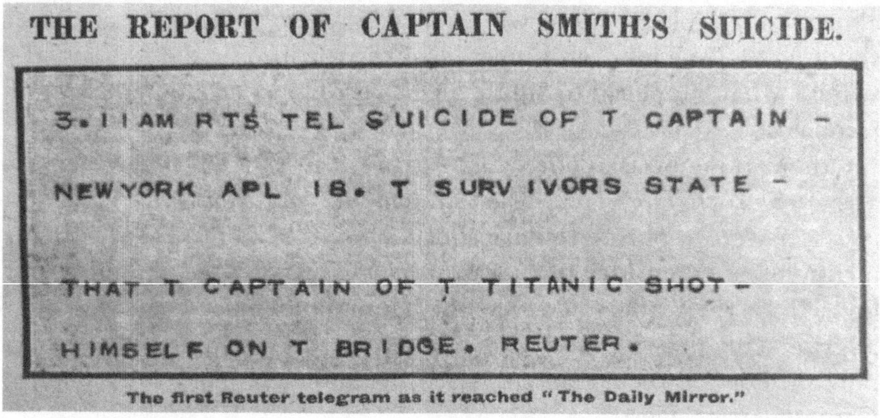

THE REPORT OF CAPTAIN SMITH'S SUICIDE.

```
3.11AM RTS TEL SUICIDE OF T CAPTAIN –
NEWYORK APL 18. T SURVIVORS STATE –
THAT T CAPTAIN OF T TITANIC SHOT –
HIMSELF ON T BRIDGE. REUTER.
```

The first Reuter telegram as it reached "The Daily Mirror."

Figure 48: Telegram printed in the 20 April 1912 edition of the *Daily Mirror*, the source of the suicide rumours. (Author's collection)

that the disgraceful story circulated in some newspapers yesterday that Captain Smith shot himself are hysterical inventions.' On the same day, *The Daily Mirror* reprinted a Reuters' telegram they had received on which they based their accounts, in an effort to absolve themselves from blame (Figure 48). The abbreviated telegram, dated 18 April, read:

> 3.11AM RTS TEL SUICIDE OF T CAPTAIN –
> NEW YORK APL 18. T SURVIVORS STATE –
> THAT T CAPTAIN OF T TITANIC SHOT –
> HIMSELF ON T BRIDGE. REUTER.[183]

In the accompanying copy, the *Mirror* reporters make no apologies of their own, writing that Reuters 'prides itself upon being the most reliable agency in the world' and the articles were 'published on Reuter's authority'. They then asked Reuters to 'explain their unfortunate blunder' and queried why the reports of suicide were being subsequently denied, to which the agency responded: 'The tragedy was reported by some of the passengers on the Carpathia during the confusion of the landing of the Titanic survivors, and that afterward, in the hurry of sending out messages to the various newspapers, two telegrams were confused. Reuter's Agency expressed their apologies for any trouble caused by their mistake.' To confuse matters further, the *Daily Mirror* ran contradictory headlines stating, 'Mystery of Captain E.J. Smith's Death' alongside 'Captain Smith Dies Like a British Sailor.' It then asked:

> How did Captain Smith die? Did he die by his own hand at the moment when the Titanic prepared for her last plunge below the waves or did

he remain on the bridge, silent, immovable, until the ocean that had known him all his life drew him to her breast? The cables as yet do not say. So contradictory are the stories bearing on the point that it would be as well for the public to reserve judgment and wait for a definite pronouncement.[184]

There was further condemnation on the same day. The *Daily Mirror* described it as a 'cruel slander on one of the noblest of the dead we mourn' while the *Daily Sketch* declared 'of all the cruelly heartless fabrications which the sensation-mongers have woven about this tragedy of the *Titanic*, the most stupid and senselessly false is the tale that Captain Smith killed himself on the bridge.'[185]

On 20 April, *The New York Times* astutely observed: 'How different were the impressions made on different persons was illustrated by the many versions told by witnesses of how Captain Smith died.'[186] The London *Times* expressed caution over the reports:

> These personal narratives, which flooded the evening papers yesterday, have been received with extreme interest, but a certain amount of scepticism is amply justified by previous experience, and the public will do well to exercise caution in accepting particular incidents. Some, such as the alleged suicide of Captain Smith, are obviously apocryphal. No one with any knowledge of the manly profession he adorned, and of the qualities required to reach the enormously responsible position he occupied, will give it a moment's credence. Other details have been published which may be disregarded not as intentionally false, but as due, perhaps, to excitement or defective observation. Every incident which people believe they witnessed on such an occasion did not necessarily happen. But when all allowances have been made, a coherent and intelligible story clearly emerges.[187]

The *Daily Mail* was condemnatory of the rumours in its Saturday coverage:

> The reports circulated in New York immediately after the Carpathia's arrival that Captain E.J. Smith, the Titanic's commander, committed suicide on the bridge were baseless slanders on a brave man dead. Our New York correspondent's prompt information enabled us to suppress the story almost as soon as it was published.
>
> The fuller reports available today combine to show that the captain was on the bridge at the time of or immediately after the slight shock caused by the collision with the iceberg. He took all steps humanly

possible to minimize the consequences... 'Captain Smith's unparalleled self-sacrifice and heroism,' says one account 'are commended by high and low...' All accounts agree that he did his duty to the last, and died with the traditional heroism of the British captain.[188]

Captain Rostron of the *Carpathia* – perhaps noting the number of *Carpathia* sources of the suicide rumour – also waded into the furore. He made it plain when he stated to a journalist: 'I wish you would deny in as strong language as permissible the persistent report sent out by some press concerns that Captain Smith killed himself when he realized that the *Titanic* was doomed. I have it from the lips of members of his crew who tried to save his life that he did not commit suicide.'[189] First class passenger Robert Williams Daniel, who claimed he remained until the end, responded to the suicide rumours by saying: 'I do not believe the stories that Capt. Smith ended his life. He stuck to his post to the last. He was a brave man.'[190] He also provided an alternative suicide victim: First Officer Murdoch.

Eyewitness Harry Senior, a fireman, put it more forcefully: 'It is a dirty lie to say that such a man as he shot himself.'[191] Similarly, author Walter Lord dismissed the suicide accounts ('there's not a shred of evidence') as he was sure that Captain Smith was more of a 'fighter'.[192]

Doubt over the exaggerated suicide rumours was too late for the 20 April 1912 edition of the French newspaper *L'Excelsior* (Figure 46). In addition to dramatic sketches of Isidor and Ida Straus clutching each other aboard the sinking ship and survivors clambering over an upturned lifeboat, artist Paul Thiriat drew a horrifying image of the Captain standing on the boat deck, with wild eyes and a gun pointed to his mouth. Behind, a lifeboat is being loaded and an officer rushes toward the Captain. The caption below explains that 'Captain Smith shot himself while the fight to find a place on board the boats was fierce. With strong resolve he went on deck, grabbed a gun from his pocket, placed the barrel in his mouth and fired.' In brackets below the caption was another, rather crucial sentence: 'According to the accounts of some survivors'.

'The captain went down with the ship'

Before examining the eyewitness accounts as to the Captain's fate, it is worth noting what the man himself allegedly spoke on the matter. On 20 April 1912, there was a meeting in Belfast and a Harland & Wolff managing director named Kempster recalled asking Captain Smith just before the *Titanic* departed Belfast 'if the old-time seamen's courage and fearlessness in the face of death still existed'. The Captain was said to have replied: 'If a disaster like that to Birkenhead happened they would go down as those men went down.'[193] He was making reference to the 1852 sinking of the British troopship the *Birkenhead* off Cape Town after striking an unchartered rock. It is believed to be the origin of the naval tradition of 'women and children first'[194] in which 454 of the 638 aboard perished, including its master, Captain Robert Salmond. One of Smith's schoolfriends, Joseph Turner, would later recall a class lesson on the loss of the *Birkenhead*: 'None of us thought at that time that we had one amongst us who would become a hero of a very similar tragedy.'[195]

An unnamed wife of a White Star Line officer, whose husband worked aboard the *Irishman*, recalled that there was a gathering of the officers of the *Olympic* and their wives not long before *Titanic* was to embark. When a reference was made that *Titanic* would take the *Olympic*'s laurels as the largest ship afloat, it was pointed out that there was a 'prophesy' about such a ship sinking – likely in the novella by author Morgan Robertson. In an account published in the *Chicago Tribune*, Captain Smith responded to this morbid reference by saying: 'Well, if the largest liner in the world sinks, I shall go with it.' The quote had been provided by 'the wife of one of the Titanic's officers, who was then attached to the Olympic', and the memory of the Captain 'upset her completely and caused apprehension about her husband's transfer to the Titanic. The husband is supposed to have been one of the officers lost in Monday's disaster.'[196] Through a process of elimination, the officer's wife, the one who originally related the story, must have been First Officer William Murdoch's widow, Ada Murdoch.

In another earlier account, Smith indicated some sense of self-preservation – although this was during his time as an officer aboard the *Republic*, during the late 1880s, when he was without the same responsibilities as a captain. A fellow officer named Wagner recalled a time they were at the Liverpool docks and 'the marine superintendent and Smith inspected the lifeboats, and Smith asked me to work out the carrying capacity of the boats: I casually referred to the well-known fact that in case of foundering at sea the boats could only accommodate a comparatively small number of passengers and crew. "Ah, well," said Smith, "if it ever comes to that, Wagner, you and I will have to swim for it."'[197]

Associates of Smith were certain of his behaviour. Mr Willis, who dined with the captain just prior to his taking command of *Titanic* and recorded how much faith E.J. had in the ship design, said that 'from what I know of Captain Smith, he would be the last man to leave the ship if it were sinking.'[198]

There was doubtless an expectation that a captain would go down with his command. In 1886, in the London edition of *Harper's Monthly Magazine*, in an article on 'The Transatlantic Captains,' it describes the men as 'master-sailors ... worthy of admiration and esteem. They are emphatically Duty's children, and whenever she commands they obey, even if obedience be at the expense, not only of great personal comfort, but almost of life itself... They are brave men, and the record of an ocean disaster often ends thus: "The captain went down with the ship."'[199]

Jumping from the Bridge

There are multiple eyewitness accounts that give a better indication of where and how Simth died that do not involve a weapon. We can certainly place Smith's final movements in the bridge area. Carlos F. Hurd, the *St. Louis Post-Dispatch* reporter from whom the early suicide accounts may have originated, was also one of the first to indicate Smith may have jumped from the bridge, although without identifying his source: 'Captain Smith remained on the bridge until just before the ship sank, leaping only after those on the deck had been washed away.'[200]

One intriguing account by a man who had known the Captain for fifteen years, first class millionaire Frederick Hoyt, says he took a drink before the final plunge: 'The captain's room was on the bridge deck, the highest part of the superstructure. I went in to get a drink of water. The captain was perfectly calm. As I filled my glass he took a drink, too. He knew there was no hope.' In the same account, Hoyt defends the captain: 'The references to Maj. Butt shooting himself and Capt. Smith committing suicide are absolutely without foundation. Capt. Smith I know to have been a man of courage, and through long years of association with him at one time and another I am convinced he died as a sailor would die – going down with his ship.'[201] A few days later, Hoyt provided another version that revealed that the two discussed their options. When Hoyt found Smith on the bridge, he told him, 'I feel like taking a drink before I take the plunge, don't you captain?' According to Hoyt, they then went to Smith's cabin and both took a large drink to fortify them against the cold, after which Smith told him, 'You will have to jump and you had better do it soon.' Hoyt suggested doing so from a lower deck and Smith apparently agreed that was a better option.[202]

Hoyt's account was also included in Gracie's 1913 book, based on a private letter in which Hoyt related that their 'conversation that night amounted to little or nothing. I simply sympathized with [Smith] on the accident; but at that time, as I then never expected to be saved, I did not want to bother him with questions, as I knew he had all he wanted to think of. He did suggest that I go down to A Deck and see if there were not a boat alongside.'[203] Captain Smith's suggestion that Hoyt should jump saved the passenger's life. He was rescued by the occupants of collapsible D, one of whom turned out to be his wife.

Smith was also seen in the bridge area, but not alone, by 33-year-old first class saloon steward Frederick Dent Ray, who testified at the United States Inquiry that Captain Smith's personal steward, Arthur Paintin, was 'last seen on the bridge, standing by the captain'.[204] 'Tiger' Paintin was lost in the sinking. When his son was born three months later, his widow named him after her husband, Arthur James Paintin.[205]

Robert Williams Daniel, a banker and 27-year-old first class passenger, said he 'saw Captain Smith on the bridge. My eyes seemingly clung to him. The deck from which I had leapt was immersed. The water had risen slowly, and was now to the floor of the bridge. Then it was to Captain Smith's waist. I saw him no more. He died a hero.'[206] Daniel elsewhere said: 'I saw the captain holding the bridge after the ship had sunk to the level of the sea. Then he went overboard.'[207] There is some doubt whether Daniel would really have been able to see the bridge, as he likely jumped from the stern.[208]

There are two accounts of the commander crying. 19-year-old second class passenger William Mellors also said Smith did not shoot himself and instead jumped:

> I was not far from where Captain Smith stood on the bridge, giving full orders to his men… The brave old seaman was crying, but he had stuck heroically to the last. He did not shoot himself. He jumped from the bridge when he had done all he could. I heard his final instructions to his crew, and recall that his last words were: 'You have done your duty, boys. Now every man for himself.'[209]

Mellor's account is made all the more credible by the fact he also survived aboard collapsible A, the last of two lifeboats that floated off the ship as it took its final dip into the ocean. His reference to the Captain crying ties into fireman James McGann's description of the captain 'trying to keep back the tears'.[210]

The most common end has Smith diving into the ocean. For example, first class passenger Eleanor Widener, who hosted the dinner honouring Captain Smith just hours before, stated that she 'went on deck and was put into a life boat. As the boat pulled away from the Titanic I saw one of the officers shoot himself in the head, and a few minutes later saw

Capt. Smith jump from the bridge into the sea.'[211] Mrs Widener was in boat no. 4 – the lifeboat that was greatly delayed by Lightoller's mismanagement – so it was possible she saw him.

The sight of Smith diving off the bridge was corroborated by someone else who had spent much time with the Captain that night, Harold Bride. In a letter to 'Mr. Cross, the traffic manager of the Marconi Co' that was submitted to the Senate Inquiry, Bride said he 'assisted in pushing off a collapsible lifeboat, which was on the port side of the forward funnel, onto the boat deck. Just as the boat fell I noticed Capt. Smith dive from the bridge into the sea.'[212] Under questioning at the Senate Inquiry, he added, 'The last I saw of the captain of the Titanic, he went overboard from the bridge about, I should think, three minutes before I left it myself... He had not a life preserver on the whole of the time when we were working; when he came into the cabin at frequent intervals.'[213] Archibald Gracie included Bride's account in his 1913 book on the disaster adding that 'the junior Marconi operator ... saw him [Smith] at the last on the bridge of his ship, and later, when sinking and struggling in the water.'[214]

Second class passenger and schoolteacher Lawrence Beesley described Smith as 'dropping' into the sea: 'The captain stood on the bridge and continued directing his men right up to the moment when the bridge on which he stood became level with the water. He then calmly climbed over the rail and dropped into the sea.'[215] Since Beesley was in lifeboat 13 rowing off the starboard side, it is questionable how much he would have seen from that distance.

Others thought that the Captain was washed from the bridge as the ship sank. Steward Edward Brown was quoted as saying that the Captain 'was washed off the bridge as the forward funnel dipped and that the captain was on the bridge at the time'.[216] Captain Rostron in his defence of the Captain added that Smith 'stuck to the ship until he was washed from the bridge'.[217]

31-year-old Isaac Maynard, a cook, described a 'rush of water':

> I saw the captain standing on the bridge. He was fully dressed and had his cap on. When the water rushed over the top deck, the remaining boats were carried away. Another rush of water washed me overboard, and as I went I clung on to one of the upturned boats. There were some six other men clinging to the woodwork when we were in the water. I saw Captain Smith washed from the bridge, and afterwards saw him swimming in the water.[218]

A 'George A. Boden' said he had seen the Captain knocked over by the seawater as he struggled to keep a foothold on the slanting deck, although there is no crew member by that name listed aboard *Titanic*.[219] 'Boden' may have been 37-year-old first class passenger and gambler George Brereton (also known as Brayton or Braden), who said Captain Smith lost his balance: 'Brayton was standing just below the captain when the latter lost his balance and fell from the bridge into the sea.'[220] In another account by Brereton, Smith was hit by two waves: 'I saw Captain Smith while I was in the water. He was standing on the deck all alone. Once he was swept down by a wave, but managed to get to his feet again. Then, as the boat sank, he was knocked down by a wave, and then disappeared from view.'[221] A separate account from Brereton says that he 'saw him swim back onto the sinking ship. He went down with it in my sight.'[222] Augustus Weikman, the ship's barber, told a similar story: 'When the forward part of the ship listed I was washed overboard by a huge wave. Looking backward, I could see Captain Smith, who had been standing on the bridge, swimming back to the place where he had stood, having been washed off the Titanic by the same wave that had washed me from the ship into the water.'[223]

Smith may have not been alone when he jumped. 21-year-old *Titanic* mess steward Cecil Fitzpatrick was involved in the aborted attempt to launch one of the final collapsible lifeboats and in a detailed account described the Captain jumping with the shipbuilder Thomas Andrews:

> I then went for'a'd on the port side, and I was passing through the bridge when I saw Capt. Smith speaking to Mr. Andrews, the designer of the Titanic. I stopped to listen. I was still confident that the ship was unsinkable, but when I heard Capt. Smith say, 'We cannot stay any longer: she is going!' I fainted against the starboard side of the bridge entrance… Just before I went overboard I saw the captain and Mr. Andrews rush past me. When I looked again they were gone, and I did not see them again. I suppose they went overboard.[224]

Fitzpatrick ended up on the upturned collapsible B, and by all accounts his statement has been considered reliable. *On a Sea of Glass* notes that not only was he in a position to see Smith and Andrews, but that his observation is supported by other individuals who saw Smith dive from the bridge. There is even further corroboration in the form of a private letter written by Thomas Andrews' friend, David Galloway, to Andrews' uncle, Lord Pirrie, on 27 April 1912, in which he recounted that 'near the end, a "young mess-boy" saw Andrews and Captain Smith on the Bridge. Both men put on lifebelts, and then the witness heard Smith say, "It is no use waiting any longer." When water reached the Bridge, both men entered the sea together.'[225] The 'young mess-boy' was, in all likelihood, Cecil Fitzpatrick.

Collapsible B

From the number of accounts that place Smith diving into the water from the bridge, likely the port side, it seems this is the most probable outcome. To some eyewitnesses, that was not the end, there was more to be seen of the Captain, still fully dressed, and some reported there was even an attempt to rescue him.

D. W. McMillan quoted his sister, Elizabeth Robert, in lifeboat no. 2, who said that 'Captain Smith went down with the ship and came up again, but sank before they could reach him with the boat.'[226] She was likely paraphrasing other accounts, as lifeboat no. 2 was rowing much further aft of the sinking ship, on the starboard side. Quartermaster Rowe, in collapsible C, also later reported that 'Captain Smith was one of the men who, at the very last, clung to an overturned boat as the Titanic went under.'[227]

Another of the *Carpathia* stories reporter Carlos Hurd managed to include in his scoop was from an unnamed cook: 'It is also related that when a cook later sought to pull him [Captain Smith] aboard a lifeboat he exclaimed "Let me go", and jerking away, went down.'[228]

Hurd's source was almost undoubtedly 31-year-old cook Isaac Maynard who was aboard collapsible B and described Smith refusing rescue:

> I saw Captain Smith washed from the bridge, and afterwards saw him swimming in the water. He was still fully dressed, with his peak cap on his head. One of the men clinging to the raft tried to save him by reaching out a hand, but he would not let him, and called out "Look after yourselves, boys." I do not know what became of the captain, for I could not see him at the time, but I suppose he sank.[229]

The *Hampshire Independent* reported an unnamed trimmer on collapsible B who gave a parallel account: 'We pulled Captain Smith on, but he was washed off. We pulled him on again, but he said "Let me go boys," and that was the last I saw of him.'[230]

Colonel Archibald Gracie, one of the passengers fortunate enough to have made his way to upturned collapsible B, reported that he witnessed a man who was refused boarding out of concern it would jeopardise stability.

> There was one transcendent piece of heroism that will remain fixed in my memory as the most sublime and coolest exhibition of courage and cheerful resignation to fate and fearlessness of death. This was when

a reluctant refusal of assistance met with the ringing response in the deep manly voice of a powerful man, who, in his extremity, replied: 'All right, boys; good luck and God bless you.' I have often wished that the identity of this hero might be established and an individual tribute to his memory preserved. He was not an acquaintance of mine, for the tones of his voice would have enabled me to recognize him.[231]

While Gracie, a reasonably reliable witness, did not recognise the man with any degree of certainty, others have insisted that it was the Commander himself, due to other similar accounts placing him at collapsible B.[232]

For example, fireman Walter Hurst, who survived on top of Collapsible B, wrote a letter to author Walter Lord stating that he apparently tried to reach an unidentified man with an oar, but the rapidly rising swell carried the man away before he could reach him: 'I can state definitely Captain Smith did not reach the raft but I always had the idea he was the man that spoke to us in the water but I could not be sure.'[233] Lord summarised his account in his 1955 book, describing Hurst as holding out an oar, but the man spun around like a cork as he was too far gone. Lord added that to this day Hurst still believes it was the Captain.[234] Hurst's account was also confirmed by his daughter Rosina Broadbere, who said her father told her he was on the upside down collapsible and 'somebody swam up to the boat and he couldn't get on because there were so many on there and he said, "Good luck boys" ... and my dad swore that was the captain that said that.'[235]

There were other firemen who mentioned Smith refusing to be saved. The *Daily Telegraph* included a report from steward Samuel Rule who said he 'heard from one of the firemen that he [Smith] could have been saved, but he would not let them pull him out of the water. He did not want to live.' The same newspaper quoted an unidentified fireman, possibly Rule's source, who added: 'We did not get far away from the ship before she went down. I saw the captain in the sea after the Titanic sunk. He was within a few yards of us, and could have been saved if he had only allowed himself to be pulled into the boat. But he refused.'[236]

There was a general expectation that Smith would make it to the upturned collapsible that was later commanded by Second Officer Lightoller. 17-year-old first class passenger John 'Jack' Thayer managed to swim to the collapsible after jumping from the ship:

One call that came around was, 'Is the Chief aboard?' Whether they mean Mr. Wilde, the Chief Officer, or the Chief Engineer, or Captain Smith, I do not know. I do know that one of the circular life rings from the bridge was there when we got off in the morning. It may be that Captain Smith was on board with us for a while. Nobody knew where the 'Chief' was.[237]

Irish able seaman in lifeboat no. 9, George 'Paddy' McGough, told a story of Smith and Murdoch's last moments: 'Both Captain Smith and Junior Chief Officer Murdoch were now together on the bridge, the water being up to their armpits. The next I saw of Captain Smith was in the water holding a child in his arms. He swam to the raft on which was Second Officer Lightoller and gave the child to the mate. That was the last. He and the ship went down, and Murdoch – God help me; don't ask me what I saw.'[238] In a differing account, he said he saw the Captain from the boat deck: 'I distinctly saw Captain Smith at some distance swimming towards another boat. When they reached out to help him he shouted to them, "Look after yourselves men. Don't mind me. God bless you." Then he threw up his hands and disappeared.'[239]

Another occupant of a lifeboat unlikely to have been able to see what really happened was second class passenger Charlotte Collyer, in lifeboat 14, who was 'told afterward by more than one trustworthy person that Captain E.J. Smith was washed against a collapsible boat and held onto it for a few moments. A member of the crew assured me that he tried to pull the captain on board, but that he shook his head, cast himself off, and sunk out of sight.'[240] A survivor in lifeboat 11 that was also too far away was saloon steward Arthur McMicken: 'The Captain was seen not far from where the Titanic went down. He wore oilskins, which weighed him down, and he seemed so exhausted he could barely keep afloat.'[241]

Captain Rostron repeated what he had heard aboard the *Carpathia* and added that Smith may not have had the energy to survive: 'Then some men caught him [Smith] in the swirling waters and landed him safely on the edge of a lifeboat. But he tumbled back into the ocean and went down. He had been too weakened by hard knocks while being tossed about the sinking *Titanic* to hold onto anything. The buffeting he encountered on the wrecked ship undoubtedly had dazed him and left him in no condition to exert even his remaining strength.'[242]

In a similar account, able seaman George Hogg told a newspaper reporter that 'as the Titanic sank, a big wave washed him over the side and he landed on a raft carrying thirty-five persons. 'The next moment I saw Capt. Smith in the water alongside the raft. "There's the skipper," I yelled, "give him a hand," and they did. But he shook himself free and shouted to us, "Goodbye boys, I'm going to follow the ship." That was the last we saw of our skipper.'[243] Hogg was most likely rescued in lifeboat no. 7 – one of the first to depart.

The Convergence of the Twain

Figure 49: 'The Death of Captain Smith' by Douglas MacPherson (1871–1951) featured on the front page of the Saturday, 4 May 1912 edition of *The Daily Graphic*. (Courtesy of Paul Lee)

Saving a Child

In addition to reaching the upturned collapsible Engelhardt lifeboat B, there were further reports of heroism. An unnamed survivor who had arrived in England was quoted in the London *Times*: 'Another of the arrivals spoke of the devotions of Capt. Smith, who struck to his post until the bridge disappeared beneath the waves. Once he leapt overboard clutching an infant, swam with it to a lifeboat, and then returned to the sinking ship.'[244]

Harry Senior, a verified collapsible B survivor, had earlier described the Captain heroically carrying a baby:

> It only took a few strokes to bring him [Smith] to the upturned life boat, where a dozen hands were stretched out to take the little child from his arms and drag him to safety. 'Captain Smith was dragged on the upturned boat,' said the fireman, 'he had on a life buoy and a life preserver. He clung there a moment and then he slid off again. For a second time he was dragged from the icy water. Then he took off his life preserver, tossed the life buoy on the inky waters, and slipped into the water again with the words: 'I will follow the ship.'[245]

Senior's 19 April account formed the basis of a dramatic painting by New York maritime artist Henry Reuterdahl (1870–1925), that was later printed on postcards (Figure 50). One interesting aspect of Senior's story is the mention of the 'life buoy' as it aligns with Jack Thayer's observation that there was 'one of the circular life rings from the bridge' on collapsible B. Ten days later, a very similar account by Harry Senior appeared in the London *Times*:

> Harry Senior, a fireman, in conversation with a press representative, said that as he was swimming to the boat after diving from the ship he saw Captain Smith in the water. The captain was swimming with a baby in his arms, raising it out of the water as he swam on his back. He swam to a boat, put the baby in, and then swam back to the ship.[246]

The account was corroborated by 29-year-old fireman, James McGann, who told of Smith taking a child before jumping:

> I had gone to the bridge deck to assist in lowering a collapsible boat. The water was then coming over the bridge and we were unable to launch it properly. It was overturned and was used as a life raft, some 30 or more of us, mostly firemen clinging to it. Captain Smith looked as if he was trying to keep back the tears as he thought of the doomed ship... He then took one of the children standing by him on the bridge and jumped into the sea. He endeavoured to reach the overturned boat but did not succeed. That was the last I saw of Captain Smith... He held the little girl under one arm as he jumped into the sea and endeavoured to reach the nearest lifeboat with the child. I took the other child into my arms as I was swept from the bridge deck. When I was plunged into

the cold water I was compelled to release my hold on the child and I am satisfied that the same thing happened to captain Smith.[247]

In another account, McGann said Smith 'took one of the two little children who were on the bridge beside him. They were both crying. He held the child, I think it was a little girl, under his right arm, and jumped into the sea... I looked around for the captain after I got to the overturned boat, but he was nowhere in sight.'[248]

Fireman Frederick Harris, who was in lifeboat 14 reiterated the story, saying that 'he saw the captain jump into the water and grasp a child, which he placed on one of the rafts, of which there were all too few. He did not see the captain afterwards.'[249]

23-year-old Charles Eugene Williams, a champion racquet player from Harrow School, related a similar occurrence to his 'friend George E. Standing' who in turn passed it on to a reporter for *The Daily Sketch*. 'I saw Captain Smith swimming around in the icy water with a baby in his arms and wearing a lifebelt. He handed the baby to someone in the lifeboat, but refused to get in himself. The Captain did ask what became of First Officer Murdoch. We told him that he had blown his brains out with a revolver. Upon hearing this, Captain Smith pushed himself away from the boat, took off his lifebelt, and sank beneath the surface.'[250]

Gambler George Brereton, who had earlier observed Smith 'lose his balance' and fall into the sea, also told a story of an infant rescue: 'Smith appeared on the surface of the water and swam toward the sinking vessel. Fifteen yards away was the body of an infant which attracted the struggling sailor. He caught hold of the child and then with his right arm made for a lifeboat. The little one was safely put aboard and the captain resumed his struggle for the sinking Titanic.'[251]

Brereton went even further, saying that Smith refused to grab a line that was thrown to him by a junior officer and returned to *Titanic*, saying 'This is my place and I will remain here and go down with the ship.' Although the claim is unlikely, Sir Cosmo Duff Gordon, seated in lifeboat no. 1, is also said to have witnessed Smith rescue an infant from the freezing water and deliver it to a lifeboat.[252]

According to able seaman 'Cyril Handy' – although nobody of that name exists on the *Titanic*'s crew list – Smith saved more than just a baby. Handy first mentioned that he was 'on the boat deck near the bridge when the captain was washed off by the encroaching waters. A moment later he found himself in the sea alongside a boat, and the captain beside him supporting a woman with a baby he had evidently picked up as he fell. Lifting the woman and child aboard the captain deliberately turned in the icy water and swam back towards the vessel in spite of the attempts of several sailors to put him aboard in safety.'[253]

Another purported eyewitness of an infant rescue was first class steward Thomas Whiteley who survived aboard upturned collapsible B: 'When I last saw the captain he was in the water trying to place a baby in one of the lifeboats crowded with people. Some women tried to drag him on the boat, but he pulled away from them and said: "Save yourselves." I saw him go under, and he never came up.'[254]

Carpathia passenger Fred Beachler heard a similar story, although in his case he believed it was more reliable as it came from an unidentified officer: 'I also learn on the same reliable authority, verified by others, that Captain Smith ... was in the water with a child in his arms, which he succeeded in placing in one of the boats. He was begged to come aboard himself, but refused and turned back as though to aid others, and was not seen again.'[255]

There were several more second-hand accounts, such as quartermaster William Wynn who said on his return to England: 'I heard from one of the last men to leave the ship that the last seen of Capt. Smith was when he swam up to one of the boats with a baby in his arms. He handed the child to one of the occupants of the boat, but the poor mite died soon afterwards. Efforts were made to get the captain into the boat, but he refused assistance, and swam back to where the Titanic sank and was never seen again in the darkness.'[256]

Figure 50: A 1912 postcard with an illustration of Captain Smith rescuing a child and bringing it to upturned collapsible B. (Kevin Saucier, Titanic Items Collection)

Second class passenger Elizabeth Nye, rescued in lifeboat no. 11, likely recounted a story based on what she had heard from others aboard the *Carpathia*: 'Just before the ship went down the Captain ... jumped into the sea and picked up a little girl who was hanging to the ship, and put her on the raft. They pulled him on, too, but he would not stay... He swam back through the icy waters and died at his post.'[257]

In the *Folkestone Herald*, there is an important extra line to Nye's account: 'The little girl died too.'[258] While the *New York Herald* confirmed that one of the men 'who was on the raft' told her that 'the girl whom the Captain saved died half an hour later.'[259]

That the child died is a distinct possibility referred to by several witnesses. Able-bodied seaman Albert Horswill manned lifeboat no. 1 that departed early in the evacuation with only twelve aboard. Nevertheless, on his return to England he said he 'saw Captain Smith in the water, swimming, with a baby in his arms, towards a raft. The captain afterward disappeared.'[260] Other accounts from Horswill added a gruesome detail: 'Asked if he saw anything of the master, Horswell [sic] said he saw Captain Smith swimming about with the dead body of a child in his arms.'[261]

There are also problematic accounts, such as those from an alleged 'Steward Charles Collins' who does not appear in crew lists, although it could well be journalists confusing the name of scullion John Collins. In his account, Captain Smith was seen swimming with a woman and child, both of whom he managed to get to a lifeboat, only for the child to die.[262]

The infant has never been identified. Author Stephanie Barczewski commented that it was noteworthy that no one could clearly point out the child in question. Despite all the confusion, she believes it is certain that someone would remember the Captain rescuing a child, but no one did.[263] Barczewski was not aware of some newspaper reports that may help identify the child. First is another account from fireman Harry Senior. In New York on 19 April, he recorded seeing 'an Italian woman holding two babies. I took one of them and made the woman jump overboard with the baby, while I did the same with the other. When I came to the surface the baby in my arms was dead.'[264] Later in England, a more detailed account by Senior appeared on 4 May:

> The mate, the captain, the second officer and myself, all happened to be together on the boat-deck. There was an Italian woman standing near us with two babies, and there was another little baby running about. The captain took one baby, I took one of the Italian woman's babies; and she kept the other... When I came up the baby I had in my arms was dead from the shock of the water.'

Titanic Legacy: The Captain, the Daughter and the Spy

'Italian' was a term frequently used by British crew to describe foreign individuals; Fifth Officer Lowe had to retract such a description from his Senate Inquiry testimony. According to a parallel account, it is quite likely the woman he described was actually Swedish.

27-year-old third class Swedish passenger, August Wennerström, survived aboard collapsible A – the last lifeboat that was partially launched and flooded as the *Titanic* sank. He knew a fellow Swedish third class passenger, Alma Cornelia Pålsson, who was travelling with her four children, two boys, Paul Folke (aged 6) and Gösta Leonard (2), and two girls, Torborg Danira (8) and Stina Viola (3). Biographies frequently contain reference to Wennerström meeting Pålsson and her children during the ship's final moments near collapsible A where 'Wennerström tried to hold on to two of the children as she had asked him to but when water came up then Wennerström lost his grip and both disappeared.'[265] In a 1913 newspaper account, Wennerström added an extra detail:

> He [Wennerström] was on the Titanic when a Mrs. Paulson [Pålsson] came up from below with four children. All the lifeboats were gone and Capt. Smith took one of the children in personal charge and told the mother that there was no way to be saved. The grief of the mother and children was heartrending.[266]

Figure 51: Family photographs of Stina Viola (age 3) and Gösta Leonard Pålsson (age 2) who Captain Smith possibly attempted to save. (Photographs courtesy of Kerstin Nilsson/fam-nilsson.eu)

The Convergence of the Twain

Based on the other witness accounts that describe Smith holding a baby, this could well narrow down the possibilities to the two youngest of Pålsson's children: the boy Gösta Leonard (2) or the girl Stina Viola (3). Odds of their survival after exposure to water and then aboard the upturned lifeboat would have been very low. Indeed, Alma Pålsson and her four children all perished in the disaster. Her body was later recovered, but none of her children were ever found.

There is also a tantalising possible identification of the individual who took the baby from Captain Smith's arms: the assistant cook, Isaac Maynard. Although he does not reference such a moment in his accounts published in the press, on his arrival in Plymouth along with many of *Titanic*'s surviving crew on Sunday 28 April 1912 aboard the *Lapland*, he was photographed and identified. The newspapers who subsequently printed his photograph, including the *Daily Sketch* and the *Sheffield Daily Telegraph* included a caption: 'G. Maynard, steward [sic] who took the baby out of Captain Smith's arms' (Figure 52).[267]

Figure 52: Maynard was identified in the press as the person who 'took the baby out of Captain Smith's arms'. *Sheffield Daily Telegraph*, 30 April 1912. (Author's collection)

There were reports of Smith interacting and caring for children during the early days of the voyage – in particular seven-year-old Eva Hart and fifteen-year-old Edith Brown. It is not a huge stretch of the imagination to believe that in Smith's final moments his thoughts were not only about his dear wife and daughter. He must have also been concerned for any children nearby facing an unthinkable demise.

Colonel Archibald Gracie in his 1913 book quoted the previous statements as given by Senior and Maynard, that spoke of Smith reaching the overturned collapsible and yet unable to maintain a hold. Gracie adds a small detail that may explain why – that Smith was washed away by the collapse of the forward funnel as the bridge area was submerged: 'From several sources I have the information about the falling of the funnel, the splash of which swept from the upturned boat several who were first clinging thereto, and among the number possibly was the Captain.'[268]

The many reports that place Smith at collapsible B ignore one important point – Second Officer Lightoller sought refuge there and took command, but never gave an indication his Captain was ever present. Is it feasible that it took place prior to Lightoller's arrival? Or in the chaos of life-and-death survival did he simply miss the appearance of *Titanic*'s Master?

On a Sea of Glass concludes that the various accounts indicate that 'he leapt overboard and at some point shortly after the sinking, reached Collapsible B... Jack Thayer saw a life ring from the Bridge floating near Collapsible B in the morning. If Captain Smith had indeed been alongside Collapsible B, this life ring may have marked the very spot where he met his end.'[269] Gary Cooper is rightly sceptical of the many stories of Smith in the water, but concludes that it was possible that 'Smith could have swum around in the water for a time and may have refused to let himself be rescued as some statements say... Considering the odium heaped upon the likes of Ismay and Captain Lord, it was probably just as well that Smith died, as had he lived the scandal would probably have destroyed him.'[270]

Author Phillip Gibbs, in his 1912 account of the disaster, after discussing the death of Captain Smith that he described as 'sublime in its heroism,' added two lines of poetry:

Beautiful was death in him, who saw the death and kept the deck,
Saving women and their babies, and sinking with the sinking wreck.[271]

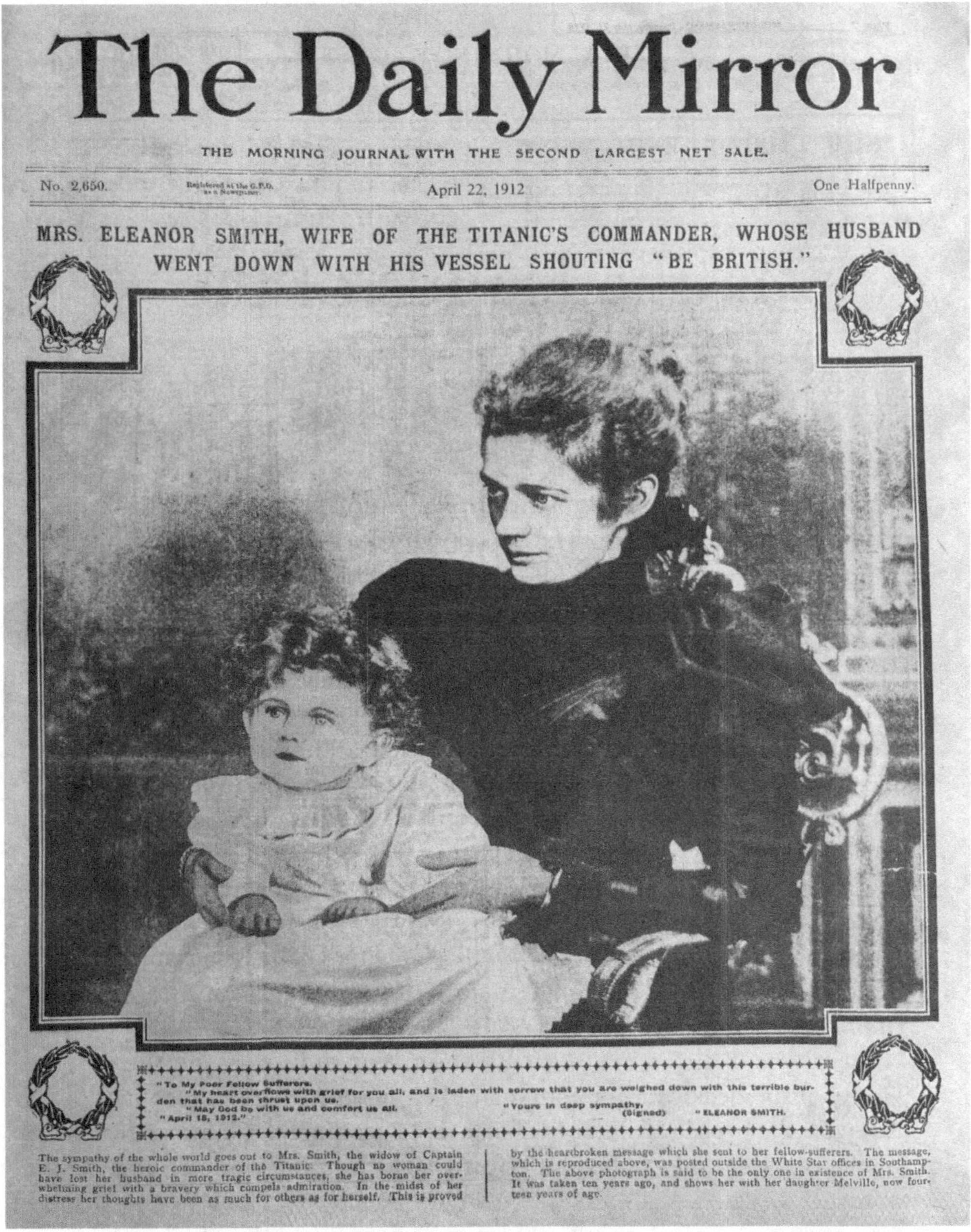

The Daily Mirror

THE MORNING JOURNAL WITH THE SECOND LARGEST NET SALE.

No. 2,650. Registered at the G.P.O. as a Newspaper. April 22, 1912 One Halfpenny.

MRS. ELEANOR SMITH, WIFE OF THE TITANIC'S COMMANDER, WHOSE HUSBAND WENT DOWN WITH HIS VESSEL SHOUTING "BE BRITISH."

"To My Poor Fellow Sufferers.

"My heart overflows with grief for you all, and is laden with sorrow that you are weighed down with this terrible burden that has been thrust upon us.

"May God be with us and comfort us all.

"Yours in deep sympathy,
(Signed) "ELEANOR SMITH.

"April 18, 1912."

The sympathy of the whole world goes out to Mrs. Smith, the widow of Captain E. J. Smith, the heroic commander of the Titanic. Though no woman could have lost her husband in more tragic circumstances, she has borne her overwhelming grief with a bravery which compels admiration. In the midst of her distress her thoughts have been as much for others as for herself. This is proved by the heartbroken message which she sent to her fellow-sufferers. The message, which is reproduced above, was posted outside the White Star offices in Southampton. The above photograph is said to be the only one in existence of Mrs. Smith. It was taken ten years ago, and shows her with her daughter Melville, now fourteen years of age.

Figure 53: Eleanor and Mel appear on the front page of the *Daily Mirror* on 22 April 1912. As the caption pointed out, the photograph was a decade old as Mel was actually aged 14 at the time the *Titanic* sank. (Author's collection)

4

'In the Hands of the Evil One'

When the *Titanic* sank, it created two widows among the rank of deck officers, Eleanor Smith and Ada Murdoch, wife of First Officer William Murdoch who was lost and whose body, along with Smith's, was never recovered. Chief Officer Wilde had already lost his wife at the end of 1910 and the youngest officer who died, 24-year-old Sixth Officer James Moody, was single. Separate from the deck officers, there was also Chief Purser McElroy, the man beside Smith in one of his last known photographs, who had married Barbara Ennis two years earlier. The 38-year-old Ada Murdoch never married again and eventually returned to her homeland, New Zealand; 33-year-old Barbara McElroy remarried two years later to a John Clancy. The orphaned Wilde children, now bereft of both a mother and father in the space of two years, were looked after by Henry Wilde's sister-in-law Annie Jones Williams and were later supported by the *Titanic* Relief Fund. The other surviving officers – Lowe, Boxhall and Pitman – did not marry until after the *Titanic* disaster (in 1913, 1919 and 1922 respectively).

There was a difference with Eleanor. Not only was she the sole widow of the deck officers with a child to support, but she also had to deal with the prospect of her husband fast becoming the focus of blame for the disaster and the lasting effect that would have on her and her family.

As early as 17 April, the *Washington Times* opined that 'had he been saved, Captain Smith's career was ended.' This was based on the series of incidents that had occurred prior to the *Titanic* disaster – the *Olympic/Hawke* collision, the *Olympic* striking a submerged wreck in February 1912 and the *New York* near-miss in Southampton – that the journalists concluded he was already on notice for, and that he had 'violated a deep sea tradition':

He had twice escaped the rule that the victim of an accident to a vessel must give up his post, but in previous accidents no lives were lost. It was considered because of Captain Smith's previous excellent career that the officials at the White Star line retained him in its service after the two mishaps to the Olympic, thus violating a deep sea tradition that has been more rigorously maintained by the British merchant marine than by that of any other nation. The rule has been almost invariable among steamship companies to dispense with the services of officers in command of vessels that met with disaster. One reason for this is the insistence of the insurance companies.[1]

Within days of arrival in New York, the survivors of the *Titanic* sinking were already criticising Captain Smith. Women who lost their husbands saw the Captain as responsible for their loss by not allowing their husbands into lifeboats. Second class passenger Mrs Amin Jerwan was reported as saying on 19 April 1912: 'Everybody on the ship blamed the Captain. The sailor who rowed our boat told me that he had followed the sea for 45 years and had never been in any kind of accident before, except on the *Olympic* when she rammed into the *Hawke*. "That was under the same Captain," he said, "and now I am having my second experience under him."'[2]

On the other hand, in early press reports there were those quick to defend Smith. Captain Inman Sealby of the *Republic* (which was lost in 1909 after a collision) stated on 17 April that 'Captain Smith was one of the safest seafaring men in the world. I believe he did everything in his human power to avert the accident.' Captain Charles Campbell noted that it is a 'mistaken idea that slow boats are less perilous than fast steamers. Fast ships are much safer.'[3]

Eleanor must have been inundated with messages of support from family and friends, if the experience of Second Officer Lightoller's Australian wife Sylvia is anything to go by. Sylvia said she received 50 telegrams congratulating her because the Second Officer had survived and 50 telegrams of condolence because the First Officer had been lost. It took five days until she received her husband's cable from New York telling her that he was safe.[4] In Eleanor's case, it may have been substantially more, if a friend's account in the *Daily Record* is accurate: 'Most of Mrs. Smith's time is occupied by answering letters and telegrams of condolence, which continue to pour in at the rate of two or three hundred a day.'[5]

Sylvia was also likely one visitor at the Smith residence in Winn Road, to console the Captain's widow. On Wednesday, 17 April – on the day when the first message came through naming Lightoller as the senior surviving officer – Sylvia travelled from their home in Netley on the outskirts of

Southampton. A *Southern Echo* reporter wrote: 'Mrs. Lightoller, who has two little boys, had just returned from Southampton, where she had been visiting the wives of other officers less fortunate than herself, and said how terribly anxious she had been, but how thankful she felt now that she was assured of her husband's safety.'[6] There were only two possible people to visit in the city – First Officer Murdoch's widow, Ada, in Belmont Road, and Eleanor Smith, a three-minute drive away in Winn Road. A newspaper account the following week related that Mrs Smith was 'still suffering greatly from the shock of her gallant husband's death, and she receives no one but the wives of the other officers who went down in the Titanic.'[7]

Eleanor herself was publicly lending assistance. In the Friday, 19 April 1912 edition of *The Southern Daily Echo*, her name is mentioned as contributing to the Titanic Relief Fund that was organised by Henry Bowyer, the Mayor of Southampton. Under 'To-Day's List' it details 'Mrs. E.J. Smith, wife of the Captain £10 39s.'[8] The amount would be about £1,260 today, so not an insubstantial sum. However, it was listed at the bottom of a column of other individual donations that were upwards of £315 (£33,000) each. The newspaper noted that by 3 pm that day the fund had reached a total of £35,000 (£3.6 million).[9]

Lapland Letter

There were two private letters shortly after the disaster that reveal the impact on the Smith family. Within days of the disaster, Smith's nephew, Frank Hancock in the United States, received an emotional letter of support from Christian Mallock written aboard the SS *Lapland* on 23 April 1912 in response to the 'horrible papers – packed full of details which had no relation whatever to truth and were manufactured by ignorant reporters for an ignorant public. It made me sick and angry when I thought of the dear brave man.'[10]

Mallock knew Smith personally; he and his wife were mentioned in previous letters Smith had written to Hancock. Additionally, the SS *Lapland* had been home to the four surviving *Titanic* officers – Lightoller, Pitman, Boxhall and Lowe – only a few days earlier when they were 'placed aboard the Red Star liner *Lapland* for the night. They refused to talk, saying they were under instructions to give no information except to the Senate committee.'[11] So it is perhaps unsurprising that Mallock quotes from the captain of the *Lapland*, a man he described as a 'Norwegian – with no brief for the 'White Star Line' and who was 'indignant at the mischievous and cruel insinuations which appeared before one word of real information was received; and says absolutely distinctly, as do all other honest seamen, that our Captain was sailing his ship as every other man would have done on a clear still night, and was 15 miles south of the ordinary April route!'

The master of the SS *Lapland* was Captain H. D. Doxrud, the Commodore of the Red Star fleet and a personal friend of Captain Smith. He was something of a legend in his own right, having been at sea for 45 years and coming to the aid of several ships during that time, so that by 1897 he held the 'world's record for saving life'.[12] He had even warned Smith of an icefield on the 11 April – although at the time the *Titanic* had only just departed Southampton. Smith responded with a thank you, nonetheless. When Doxrud was informed of the disaster, he initially refused to believe it until they reached New York and saw the headlines.

Mallock even claimed to have obtained an eyewitness account from 'Capt. Smith's own steward who was saved and is here.' Smith's private steward, James Arthur Paintin, did not survive the disaster, so Mallock must have spoken to another steward who had either attended to the Captain or at least seen him during his final moments. Based on this account, Mallock wrote that Smith 'swam off at the last and was picked up'. He personally vouches for Smith's behaviour, explaining that 'anyone with any knowledge whatever knows that Capt. Smith before and after the accident did everything a brave seaman would, and did it as a matter of course.' Mallock was also aware of the pain the rumours were causing to the family: 'It is more than possible that those rumours and misstatements have hurt you,' he wrote.[13]

Beesley's Commentary

On arrival in New York, school science teacher Lawrence Beesley was asked by the editor of *The New York Times* his opinion as to the cause of the disaster. His long answer was printed on 29 April 1912 and contained much criticism of speed, design and regulations – but not of the Captain.

He warned that we must 'analyse the whole circumstances in a just manner. Let us not form hasty judgements or make rash statements ... as commander the Captain is responsible directly for course and speed ... and at first sight it seems difficult to see how he can escape responsibility for the disaster. But here we must be cautious.' Beesley proposed a series of questions:

Did he [Smith] do anything which was in defiance of all custom in running his ship at full speed through the iceberg region? Did he do

> anything that has not been done by many Captains for years past? (I do not say every Captain, but many Captains of fast mail-passenger steamers.) Did he defy and outrage all precedent in not slowing down? I think the answer to all these is 'No.'... I do not wish to seem to take away any responsibility that should be laid on Captain Smith, but as he is not here to defend himself, let us all see that no undeserved censure be meted out to him. He took the risk which many other Captains have taken. What the chances were in taking the risk no man can say, but in his case the awful thing happened that should never have happened. In the case of all other Captains who have taken a similar risk it did not happen. If he is to be blamed it seems they are all equally blamable for the disaster, for he took the same risk as they did – no more or no less. Remember how the fastest boats are timed to run: 'Leave New York Wednesday, dine in London the following Monday,' and it is done...
>
> I am convinced, but for the sake of Captain Smith it seems important to know what the custom has been, for if he has taken a risk many take, the responsibility for such loss of life is fixed on a common system, to which many owners and Captains have agreed, perhaps unconsciously. If he took an uncommon and extraordinary risk, then it seems he is largely to blame.[14]

Beesley notes that even when supplied with the precise latitude and longtiude of icebergs, on reaching the position, often no trace of them can be seen, while temperature is never a guarantee of ice.

> From what has been said in some sections of the press, it would seem as if the boat was deliberately run through a locality in which it was certain an iceberg was floating in a particular position and no precautions were taken to avoid such a position – in fact, that the utmost criminal negligence was observed; but to say so is to become hysterical. What seems likely is that the risk was taken which it is a frequent custom to take, and the unusually southern position of the field and bergs as well as the large number of the latter, united to increase enormously the probabilities of collision.
>
> So that if you blame Captain Smith you must blame a large number of other people. Shall you blame Captain Rostron of the Carpathia, who 'knew icebergs were there but went ahead at full speed,' stopped at 4:10 because of iceberg ahead, and when the day dawned icebergs were around his ship and on every part of the horizon? He must have been near them many times in the night. He took the risk in a splendid cause, and no one is more grateful to him than I am that he did so, and never did a day dawn with greater rejoicing for me than when I climbed

aboard his ship. But he did take the risk. I admit there is no comparison between the reasons why he took the risk and why Captain Smith took his, but after all Captain Rostron had his own ship and passengers to consider, and he could not take too great a risk; the fact that he took it at all means it was not considered to be such a danger as we, who have known only the abnormal and not the normal result of taking the risk, might suppose.

I do not think anyone can say Capt. Smith can be held solely responsible.

Beesley blamed a much wider group than the Captain. He asked if White Star had been 'negligent' then why did the United States not stop their ships from entering? The general public's demand for larger and faster ships also played a critical role: 'Let every man who has ever grumbled to a ship's officer about slow speed, take it to heart. He had perhaps, something to do with the sinking of the Titanic'.

Senate Inquiry

Mallock's disdain for misinformation spread in the papers and Beesley's reasoned approach to Smith's accountability was to be followed by something far more serious: condemnation from the first official inquiry into the disaster. The four senior surviving officers would undoubtedly have wanted to be aboard the *Lapland* on its return to England. Instead, they were served with subpoenas to appear at the Senate Inquiry.

Wasting no time, the hearings began in New York on 19 April 1912, at the Waldorf-Astoria Hotel, New York, the day after the *Carpathia* had arrived with the *Titanic* survivors. It was soon moved to Washington, D.C., concluding on 25 May 1912 with a return visit to New York, taking a total of eighteen days.

It was presided over by Senator William Alden Smith, a Republican from the state of Michigan who, with a background in railroad law finance, had little experience in maritime matters. In an interesting coincidence, the Senator and his son had made a North Atlantic voyage aboard the *Baltic* in 1906 and had been invited to dine at Captain Smith's table when the conversation ostensibly turned from railway regulation to steamship safety. According to author Wyn Craig Wade, the Captain invited the Senator and his son on a tour of the ship that also included a visit to the bridge, where he saw the mechanism that activated the watertight doors. William Alden was said to be duly impressed.[15] He would soon change his mind on that point.

Author Richard Davenport-Hines gauged the Senator as 'an incoherent, unsystematic questioner, who hated the Demon Drink and hoped to elicit that Captain Smith or other officers had been drunk. He cross-examined Henry Stengel, in Ismay's presence, to discover if Smith, Ismay and the ship's officers had participated in the pool betting on the ship's speed and arrival time. His implication was that Smith or Ismay had ordered the ship to race into the ice zone to win a bet.'[16] Of course, there was no truth to the claim. Other allegations went unchallenged, such as the unfounded story that second class passenger Imanita Shelley repeated before the inquiry, that 'a first-cabin passenger a Mme. Baxter, of Montreal, Canada, told Mrs. Shelley that she had sent her son to the captain at the time of the collision to find out what to do. That her son had found the captain in a card game, and he had laughingly assured him that there was no danger and to advise his mother to go back to bed.'[17]

All eight senators involved in the questioning were not nautical authorities, and Lightoller was frustrated by their lack of expertise. He described the inquiry in his book as

> ...a colossal piece of impertinence that served no useful purpose and elicited only a garbled and disjointed account of the disaster; due in the main to a total lack of co-ordination in the questioning with an abysmal ignorance of the sea... With all the goodwill in the world, the 'enquiry' could be called nothing but a complete farce, wherein all the traditions and customs of the sea were continuously and persistently flouted.[18]

Not that Lightoller made it easy for the senators, with often ambiguous and elusive responses to the questioning, along with sometimes contradictory statements.

There is one interesting piece of evidence that Lightoller gave in response to criticism that Captain Smith should have changed their course further south due to the ice reports they had received. It seems like a valid observation – and is still to this day used in claims of negligence. Lightoller was clear on why:

> We receive our orders; the routes are laid down. As a matter of fact, these routes are laid down by some of your naval men in the United States, and we adhere to them. We have an ice route. When ice is very prevalent and we know that a lot of ice is coming down from the north and we have been notified of it, we sometimes are instructed to take what we call the ice track, or extreme southern route, coming west

> ... they come from the company... You get it before you leave port... I have never known the route to be changed by the commander.[19]

While a captain would obviously alter course to avoid an immediate danger such as a derelict, it was not the custom for another track to be taken without having received authority to do so from the company. Ismay would later reiterate this point in a written statement on 21 April 1912: 'The tracks, or lanes, were designated many years ago by agreement of all the important steamship lines, and all captains of the White Star Line are required to navigate their vessels as closely as possible on these tracks.'[20]

Despite Fourth Officer Boxhall arriving in New York in serious pain, he answered around 900 questions during an intense, three-hour session, surrounded by a throng of almost 600 people. He was scheduled to continue the following day but was too unwell to do so, with a doctor diagnosing that the officer was suffering from pleurisy and physically unable to appear.[21] Third Officer Pitman appeared in Boxhall's place and was similarly subjected to intense questioning, although this time without the huge crowds that had followed Boxhall's every word. Pitman broke down at one point when forced by Senator Smith to describe the sounds he heard when people were dying in the water. One description noted that Pitman's voice 'choked when he came to the death scene, and he begged the committee not to question him further along that line'.[22]

Fifth Officer Lowe was especially involved in a particularly tense and combative round of questioning. On one occasion, when Lowe was asked by Senator Smith if he knew what an iceberg was made of, the Welshman responded, 'Ice, I suppose, sir.' The Senator, frustrated by frequent 'I do not know' and 'I cannot remember' responses, at one point said bluntly to Lowe: 'I am not having a very easy time with you, because you do not seem to be willing to answer my questions.'[23]

Lowe's reluctance to answer was perhaps justified when he was unfairly accused of drinking, an allegation that as a teetotaller resulted in him demanding a statement be put on record clarifying that he did not drink any alcohol at all. Claims of racism were more difficult to defend. In an affidavit, he admitted to describing as 'Italians' those who caused him to fire his gun when they jumped into his lifeboat. He then asked for the record to be changed, to substitute 'Italians' with 'immigrants belonging to Latin races'. The declaration was made in the presence of the Royal Ambassador of Italy.[24] While the damage to Italian reputation had been somewhat corrected, the image of Captain Smith and his officers had made a decidedly bad impression at the Senate Inquiry, and Senator Smith did not hold back in his condemnation of the legendary commander in his conclusions.

Titanic Legacy: The Captain, the Daughter and the Spy

After 18 days, 86 witnesses and over 1,000 pages of testimony, Senator Smith submitted his final report on Tuesday, 28 May 1912. It began with some kind words for the Captain:

> Captain Smith knew the sea and his clear eye and steady hand had often guided his ship through dangerous paths. For 40 years storms sought in vain to vex him or menace his craft. Not once before in all his honorable career was his pride humbled or his vessel maimed. Each new advancing type of ship built by his company was handed over to him as a reward for faithful services and as an evidence of confidence in his skill. Strong of limb, intent of purpose, pure in character, dauntless as a sailor should be, he walked the deck of his majestic structure as master of her keel.[25]

There was a section that addressed rumours of drinking:

> It has been said many times – often in my hearing and often by letter – that the last dinner which he [Captain Smith] had partaken in the café of the ship, given by Mr. and Mrs. Widener, of Philadelphia, might have had some influence upon the action of the captain, but I have the word of the hostess, whose husband was lost in this catastrophe, that at that dinner Captain Smith touched no liquor of any kind; indeed, that he asked that all glasses be removed from his plate. I make this statement because I think it is due to the memory of the dead, whose habits of life are worthy the highest praise.

Then damning words that would make headlines:

> *Titanic* though she was, his indifference to danger was one of the direct and contributing causes of this unnecessary tragedy, while his own willingness to die was the expiating evidence of his fitness to live. Those of us who knew him well – not in anger, but in sorrow – file one specific charge against him: Overconfidence and neglect to heed the oft-repeated warnings of his friends. But in his horrible dismay, when his brain was afire with honest retribution, we can still see, in his manly bearing and his tender solicitude for the safety of women and little children, some traces of his lofty spirit when dark clouds lowered all about him and angry elements stripped him of his command. His devotion to his craft, even 'as it writhed and twisted and struggled' for mastery over its foe, calmed the fears of many of the stricken multitude who hung upon his words, lending dignity to a parting scene as inspiring as it is beautiful to remember.

'In the Hands of the Evil One'

As if to re-emphasise the 'indifference to danger' line, the Senator also added: 'The mastery of [Captain Smith's] indifference to danger, when other and less pretentious vessels doubled their lookout or stopped their engines, finds no reasonable hypothesis in conjecture or speculation.' Indifference was the key word, and he used it to describe the crew in general, that 'the warnings of shipmasters fell upon deaf ears and officers and crew seemed to have regarded the paper bulletins of danger with absolute indifference.' After the collision, he claimed that 'no ship's officers formally assembled, no orderly routine was attempted or organized system of safety begun.'

To the Senator, Captain Smith was not just indifferent, but overconfident and neglectful. The Senator was essentially pointing the finger of blame at a man who could no longer defend himself. That did not mean his condemnation did not extend to the living. He surprisingly even singled out *Titanic*'s junior officers, with unfounded claims of cowardice:

> Among the passengers were many strong men who had been accustomed to command, whose lives had marked every avenue of endeavour, and whose business experience and military training especially fitted them for such an emergency. These were rudely silenced and forbidden to speak, as was the president of this company, by junior officers, a few of whom, I regret to say, availed themselves of the first opportunity to leave the ship.

Finally, there was also anger at the British Board of Trade, to which he believed 'the laxity of regulation and hasty inspection the world is largely indebted for this awful tragedy.'

Perhaps thankfully, *Titanic*'s surviving deck officers were not in the United States when the report was submitted. Several weeks earlier, at midday on Thursday 2 May, the four officers, in addition to thirty crew members and White Star managing director Bruce Ismay departed for England, boarding the *Adriatic* from New York City. They arrived in Liverpool on 11 May 1912, ready to face another inquiry, this time by the British Board of Trade itself.

The Senate Inquiry report did not go down well in England. Newspapers mocked the Senator's apparent lack of credibility and dismissed most of the findings. In response, the *New York Herald* wrote that British criticism was 'arrogant insularity' from 'slow-witted Englishmen' and 'self-complacent moguls in England', and that the report explained why 'so many American lives were wasted by the incompetency of British seamen.'[26]

Senator Smith's rebuke of the *Titanic*'s captain and officers struck at the heart of British maritime pride, in an empire that in 1912 still – only just – 'ruled the waves'. It was no surprise then that the Imperial Merchant Service Guild, based in Liverpool, sent a letter dated 8 July 1912 to the Senator describing his report as an 'attack on the executive officer of the *Titanic*' and referring to the 'malevolence which characterised your speech'. In particular, they stated that 'without a shred of evidence or a particle of truth, you accuse officers of the British mercantile marine of despicable cowardice.' They specifically singled out the charge of cowardice levelled at the junior officers: 'It has been proved up to the hilt that in the midst of an appalling emergency perfect discipline prevailed, which was worthy of the best traditions of the British mercantile marine.' The letter then clarifies: 'The four officers who left the ship in charge of the four boats did so acting upon definite instructions from their superior officers.' It asked Senator Smith to acknowledge his 'error' and withdraw it.[27] There was another reason for the Guild's outrage over the Senate report: in early July the British Board of Trade Inquiry was wrapping up and it was clear that the Senator had made some demonstrably unfair accusations.

The British Inquiry

The British Wreck Commissioner's Inquiry on behalf of the British Board of Trade began on the very day that the four surviving officers had boarded the *Adriatic* in New York for their journey home, so it started in their absence. There was an obvious irony that the Board of Trade was conducting these hearings, as it was their own regulations that had led to ships sailing without adequate lifeboats – a fact that lay at the very heart of the tragedy. With a total of 42 days of investigation spread over three months, with nearly 100 witnesses, the hearings took place primarily at the London Scottish Drill Hall at 59 Buckingham Gate, London and were presided over by High Court judge Lord Mersey (John Charles Bigham, 1st Viscount Mersey) who had a background in commercial law and politics. Unlike the Senate sessions, Mersey called upon the services of those with specific experience at sea, with nautical assessors such as Captain Arthur Wellesley Clarke and Commander Fitzhugh Lyon, RNR.

Second Officer Lightoller, who appeared over the course of three days – the twelfth, thirteenth and fourteenth days of the Inquiry (21–23 May 1912) – held a much higher opinion of the proceedings compared to his experience in the States:

> Such a contrast to the dignity and decorum of the court held by Lord Mersey in London, where the guiding spirit was a sailor in essence,

'In the Hands of the Evil One'

and who insisted, when necessary, that any cross-questioner should at any rate be familiar with at least the rudiments of the sea... In Washington it was of little consequence, but in London it was necessary to keep one's hand on the whitewash brush. Sharp questions that needed careful answers if one was to avoid a pitfall, carefully and subtly dug, leading to a pinning down of blame on to someone's luckless shoulders.[28]

The Board of Trade's conflict of interest was not lost on Lightoller. He wrote of having his 'hand on the whitewash brush' and described himself as 'more like a legal doormat than a Mail Boat Officer.' Following the unfavourable outcome of the Senate Inquiry and the occasional instances of the four deck officers divulging more information than required, resulting in complications, they exhibited a more cautious approach on this occasion. Their responses were conservative and limited to essential information, refraining from providing any unnecessary additional details that could unfairly incriminate them. They were

Figure 54: The surviving deck officers of the *Titanic*, photographed shortly after the disaster, probably in May 1912, along with their signatures. From left: Fifth Officer Harold Lowe, Third Officer Herbert Pitman (seated), Second Officer Charles Lightoller and Fourth Officer Joseph Boxhall. (Mary Evans Picture Library / Onslow Auctions Limited)

doubtless under legal instructions from the White Star lawyers to weigh their answers carefully.

This caused frustration for Mersey, who described Lightoller's testimony as 'not at all satisfactory ... it seems to contain contradictions and statements which it is very difficult to reconcile with what we know to have been the facts.'[29]

Titanic's second officer did take the opportunity to defend his captain. When confronted with the claim that it 'was recklessness, utter recklessness, in view of the conditions to proceed at 21½ knots' Lightoller replied: 'Then all I can say is that recklessness applies to practically every commander and every ship crossing the Atlantic Ocean.'[30]

Lightoller's fellow surviving officers (Figure 54) appeared over a similar time – Pitman on day thirteen and Boxhall and Lowe on days thirteen and fourteen. Fifth Officer Lowe in particular provided muted, short answers, clearly on the advice of his legal counsel after the issues of drinking and racism had blighted his America evidence. Lightoller was the only married man of the four officers. Author Daniel Allen Butler wrote that Sylvia Lightoller 'faithfully attended every session of the Board of Trade Inquiry. To her it was a question of keeping faith with her husband's colleagues, living and dead.'[31]

Eleanor's Letter

If Eleanor Smith ever attended any of the sessions is unknown. She was likely disinclined and too busy managing correspondence. A few weeks after the officers testified, on Thursday 6 June 1912, she wrote a letter to Frank Hancock to answer correspondence she had received from him that had included a photograph of his family. He had, in all probability, written a letter of both sympathy and encouragement, especially after receiving such words of confidence from Mallock aboard the *Lapland*. Eleanor's response is a seven-page letter, written in pencil on Woodhead letterhead, on black-bordered mourning stationery (Figure 56). In parts it is barely legible; grief may have affected her, or simply the number of letters a 50-year-old widow was expected to write in response to an outpouring of affection for her lost husband may have taken its toll. To Frank, she even admits that she cannot write 'a decent letter as I would like, it is too trying even yet, so please excuse.'

The volume of correspondence was immense, so it is not surprising that Eleanor made use of a printed thank you card, four and half inches by three inches, that she could post in response to all the messages of sympathy she was receiving (Figure 55).

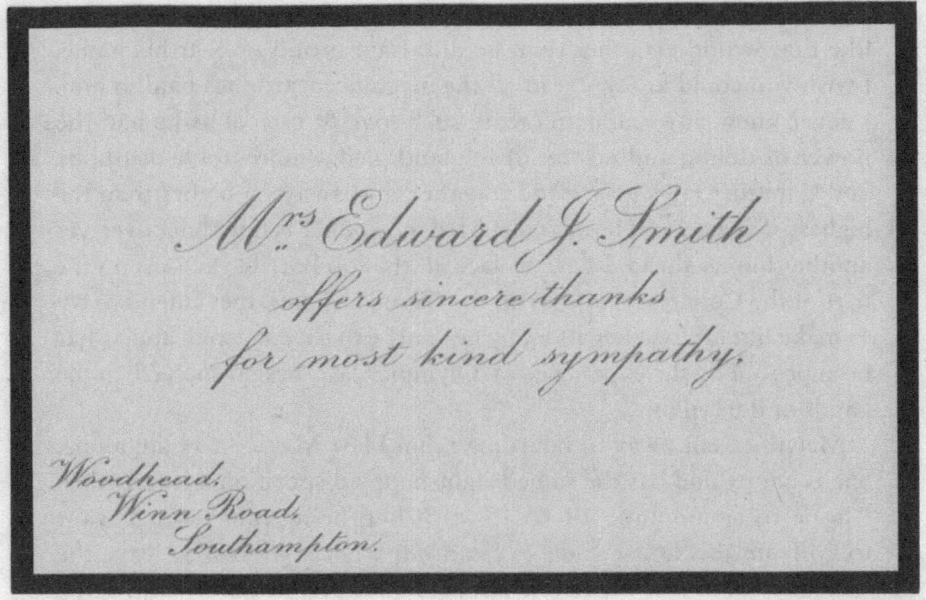

Figure 55: An example of the card Eleanor sent in response to many messages of sympathy she received, with a black mourning border. (Courtesy of Donald J. A. Smith)

The more in-depth letter to Frank reveals she was aware of news reports and offers glimmers of hope for Mel, the 'vivacious golden-haired' girl who had lost her father:

Telephone 1400.
Woodhead,
Winn Road,
Southampton.

Dear Frank
I'm sorry to be long in answering your letter and picture of your family which I am pleased to have. What a lovely outlook from your home. By the 'Olympic' I have sent to you a Menu of 'The Dinner', Dec. 28th, 1911, my dear one said only in March, 1912, he wanted you to have a copy, which of course I could not send not having your address. I am more than proud of that picture – I have a large one of 'the dinner' – it's a great souvenir to hand down to his Gillie and her children please God, and he seemed to think you also might be proud to possess a menu, his own was bound in white Morocco, edged with silver bands. I suppose you have a nice picture of him, the last one taken on 'Olympic' in his white uniform, if not I could let you have a copy taken from it, it's

a glorious picture so spirited and fearless, no one with an expression like that would do other than he did. I am proud to bear his name, I wish you could know – read all the magnificent tributes paid to him. I never knew any one man create such love & esteem as he had the power of doing, and no son of England died a more noble death, he and Captain Oates may stand together, and away up higher than the highest. The way has been and is hard, no sooner is one thing over, yet another looms ahead. I have to face all the too horrible actions on the part of the Congress working up the 'Titanic' claims, they intend to try to make out faulty navigation, by lies only can they succeed, and as has been proved by the experience of 'Olympic' case, lies do succeed, in the hands of the evil one.

Melville went away to boarding school last May 7th so I am alone. She is happy and has the same bright-happy disposition as her Father. I hope to spend June 14 & 15 with her, being mid-term. I want to go from this house soon as I can but what a wrench to leave the sacred room of his, where one last said goodbye. I cannot write you a decent letter as I would like, it is too trying even yet, so please excuse. I wish I had a picture of myself to send you, my dear Ted was always asking me to have one done, as Melville now is. Did you know of the memorials they have put up in Hanley? A brass tablet & two pictures in the old school. There is also to be something in New York, in the Seamen's Church Institute and now I hear there is something on foot in England. I believe the Duke of Sutherland is the chairman, and some very prominent men on Committee including Lord Pierre, Bishops of Ripon and Willisden. Did you ever hear of dear Ted saving the child? it is quite true and so like him.

I should much like to hear from you again. Receive my Kindest message for yourself and family to whom I hope enjoy good health.

Very Sincere Love
S. Eleanor Smith

Eleanor included with her letter a copy of the menu from the memorable 'Dinner' that was held in his honour in December 1911. In referencing the famous photograph taken of Smith aboard the *Olympic* in his white summer uniform (that she gave *The Sphere* permission to reproduce on 27 April 1912 – see Figure 22) Eleanor described her lost husband as 'so spirited and fearless ... I am proud to bear his name.' There is no hesitation in her support. One particular detail catches her attention – of 'dear Ted saving the child' which she states, 'is quite true and so like him'.

'In the Hands of the Evil One'

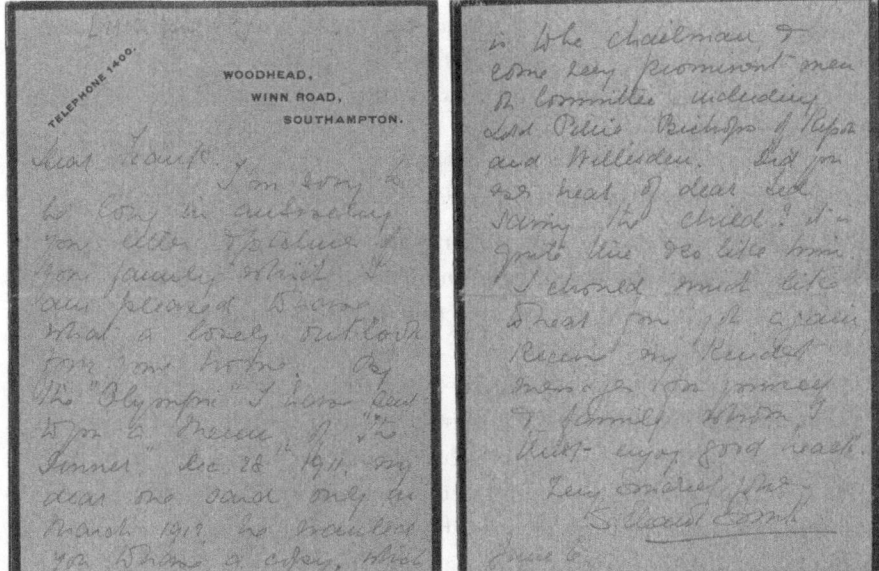

Figure 56: First and last page from a seven-page letter by Eleanor Smith to Frank Hancock, shortly after the *Titanic* tragedy, written in pencil on mourning stationery. (Reprinted by kind permission of the Mystic Seaport Museum: VFM 194, Manuscripts Collection, G.W. Blunt White Library, Mystic Seaport Museum)

She compares her Ted to 'Captain Oates' – a reference to Captain Lawrence Oates, a 32-year-old British army officer who sacrificed his life for his team during the doomed Robert Scott expedition to the South Pole only a month before, on 17 March 1912.[32] Tributes, such as his monument in Holy Trinity Church, Meanwood, Leeds, use the phrase 'A Very Gallant Gentleman', a parallel of how 'Be British' became Smith's Edwardian mantra. On the other hand, Eleanor's letter reveals she was painfully aware of the bad press, especially after the 'horrible actions on the part of the Congress'.

When Eleanor returns to writing about Mel, she says she will visit her on 14 and 15 June as that is 'mid-term', which suggests that Mel is boarding some distance away from the Southampton home. The loss of her father may have also prompted Mel to ask her mother for a photograph, which she admits she does not have. The memorials in Hanley and in New York would be realised in the years to come.

Mersey's Final Report

The final report of the British Wreck Commissioner's Inquiry was not published until 30 July 1912 and ultimately decided that the disaster was 'due to collision with an iceberg, brought about by the excessive speed at which the ship was being navigated', but it did not blame the Board of Trade, the White Star Line or the *Titanic*'s Captain.

Regarding the accusations of excessive speed, Mersey firstly established the historical context:

> It was shown that for many years past, indeed, for a quarter of a century or more, the practice of liners using this [southern] track when in the vicinity of ice at night had been in clear weather to keep the course, to maintain the speed and to trust to a sharp look-out to enable them to avoid the danger. This practice, it was said, had been justified by experience, no casualties having resulted from it. I accept the evidence as to the practice and as to the immunity from casualties which is said to have accompanied it. But the event has proved the practice to be bad. Its root is probably to be found in competition and in the desire of the public for quick passages rather than in the judgment of navigators. But unfortunately experience appeared to justify it.[33]

Indeed, during the inquiry several captains had testified confirming that maintaining speed under such conditions was standard practice. This was supported by the statistics. Sir Walter J. Howell, Chief of the Marine Department at the Board of Trade, testified that between 1892 and 1901, 3¼ million passengers were carried in British ships and, of those, there were a total of 73 casualties. Between 1902 and 1911, there were twice as many passengers – 6 million – and yet the number of casualties was 9.[34] Even with the greater size of ships built and the increasing number of passengers, the number of deaths was decreasing.

Specifically, in regard to Captain Smith's behaviour, the report freed him of blame:

> I am not able to blame Captain Smith. He had not the experience which his own misfortune has afforded to those whom he has left behind, and he was doing only that which other skilled men would have done in the same position. It was suggested at the bar that he was yielding to influences which ought not to have affected him; that the presence of Mr. Ismay on board and the knowledge which he perhaps had of a conversation between Mr. Ismay and the Chief Engineer [Bell] at Queenstown about the speed of the ship and the consumption of coal probably induced him to neglect precautions which he would otherwise have taken. But I do not believe this. The evidence shows that he was not trying to make any record passage or indeed any exceptionally quick passage. He was not trying to please anybody, but was exercising his own discretion in the way he thought best. He made a mistake, a

very grievous mistake, but one in which, in face of the practice and of past experience, negligence cannot be said to have had any part; and in the absence of negligence it is, in my opinion, impossible to fix Captain Smith with blame. It is, however, to be hoped that the last has been heard of the practice and that for the future it will be abandoned for what we now know to be more prudent and wiser measures. What was a mistake in the case of the 'Titanic' would without doubt be negligence in any similar case in the future.[35]

So Smith's navigational practices were so common that they could not be considered negligent, but they would be considered negligent going forward. There were also contradictory headlines in the press. On 31 July 1912, the day after the final report was submitted, the *Daily Herald* ran with 'CAPTAIN SMITH'S ERROR' while the *Evening Mail* printed 'CAPTAIN SMITH NOT TO BLAME' and the *Daily Mirror* 'NO NEGLIGENCE' and 'NO BLAME FOR CAPTAIN' while the *Evening Standard* ran with 'CAPTAIN NOT BLAMED'.

Eleanor and Mel must have been somewhat relieved at the news. Yet, there were to be more court cases to follow – and not all of them favourable.

Fourteen Captains

One of the key reasons Mersey's final report did not blame Captain Smith was the testimony of fourteen contemporary captains of similar experience on the North Atlantic service brought in to give their unique professional perspective on what happened. Their statements, made under oath, are important for the simple reason that not only was Smith no longer alive to defend the claims made against him, but also his Chief Officer (Wilde) and First Officer (Murdoch) were lost in the disaster. There was a large amount of critical evidence lost to the sea.

There were also some ethics at play here, as it was considered morally unacceptable to lay blame on the shoulders of a man unable to defend himself. Lord Mersey stated that he had been told it was 'not the practice to find negligence against a dead man', which was confirmed by Mr Aspinall, an Admiralty counsel for the Government, who said: 'I have never known a case, and I have always known this, that the Court has shown the greatest reluctance to accede to any such suggestion.' Lord Mersey agreed saying he felt 'the greatest reluctance to finding negligence against a man who cannot be heard'.[36]

So, these highly skilled captains with decades of experience were as close as one could get to hearing Captain Smith defend himself. Although working in competitor lines, they all agreed on basic protocols common to every seafaring ship regarding speed, ice warnings, binoculars and lookouts – all of which essentially freed Smith of blame. The eleven captains who testified during the British Inquiry were:

1. **Captain John Pritchard (retired)**, who formerly commanded Cunard's record-setting *Mauretania*, which was capable of 26 knots (at least 3 knots faster than *Titanic*). He testified on day 27 of the British Inquiry that even with 'information that there was a probability of your meeting ice on your course' he would maintain speed: 'As long as the weather is clear I always go full speed.' Pritchard also explained that this was in his experience a 'universal practice' – based on his time commanding Cunard ships between Liverpool and New York for 18 years. He also noted that if following the southern track – as did Captain Smith – he had 'never got into an ice-field. We do not go North, you know; we go on the southern tracks this time of year.' As for lookouts, he would not double them when in 'clear weather'.[37]

2. **Captain Hugh Young (retired)**, of the Anchor Line, with 37 years' experience crossing the Atlantic on the New York trade, testified under oath that if ice were reported, he 'should keep my course and maintain my speed' in clear weather. He also confirmed this was a 'universal practice'.[38]

3. **Captain William Stewart (retired)**, Canadian Pacific, worked for 38 years on the route between Liverpool and Canada. He was posed the question, if you 'were given information that you might meet ice and that your course would take you through the place where you might meet ice, and meet it at night, would you reduce your speed?' His answer was: 'No, not as long as it was clear.' Then, 'if you had information that you might meet field ice, would you still maintain your speed?' and he responded similarly: 'Until I saw it, and then I should do what I thought proper.'[39]

4. **Captain John A. Fairfull (retired)**, of the Allan Line concurred with the previous evidence of Pritchard, Young and Stewart. He had worked the Atlantic for 21 years. He was asked: 'Is your practice in accordance with theirs?' And he answered, 'All except that when we get to the ice track in an Allan steamer, besides having a look-out in the crow's-nest, we put a man on the stem head at night.'[40]

5. **Captain Andrew Braes (retired)**, who commanded steamers of the Allan Line for 17 years, also confirmed not changing speed or course

in good visibility – 'Just the same. I never slowed down so long as the weather was clear... I kept my course... I never knew any other practice.'[41]

6. **Captain Frederick Passow**, who had been a captain on the North Atlantic for 28 years, for the Inman and American Lines, and who had crossed about 700 times, testified that he 'had a very large experience of ice' and yet did not slacken his speed for ice as long as the weather was quite clear: 'Not as long as it was quite clear – no, not until we saw it ... when it is absolutely clear we do not slow down for ice.'[42]

7. **Captain Bertram F. Hayes**, of the White Star Line, testified that with a position of reported ice he would continue 'at the same rate of speed ... No alteration ... it is the practice all over the world so far as I know – every ship that crosses the Atlantic ... Ice does not make any difference to speed in clear weather. You can always see ice then.'[43]

8. **Captain Benjamin Steele**, marine superintendent at Southampton for the White Star Line and master mariner with an Extra Master's certificate of 19 years having been at sea 'about 26 or 27 years' confirmed the practice of 'not slackening speed on account of ice as long as the weather is clear' by responding 'It is. I have never known any other practice.'[44]

9. **Captain Richard Jones**, master of the SS *Canada* of the Dominion Line and in the Canadian service for 27 years, testified that his ship was stopped by ice on 11 April 1912. However, he also confirmed that after receiving messages about the ice he continued at full speed ahead, considering it a usual practice. He said: 'I should think it would be just as safe to go full speed with 22 knots ... we always make what speed we can ... we always try to get through the ice track as quickly as possible in clear weather.'[45]

10. **Captain Edwin Galton Cannons** of the Atlantic Transport Company with 25 years' experience in the North Atlantic, noted that he had 'never seen field ice on the southern track'. He testified if an iceberg is sighted that 'I keep my speed ... Both day and night ... I have never had any difficulty to clear when I have met ice ahead.' If ice is reported, he said: 'I should maintain my speed and keep an exceptionally sharp look-out ... to maintain speed until the ice is seen.' If it was clear, he confirmed he would not double the look-out.[46]

11. **Captain John Ranson** of the White Star Line's *Baltic* on the Liverpool-New York run, and who had been in communication with the *Titanic*, sending details of ice in a message that Smith

handed to Ismay, also confirmed the standard practice: 'We go full speed whether there is ice reported or not.' He also stated that it is the practice of all liners on that course 'for the last 21 years to my knowledge' and that he would not double the look-outs at night – 'not in clear weather'.[47]

There were so many captains ready to confirm that Captain Smith followed standard procedures, at one point Mersey said: 'May we take it they say the same?' To which Aspinall replied: 'They do according to their proofs.' There was one dissenting voice, and from a surprising witness to take the stand at the British Inquiry – Sir Ernest Shackleton. He did not need an introduction, even for the record, such was the Antarctic explorer's fame. When posed with a similar question to the previous captains on day 26 of the inquiry, he responded:

> I would take the ordinary precaution of slowing down, whether I was in a ship equipped for ice or any other... You have no right to go at that speed in an ice zone... I would put a look-out man in the bow or as near to the waterline as possible, even on a clear night, but I would only have one man in the crow's-nest.

He was a polar explorer, however, not a North Atlantic captain on a regular transatlantic Royal Mail service. His experience was vastly different. And only three years later, he was to lose a ship himself – the 1912 ship *Endurance* – to the very ice he warned the inquiry about. In a bitter irony, he had ignored warnings about ice conditions when he embarked on his fateful Antarctic expedition.

Despite Mersey's conclusion that Smith was not to be blamed, Eleanor's ordeal was not over, as in June 1913 there was yet another court case, with a much less favourable outcome. Billed as the 'third Titanic inquiry', Ryan v. OSNC was brought before Justice Bailhache and a special jury in a case in which Thomas Ryan sued the White Star Line (Oceanic Steam Navigation Company Limited) for the loss of his 29-year-old son, Patrick Ryan, a third class passenger who was travelling aboard *Titanic* to start a new life in the New York Police Department. His body was never recovered, and the father took legal action to recover damages.[48] All of *Titanic*'s officers were questioned again, as well as six captains – three of whom had already testified at the British Inquiry, plus Captains Apfeld, Roberts and Warr. Once again, these were captains from various competitor lines with considerable experience and when questioned on day two and three of the case (23 and 24 June 1913), they were unanimous about Smith's behaviour:

'In the Hands of the Evil One'

1. **Captain Edwin Galton Cannons** knew Captain Smith personally and said he was 'an officer of great experience and high position and a man they all admired'. According to the transcript for the prècis Law Report for the case, Cannons was asked by Henry Duke K.C., for the defendant: 'When you are in the North Atlantic and ice is reported, what is the usual course with regard to speed in fair weather?' To which Cannons responded: 'We maintain the course and speed.' When asked, 'How long has that been the practice?' he said it was 'during the whole of my sea service'.[49]
2. **Captain John Pritchard (retired)** stated that while the *Mauretania* had a speed of 26¼ miles an hour and she and the *Lusitania* were 'the fastest ships afloat,' he was adamant that 'in clear weather his practice was to maintain his course and speed in the ice area until he saw ice ... he would not reduce speed in the neighbourhood of ice.'
3. **Captain Gerhard Christopher Apfeld**, a marine superintendent of the Red Star Line, had been 39 years at sea and 'had considerable experience in navigating in the ice region of the North Atlantic. In clear weather, it was his practice to maintain course and speed. On a clear dark night, an iceberg could be seen about four miles away.'
4. **Captain Bertram Fox Hayes** of the White Star Line said that when he received reports of ice in clear weather, his practice was to carry on the ordinary routine of the ship. 'The danger of the ice region was not a danger of ice, but a danger of fog. In clear weather a berg could be seen from five to six miles away at night.' Hayes was an interesting witness, as he had worked as an officer under Captain Smith for five or six years and was able to testify that the Captain 'was a careful navigator, and never took a risk or in his opinion came to an unwise decision. He [Hayes] also knew Mr. Murdoch, who had been an officer under him. He was a capable, efficient, and zealous officer.'
5. **Captain Roberts** of the American Line, with 37 years' sea experience, 'agreed with the evidence given by the previous witnesses as to the practice in clear weather in the ice region of the North Atlantic ... on a dark night with a smooth sea he had himself detected an iceberg as far away as eight miles.'
6. **Captain Warr (retired)** of Cunard, with 49 years' experience, was the last of the captains to testify and stated that 'the practice in the ice region in fair weather was to maintain course and speed until ice was sighted. A normal berg can be seen on a clear dark night four or five miles away.'

With such consistent evidence, it would seem impossible to accuse Smith of negligence. It must have come as a shock when the jury returned a verdict on 25 June that 'there had been negligence as regards to speed.' It seemed a judgement that flew in the face of the fourteen captains' 478 years of combined maritime experience. To understand the verdict, it must be seen in context. The primary objective of the court case was not to establish the cause of the disaster but to win compensation for the loss of a son, with much of the evidence discussing ticket conditions. It analysed a passenger's position in law, the meaning of a ticket as a contract and explored how the son's ticket had conditions that were not in a form approved by the Board of Trade, and he was unlikely to have been aware of the details. It became a test case for consumer rights. It did not change maritime law.[50]

Shaw vs Doyle and Captain Turner

The unfavourable result of the Ryan case was not the only criticism of Smith in the year following the disaster. Irish playwright George Bernard Shaw, in response to Captain Smith's heroic portrayal, wrote a scathing article entitled 'Some Unmentioned Morals' that was published in the *Daily News* of 14 May 1912, to counter what he believed was a romanticising of the tragedy:

> Though all the men must be heroes... the captain must be a super-hero, a magnificent seaman, cool, brave, delighting in death and danger, and a living guarantee that the wreck was nobody's fault, but, on the contrary, a triumph of British navigation. Such a man Captain Smith was enthusiastically proclaimed on the day when it was reported (and actually believed, apparently) that he had shot himself on the bridge, or shot the first officer, or been shot by the first officer, or shot anyhow to bring the curtain down effectively. Writers who had never heard of Captain Smith to that hour wrote of him as they would hardly write of Nelson. The one thing positively known was that Captain Smith had lost his ship by deliberately and knowingly steaming into an ice field at the highest speed he had coal for. He paid the penalty; so did most of those for whose lives he was responsible. Had he brought them and the ship safely to land, nobody would have taken the smallest notice of him.[51]

Sir Arthur Conan Doyle responded to Shaw's article in the same newspaper five days later, containing a point-by-point rebuttal of the claims – 'How a man could write with such looseness and levity of such an event at such a time passes all comprehension.'

> His next paragraph is devoted to the attempt to besmirch the conduct of Capt. Smith. He does it by his favourite method of 'suggestio falsi' – the false suggestion being that the sympathy shown by the public for Capt. Smith took the shape of condoning Capt. Smith's navigation ... the sympathy was at the spectacle of an old and honoured sailor who has made one terrible mistake, and who deliberately gave his life in the reparation, discarded his lifebelt, working to the last for those whom he had unwillingly injured, and finally swimming with a child to a boat in to which he himself refused to enter.[52]

Doyle's defence included a pledge to contribute £100 to the Fabian Society if Shaw could show him any newspaper report wherein Smith was described 'in the terms of Nelson'. Two days later, Shaw rejected the offer 'of £100 to the Fabian Society for every hyper-Nelsonic eulogy of the late Captain Smith' stating that while he wanted the Fabian Society solvent, he would not wish it at the cost of 'utter destitution to a friend'. More interestingly, he addressed concerns over adding to the suffering of Captain Smith's family:

> I should not run the risk of adding to the distress of Captain Smith's family by adding one word to the facts that speak only too plainly for themselves if others had been equally considerate. But if vociferous journalists will persist in glorifying the barrister whose clients are hanged, the physician whose patients die, the general who loses battles, and the captain whose ship goes to the bottom, such false coin must be nailed to the counter at any cost. There have been British captains who ... have kept discipline in the face of death and not lost one life that could have been saved... These are the men who I admire and with whom I prefer to sail... No excuse, however good, can turn a failure into a success...
>
> The Captain of the Titanic did not, as Sir Arthur thinks, make 'a terrible mistake'. He made no mistake. He knew perfectly well that ice is the only risk that is considered deadly in his line of work, and, knowing it, he chanced it and lost the hazard. Sentimental idiots, with a break in the voice, tell me that 'he went down to the depths.' I tell them, with the impatient contempt that they deserve, that so did the cat.[53]

Doyle decided to respond with a simple statement that expressed his intent to close the discussion 'without continuing a controversy ... the worst I think or say of Mr. Shaw is that his many brilliant gifts do not include the power of weighing evidence, nor has he that quality – call it good taste, humanity, or what you will – which prevents a man from needlessly hurting the feelings of others.'[54]

There was another moment when Smith came in for criticism – and this time from a captain of similar ilk. Two years after the compensation case against White Star was won, the United States District Court held a series of Limitation of Liability Hearings in 1915, a civil court action to determine financial liability. One of the witnesses was 59-year-old British Captain William T. Turner, from Liverpool, who had worked for Cunard for 32 years and appeared before the hearing on 30 April 1915. He was asked what he would have done differently and said that he would have gone farther south to avoid the ice and 'if she was a big ship I could slow her down much more than a small one.'[55] He even drew a pencil sketch on a yellow pad detailing the southern course deviation of 65 miles, claiming that the practice of a course change and speed reduction has 'always been the practice in the Cunard Company with everybody; the Company's explicit orders'. And that when in the vicinity of ice, they would 'take all due precautions and slow the ship down'.

Turner's testimony obviously contradicted that of his colleagues at Cunard – specifically Captain Pritchard and Captain Warr at the earlier 1912 and 1913 hearings. This was pointed out to him during the questioning, that according to them 'the Cunard boats kept their course and speed in clear weather at night, even when they had reports of ice in the track,' to which Turner responded: 'I generally slowed down; I don't know what other Captains did.' Surely, if it was 'Company's explicit orders' the other captains would have no choice but to follow suit. When asked if 'in clear weather by night or by day in the ice region' would he slow down or continue at full speed, Turner answered, 'I continue on at full speed in clear weather in daytime.' And when asked about night-time he concurred he would do the same. So essentially once in an ice region, Turner would maintain speed.

The following day at 10 am he joined his ship in New York, the *Lusitania*. She departed on her return trip to Liverpool and on 7 May – a week after Turner's evidence against Captain Smith – he faced his own moment of reckoning when his ship was struck by a German torpedo. Swept off the bridge, Turner survived. He had received several warnings about U-boat activity prior to sailing and an investigation into the tragedy was presided over by the same Lord Mersey as the *Titanic*'s Board of Trade Inquiry. Turner faced an Admiralty who attempted to lay the blame on him – this time for failing to travel at high speed or take other precautions. In the end, he was absolved of any negligence.

If only Captain Smith had been so fortunate.

5

'A Deathless Crown at Duty's Post'

Just two days after the *Titanic* sinking, the Cable Ship (CS) *Mackay-Bennett* was the first of four ships chartered by the White Star Line to search for bodies, departing on 17 April 1912. After seven days of searching, the crew recovered 306 bodies, of which 116 were buried at sea. Despite an extensive search, the body of Captain Smith was never found, or at least never identified. The highest-ranking crew member to be retrieved was Chief Purser Hugh McElroy – the man who stood beside Smith in one of their last known photographs. McElroy's body, in a white 'ships uniform' was initially misidentified as 'Steward D. Lily' and buried at sea.[1] For all we know, Smith's body could have endured a similar fate. Recovering his body would have likely helped Eleanor and Mel in the grieving process, but was not to be. The lack of a body led to one very curious story.

Sightings

On 21 July 1912, a syndicated article appeared headlined 'COMMANDER OF TITANIC IS SEEN' – claiming Smith had not perished but had escaped and was living in Maryland in the United States. The account came from a Peter Pryal of Baltimore who was 'quartermaster on the SS *Majestic* of the White Star line 30 years ago when Smith was its captain':

> Pryal declares he saw Captain Smith first last Wednesday, and again yesterday when he talked with him. He says that when he saw the Captain on Wednesday he was dressed in a neat business suit, carrying two suit cases and appeared unconscious of his surroundings, failing to reply when spoken to by Pryal.

Returning to the same place yesterday Pryal declares Captain Smith again appeared after some time had elapsed, and as he approached Pryal greeted him with: 'Captain Smith, how are you?'

'Very well, Pryal, but please don't detain me. I am on business,' was the reply, says Pryal.

Pryal followed his old commander who turned and seeing him made an unsuccessful attempt to shake off his pursuer. Pryal followed him to the B. & O. depot, where Smith purchased a ticket for Washington and as he passed through the train gate, he turned and with a smile, said: 'Be good to yourself until we meet again.'

Pryal declares he will take an oath to the incident and is confident that Captain Smith was the man he talked with, as he would know him anywhere even without his whiskers.[2]

In another account Pyral described Smith as 'attired in a neat-fitting business suit of a light brown color, straw hat, and tan shoes, the man carried two suitcases and was staring straight ahead.'[3] Pryal was adamant about this story and in a *Washington Herald* follow-up article – which described him as 'still emphatic in his assertions' – he even went so far as to propose a method of escape for Smith:

> It would have been an easy matter for Capt. Smith, of the Titanic, to have gotten into a lifeboat attired as a passenger, and again, knowing as he did the proximity of Barren Island, might have, under difficulties, of course, made his way there and thence to Cape Sable. Whether or not he did this or was saved in another way, I do not know, but I do know that he is alive and that I saw him. I would know him anywhere and under any circumstances.[4]

A separate account in August 1912 revealed that Pryal was 'on his way to the office of Dr. Mactier Warfield for treatment for an internal disorder' when the sighting occurred and that the same doctor treating Pryal 'felt he was perfectly sane'.[5] That sanity was later called into question when in 1914 Pryal was once again in the news as the 72-year-old proclaimed he had found the cure for cancer. The article stated: 'In answer to his prayers to the virgin mother for two years a cancer on his nose from which he has suffered for the last 27 years has been cured... The old man said he retired one night, and on awakening he discovered that the cancer, which had been eating its way into his left eye and into his brain, had been cured.'[6] It is quite plausible that his cancer had a part to play in his vision of Captain Smith.

The White Star Line was certainly of the opinion that Pryal's sighting of Smith was not to be taken seriously. Pryal's claim was 'received with incredulity ... This Baltimore captain's story must be either the result of delusion or mistaken identity.'[7]

There was yet another story later in 1912 of someone meeting Captain Smith in the United States, with far darker undertones. Sophie Adelaide Radford de Meissner (1854–1957) was an American author who became a proponent of spiritualism, publishing a book entitled *There Are No Dead* in 1912 in which she claimed, after the death of her only son, to have conversations with deceased family, friends, and those who died aboard the *Titanic*, including Captain Smith:

> I will here state what came to me as I read the verdict of the British court of inquiry pronounced on July 30th by Lord Mersay [sic], the presiding Judge. In reading the words: 'In the circumstances I am unable to blame Captain Smith. Other skilled men would have done the same thing in the same position,' I hear Captain Smith say: 'I thank God for that – I have wished and wished and wished I might know how that investigation ended and now I have read it when you read it, and I cannot sufficiently thank God for showing it to me. I don't see how I could have done otherwise than as I did. I had done it hundreds of times before and nothing had ever happened. Every captain who crosses the ocean does it. It is wrong of course but then it is the custom. Could we know such terrible conditions as had never been known before prevailed? As I said before, those long ships are too unwieldy to use in crossing the ocean or in any other place. Tell them if they use them again there will be just such another accident and they must give them up. No other ship must be built of the size of the 'Titanic'. It will be fatal to many more people than were lost on her. I insist upon your publishing this. It is most important. That is all. Smith – late Captain of the Titanic.'[8]

This press-inspired fantasy was not the end of it. Several years later, there was another sighting involving a 'down-and-out' in Ohio, who was known locally as 'Whispering' Smith' and 'who claimed shortly before his death that he was the former captain of the Titanic!'[9] *Life* magazine, in 1940, carried a similar story that three years after the sinking an 'unknown, penniless man, whom local police called "Silent Smith" died in Lima, Ohio.' The Irish seaman, with 'The Rock of Ages' tattooed on his chest, would not speak other than to mutter 'Smith'. His body, which allegedly matched the weight and height of the *Titanic* captain, was embalmed by a local undertaker to allow time to identify him. In a dramatic extra detail, the article, which includes a grisly photograph, claims that the hair on the mummified body continued to grow and every now and then needed to be cut.[10] Stories such as these inspired the satirical tabloid the *Weekly World*

News to run the headline, 'Titanic Captain Found in Lifeboat' in 1991, insisting he was picked up by a Navy ship still wearing his 'fresh 1900s officer's uniform' and 'thinks it's April 15, 1912 – and his pipe is still lit!'[11]

In subsequent years, there have been further paranormal stories about the Captain. One was that Eleanor Smith was in her drawing room in 1912 when the door opened and she watched Ted walk across toward the window. He ignored her and then disappeared. News of the *Titanic* disaster had not yet been published and yet, as the story goes, 'she knew' he had died.[12] In 2018 the *Titanic* Captain's 'Haunted Mirror' came up for auction in Lichfield, with an associated story that it once belonged to Smith's housekeeper and she saw the Captain's face in the silver-framed easel mirror every year on the anniversary of the sinking.[13] Closer examination of the facts related to the alleged artifact raise considerable doubt as to its provenance.[14]

In August 1912, 19-year-old John Smith in Salt Lake City, Utah, claimed to be the son of the Captain when he was arrested for trying to pawn a suit that he did not own, stating at the police station: 'I don't care what you do with me, for my life is worth nothing to me since my father, Captain Smith, went down in the Titanic.'[15]

St Mary's Church Service and Personal Tributes

On the sunny afternoon of Saturday 20 April 1912 – just five days after the sinking – Eleanor made an appearance at an elaborate church service in Southampton. Curiously, no local Southampton newspaper referred to her attendance. Syndicated accounts in various regional newspapers in their Monday 22 April editions noted it. The *Staffordshire Sentinel* printed the following:

> CAPTAIN'S WIDOW AT SERVICE
>
> Mrs. Smith, the widow of Captain Smith, was present at a memorial service at St. Mary's Church, Southampton. The Bishop of Winchester, who preached the sermon, said the disaster was a mighty lesson against our security and confidence and trust in the strength of machinery and money. The name Titanic would stand as a monument of warning against human presumption.[16]

This was a large-scale event. There were prominent representatives (Lord Winchester as Lord Lieutenant of the County represented the King), and a grand procession from High Street to the church grounds, with sailors and officers from White Star and the American Line that journalists described as 'In Memory of the Brave, Southampton's Tribute to Her Sailor Sons.'[17]

With more than a thousand in attendance there was not enough room in the church, so crowds gathered outside. The service began with the hymn 'Rock of Ages' followed with a sermon by the Bishop of Winchester, who was perhaps thinking of Eleanor when he warned the congregation 'against anger and recrimination', which, he felt, would 'tarnish the holy sorrow of the day'.[18] The service concluded with the hymn 'Eternal Father, Strong to Save'. There was scarcely a dry eye in the building. There were reports of grieving women sobbing and some who had broken down completely and had to be escorted outside during the service.

Attending such an event, when eyes would have been focused on the Captain's widow, must have taken a huge toll on Eleanor. One report indicates that she was 'accompanied by a close family friend, Mr G Dominey [sic], but her brave attempt to conceal her sorrow presented him with a source of deep concern'.[19] The family friend was a Mr George Dominy, J.P. of Southampton, who later wrote a tribute: 'We all of us here had great regard for the Commander of the 'Titanic' and shall always mourn his loss to his family, his country and ourselves.'[20] It is maybe not surprising that there is no record of her attending any other of the large *Titanic* services that took place.

In the absence of a recovered body and subsequent funeral, which would have provided some sense of closure, Eleanor and Mel would likely have taken comfort in the number of tributes paid to Captain Smith in the wake of the disaster. And there were many. Some were official. On the same day as the Southampton memorial service, Eleanor received a personal message from the King of Spain via the White Star Line: 'Please accept sincere condolence for awful disaster of Titanic, and express to family of Captain Smith, whom I met last year on board the Olympic, our heartfelt sympathies. Alfonso R.' The White Star Line replied, 'Your Majesty's kind message is deeply appreciated and its contents have been communicated to Captain Smith's widow.'[21] It seems that the Captain met the King and Queen of Spain while they were on a visit to Princess Henry of Battenberg on the Isle of Wight and took an opportunity to inspect the *Olympic* at Southampton. According to a lady friend, Eleanor wrote a personal reply to King Alfonso, 'who was a great admirer of Captain Smith'. This same friend indicated that Smith had rubbed shoulders with a number of royal and celebrity passengers: 'When the Titanic went down a book of the captain's containing the autographs of Royal passengers and eminent public men was lost.'[22]

Miss Lucy McNeill and the Larne Women's Unionist Association wrote to Mrs Smith and the White Star Line on 23 April 'to offer a tribute of heartfelt sympathy...We view with feelings of the highest admiration and pride the heroic manner in which the captain, officers and crew, aided by the passengers, upheld the honour of the Flag, and the best traditions of the sea, by sacrificing their lives to save the women and children.' They received a reply from Eleanor in early May:

> Dear Miss McNeill, – It is with the utmost gratitude I receive your very kind resolution of sympathy and condolence passed on behalf of myself, relatives of the officers, crew and passengers. I am indeed greatly touched by the Unionist women of Larne towards their sorrow-stricken fellow-creatures, and I beg you will convey to each member of your Association my most sincere and heartfelt thanks.[23]

British politicians also took opportunities to formally express their admiration for Captain Smith, such as when Lord Mersey's Board of Trade report was submitted to the House of Commons on 7 October 1912, Richard Holt (1868–1941), a Liberal Party politician with interests in shipping, remembered Captain Smith as 'an officer with whom I had the pleasure of sailing on many occasions, and for whose character and special abilities I had the very greatest respect. If he could be brought to life again I should still have the utmost confidence in him.'[24]

One of the earliest personal tributes was from a Colonel William Hester in Brooklyn, New York, who, along with John J. Sinclair, had expected to entertain the Captain at noon on Thursday 18 April. Hester submitted a eulogy to the *Brooklyn Eagle* newspaper that was printed on Wednesday the 17th:

> I have known Captain Smith a number of years and have crossed with him on the Baltic, Adriatic and Olympic and expected to cross with him again this summer on the Titanic. Except when I was out of town, I always met him when he was in New York and together with an old friend, John J. Sinclair, had expected to lunch with Captain Smith on Thursday (tomorrow). I have visited his home in Southampton and met his wife and daughter. Captain Smith had many friends in this city and was a frequent visitor at Glen Cove. Among those who entertained him there was Henry W.J. Bucknall, a fellow Englishman and a friend of long standing.
>
> Captain Smith had nothing of the old salt in his appearance. He was over six feet in height, well proportioned, fair complexion, and had the appearance of a military or naval officer. His manner was quiet and his address pleasing. It was not necessary for him to be severe in his tone on shipboard to command respect. His whole appearance did that, and as a prominent lady remarked, when introduced to him, 'His countenance inspired confidence.' He was very little in evidence on shipboard, being

'A Deathless Crown at Duty's Post'

only where his duty called him. The large circle of friends among ocean travellers that he had was not created by his catering to their society.[25]

In London, the Right Reverend William Wilcox Perrin wrote a letter published in a Southampton newspaper on Friday 19 April 1912, printed at the top of the correspondence section:

TRIBUTE TO CAPTAIN SMITH

Sir, – Amid the appalling gloom which must overshadow the town, it is some comfort to my mind to recall the character of the late captain of the Titanic. I have had the good fortune to have often crossed the Atlantic with Captain Smith, and he certainly was one of the strongest men I have ever known. I well remember once speaking to him of the immense responsibility he had with so many lives depending upon him, and he realised it to the full. Familiarity with him had not bred contempt, and he took no risks. He was a splendid specimen of a British sailor, and I can imagine how he would have done his duty to the very last, for it seems certain that as he would have wished, he has gone down with his ship. May God comfort those near and dear to him, and at who at this awful trial are mourning their lost ones, and may England never fail to have such men in her mercantile marine.

Yours faithfully,
W. W. PERRIN
Bishop of Willesden

P.S. Will you kindly add the enclosed cheque for £5 5s. to the Relief Fund.[26]

Elsewhere, the Bishop of Willesden described Smith as 'the truest and best friend of every seaman and fireman on his ship [who] looked after steerage passengers as well as more favoured individuals.'[27] He would later be part of the ceremony unveiling a statue to Smith in Lichfield.

There was early poetry. Francis Seymour Stevenson wrote a poem that was published on 20 April 1912 in *The Southern Daily Echo*:

'The Bridge of the Titanic'
April 14th to 15th 1912
IN MEMORIAM
COMMANDER E.J. SMITH, R.D., R.N.R.

From fiery flames and frenzied force
Of raging hurricane, and shock

Of sunken reef or beetling rock,
Heaven shield, we pray, the vessel's course!
But, fiercer far than storm or fire,
Than reefs or rocks a subtler foe,
In silence floats the berg or floe,
Relentless broods the ice fiend's ire.

And he, whose strength of heart and brain
Has guided through the allotted span,
The short-lived Titan work of man
With skill and courage, dies to gain,
Amid death's grim and icy host,
A deathless crown at duty's post.[28]

Stevenson was a British Liberal politician with a penchant for poetry. The year before he had published *Poems: In Various Moods for Various Ages* (1911). He became the secretary for the Captain Smith Memorial Committee.

A poem appeared in the Monday 22 April edition of the *Southern Daily Echo*, which made comparisons to Smith with seafaring legends Francis Drake, Walter Raleigh and Lord Nelson and proposed that Viking blood ran in his veins:

Captain E.J. Smith.

His name was Smith! A common name,
Ay, common of the common place.
It stands today before the world,
Blessed with as fair a grace,
As any on the Scroll of Fame
Of our proud island race.

That Viking grim with dauntless pride,
His Raven from the Fjords flashed,
To brave the roarings of the gale;
The battle thunder crashed
When Drake his game of war-bowls plied,
Where helpless Spaniards lashed.

Lord Nelson in Trafalgar Bay
Sailed proudly through the Frenchmen's van,

'A Deathless Crown at Duty's Post'

While through the fleet like lightning fire
The famous signal ran
And the spirit of that bygone day
Lived in this Englishman.

His was the blood of Viking bold,
His was the heart of mighty Drake
He came of the Trafalgar stock,
Of Grenville, Raleigh, Blake.
In one short line his tale is told –
He died for Honour's sake.

C.L. Ross.[29]

Another poet, Edith Whitford, from the Isle of Wight, wrote a letter to the editor of the *Southern Echo* in which she proposed a memorial.

> I am sorry such base reports were circulated over the brave old skipper, Captain Smith. He died, as we all know, like the crew, a hero's death, and to their memory we can add 'Nobler in Heaven's sweet climate yet the same.' Southampton will no doubt erect a fitting memorial to her brave dead, and as a townswoman I shall be proud to send my subscription.[30]

Whitford's suggestion for a Southampton memorial to Captain Smith was not the only one published on 23 April. *The Times* of London, in its coverage of a tribute to Mr Hays, president of the Grand Trunk Railway, who was lost, added: 'It is suggested at Southampton that a memorial should be erected there to Captain Smith, commander of the Titanic.'[31] Such calls for a Southampton memorial fell on deaf ears. It is easy to see why. Directly following Whitford's letter to the *Southern Echo* editor were submissions from those seeking tribute for the 'sea post victims' and five emphatic letters about the heroism of the engineers, which the correspondents felt had been overlooked. An 'Engineer's Wife' wrote: 'There is a lot of praise given to various officers of the Titanic, but I have never seen a word mentioned of the engineers.' As it happened, impressive memorials were later erected in the city recognising the engineers, sea-post officers, restaurant staff, and musicians, while a 'Titanic Crew Memorial' lists the 'stewards, sailors and firemen' – short of any mention of the deck officers or indeed the ship's captain.[32]

Titanic Legacy: The Captain, the Daughter and the Spy

A year after the disaster, on 15 April 1913, the *Southern Echo* included another piece of poetry on Captain Smith, from the book *In Memoriam – The Titanic Disaster* by H. Rea Woodman of New York:

'Row toward that light,' the Captain said,
And he spoke full cheerily,
As from the side of the wounded ship
The little lifeboats swung free.

'Row toward that light,' the Captain said,
And his smile was sweet to see,
As he pointed to a dimming disk
That burned on the bitter sea.

'Straight for that light,' the Captain said,
And 'God speed you all!' cried he,
And waved adieu as the last lifeboat
Dropped into the bitter sea.

'God keep you safe,' the Captain said,
And 'A stout heart lives!' cried he,
Then leapt adown, as lover might,
To peace in the bitter sea.[33]

American writer Kate Douglas Wiggin, who had known Smith for many years, was almost poetic in her tribute: 'If I had gone down into the sea with him on that tragic, never-to-be-forgotten night, I believe with all my heart, that in the very midst of my terror and suffering I should have called out to him as I rose for the last time: "Good-bye, Captain! I'm sure you did your best! God bless and help us both!"'[34]

Passengers George Sherman and his wife of Honolulu, Hawaii, counted themselves as 'close personal friends', calling him 'their Captain Smith'. It was his ship that had taken them on their honeymoon, and they crossed a further six times while he was Master. They had even visited him at his home in Southampton and were 'close friends of Captain Smith's widow and daughter'. Mrs Sherman said that the Captain's ambition was to cross the Atlantic in 'a thousand-foot steamer'. Mr Sherman paid tribute to the man's character:

> He was a man in a class by himself, and the White Star Line for many years gave him command of the newest ships and of course the largest. He counted among his friends dozens of the best-known Americans,

many of whom would cross the Atlantic every year in whatever ship he commanded, spend their summers abroad and return with him, and him only, in the fall. One man boasted crossing more than twenty-one consecutive years with him. Captain Smith was genial, kind hearted and devoted to his friends. He was a loyal Briton and duty was always foremost with him.[35]

Another passenger, J. E. Hodder Williams of Hodder and Stoughton Publishers, was quoted in 1914 as saying:

> We crossed with him on many ships and in many companies, through seas fair and foul, and to us he was, and will ever be, the perfect sea-captain. In the little sea parties in his private state-room we learned to know the genial warm-hearted family man…
>
> He was amazingly informed on every phrase of present-day affairs, and that was hardly to be wondered at, for scarcely a well-known man or woman who crossed the Atlantic during the last twenty years but had sometime sat at his table. He read widely, but men more than books. He was a good listener … although he liked to get in a yarn himself now and again, but he had scant patience with bores or people who 'gushed'. I have seen him quell both…
>
> He had two passions, his home and his country. He was very British, almost insular for a man who had travelled so widely… An inspiring man to meet, was our friend Captain Smith, an inspiring man to serve under, if need be, to die with.[36]

Mrs O'Donnell in San Francisco, who knew Ted as a young boy in Hanley, considered him

> … a kindly, thoughtful and genial man. He never rose above his position, and I never knew him to forget that once he was listed on the ship's books as merely an able seaman. He never forgot his friends and loved to cherish memories of the days spent in the little town in England. Capt. Smith was one of the bravest men that ever lived. He was never known to have flinched in the face of the most serious danger. The utmost confidence was always placed in him by the owners of the ships he commanded. He was thoroughly reliable and conscientious, and was loved by everyone who knew him. They could not help it, for he seemed to be a man who was a friend to all who understood him.
>
> He always expected to go down with this ship, and I know he tried to do all in his power to save the lives of as many passengers as possible.

While he was supervising the taking off of the women and children, I know there was never a thought for himself. His family has been bereft of a loving husband and father, and I know his thoughts at the last moments were for them.[37]

William Jones, of Edmund Street in Hanley, supplied a touching tribute in the *Daily Sketch*, describing his schoolfriend 'Teddy Smith' as a 'genial and good schoolfellow; one always ready to give a kind of helping hand in any way to his mates ... he was a brave soul as a boy.' He expressed contempt at the suggestion of suicide and said that if any man had predicted Smith would react in such a way to an emergency he 'would be minus a few teeth before the words were well out of his mouth'. Mr Jones then observed: 'Teddy Smith has gone down with his ship, and out of the six of us lads who used to be schoolmates together only one is now left – myself.'[38]

David Thomson wrote that 'a more high-minded, clear-headed leader of men and things never lived, and we consider it one of our highest privileges to have known him.' Mr George Riggs noted an intangible quality: 'I have read many of the tributes to him who was ever my loving friend, but none of them as yet have portrayed the loveliness of his true soul. It could not be told, one must only have felt it.' John Hay went as far as to call it love: 'To know Captain Smith as I knew him was really to love him, and caused me more than once to delay my sailing date to have the privilege of going with him, sitting at his table and enjoying his many stories. How confident we all felt while under his care! God has seen fit to take to Himself one of the noblest lives He ever created!'[39]

Colleagues Pay their Respects

In addition to those who attended the inquiries and went on record defending Captain Smith's actions, there were other captains and officers who were willing to risk their reputation by going public with their admiration. One colleague was also a relative. James Harrington was the Captain's nephew and served two-and-a-half years under his uncle aboard the *Lizzie Fennell*. Just one day after the *Titanic* sinking, on 16 April, Harrington was already defending his uncle, as he was 'much depressed at the character of the latest dispatches. He has such faith in the skill and judgment of his distinguished relative, however, at present he is strongly inclined to the belief that subsequent telegrams will prove the inaccuracy and exaggerated character of much that has so far transpired.'[40]

'A Deathless Crown at Duty's Post'

Two days after the sinking, an article about 79-year-old Captain J. R. Mullet was published in *The Chicago Daily Tribune*. Mullet said of Smith:

> I was about ten years his senior, and he used to look to me for advice. He read day and night. I never knew a sea dog to study as Smith did. He was a man who saw far ahead. I never will forget how he would ask questions regarding navigation. Nothing else interested him. I watched his rise, and I was the happiest man in Chicago when I learned the White Star lines had made my former pupil the boss of the giant Titanic. There are few men like Capt. Smith.[41]

Another White Star captain, by the name of Anning, who knew Smith, described him as 'one of the smartest navigators':

> For some time past there has been in Brisbane, Captain Anning, who at one time was commander of the White Star liner Persic, trading to Australia. He said, in reply to a question to-day, that he knew the late Captain E.J. Smith, of the Titanic, whom he said was a man absolutely devoid of nervousness, and was one of the smartest navigators on the Atlantic. He had had a splendid career, serving at different periods in the Pacific trade, between San Francisco, Japan, and China before being transferred to the Atlantic… Captain Smith was about 60, and was going to retire at the end of the year.'[42]

Captain J. H. Rinder of Berkeley, Northern California, had tears in his eyes when he expressed confidence in his former colleague:

> He was one of the greatest mariners in the world. And I am sure that he died like a hero, going to his death into the same grave that covers the greatest vessel ever built. The Titanic was worthy of such a master as 'Ted' Smith and 'Ted' was worthy of such a ship as the Titanic. I knew him when he sailed out of San Francisco and he had the reputation of being the inferior of no man that ever trod a ship's bridge.[43]

When the White Star liner the *Afric* arrived in Melbourne from Liverpool shortly after the disaster, the unnamed ship's officers, some of whom described themselves as 'personal friends', were most complimentary:

> 'Captain Smith was an ideal sort of skipper,' said one officer who had served under the commodore of the fleet for over a year whilst the latter was in charge of the *Adriatic*. 'He was a fine looking chap,' the officer

continued, 'standing well over six feet in height, and with the carriage and bearing of a man of only half his sixty odd years. Distinction and a somewhat patriarchal demeanour were conferred upon him by his carefully trimmed white beard. Captain Smith by reason of his sociability was a great man amongst the passengers. He was very well read, had a great knowledge of the world, and was an excellent narrator of a fund of excellent stories.'[44]

The officers also touched on rumours of his retirement stating that 'he had decided to leave the service, but had not fixed upon any date.' One of the quoted *Afric* officers added further detail:

Mr. Simpson, first officer of the steamer 'Afric' said that Captain Smith was a fine man in every sense of the word. Standing over 6ft. high, with a white beard that gave him quite a patriarchal appearance, Captain Smith presented a striking figure. He was at the time of his death 62 years of age. Of a kindly, cheerful disposition, the commander was a great favourite with all who worked under him, and the thousands who travelled in his ships between Britain and America have no doubt shed a tear for the old man… Captain Smith was a master for something like 30 years, and until his ship the *Olympic* and the *Hawke* came into collision had not been concerned in a single accident. Captain Smith was to have retired towards the end of the present year. When I read the report that Captain Smith had shot himself I refused to believe that it was correct. He is not that kind of man. It must have been heart-breaking for him to lose such a fine ship, but that he fully maintained the highest traditions of the British sailor and went down like a hero is shown by the latest accounts of the *Titanic*'s end.[45]

Chief Officer Robinson of the *Euryalus* spoke to a Melbourne *Argus* reporter: 'Captain Smith was a cool, calm, self-contained man. In the stress of danger the more level-headed he would become. I can imagine him smoking his pipe while the vessel was sinking. He was not the man to commit or even think of suicide.'[46]

Second Officer Lightoller of the *Titanic* considered Smith the 'beau ideal of a western ocean mail boat captain.'[47] He went further in a touching passage about Smith in his autobiographical book *Titanic and Other Ships* that his wife Sylvia had pushed him to write in 1935:

Captain Smith, or 'E.J.' as he was familiarly and affectionately known, was quite a character in the shipping world. Tall, full whiskered and broad. At first sight you would think to yourself 'Here's a typical Western

Ocean Captain. Bluff, hearty, and I'll bet he's got a voice like a foghorn.' As a matter of fact, he had a pleasant quiet voice and invariable smile. A voice he rarely raised above a conversational tone—not to say he couldn't; in fact, I have often heard him bark an order that made a man come to himself with a bump. He was a great favourite, and a man any officer would give his ears to sail under... Captain E.J. was one of the ablest Skippers on the Atlantic, and accusations of recklessness, carelessness, not taking due precautions, or driving his ship at too high a speed, were absolutely, and utterly unfounded; but the armchair complaint is a very common disease, and generally accepted as one of the necessary evils from which the sea-farer is condemned to suffer.[48]

Lightoller told a story in his autobiography which, although it should be treated with caution as he was prone to exaggeration, does give us an insight into a captain who had earned respect from his fellow seafarers:

> I had been with him many years, off and on, in the mail boats, *Majestic*, mainly, and it was an education to see him con his own ship up through the intricate channels entering New York at full speed. One particularly bad corner, known as the South-West Spit, used to make us fairly flush with pride as he swung her round, judging his distances to a nicety; she heeling over to the helm with only a matter of feet to spare between each end of the ship and the banks.

Taking a ship the size of the *Majestic* at full speed through such narrow channels could well be considered foolhardy. Lightoller did not think so – even though he was often quick to dismiss another sailor's competency in comparison with his own. In his opinion, this was because Smith had confidence in his ship and equally his own handling abilities.

White Star officer Henry Cater was the Third and Second Officer aboard the *Olympic* under Smith and at the time of the disaster was in Wellington, New Zealand, aboard the *Corinthic*.[49] In a *Manawatu Times* article, he described Smith as a 'careful commander ... most particular about boat drills and the other precautionary measures':

> 'Do you know,' continued Mr. Cater, 'I was on board the Olympic with Captain Smith on one occasion when we had every chance of breaking the record between Southampton and New York easily. We were well ahead of it at a distance of a few hundred miles from the American coast when we ran into a fog. At once the order was given for the engines to go slow, and although it was most disappointing, the safety of the passengers and ship was the first consideration.'[50]

In another account, Cater elaborated on Smith's attitude to boat drills:

> In the White Star Line very particular attention is paid to boat drill, and every man knows his station. Boat drill was carried out regularly on board the Olympic when I was on her, and everything worked smoothly. Captain Smith was most particular about this when I was with him, and there is no reason to doubt that the same conditions prevailed on board the Titanic… Captain Smith was too careful a navigator to run any risks… It is said that the Titanic was warned by wireless the day before the mishap that she was nearing an icefield. This in itself would make her commander more careful still… I don't think for one moment that the Titanic was out to break records on this trip. There was too much at stake.[51]

First class bathroom steward Samuel Rule had worked aboard ships commanded by Smith for many years:

> During most of my service I have been on ships with Capt. Smith, of course, starting when he was a junior officer. A better man never walked a deck. His crew knew him to be a good kind hearted man, and we looked upon him as a sort of father… A better commander never walked a bridge. All the officers were good men. In my opinion the cream of the White Star Line went down in the Titanic.[52]

Family Memorials

Eleanor paid tribute to her lost husband by initiating a yearly tradition: on St George's day (23 April) she would send the Mayor of Southampton a 'buttonhole of red and white roses' in his memory.[53] Wearing a red rose in the lapel of one's garment was once a traditional custom on St George's Day. Eleanor's sent the first buttonhole shortly after the disaster, on Tuesday, 23 April 1912. 'Many mourners in Southampton today were wearing red roses not only in honour of St. George's Day but as a tribute to the memory of Captain Smith of the Titanic who was a staunch believer in the Empire and always celebrated St. George's Day.'[54]

The following year, William Bagshaw assumed the mayoralty from Henry Bowyer, who had established the Titanic Relief Fund. The act of sending flowers was not about the recipient. Eleanor continued the tradition every year until her death.

On Sunday 5 May 1912, Stoke-on-Trent held a memorial service at St Mark's Church, in Shelton, Hanley, which attracted a large congregation made up of family and friends, notably Mrs Thyrza Harrington (half-sister), Mr James W. Harrington (nephew) Mayor and Mayoress Geen and a roll call of schoolmates. Eleanor and Mel were not in attendance. The service had been advertised on the front page of the *Staffordshire Sentinel* three days prior, calling for 'British schoolmates, friends, and all wishing to honour the memory of the late Edward John Smith'.[55]

As the congregation assembled, Beethoven's and Chopin's funeral marches were played before the service commenced at 11 am with a lesson taken by The Rector, the Rev. Percy Gordon. After the reading of scripture and the choir singing 'Blest are the departed' from Spohr's 'The Last Judgment', the Rector remarked that it was 'generally the last act in the drama that they remember best'. He gave several examples, from the Venerable Bede, the Apostle John to Lord Nelson and concluded that it was 'the same with him of whom they were thinking more especially that day – Commander Edward John Smith.' The Rector addressed Smith's school friends in attendance:

> Some of you here remember him well as your school mate. It seems a long way back to those school days, but the most vivid impression left upon the minds of those who knew Captain Smith in his school days is as the boy who always stuck up for the weak against the strong. Possessed even in those days of a fine physique and indomitable pluck, combined with a kindly, generous nature, he was once the admiration of all and the fear of some of his fellows. The bully who delighted to ill-treat the boy who was smaller and weaker than himself had to reckon with a formidable opponent in Edward John Smith...
>
> He was a British sailor of the best type. He lived his whole life on the sea and loved it, but he always had an infinite respect for the sea. He had seen it as few others had seen it, and he knew something of its vagaries and its hidden terrors... Shipbuilders and others might say and think a vessel unsinkable, but (though absolutely fearless) Captain Smith had 'never any illusions as to man's power in the face of the infinite'. Often questions would be put to him, but he would never prophesy an hour ahead. His invariable reply was: 'If all goes well.'...
>
> I have not heard whether his body has been found: it does not much matter. We have not come here to praise Captain Smith. He is far beyond either our praise or our blame... So far as I know there is no grassy mound to mark the earthly resting place of Edward John Smith; but if you, his old schoolmates and friends, have any tribute of affection which you desire to place upon the icy waters that cover him, be British: revise the standard of your life, so that when your time

comes you may be honoured too in the affectionate remembrance of your friends.

At the end of the service, it was announced that any money left over after deducting the customary morning offertory would be forwarded to the Titanic Disaster Fund. The *Staffordshire Sentinel* described an emotional ending: 'The offertory hymn was Whitney's [sic] "Eternal Father" to Dr. Dyke's tune. The organist played the Dead March from "Saul" with a sincerity of feeling as rare as it was appropriate. For the final Amen Sir John Stainer's sevenfold version, was used. It was beautifully done, and was a fitting close to a memorable service.'[56]

US Tribute: Seaman Church Institute Memorial Tablet

Considering the Senate's scathing appraisal of Captain Smith, it may be surprising that one of the first memorials to the *Titanic*'s Master was in New York. The 30 April 1912 *Times* of London reported that 'a committee of American friends of Captain Smith, including Mr. J.P. Morgan, jun., and Mr. Charles Lanier, has been organised to arrange for a testimonial to raise a fund for his family.'[57] This was likely based on a report the previous day about a meeting at the Union League club in New York:

> A conference of the American friends of Captain Edward J. Smith, late commander of the Titanic, was held in the Union League club to arrange a fitting testimonial in his memory and create a fund for his widow and daughter. A committee consisting of Charles Lanier, J. Pierpont Morgan, Jr., William A. Nash, William L. Sloane, John J. Sinclair, William Hestor and others was appointed. William Nash, of the Corn Exchange bank, will be treasurer.[58]

While nothing further was heard about the committee – likely due to the unfavourable outcome of the Senate Inquiry – Eleanor Smith referenced similar in her 6 June 1912 letter to Frank Hancock: 'There is also to be something in New York in the Seamen's Church Institute.' She was correct. The Institute, an agency supporting US and international seafarers, had coincidentally laid a cornerstone in a ceremony held at its headquarters at 25 South Street, New York City, on the morning of 15 April 1912 – the very same day the *Titanic* sank. That coincidence was not lost on the Institute. They donated much needed clothing to the *Titanic*'s surviving crew once they arrived in New York. And exactly a year later, on 15 April

'A Deathless Crown at Duty's Post'

Figure 57: A lantern slide of Smith's memorial tablet installed in the Seamen's Church Institute building. ('Memorial Tablets,' Seamen's Church Institute Archives).

1913, they dedicated a Titanic Memorial Lightouse built on the roof of their South Street headquarters, which operated as a fully functional lighthouse, with a time ball that dropped at noon. It ceased operating in 1967.

More specifically, a memorial tablet was installed inside the Seamen's Church Institute (Figure 57), with some touching words dedicated to the *Titanic* captain:

> IN MEMORY OF
> CAPTAIN EDWARD J. SMITH
> R.N.R.
>
> WHO LOST HIS LIFE WHILE IN COMMAND OF
> THE S.S. TITANIC, APRIL 15, 1912
> HE SAILED THE SEA FOR FORTY YEARS
> FAITHFUL IN DUTY, FRIENDLY IN SPIRIT
> FIRM IN COMMAND, FEARLESS IN DISASTER
> HE SAVED THE WOMEN AND CHILDREN
> AND WENT DOWN WITH HIS SHIP
> GIVEN BY F.R.A.

Titanic Legacy: The Captain, the Daughter and the Spy

Madame Tussauds

A wax model of Captain Smith was created at the Madame Tussauds Exhibition in London. Captain Smith's figure, located near the portrayal of telegraph inventor Guglielmo Marconi, proved to be very popular. The London *Times* carried an advertisement on 7 May 1912 proclaiming "Madame Tussaud's exhibition, The loss of the Titanic. Lifelike Portrait Model of the Late Captain Edward J. Smith."[59] On the same day, the *Daily Sketch* newspaper noted: "An excellent model of Captain Smith, the brave captain of the *Titanic*, has just been added to Mme Tussaud's Exhibition. Mr. John Tussaud has modelled the figure from a 'Daily Sketch' photograph taken on the *Titanic* shortly before she started on her fatal voyage."[60] The *London Evening Standard* described Smith as "wearing a full captain's uniform. On his breast are two decorations one of which is for long service and good conduct in the Royal Navy."[61] The *Lloyd's Weekly Newspaper* added that "Mr. John Tussaud has gone to great pains to make a faithful representation of the original…The model, which is life-sized, occupies a prominent position by itself on a dais in the principal room at the exhibition."[62] Originally, it stood near "an effigy of Mr. Marconi"[63] and proved a "centre of attraction" during May 1912.[64]

From one of two only known photographs of the model, he is positioned standing in between the equally ill-fated Antarctic explorer Captain Robert Scott on the left and English Methodist preacher General William Booth on the right (Figure 59).

TITANIC'S CAPTAIN IN WAX.

An illustration of the figure in wax of the late Capt. Smith, of the Titanic, which has just been placed in Madame Tussaud's Exhibition in London.

Figure 58: Madam Tussauds wax model of Captain Smith in *The Illustrated Chronicle*, 8 May 1912. (Courtesy of Paul Lee)

'A Deathless Crown at Duty's Post'

In 1919, the model was listed in the Madame Tussaud & Sons Catalogue entry 27, with the following description:

> Commander Edward J. Smith, R.N.R., born 1853 [sic]. Commander Smith was Captain of the White Star liner "Titanic" which went down in the Atlantic on 14 April, 1912, during her maiden voyage to America. In this terrible disaster, which was the result of collision with an iceberg, 1,503 [sic] lives were lost, including those of her heroic Captain and Colonel Astor.[65]

Figure 59: The model of Captain Smith was displayed between 1912 and 1925. (*Daily Graphic* 22 February 1915)

The wax image went on a touring exhibit with other celebrity models during 1913 and 1914 but was sadly lost during a fire at the London venue on 18 March 1925. Discovered at 10:30 in the morning, it took until midnight to extinguish the flames during which time almost all of the collection was lost.[66] The attraction took only three years to recover, as fortunately wax moulds had been stored in a separate location. By that time, interest in the *Titanic* and Captain Smith specifically was all but non-existent and so his model was never rebuilt.[67]

Southampton Sword and Hanley Memorial

The fifteenth-century Tudor House in Southampton's Old Town was opened as a museum on 31 July 1912, just months after the sinking of the *Titanic*. Appropriately, Eleanor thought she must contribute something to the newly established museum and so on 15 April 1913, the first anniversary of the sinking, she donated her husband's Royal Navy Reserve sword, with the RNR initials clearly inscribed on it. It was later part of the Southampton Maritime Museum in what is now known as the SeaCity Museum, where it is still on display, with the following caption:

> Like most officers who work for White Star Line, Captain Smith is in the Royal Naval Reserve. As a former Honorary Commander of the Royal Naval Reserve, Captain Smith can fly the Blue Ensign flag from any merchant ship under his command.

In Smith's hometown, Hanley, in Stoke-on-Trent, the council initially made no move to officially commemorate Captain Smith. He was hardly known beyond his circle of close friends, and a *Titanic* connection to the area was probably not seen as good publicity. It took a local individual initiative to propose a memorial, that of an old friend, William M. Hampton. The local *Staffordshire Sentinel* printed Hampton's request two days after the disaster:

> Sir – Might I suggest it would be a gracious act to place a memorial tablet in some public building in Hanley to the memory of the late Captain E.J. Smith of the Titanic? It is well known that he was a native of Hanley, and I have (amongst many others who are now with us) known him personally since his schooldays, and have watched his career and have been proud that Hanley has produced such an eminent seaman. There are no doubt many who would like to show respect to his memory by subscribing towards the memorial. I would like to name 2s.6d. as the

'A Deathless Crown at Duty's Post'

limit of the subscriptions. Would it be asking too much for your sympathy in the matter, [for you to] receive any subscriptions which may be sent?

– Yours etc. W.M. Hampton. Eastwood and Mousecroft Fire Brick and Marl Works, Hanley, April 17 1912.[68]

Local support was muted, even with donations from Smith's fellow old boys at the Etruria British School. This was primarily due to unfamiliarity with Smith, combined with the general poverty of those in the Potteries, and some uncertainty as to whether he was really to be celebrated as a hero. It took a year to gather enough contributions from about ninety subscribers to make a memorial tablet feasible, with a total of £21 0s, 6d raised,[69] equivalent to about £2,000 in 2023.[70]

In February 1913 during a Stoke-on-Trent Town council meeting there was a very short note 'that the Council has given permission to a tablet being placed in Hanley Town Hall, as a memorial to the late Capt.

MEMORIAL TO THE CAPTAIN OF THE TITANIC.

Tuesday was the anniversary of the loss of the Titanic, and a memorial to Captain Smith was unveiled in the Town Hall, Hanley, by the Mayor. Our picture shows the unveiling ceremony.

Figure 60: 17 April 1913 *Daily Graphic* newspaper article on the Hanley Town Hall unveiling. (Courtesy of Paul Lee)

Smith, of the Titanic, who was a native of Hanley'. During the meeting, Mr Hampton submitted a design for the proposed tablet.[71]

Precisely a year after the sinking, there was a ceremony at the Hanley Town Hall (Figure 60). A brass tablet was installed in the apse facing the entrance to the Town Hall (Figure 61), with a ceremony at 3 pm on Tuesday, 15 April 1913, unveiling the tablet with the following inscription:

> THIS TABLET IS DEDICATED TO THE MEMORY OF
> COMMANDER EDWARD JOHN SMITH
> R.D. R.N.R.
> BORN IN HANLEY, 27TH JANUARY 1850,
> DIED AT SEA, 15TH APRIL 1912.
> BE BRITISH.
>
> WHILST IN COMMAND OF THE WHITE STAR SS 'TITANIC'
> THAT GREAT SHIP STRUCK AN ICEBERG IN THE ATLANTIC OCEAN
> DURING THE NIGHT AND SPEEDILY SANK, WITH NEARLY ALL WHO WERE
> ON BOARD. CAPTAIN SMITH HAVING DONE ALL THAT MAN COULD
> FOR THE SAFETY OF PASSENGERS AND CREW REMAINED AT HIS POST ON
> THE SINKING SHIP UNTIL THE END.
> HIS LAST MESSAGE TO HIS CREW WAS 'BE BRITISH.'

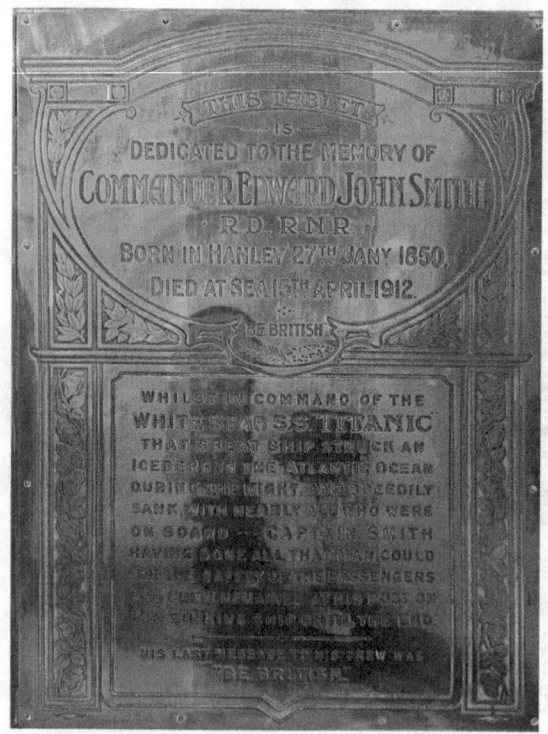

Figure 61: The brass tablet installed in the Hanley Town Hall in 1913, as it looked in 2023. (Photograph: Dan Parkes)

'A Deathless Crown at Duty's Post'

The *Staffordshire Sentinel* transcribed the Mayor's address in which he proclaimed that Smith was a 'Hanley man, and prior to the Titanic disaster had done so much to make a name for himself, and in that way to glorify the town to which he belonged.' It was hard to ignore that the Mayor used the expression 'prior' to the *Titanic* disaster, as if acknowledging there was doubt over whether that honour remained. Nevertheless, he also noted that Smith 'always carried out his duties faithfully and honestly, and on every occasion justified his appointment even in that lamentable disaster to the Titanic... Those present that afternoon were quite certain that Captain Smith did all that was humanly possible to save not only the lives of the passengers and crew, but the ship itself.'

Edmund Jones, an old friend, at the request of the Mayor spoke next and said he 'remembered him first as a senior boy in the old Etruria school. He remembered him as a quiet, respectable, courageous lad. He never put himself to the front very much, but was always ready to defend the weaker and lesser lads.' Nephew James Harrington thanked the Mayor on behalf of the family and 'spoke under some emotion. He pointed out that he had had the honour and pleasure of serving under his uncle at sea.'[72]

One person who did not attend, through undisclosed indisposition, was the man who had taken the initiative of arranging the tablet in the first place – William Hampton. He had passed on details of the event to Eleanor who wrote a letter of thanks to all involved in reply:

Dear Mr. Hampton,
I am greatly touched by the beautiful tribute raised by the townsmen of Hanley to the memory of my dear husband. I offer to you and each subscriber my deep and heartfelt appreciation of the honour paid him and beg you will convey to each one my most sincere thanks. It is indeed sweet consolation that my husband created such a wonderful and profound esteem among those with whom he came in contact, and all through life and in those last moments proved how truly he was worthy of all honour paid to him.
    He was a magnificent example of one of 'England's best sons,' loyal and true to his last breath.

Yours with grateful appreciation,
S. Eleanor Smith
May 24th.[73]

The *Birmingham Gazette* of 17 April 1913 printed a photograph of Alderman Geen, the Mayor of Stoke-on-Trent, unveiling the memorial tablet beneath a large portrait of who is likely a Hanley council dignitary (Figure 60). Sometime later, this painting was replaced with a similarly large portrait of Captain Smith standing dressed in his full RNR uniform (Figure 62). This may have occurred when the plaque was removed in 1961 during renovations at the hall and given to the Etruria British School, or when the plaque was later returned to the Town Hall in 1978, this time relocated to a central courtyard not far from the impressive old courtroom.

Smith's old school, the Etruria British School, was a logical locale. A week after the Town Hall unveiling in 1913 it had its own similar ceremony.

Etruria Portraits

What was described as a 'very interesting function' took place on the evening of Tuesday, 22 April 1913 at the Etruria Council Schools. It had been arranged by Edmund Jones of the Etruria Old Boys' Committee who wrote to Eleanor Smith via Spencer Till, a close friend of the late Captain, regarding their intentions soon after the Hanley church service in May 1912:

> Many of the surviving school fellows attended the recent special memorial service to the late Captain Smith at Shelton Church, and we have since held a meeting at our old school in order to arrange for a permanent memorial of your late husband, as our most distinguished schoolfellow. For this purpose we should be very much obliged if you could send us a copy or say where we could obtain a copy of the most approved photograph of the late Captain Smith in his official uniform.[74]

Till's letter also quoted several school songs, the first of which included the lyrics 'the bravest of the brave ... rule the stormy sea.' The other song referenced the need for sympathy and they passed on their desire 'to express to you our most sincere sympathy with you and your daughter in your terrible sorrow and bereavement'. Eleanor replied:

> Southampton, June 9th 1912,
>
> Dear Mr. Spencer Till, – How deeply my sore heart is touched by the loving words of sympathy for myself and little daughter, from my husband's 'old schoolfellows.' It is indeed a source of great consolation that his old friends are loyal to his memory, and cherish, as he did

most dearly, the happy reminiscences of his school days. It was a great joy to him to be present at the re-union of which you speak, and it would have made him sad to hear of so many having 'passed on' since that memorable event. I beg you will convey to each member of your committee and to each 'old schoolfellow' my warmest gratitude for their kind feelings toward me and my child, and for the beautiful tribute to my dear husband; may I say that, honourable and true as you found him as a friend and school-fellow, even so he proved to me to be one of the best and noblest men ever created by God. His devoted, beautiful, unselfish life, his high standard of discipline, gave him calm courage (as we all knew they would, should the demand ever be made upon him) to make his last glorious stand and 'Dare to do right.' He has left a golden heritage for his child, his crown of laurel is won, but oh! at what a cost! May men and women be raised to the highest type of man and woman hood by his beautiful example—Yours, with heartfelt gratitude,

S. Eleanor Smith[75]

Joseph Turner, a manager of an explosives factory in Cornwall, wrote a letter to the Old Boys' Committee recollecting his school days: 'One of my earliest recollections was of Edward John Smith, who then lived at Well Street, Hanley, and came as a daily scholar. He was my senior, I think, by two years. He was what our dear old schoolmaster would call a "high-spirited lad."' Turner gave a specific and quite violent example of what he meant:

> While at Etruria School, Commander, or rather Ted Smith, quarrelled with me many times and used to punch my head, and I returned the obligation. These quarrels became so incessant that our dear old school master cautioned us before our class that they must be stopped, but if we wanted to cudgel ourselves, we must go out in Hall Fields and cudgel each other to our hearts' content. I am sorry to say that we both took such advice and met after close of school. My second was Herbert Greatbatch (still living). Ted Smith's was my brother Edward. After the fight had progressed for some time with sword sticks, I inadvertently struck Ted Smith on his neck, and this so infuriated Smith that he rushed on me, put down my guard, and thrashed me until I howled. Like all school-boy quarrels, ours was soon made up.[76]

After this brutal encounter, they became friends, although an attempt by Turner to join Smith at sea was thwarted when Captain Hancock refused to take him on. He completed his account by stating: 'All honour to Commander Smith and his brave officers and crew, and I, as a school fellow of his, am also honoured by having known him.'

The ceremony at Etruria was presided over by Alderman Elliot, Chairman of the Stoke-on-Trent Education Committee. Elliot admitted he did not know the Captain personally, but as the portrait would hang in the school wanted to ensure it was pointed out to the boys that the picture was of one who was 'a brave, dignified, noble-hearted man, whose life and the position he attained in his profession should be a stimulus and example to the boys – that he had attained to so exalted a position was a tribute to the good training he received.'[77]

Major Cecil Wedgwood then performed the unveiling ceremony: 'In the present day one heard a very great deal about rights and not so much about duty' and the consolation of the tragedy was that it 'produced examples of heroism and of duty nobly done'. Wedgwood's emphasis of duty elicited a 'hear, hear' from the audience:

> Captain Smith evidently from the time he was a boy had what was called a high spirit – a spirit which made him as a boy the protector of the weak. Thus, he was on the right path from the beginning... Surely the highest praise that anyone could have inscribed upon his tombstone, or remembered in connection with his life, was that he tried to do his duty.[78]

The portrait of Captain Smith would, he hoped, 'long hang in that schoolroom so that when future generations of boys came to the school, they might look at the picture and ask "Who is that?" and be told, "That is the portrait of a man who did his duty."'

As the room resounded with applause, Major Wedgwood unveiled the portrait, with an inscription beneath that read: '"Be British." The last words of Captain Edward John Smith, R.D., R.N.R., who lost his life with his ship, R.M.S. Titanic, after collision with an iceberg in the Atlantic, on April 15th, 1912. The accompanying photograph of Captain Smith is provided by the voluntary subscription of old boys of the British School, Etruria, in memory of the bravery of an old schoolfellow.'

The photograph itself was described as a 'most efficient piece of work executed by Mr. Harrison, photo artist, of Newcastle-under-Lyme. The portrait, enclosed in a substantial frame, was much admired for its 'accuracy of likeness and pleasing finish'. The next speaker at the ceremony, Spencer Till, knew Ted and Eleanor personally and remarked that Smith was in the Royal Naval Reserve, with 'Royal Distinction', so it was fitting that 'it was in his uniform as a captain of the Naval Reserve that he was represented in the memorial portrait.' The impressive portrait can still be seen today, although sadly it is presently behind closed doors (Figure 62).

The proceedings then terminated with the singing of the hymn 'Nearer, My God, to Thee.' There was an adjournment to the Old British Schools for a second ceremony presided over by a Mr Jesse Shirley, who reminded those gathered that this was where the late Captain had received his education. He said that they 'admired the manner in which he stuck to the bridge to the last, the true grit and the true courage, the true backbone he displayed, and remember with pride that those traits were installed in him within the walls of that little room.' Shirley finished by stating that they would 'all revere the memory of the man who above all had shown himself to be a true Christian'.

A second, smaller version of the portrait was unveiled by Major Wedgwood, then nephew James Harrington 'spoke with emotion of love and esteem for his uncle, and of the irreparable loss the family had suffered by his tragic death. He particularly wished on behalf of the widow and family to thank all who had helped to place the portraits in the school as memorials.' The meeting then closed with the singing of the National Anthem. This smaller portrait was likely the version originally owned by Eleanor and supplied to the press, rather than a smaller version of the RNR portrait. This can be determined due to the

Figure 62: The large portrait of Captain Smith in his R.N.R. uniform that hangs in the Hanley Town Hall, Stoke-on-Trent. (Photograph: Dan Parkes)

framed subscription note turning up at auction, along with a similarly aged framed photograph of Smith with his arms folded (Figure 63).

The Town Hall plaque joined the large RNR portrait in 1961, but when the school closed in 1978 the plaque was returned to the Hall – notably not in the entrance as before. In an indication of waning enthusiasm, the plaque and large portrait were moved to an interior location in a small apse in a central hexagon area, with the Hanley coat of arms on the wall opposite. The bright, naturally lit area was often used by photographers, as it was near the registrar's office. Gary Cooper thought that the large portrait made Smith look like 'some Ruritanian master of ceremonies' as 'he stares down benignly on the newlyweds and their families and friends'.[79]

By 2020 the Hanley Town Hall was closed and the Grade II building listed up for sale, meaning the Captain Smith memorial is no longer accessible to the public. After several years of unsuccessful attempts to find a buyer, by 2023 it was on the market for just half a million pounds. With an uncertain future in the hands of residential, leisure or hospitality developers, it remains to be seen whether Captain Smith's Hanley tribute will ever be available to the public again.

There was another photographic memorial located in an area connected to the life of the Captain, a portrait that hung in the Winwick schoolhouse until the 1930s at least. Edward and Eleanor had married in Winwick, Warrington, with her family from this area of Cheshire. Every year on Armistice Day the pupils of the Winwick schoolhouse not only

Figure 63: The smaller of the two Etruria portraits turned up at auction, along with the framed 'Be British' phrase and the note: 'The accompanying photograph of Captain Smith is provided by the voluntary subscriptions of The British School, Etruria, in memory of the bravery of an old school fellow.' (© Henry Aldridge & Son Ltd. / Mary Evans)

observed a minute's silence for those lost in the First World War, but they also turned in the direction of the photograph of the *Titanic*'s master and remembered him, too.[80]

Lichfield Statue

In 1914, only months before the Great War, one of the finest memorials to the Captain was unveiled: a huge, larger than life bronze statue, nearly 8ft tall. Even Eleanor and Mel attended the ceremony (Figure 64). But it was not without controversy.

Its location is the first oddity. The cathedral city of Lichfield, while situated in Staffordshire, has no other connections to *Titanic* or to Captain Smith. It is as far from the sea as is physically possible.

The concept originated in November 1913 when a Captain Smith Memorial Committee was formed by the Bishop of Willesden, Lady Astor, and the Duke and Duchess of Sutherland, among others, who had been passengers and personal guests of the Captain during his career. The committee would later comprise several more esteemed individuals including the Mayor of Southampton and significantly, the Mayor of Lichfield. Eleanor referenced the committee as far back as 6 June 1912 in her letter to Frank, so something had been in the works for a year or so. The issue now was finding a location. Rumour has persisted that placing a statue in Hanley was rejected, 'shunned by the outraged folk of the Potteries', an idea that was debunked in 2013 by volunteers at the Lichfield Heritage Centre and the Lichfield Titanic Commemoration Group, who concluded that it was a strategic location: 'It is in Lichfield because, when it was commissioned, this was a major coaching route between London and Liverpool.'[81]

The memorial booklet that accompanied the unveiling ceremony notes in its introduction that Lichfield 'fulfilled most of the qualifications required for a monument to this brave Staffordshire man' due to several specific claims:

> Being about half-way between Liverpool and London, Lichfield would be convenient alike to British and to American subscribers, and its selection would enhance the interest they already feel in that City owing to the beauty of its Cathedral and the wealth of its literary and historical associations.It is situated in the county, and is the Cathedral City of the Diocese in which the Captain was born, and the proposal has met with local encouragement as well as with the approval of friends from a distance.[82]

Whether there was any merit in these geographic claims is debatable. Cooper described it as an 'artificial excuse' although notes that a more germane factor was that Lichfield was a 'much prettier place than the hard industrial landscape of the Potteries'.[83] And as pointed out in the memorial booklet, that there were already two memorials in Hanley. What is for sure is that the residents of Lichfield were not all comfortable with the concept when first proposed.

The original intent was to include the ports from which Smith had sailed. The 'Memorial Scheme' was to install a stained-glass window in the new Cathedral in Liverpool and the surplus allocated to the Seamen's Orphanage for Boys of Southampton. Neither of these initiatives followed the Lichfield unveiling, the lack of enthusiasm the result of the outbreak of a devasting war.

The concept was initially embraced by the Mayor of Lichfield, H. J. C. Winterton, who, when approached by the statue committee in April 1913, responded by assuming that 'the citizens generally would welcome a Memorial ... and would consider it an honour to the City... There is some fitness in the thought that Lichfield, the "field of the dead," may help to keep alive for the sake of future generations the memory and example of one who was foremost among many in courage, devotion to duty, regard for others, self-abnegation and heroism.'[84]

Figure 64: Mel unveils the statue of her father on 29 July 1914 in Beacon Park, Lichfield. Her mother sits just to her left. From 'Captain E.J. Smith Memorial – A Souvenir of July 29th, 1914'. (Author's collection)

'A Deathless Crown at Duty's Post'

Mayor Winterton had not accurately read the mood of his citizens. Letters to the editor were published in the June 1914 editions of the *Lichfield Mercury* that expressed quite a different opinion. They were more or less based around the premise that a captain dying along with almost 1,500 others did not in itself make him a hero. The official inquiries, and especially the newspaper reports, had queried his culpability in the disaster. For example, on 3 June 1914, Reverend Wilfrid Fuller, a vicar at St Chad's, a local parish church, wrote that 'we ought to bear in mind some of the findings of the Court of Enquiry [sic]. If my memory serves me clearly, it was proved that on the day of the disaster the officers received warning of the existence of ice in the region they were to enter that night, and that the speed of the ship was not reduced. I think, therefore, that the point of view should not be lost sight of from which the relatives of the 1500 lost lives may regard this proposal.'[85] Another correspondent, 'A. Layman', supported the Reverend, writing three days later that he was 'delighted' to see Fuller's letter. His argument first rested on the opinion that 'it would be a pity to allow our gardens to become a dumping ground for monuments of men who have no connection with the City, and are unknown to fame.' Under the cloak of anonymity, he went a step further:

> We must face the facts, and I believe it is a fact (and I say this at the risk of being labelled uncharitable) that the late Commander of the *Titanic* was unknown to fame before he committed the error of judgment, which humanely speaking, led to one of the greatest catastrophes of modern times. He was no doubt plucky, and met his death in a truly British and seaman-like manner – but so did many others.[86]

The sentiments were clear. This captain he mistakenly considered 'unknown to fame' had made an 'error of judgment' that did not warrant a statue in their city. The thoughts were not confined to editorial. Those against the proposal went so far as to present a petition to the city council in protest. On 17 June 1914, weeks before the scheduled unveiling, 73 signatories submitted a petition that laid out reasons for their objection: that Smith was not born in Lichfield, that it was not decided by general consensus and that there was no historical connection. They did not 'suggest any sense of reproach upon the memory of an admittedly brave sailor' but then also urged caution about placing it so near to the statue of the King Edward VII 'of which we are all justly proud'.[87] In response Councillor Raby proposed that Smith was a 'Staffordshire hero' and the Council 'would be doing ill to themselves and the City if they listened to that belated and ungracious petition'.

Titanic Legacy: The Captain, the Daughter and the Spy

It was when the list of those supporting the proposed statute was read out – dignitaries from both sides of the Atlantic, including Queen Alexandra herself – that further debate seemed futile. Raby's motion was seconded by Alderman Harrison who said he 'thought it an honour to have the statue in Lichfield, which had been selected because it was easier of access than North Staffordshire'. Councillor Jones, an old sailor, also supported Raby's motion with 'great pleasure'. Councillor Longstaff agreed but on the grounds that it was too late to change the decision. If it was a 'year ago it might have been arguable whether it would have been better to put the statue at Hanley, or elsewhere in the Potteries, rather than in Lichfield'. To make his point, Alderman Haynes announced that the work of 'getting out the foundation' was to be commenced on the following morning.

Even the story of the sculptor was marked by sad coincidence. It is the work of Lady Kathleen Scott, the wife of the Antarctic explorer Captain Robert Falcon Scott. She was noted for her large public monuments and war memorials, including those to her husband, so she was a perfectly natural choice. Captain Scott had died at the young age of 43, two weeks before the *Titanic* sank. They had only been married four years, so the relationship was not a direct comparison to Eleanor's, yet they were united in widowhood nonetheless, and both with a young only child. An end note in Cooper's *Titanic Captain* biography points out that 'Lady Scott was aboard a ship, reading an account of the *Titanic* disaster, when she received news that her husband's remains had been found.'[88] Her involvement also swayed the Lichfield council to reject the petition. Councillor Longstaff noted that Captain Smith had 'showed them how to die in the same way that the husband of the lady who had carved the statue had showed them how to die.'[89]

In the end, the statue cost £740 to commission and manufacture.[90] While distinguished patrons took prominent billing, there were two notable contributors to the cost of the statue as listed in the commemorative booklet that accompanied the unveiling: 27-year-old domestic housemaid Ann Brett, and 22-year-old domestic cook Mabel Lucy Inkpen. They were employees of the Smith family at Woodhead in Southampton (Brett had also worked for the family in Liverpool).

It was 16-year-old Mel who unveiled the impressive bronze statue of her father, 7ft 8 inches (2.34 metres) high mounted on a 7ft-high pedestal. Located in the Museum Gardens, Beacon Park, it was uncovered on a sunny Wednesday afternoon before a large crowd on 29 July 1914, an event captured on film. Eleanor sat in front of a purpose-built temporary platform beside the statue. Mel was in a bright white dress and white hat that shines among the mostly black clothing of those surrounding her (white was considered an alternative to black for young Edwardian

'A Deathless Crown at Duty's Post'

Figure 65: Mel (in white) sits next to her mother (in black) at the unveiling of the statue. (Still extracted from the 1914 film reel, courtesy of British Pathé)

women in mourning). She is seen on film sitting with her mother as Millicent Leveson-Gower, the Duchess of Sutherland, gives a speech, to which Eleanor enthusiastically applauds, although Mel does not. Mel, on the Duchess' request, stands up and pulls a cord that reveals the statue and then returns to her seat next to her mother as the bugles sound the 'Last Post'.

During the ceremony, reference was first made to the location, with Lord Charles Beresford MP referring to it as 'the ancient capital of Staffordshire'. According to the recollection of columnist Vivian Bird, Mel said in 1967 that she seemed to remember 'something about a town refusing the statue'.[91] She also later revealed that the unveiling and 'The Last Post' had no significance for her. But she remembered Captain Smith as 'a funny man, always laughing; the man who came home on Wednesday – every fourth Wednesday between voyages'.[92] Although the significance may have been somewhat hazy to the 16-year-old at the time, Mel kept a copy of the memorial booklet to her dying day.

There were other family members who attended. Thyrza Harrington, the Captain's older half-sister, aged 78, was present with her children and grandchildren, including James Harrington.[93] A Mr Owen Williams from Liverpool represented the family of Henry Wilde, the lost chief officer of the *Titanic*, while friend Thomas Jones from Runcorn was also in attendance (he was one of the five witnesses listed on Ted and Eleanor's marriage certificate). There was even a message from Queen Alexandra: 'Her Majesty, as you are well aware, feels the most sincere and sympathetic interest in this movement, and thinks this tribute to the memory of the good and brave man who died in the performance of his duties a most appropriate one.'[94]

Other eloquent messages from absentee guests were read, including that of the Marquis of Salisbury who described the 'gallant death of the brave man whose acquaintance I had the opportunity of making four years ago,' while the commander of the *Megantic* called it the 'last tribute of respect and reverence to the memory of one of the best of England's merchant seamen'. The Dowager Countess of Arran wrote that the 'extraordinary impression Captain Smith made on my mind [was] through the "love" all his ship's people had for him (one can describe it in no other way), and through his intense sense of his responsibility for the lives he had depending on him.'[95]

There were messages from further afield, such as from Mr and Mrs John Thallon in the United States, who had sailed with the Captain for nearly thirty years, following him from ship to ship, and who would have been aboard the *Titanic* if their schedule had allowed it: 'We always felt so safe with him, for one knew how deeply he felt the responsibility of his ship and of all on board. He has been a deeply cherished friend on sea and land all these years, and we hold him in love and veneration, and are proud that we could count so noble a man among our closest friends.' Their sentiments were echoed by another American, Mr John Sinclair Armstrong: 'Our lives, even in sad reminiscence, are made more sweet with the memory of that noble man, whom we loved.' Ernest Thompson Seton, an author and co-founder of the Boy Scouts, asked that he could add his 'word of appreciation of the man who left an undying record of peace-time heroism; a standard of nobility that must for ever have helpful results among all those who go by the waters.' A Mr Bonbright described 'one of the true heroes of this generation', while Mr Lanier from New York proclaimed: 'A better and truer man never lived than Captain E.J. Smith.'[96] Lanier was Charles Lanier, the host who took Smith and J.P. Morgan on a high-speed automobile dash in 1907 and who had been involved in proposing a New York memorial.

The following speeches were long and eloquent. The Bishop of Willesden, Right Reverend William Wilcox Perrin, spoke about enjoying the privilege of intimate acquaintance with the late Captain, having crossed the Atlantic three or four times with him.[97]

The Duchess of Sutherland gave what was described as a 'touching eulogy' explaining 'the chief reason she was there was because Capt.

Smith was a man who her husband respected and admired.' She touched on the Captain's reputation and remarked on what the focus should be:

> We all pass through this world, as it were, partly masked, and therefore partly misunderstood ... sometimes the power of complete revelation of character is given to us in the face of crucial situations in life or at the command of our unbending taskmaster – 'Death'... Do not grieve that Captain Smith lies in the mysterious sea ... take heart now, in this solemn scene, so that we too may never be lacking in any supreme hour.

It was at this point that Eleanor enthusiastically applauded and the Duchess requested that Miss Smith unveil the statue, at which Mel stepped forward and pulled the cord. According to one description, she 'reverently performed the ceremony' and then said to those in attendance: 'I hereby declare this statue unveiled.'[98]

Then Lord Charles Bereford, himself a Naval officer of 52 years, delivered his tribute, telling those assembled that he 'knew Captain Smith most intimately. I had learnt to respect and esteem him. I took several voyages with him and I admired his readiness of resource and all those characteristics which appeal to all British seamen.' In a brief biographical review of his life, he noted that Smith's 'mileage at sea with the White Star Line was 2,000,000.' He described the Captain as 'a conspicuously brave man' and received a round of applause when he stated he was 'an example of the very best type of British seaman and British gentleman'. The Lord's speech was more than just a tribute – it was a rallying cry for the Mercantile Marine to assist the Royal Navy as 'Europe might be on the eve of one of the greatest catastrophes that the word had ever seen... It was men like Capt. Smith ... that they could count on ... and end the war as soon as possible.'

There were votes of thanks from the Sheriff of Lichfield, Mr T. Baxter, who stated in his resolution that 'I venture to say we have no more interesting feature in Lichfield than the statue of Captain Smith.' Alderman Morgan seconded the resolution by adding that it is 'well that we who live in this midland county... I suppose as far from the sea as it is possible for anyone to live in this country, should from time to time be reminded ... of the great dangers ... in great waters.'

Mr A. O. Worthington referenced the attendance of Mel in his vote of thanks: 'It must be a great satisfaction to Miss Smith to know that a statue of her father is placed in these grounds where the only other statue is that of our late highly respected and beloved King Edward the Seventh. I have great pleasure in proposing a vote of thanks to Lady Scott, who has carved the statue, and also to Miss Smith for unveiling it to-day.'

The spectators then joined in singing the National Anthem after which Eleanor Smith ended the ceremony by placing a wreath of evergreens and red and white roses at the foot of the statue.[99] Visitors also attended an Evensong service at Lichfield Cathedral, where the choir sang a moving rendition of Gounod's anthem 'Send out Thy light', followed by the hymn 'God Moves in a Mysterious Way.'

As the crowds filtered away and the platform constructed for the event was dismantled, the plaque on the foot of the statue could now be clearly read by all: 'Commander Edward John Smith, R.D., R.N.R. Born January 27 1850. Died April 15 1912. Bequeathing to his countrymen the memory and example of a great heart and brave life and a heroic death. Be British.'

Some thought had gone into the design of the plaque, with symbols in the four corners representing an aspect of his life (Figure 66): top left, a laurel wreath (symbolising heroism); top right, an anchor of hope; lower far left is Smith's Royal Naval Reserve Decoration medal; lower left, a sailor's knot (with 'Forty years' written in it, emblematical of seafaring

Figure 66: The plaque below the statue with the symbols representing parts of the Captain's life. Note the later addition of 'Captain of the R.M.S. Titanic' that was not on the plinth when it was unveiled in 1914. (Photograph: Dan Parkes)

life); lower right, a Staffordshire knot; and lower far right, Smith's Transport Medal (South African Clasp, 1899–1902, for his services during the Boer War.)

One curious detail that must have been observed by those in attendance or who visited afterwards was that the memorial contained no mention of *Titanic* at all, anywhere – as if to appease those who may have found the reference distasteful or because the mere mention of it might call into question his heroism. To add some needed clarification, an inscription was applied to the plinth above the plaque in 1985: 'Capt. of R.M.S. Titanic' (Figure 66). The discovery of the wreck in that year somehow made the connection acceptable once more.

Its inaccessible and unmarked placement continued to cause some confusion many decades later. In a 1958 *Lichfield Mercury* article, it was pointed out that the statue was 'situated behind some neatly maintained turf, the type which is so immaculate that only the innocent child or the naughty dog dare to tread. No direct path is laid to the memorial, and visitors, finding the approach uninviting, neither dare or bother to study the dark, heavy carving.'[100]

In 1985, it was acknowledged in a Lichfield newspaper that 'for decades, a story has been perpetuated that Lichfield accepted the imposing bronze ... as a reject from the Captain's home town of Hanley.' The article pointed out it 'appears that Stoke-on-Trent councillors may have fallen foul of the popular myth, however, in believing that the statue was originally theirs.'[101] Mythology that the statue was rejected by Smith's home town was fuelled by articles such as Mabel Swift's 1989 full-page spread in several Staffordshire newspapers, in which she erroneously stated that the statue had been 'hawked from one end of the country to another ... unable to find a home',[102] and that it was 'ordered in glory and moved in shame', explaining that Hanley felt it was 'inappropriate' to erect it.[103] *Lichfield Mercury* readers were quick to point out the error in a 'Letters to the Editor' section a week later.[104]

After standing resolute for almost a century, the elements began to take their toll on the statue, as its dark features faded into a dull green patina. While the city with a population of 30,000 had for the most part remained aloof to the memorial in their midst, it was finally given some attention in 2010, when the Beacon Park area was granted £3.9 million from the Heritage Lottery Fund's 'Parks for People' programme.[105] Not that the memorial took priority. The statue of King Edward VII was, of course, restored first.

The restoration led to a call the following year for the statue to be moved from Lichfield to Hanley, in a campaign organised by Phil Ball: 'Lichfield has got no connections to the Titanic; no connections to

Captain Smith. It was just somewhere to stick a statue.' His appeal to Stoke-on-Trent councillors fell on deaf ears. Mike Wilcox, leader of Lichfield District Council, ruled out moving the statue, offering instead to 'welcome any of the people of Hanley or Stoke ... I would personally introduce them to the statue.' Ray Johnson from the Staffordshire Film Archive suggested another solution: 'Borrow it. Let's have it as a guest visitor. Remould it. Let's have a copy. Think laterally about it. There are things we can do. I don't blame people in Lichfield for wanting to keep it because it is well loved there.'[106] It was not the first time that there had been a motion to move the statue.

In October 1985, a month after the discovery of the wreck, there were stories that Hanley had suddenly realised the commercial potential of *Titanic* memorabilia and the ill-fated commander was back in demand. The Head of Tourism in Stoke, Ted Smith – no relation – mistakenly claimed that the city had paid for the statue.[107] In November, the Stoke-on-Trent City Council formally wrote to Lichfield District Council 'asking for the statue back', which was met with a blunt refusal, including Lichfield Councillor Bob Blewitt's wry observation that Lichfield had been responsible for cleaning the pigeon droppings off the statue for 70 years. This was followed by another bid by schoolchildren in 1994 and again in 1997, fed by the film frenzy created by James Cameron's cinema blockbuster, that were also rejected.[108] While Lichfield had not appeared willing to promote the statue, neither was it willing to part with it. There was a key issue often overlooked: even if Lichfield bowed to Stoke's request, as the statue is designated a historical landmark it cannot be relocated without government permission.

The statue briefly became centre stage again during the centenary anniversary of the *Titanic* disaster in 2012. Lichfield researchers first went about debunking the myth that the statue only ended up in their city after being shunned by the Potteries, noting that it was selected due to its location as a 'major coaching route between London and Liverpool.'[109]

Part of this revision of history included the placing of an additional tablet immediately in front of the statue, as a form of local explanation. Dated 2011 and installed by Lichfield District Council, it mentions Smith was the Captain of the Titanic and was born in Hanley and then explains: 'Lichfield was considered a more accessible place for the statue. The location may also have been chosen because Lichfield was the cathedral city of the diocese that covered Hanley.'

On Tuesday afternoon, as part of a centenary observance on 10 April 2012, there was a costume drama performed in the Lichfield Heritage Centre telling the controversial story of its proposal and installation. On the following Saturday, 300 people gathered to watch a distress flare that was fired from behind the memorial, representing the flares set off from the sinking ship. Afterward, 1,500 flickering tea lights – one for each person who died – were placed around the base of Commander Smith's statue.[110] The tea lights were laid at the foot of the statue by Stafford and Rugeley Sea Cadets, as music from the era was played by solo violinist Jordan Taylor.[111] The symbolism could be interpreted in more than one way. Was the subtle implication that the lives of 1,500 were placed at the feet of a man who had frequently been blamed for causing the disaster?

The following day, on Sunday 15 April, Beacon Park hosted a moving memorial service led by the Reverend Dr Pete Wilcox, Canon Chancellor at Lichfield Cathedral. The service consisted of hymns and prayers, eight bells rang from nearby Lichfield Cathedral and the Staffordshire Young Musicians performed several songs.

Wreaths were laid by Lichfield District Council, the British Titanic Society, the Corporation of Trinity House, and the Titanic Heritage Trust. There were two other wreaths that were particularly poignant – one in memory of Carl Spencer of Kings Bromley in Staffordshire, who died while diving at the wreck site of the *Titanic*'s sister ship, the *Britannic*. And one in memory of Andrew Wright, Spencer's friend, who had worked with director James Cameron on the documentary 'Last Mysteries of the Titanic' and had died in a helicopter crash in Australia earlier that year. The statue had become a centre point of both remembrance and grief.

Shortly thereafter, the Lichfield statue retreated into relative obscurity. Visitors still sometimes struggle to find it. While it is often described as the main 'feature' of the park, the reality is that it is rarely referenced, if at all. The Lichfield visitor information website on Beacon Park omits any mention of it. Once in the park, there is no signage pointing the way. The statue to King Edward VII stands at the front of the park, clearly the centrepiece.

Those who venture to find the statue will discover a seemingly unhappy figure, almost as if he was sulking, with his arms folded and his back to the tennis courts and skateboard park behind him, with a slightly condescending look, as if to query just why he was put there. As people filter past, a mix of disinterested youth and retired folk, they seem bemused by anyone taking any interest in the sculpture.

Benches scattered around the park have plaques in remembrance of various people from the town. The seat immediately behind the Captain is dedicated to 'John and Wendy Hiorns' who are described as 'soulmates'. One wonders what feelings Ted's dearest Eleanor had of the statue to her husband in such an unusual location. Did she ever visit again?

Today, anyone looking upon his noble features will likely feel an awkward kinship with the Master. As locals stare out of the corner of their eyes, you will also be a stranger in the park, to be glanced at inquisitively.

Figure 67: The Lichfield statue to Captain Smith as it looked in 2023. (Photograph: Dan Parkes)

One of the last personal tributes to the Captain was by Quartermaster George Rowe in 1962, on the fiftieth anniversary of the disaster, printed in *The Southern Evening Echo* on 14 April:

IN EVER LOVING MEMORY of Capt. E. Smith and my dear shipmates, who lost their lives in the sinking of the Titanic 50 years ago. Ex-Quartermaster George Thomas Rowe, B.E.M. [112]

PART TWO
The Spy

Figure 68: Sidney Russell Cooke, the MI5 spy who married Helen Melville Smith. (Artwork by Paul Van Doodson)

6

London Life

Melville was a happy teenager, even after all that she had been through in 1912. She was described in the press as 'a golden-haired and hitherto vivacious girl of thirteen [sic] years'[1] while her mother, Eleanor, pointed out in her letter in June 1912 that 'she is happy and has the same bright, happy disposition as her Father.' The implication is that Eleanor herself was not as postive as her daughter in temperament.

Eleanor had reasons to be anxious. She was not only dealing with the loss of a husband, but also a debate over whether his memory should be honoured or not – or worse, if he was to be blamed for the disaster.

In June 1912, Eleanor specifically requested to meet American author Ella Wheeler Wilcox (1850–1919) while she was on tour in England promoting her latest work. Wilcox was most famous for a line of poetry that was inspired from a moment in the 1880s when she encountered a weeping widow dressed in black. She subsequently wrote the immortal lines: 'Laugh, and the world laughs with you; weep, and you weep alone' ('The Way of the World', 1883). Her poems were often about loss and death. Did Eleanor believe that somehow Cox could encourage her with a line of poetry? In her 1918 book *The Worlds and I* Wilcox described the meeting, which was just when Wilcox was about to depart aboard the *Olympic* from Southampton:

> On my departure from England in June, I learned that a large reception had been planned for me at Southampton before sailing from that port on the *Olympic*. Proceeding to Southampton a day in advance, accompanied by Messrs. Gay and Hancock, my English publishers, I was met at the train by the American Consul, Colonel

Albert W. Swalm, and several prominent citizens and conducted to the Polygon Hotel, where a luncheon of ten covers was prepared. Meantime Mrs. Smith, widow of the Captain of the ill-fated *Titanic*, was waiting to see me for a half hour alone. It was a difficult and pathetic half hour – this interview with the frail little lady filled with thoughts of her husband to whom she had been married a quarter of a century when his tragic death occurred. She felt I could say something to comfort but I fear I failed, save as there may be comfort in sympathy.[2]

Wilcox thought she had 'failed'. She was the same age as Captain Smith. Only a few years later, Wilcox lost her husband after 30 years of marriage, so found herself in a similar position, with her intense grief having no source of comfort.

Leaving Woodhead

It became increasingly obvious that living in Southampton was not conducive to someone grappling with such a heavy loss. Over 500 households in the port city had lost at least one family member and there were claims that in every street there was one casualty from the disaster. Mourning was everywhere. Worse – a large majority were male crew, the breadwinners from each family. To put this in perspective, at Northam School near the docks, 120 out of 250 pupils had lost their fathers. It was on a scale that would only be eclipsed by the Blitz, when the city lost more than 600 people.[3]

Eleanor knew that blame for the sinking could at any moment be pointed at the house of the Captain. She also knew she had to leave: 'I want to go from this house soon as I can.'[4] She knew as a widow with a child at boarding school, she needed financial support to do so.

The 'Millionaires' Captain' had left his family a modest legacy. The White Star Line had an insurance and pension scheme for captains and officers, and on 25 April 1912 the *Daily Mail* newspaper reported that Captain Smith's wife would receive £1,168 as his widow – just short of the £1,250 he was earning annually.[5] On 15 November 1912, a probate was issued to Eleanor for a total of £3,186, the value of Captain Smith's effects. Such comparisons are notoriously complex to calculate, but using a retail price index, or GDP deflator, between £336,000 and £354,000 today.[6] The probate document notes that at the time it was issued, Eleanor was based at 6 Adelaide Terrace in Liverpool, which was the home of David Cook, one of the executors of the will. The other executor was Thomas Jones of Runcorn. Both renounced their stake in the inheritance, leaving it all in favour of Eleanor.

Reports indicate that now with some financial security, Eleanor and her daughter were able to leave their home at Woodhead for good and move north. *The Daily Telegraph* dates the move: 'Three years after that tragedy [Captain Smith's] widow brought her only daughter, Melville, to London.'[7] This aligns with other references that show the house only remained in the Smith family until 1915, after which it was renamed 'Coulhurst' in 1916.[8]

Between residing in Southampton and London, there is some evidence that Eleanor and Mel may have escaped to the countryside to avoid the controversy. An anniversary article in the New York *Daily News* in 1934 summarised this time:

> When Capt. Smith lost his life in the Titanic disaster, Mrs. Smith and her daughter, Melville, went immediately into the country to live – far from London and far from the controversy which raged as to whether or not the Captain shot himself or went down with his ship, whether or not he was guilty of negligence in speeding his beautiful craft through ice-filled waters. For three years his survivors kept very much to themselves, spending most of their time working in their beautiful garden. It was a terrible tragedy for the girl. To her the big, blue-eyed, bearded sailor in his gold braid was the greatest hero in the world, no matter what people said of him.[9]

Leaving Southampton did not mean that Eleanor was attempting to isolate herself from the plight of those affected by the disaster. She took a keen interest in the welfare of Chief Officer Henry Wilde's four children, especially since they had not only lost a father aboard the *Titanic*, but their mother had died a little over a year before, due to complications in the birth of twins, who also died. The Wilde family was based in Liverpool, in a northern region closer to where Eleanor's heart lay, and she must have been touched by a family suffering such enormous loss. It was not that the Wilde family were under any particular financial duress. In fact, Henry Wilde's probate amounted to £6,783, 3s 9d – more than twice the amount of Captain Smith's. But when there was concern over the allowance that the Titanic Relief Committee was providing to support the Wilde children's education, Eleanor expressed her anxiety and appeared in person at the Liverpool Town Hall on 4 June 1915. She had a meeting with Mr Allen, an official of the Public Trustee Office, asking that the committee reconsider the children's allowances. It was noted in the following correspondence:

London Life

PUBLIC TRUSTEE OFFICE 3 & 4 CLEMENTS INN, STRAND, LONDON W.C.
4th June 1915.
Titanic Relief Fund

Dear Mr. Corkhill,
Mr. Allen had a personal interview with Mrs. Smith, the widow of Captain Smith, yesterday afternoon, who is anxious that you should be good enough to consider her claim that the allowance, in respect of the four children of Mr. Wilde the First Officer, should be reconsidered. I have no doubt the matter has been properly dealt with by your Committee, but shall be very glad if you will kindly send her a short report of what your Committee has done for them. Mrs. Smith's address is: The Nook, Runcorn, Cheshire.

Yours faithfully
P.L. Swain, Hon. Secretary, Examining Committee,
P.F. Corkhill, Esq. Town Hall, Liverpool.[10]

This confirms that Eleanor had moved north to be closer with family and was now residing at 'The Nook, Runcorn, Cheshire', the home of Captain Smith's old friend, Thomas Jones, who owned the Navigation Inn.[11] It was in Runcorn in 1901 that the baby Mel appeared in her first census record. Now they were staying at 'The Nook' a two-storey, eighteenth century house made of roughcast stone and brickwork and today listed on the National Heritage List as a Grade II building. Eleanor may have also been spending time with Thyrza Harrington, Ted's older half-sister, who lived in Runcorn. Author Pat Lacey, in her dramatisation of the life of the Captain, added in the Epilogue that prior to staying at The Nook, Eleanor had resided 'with a friend, David Cook, at Adelaide Terrace' in Liverpool.[12] Cooke, of 6 Adelaide Terrace, Waterloo, Liverpool was one of the executors of the will that Smith had drawn up on 11 May 1903. The other executor was indeed Thomas Jones of The Nook. So, it would seem that Eleanor was visiting those who had a vested interest in ensuring the Captain's last will and testament was adhered to. Smith had left everything to his wife but with a notable clause, as mentioned earlier: only if she did not remarry, otherwise all would default to Mel. Eleanor never did marry again.

This was not the first time Eleanor had made a trip north. Sometime in early 1913, Eleanor had also stayed with 'a lifelong friend of hers in Runcorn', almost certainly Thomas Jones and family. The visit was

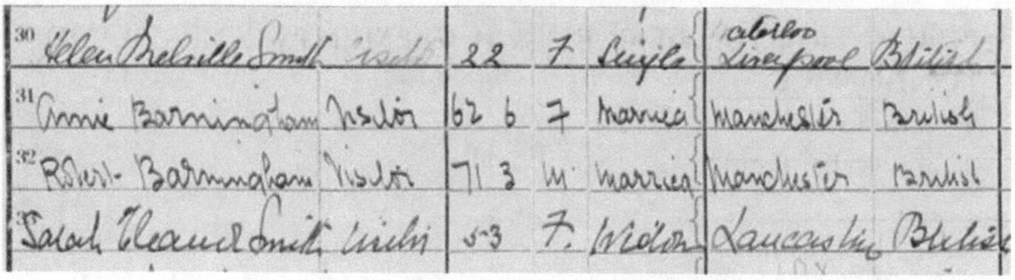

30	Helen Melville Smith	Visitor	22	F	Single	Liverpool	British
31	Annie Barrington	Visitor	62 6	F	Married	Manchester	British
32	Robert Barrington	Visitor	71 3	M	Married	Manchester	British
33	Sarah Eleanor Smith	Visitor	53	F	Widow	Lancashire	British

Figure 69: The 1921 census showing Mel (line 30) and her mother, Eleanor (line 33), residing at 41 Queens Gate Gardens. (Courtesy of Paul Van Doodson)

recalled by another friend, Spencer Till, who while there remembered Eleanor showing him

> … many interesting photographs, including one very large photograph of a banquet given in honour of the late captain at the so-called Millionaire's Club in New York [Figure 34]. Included in the company were many of the most prominent and well-known men of the United States, who had crossed the Atlantic with him on numerous occasions. He was told that Captain Smith was repeatedly referred to in the United States as 'The Grand Old Man of the Sea.'[13]

These visits north were not only a time to reminisce and stay out of the limelight. They were also an indication that Eleanor was exploring options for leaving Southampton.

Eleanor and Melville decided not to settle in the Liverpool area. By 1921, they had returned to the south, moving into the upmarket South Kensington district of London. Their location is captured in the 1921 census, placing them as 'visitors' at 41 Queens Gate Gardens (Figure 69). Sarah Eleanor Smith is listed as a 'widow' (incorrectly recorded as 53 years old, she was turning 60) and her 22-year-old daughter Helen Melville Smith as 'single'.

At the time of the census, 41 Queens Gate Gardens was the Leicester Court Hotel, once a house with royal connections and now the four-star Strathmore Hotel (formerly Grange Strathmore) owned by Gem Hotels.[14] Promotional material characterises the establishment as a delightful combination of Victorian grandeur and modern luxury, showcasing a restaurant with a colonial vibe and a bar adorned with original chandeliers and intricate carved panelling.[15]

As permanent guests, quite likely Eleanor and Mel enjoyed the same Victorian grandeur and the bar's chandeliers and fireplace that can be seen in the hotel today. Eleanor was still living there in 1931, ten years later, so she must have enjoyed the residence and its regal history as well as its easy access to the sights of London.

The Myth of Captain 'Uncle Jack'

There is another interesting detail in the 1921 census: it lists Helen Melville Smith as 'single' and her mother a 'widow'. According to a substantial number of biographies that include Captain Smith's daughter, there was supposed to be a further tragedy in the Smith family, with claims that Mel was first married to a 'Captain John Gilbertson of Liverpool' also known as 'Uncle Jack'. Gilbertson was allegedly the youngest captain in the British Merchant Navy who died of black water fever aboard the *Morazan* on a return voyage from India. If true, that would make Mel technically also a widow, as the 1921 census was the year before Mel was to be married to Sidney Russell Cooke.

The census is not the only clue that the 'Uncle Jack' story is a myth. According to the 'Index to the Captains' register of Lloyd's of London, there is only one John Gilbertson of Liverpool, born in 1884 and dying in Liverpool in 1911 (when Mel was 13). There is also a distinct lack of supporting documentation regarding a vessel named the *Morazan* or a case of 'black water fever'. The only British Merchant Navy ship called *Morazan* during this period is mentioned in an 'Index of Ships' in 'British Merchant Vessels Lost 1914-1918', a vessel that foundered on 11 November 1916.[16] More obvious is the complete absence of a marriage certificate or any marriage registry information. In Mel's 1922 marriage certificate, she is described as a 'spinster'. So 'Captain John Gilbertson' is almost unquestionably a myth.

The source of the story seems to have originated online via a comment by a 'John E. Smith' from Fredericton, Canada, repeating a story he was told by his mother. This anecdote was reprinted in a self-published eBook in 2017 entitled *Captain Edward John Smith of the Titanic* by Kathleen Alice Evans (also known as 'Lady Kathleen'. She says Captain Smith was her 'Great Great Grand Uncle'). The online book reprints a letter by 'John E. Smith':

> Prior to her marriage to Russel-Cooke [sic] I believe she was married to Captain John Gilbertson of Liverpool England. John Gilbertson (my 'Uncle Jack') died soon after their wedding (possibly less than a year) of black water fever on a voyage home from India on board his first command, a ship called the Morazan of the Bibby Line. At the time of his death Captain Gilbertson was the youngest captain in the British Merchant Navy. Another sad story. It is little wonder she later said she was afraid to form close relationships because they seemed destined to end in tragedy!!
>
> My mother told me this story. She was my uncle Jack's sister, and I have a picture of Helen and my uncle taken soon after their wedding. Unfortunately, all my family has passed away now except for my wife

and three daughters so there is no one left to get further information from here. If you can shed more light on this story I would appreciate it.[17]

This story has been oft repeated and found its way into online biographies and genealogical trees all over the internet. There is a possibility the confusion is due to the fact that Sidney was demobilised with the rank of captain in the First World War. Although not in the maritime sense, Melville did marry a captain.

So Melville (Figure 70) was 'single' in the 1921 census, but that would not be for much longer. Ten years after the loss of her father, on 18 January 1922, Mel married a wealthy stockbroker, a Mr Sidney Russell Cooke, at St Mark's Church, North Audley Street, Mayfair, London. Sidney Russell Cooke was born in Paddington on 12 December 1892 to William Russell Cooke and Margaret Mary Smith. This makes Sidney 29 years old at the time of the marriage, while Mel was 23. From an account in 1934, it appears that Mel met Sidney after they moved to London.[18]

There was, however, something unusual about this wedding. Despite the pedigree of the two newlyweds, there was little fanfare – it was not even announced in the local Isle of Wight newspaper. There is a clue in one of the names listed on the marriage certificate: a Mr Oswald Allen Harker. Harker worked for the British Security Service, also known as MI5 and was Sidney's best man. Sidney had attended Harker's wedding in 1920, as Oswald had married Sidney's sister 'Pattie' (Margaret). They were brothers-in-law.

They were also both spies.

Figure 70: Helen Melville ('Mel') Smith in an undated photograph. (Courtesy of Paul Van Doodson)

7

Cookie

For Melville, it must have been a fine match with six foot, one-inch-tall Sidney – a very wealthy stockbroker by day in London and an avid yachtsman on the weekends on the Isle of Wight, where they lived and would have twins. Maritime memories of her father must not have been far away. How much she knew of her husband's background is unknown. If she knew, she would most likely have been quite inspired by his mother.

Sidney was the only son of William Russell Cooke, who founded the legal firm Russell-Cooke (still in existence today)[1] and was legal adviser to the Liberal Party during the 1890s, the main opposition to the Conservative Party at the time. He was also a legal advisor to Princess Henry of Battenberg in her capacity as governor of the Isle of Wight (she was the fifth daughter and youngest child of Queen Victoria and Prince Albert).

Sidney's mother also had grand, perhaps more scandalous, connections and became famous in her own right as a British writer and suffragist campaigner. Born Margaret Mary Smith in 1857, William Cooke was her second marriage; she was the widow of Ashton Dilke, formerly the Member for Parliament for Newcastle-on-Tyne, with whom she had three children (Fisher, 1877, Clement, 1878, and Sybil, 1879).

After Ashton's Dilke's death from tuberculosis in 1883, it became public that his brother, Sir Charles Dilke, had an affair with Ellen Smith – Margaret's mother – which caused quite the stir and two divorces. Margaret herself (more commonly referred to as 'Maye' Dilke), trained to be a teacher in France, but instead became an active member of the women's suffrage movement, working as treasurer for the Central National Society for Women's Suffrage and giving speeches on the subject all over England. She published a book entitled *Women's Suffrage* in 1885 under the name of 'Mrs. Ashton Dilke' (later editions used the name Mary Dilke), published as part of what was called 'The Imperial Parliament Series' – essentially a political handbook dealing with 'topics of the day'. The book was a response to many of the key anti-suffrage arguments, with chapter headings such as a 'Reply to Habitual Objections – physical and mental'. Her arguments were powerful and clear:

> The idea that women should not vote because they have less physical strength than men, seems extremely difficult to eradicate, and hardly a debate or public meeting can take place without some champion appearing to insist that because women are the weaker, therefore they are not to be considered capable of performing the duties of citizenship... It certainly cannot be urged that women have no physical force ... when we see the vast amount of hard, toilsome physical work performed by women, it seems most illogical to treat them as if they had none.[2]

She also squarely addressed the argument that granting votes to women would cause 'a great loss of feminine charm and constitute a great injury to home life':

> It cannot be supposed that the mere act of marking a paper and handing it to a returning officer, makes so remarkable a change in the character and attractions of women, as they already do this in thousands of cases in municipal and other local elections... Men will continue to court favour with pretty faces, and do homage to the queens of society, be there votes or be there none.

Dilke's ideals that she held so dearly would not be realised until acts of parliament brought partial reform in 1918 and more specifically the Equal Franchise Act of 1928 that granted women over 21 the right to vote, finally attaining equal suffrage with men.

In the meantime, she remarried, to a William Russell Cooke on 19 September 1891. They had two children. Sidney was born on 12 December 1892, with a younger sister Margaret Dorothy born two years later in 1894. Maye was even the subject of artist John Sargent in an 1895 oil on canvas work entitled 'Mrs. William Russell Cooke.' (Figure 71)

Sidney's father, William, died on 30 January 1903 at age 48. He had been suffering for a month from appendicitis and after surgery did not recover. His loss was felt deeply in the community, as the Russell Cooke family had been associated with the Isle of Wight for generations. In politics he was characterised as an 'ardent Liberal', as would his son.

Cookie

Figure 71: An oil painting of Mrs William Russell Cooke by John Sargent, 1895. (Wikimedia Commons/public domain)

A local press article on his death speculated that if he had survived he would have been a possible Liberal candidate for the Island in the next election.³ In his stead, Sidney's mother, Margaret, continued in politics, moving permanently to the Island in 1905, and was the first woman to stand, albeit unsuccessfully, at the Isle of Wight county council election, before her untimely death in Newport on 19 May 1914, aged 56.⁴ She died in the family home, 'Bellecroft', after a long illness and unsuccessful surgery.⁵

Margaret Russell Cooke had been active in local politics in the year prior to her death. In addition to an attempt to stand in county council elections in 1913, she gave an address at the National Union of Women Suffrage Societies in February 1913.⁶ She then appeared as the first lady member of the Isle of Wight Education Committee in September 1913, where Margaret consented to supervise the work of student teachers and expressed her satisfaction that they were teaching boys cooking in classes.⁷ In October 1913, she opened the sale of 'very excellent work' by 'inmates' at the Island Workhouse under the auspices of the Brabazon Employment Society. At the prestigious event, under the patronage of the Royal Governor herself, Margaret declared to the crowds that the sale was open and that it was evidence of a 'spirit of care for the inmates, seeing that they made the most of the facilities and that their lives were made as happy and interesting as possible'. At one of her last engagements before her death, the Reverend F. J. Bamford proposed a

Figure 72: 'Bellecroft', the family home of the Russell Cookes, thought to be taken c. 1910. Present owner Keith Prowse believes Captain Smith was known to the Russell Cookes and appears in this photograph, the second man standing from the left, with a beard and wearing a hat. The identity is unconfirmed. (Photograph courtesy of Keith Prowse)

hearty vote of thanks to Mrs Russell Cooke who 'was always busy with good works.'[8] In November 1913, she was involved in raising funds for a new vicarage at St Paul's, donating £20 towards the cause, along with other family members. She even manned a toy stall with her 19-year-old daughter.[9] St Paul's Church bordered the Bellecroft estate property, so the family was frequently associated with events there.

There is a possible connection between Captain Smith and the Russell Cooke family dynasty during this time. In a photograph dated circa 1910 (Figure 72) in the possession of the present Bellecroft owner, Keith Prowse, there is a man standing on the far left that some believe resembles Captain E. J. Smith. He has a beard and a hat and appears to be wearing a boutonnière but otherwise little else is discernible. It would not be unrealistic to believe that Smith and his family spent time on the Isle of Wight, just an hour's journey across the waters from Southampton, and they may have joined one of the many gatherings at the sprawling estate of Bellecroft. There is presently no independent verification that he ever did so, or that the Smith family had any leanings toward women's suffrage or Liberal politics. A boutonnière would indicate a wedding. The only certain connection is that Sidney Russell Cooke married Melville in the 1920s, and that by the 1930s Mel had become owner of the Bellecroft estate.

Just a fortnight before Margaret's death, she was present at the formation of the Newport branch of the National Women's Suffrage Society in her home at Bellecroft, where she was elected vice-president. In spite of her illness, the local press reported that she 'felt great satisfaction in the realisation of her keen desire to see the branch effectively established'.[10]

After her death, Sidney and his younger sister Margaret ('Pattie') attended a memorial service for her at St Paul's Church, along with other members of the family, on Friday 22 May 1914. Household staff were also in attendance: Mrs Brown, the housekeeper, and Mr Charles Morgan, the head gardener, along with a long list of local dignitaries.

Margaret was buried the following day alongside her husband at Brookwood Cemetery near London with a well-attended funeral ceremony performed by the Dean of Salisbury. On the day of her burial, the local *Isle of Wight County Press* published an emotional and detailed account of her life: 'News of her death cast a gloom over the district and caused profound regret throughout the Island, in every part of which the deceased lady was well known and highly esteemed. Flags were flown at half-mast at the Newport and other Liberal Clubs, and deep and sincere were the expressions of sorrow and sympathy ... her strong personality and exemplary work for the public well impressed themselves with equal force on those who had the privilege of her acquaintance.'[11]

Sidney took the responsibility of responding to the outpouring of affection for his mother. He wrote a letter to the Isle of Wight Education Committee that she had worked tirelessly supporting, even visiting every school in the area on their behalf, in response to a letter of sympathy they had sent. He wrote that 'members of the family were very grateful ... mother was always deeply interested in educational work and it was a great consolation to the members of her family to find that so high a value had been set upon her powers by her fellow workers.'[12]

Upon her death, Margaret Russell Cooke left an estate of £8,479.[13] Sidney became the joint owner of Bellecroft with his younger sister Pattie,[14] who also inherited John Sargent's oil painting of her mother. As for Sidney, he had inherited a legacy that only an ambitious young man could think to imitate. And it started with his own education.

Cambridge and The Great War

Sidney Russell Cooke, unsurprisingly, had an affluent education, studying at Cheltenham College, a public boys' school in Gloucestershire, where he showed sporting prowess, listed as the 'racquet champion of Cheltenham College in 1911 and coxswain of the College boat in 1910'.[15]

He was admitted to King's College Cambridge on 5 October 1911, studying history and law, graduating with a B.A. and L.L.B. (Bachelor of Laws), in 1914 and an M.A. in 1919.[16] Whilst at university, he was the president of the Debating Society where he gained 'considerable knowledge and power as a speaker' that would stand him in good stead for a career in politics.[17]

In August 1912, the 20-year-old had a brush with the local Isle of Wight law when he was fined for 'obstruction' after leaving a 'motor-cycle with a trailer attached' at the Esplanade near the Pier Gates for a period of 35 minutes. He failed to appear before the magistrates, so evidence was given by Police Constable Warne that it occurred at 3:45 pm during a busy time and that he waited until 4:20 pm until Cooke returned. Cooke immediately admitted the motorcycle belonged to him and asked the P.C. in no uncertain terms: 'Where the deuce am I to put it?'[18] Cooke was defended by a Mr H. Eldridge who said his client instructed him to say that Cooke 'was very sorry for anything he had done or left undone'. He had been meeting a friend at the Pier and the boat was late. It was described as 'not a very serious case' and the misdemeanour was ultimately considered a 'breach of the bye-laws'. Sidney was fined 2s, 6d., with 4s. costs.[19]

In the same year he graduated – and only months after the death of his mother in May – he signed up to serve in the First World War. Cooke joined the Post Office Rifles right at the outbreak of war, 'receiving his commission on the 20th August 1914, a remarkable effort even in the early days of war. He helped to recruit the second line Battalion, and went to France in March, 1915, with the Battalion.' He saw fighting that was described as 'terrific' in the Festubert area of France where the 'battles were of the bloodiest character, and the men engaged in it remember it with horror … on one occasion every officer of the company with the exception of himself was a casualty.' After seeing active service in France, he was invalided home suffering from 'shell shock and concussion'.[20]

The Battle of Festubert was fought between 15 and 25 May 1915 in the Artois region of France and formed a part of the larger French Second Battle of Artois that ultimately resulted in minor British gains and heavy losses. The Post Office Rifles were primarily Post Office employees, with a Second Battalion formed in September 1914, the 2nd/8th Battalion, that Cooke joined, which was initially a reserve. The First Battalion embarked from Southampton on 17 March 1915 and entered the trenches near Givenchy to fight in the battle for Festubert on 11 May.[21] By the afternoon of 25 May, some 600 of the 900 officers and men of the Post Office Rifles had been killed or wounded.[22] The entire offensive resulted in less than a 2 mile advance.

His service record reveals that he was a member of the 8th (City of London) Battalion (Post Office Rifles) and that he was listed as 'wounded' on the Casualty List issued by the War Office on 28 May 1915. The *Gloucestershire Echo* of June 1915 also listed Cooke as wounded, aged 23.[23] His cousin, Oliver Paget-Cooke, would later testify that Cooke suffered from shell shock and for a time was in a hospital in Kensington until he 'pretty well recovered'.[24]

Although that ended any further service in the field, he subsequently worked in the War Office Intelligence Department and was demobilised with the rank of Captain.[25] His King's College biographical entry noted that he was in the 'Intelligence Directorate, W.O., 1915-19; Captain G.S.O. 3' which meant he was a General Staff Officer (Grade 3).[26] A 1920 biography confirmed that he was 'Capt. 8th (City of London) Batt. London Regt., attached to the Gen. Staff, War Office'.[27] As a member of staff of the Military Intelligence Directorate, he was described as having 'performed splendid service'.[28] It seemed Cooke had the makings of a spy.

The Economist

Just before Cooke went to war, he met the famous economist and architect of British economic policy, John Maynard Keynes. Born in 1883, Keynes had originally been a Civil Service clerk in the India office, was a fellow at King's College by 1909, and editor of *The Economic Journal* in 1911. By 1913, he had published his first book – *Indian Currency and Finance*. Keynes was also unusually open about his affairs, which prior to 1921 were exclusively with men. As what might be considered logical for an economist (he was known to obsessively write numerical lists of expenses and golf scores) the identity of his lovers was noted in a private diary he kept between 1901 (when he turned 18) and 1915 and later published in a book in 1992.[29] In the early twentieth century, documenting this was acutely dangerous, especially considering the 1916 example of Roger Casement, an Irish nationalist who was hanged for high treason. As a compulsive diary writer, Casement's records of his homosexual relationships were exposed and turned public opinion against him, leading to his execution.[30]

Keynes' diary includes the names of many elite men of his day: Alfred Knox (Enigma codebreaker), Daniel Macmillan (publisher and brother of the Prime Minister), Lytton Strachey (founder of the Bloomsbury Group), Arthur Hibson (Liberal politician), Francis Nelson (aspiring actor), Benoy Sarkar (Indian nationalist), Arthur Felkin (League of Nations diplomat), John Sheppard (later the Provost of King's College,

Cambridge) and Duncan Grant (Scottish artist). Not that Keyne's tastes were altogether exclusive. Towards the end of 1909 it lists a 'stable boy of Park Lane' and in 1911 a 'lift boy of Vauxhall'. In among this catalogue of encounters there is one name that repeats several times: 'Cookie,' Sidney Russell Cooke, for the years 1913, 1914 and 1915.[31]

It is most likely that Cooke met Keynes while studying at Cambridge. A Cheltenham school friend of Sidney's remembered being introduced to 'Maynard' while Cooke was an undergraduate. 'I had gone to spend the weekend with him. Sidney's rooms in college were always alive with good talk and the most fascinating argument used to come from a long-legged man lounging deep in his chair whom they called 'Maynard'... Although Sidney was an extremely good-looking young man, it never occurred to me that this was of any special interest to Maynard.'[32]

Confirming the relationship, the Cambridge University King's College Archive Centre contains four autographed letters, and an autographed postcard in 'correspondence from Sydney [sic] Russell Cooke to J.M. Keynes between 1913-1921'.[33] The first letter, dated 6 July 1913, invites Keynes, whom he addressed as 'Maynard', to visit him at the family home of Bellecroft. A short note confirms that he expected Keynes to arrive on Friday the 11th, most probably to spend the weekend there.

Their time together must have gone well, as by December of the same year Cooke wrote a long letter explaining that he could join Keynes on the continent, writing that he would 'love to enjoy the reflected glory of touring Europe (or even gambling at Monte) with so good & faithful a servant of Our Liege Lord, King George the Fifth as yourself' but that he 'really cannot manage it.' He explained that his 'people' have 'arranged a lot of visitors, dances, & other things for my benefit, not to mention that it really annoys them if I am not at home during the vacation, that I feel I should be a brute to go away.' In his absence, Cooke asked Keynes to 'put £5 on' while in Monte Carlo and additionally to help him 'gamble on the Stock Exchange' with the condition that it should be 'at least a 10 to 1 chance that I did not lose more than £50.'[34]

Cooke congratulates Keynes, as he had 'done very well on that Commission' – referring to his appointment to the Royal Commission on Indian Currency and Finance in 1913 – but then warns him not to join the Conservative government. 'I hope your admiration for Austen Chamberlain will not lead you to accept office under the next Tory government... You would become a bigoted Tory within five years, & prostitute your expert knowledge of Economics... Do tell me if I guessed right in thinking that you have one eye on the next Tory government?'[35]

Cooke was not entirely correct about Keynes' political intentions. There was no Tory government (the Liberals remained in power until the coalition of 1916) but Keynes did offer his expertise during the early stages of the First World War and in January 1915 took up a government position in the Treasury. In early 1914, Cooke wrote to Keynes from the office of the *Cambridge Review* expressing concern over reports of his illness and the effect it would have on his role in the Commission, writing that he could not 'conceive how they will be able to produce that report without you'.[36]

Later, when Cooke was invalided home to Bellecroft with shell shock, Keynes, himself recuperating from appendicitis, visited him there. Author Davenport-Hines believes that 'at this stage of life Keynes liked to change compartments at short intervals. Accordingly, he left plush Garsington to go to stay at Bellecroft ... the two invalids found sexual consolations together during their convalescence.' Davenport-Hines describes the relationship between the two men as 'gentle but solid affection' and that Cooke was 'simply gentle and affectionate'.[37]

Torquay Politics

Having only just acquired his Master of Arts in 1918, in that same year 26-year-old Cooke decided to stand for the Liberal party in Torquay in the general election that took place immediately after the Armistice. Labelled the 'women's election,' it was the first time in which women could not only stand for election but also the first in which women over 30 who met a property qualification could vote. His mother would have been equally proud and frustrated. It would be another ten years before all women over 21, regardless of property, could vote.

It was a 'three-cornered fight' with Captain Russell Cooke facing Colonel Burns of the Conservative-Unionist Party, and Major Trestrail of Labour – 'the influence of the war was evident in the fact that all three major candidates were military men.'[38]

The Western Times described Captain Cooke as 'a young man of much ability, not only as a speaker, but as a politician. His Liberalism is sound, and he gives expression to its principles with clearness and force.'[39] When he gave political speeches, he was accompanied by his younger sister and 'spoke of the importance of dealing with soldiers' and sailors' pensions as a whole'.[40]

Not unlike his suffragette mother, he once addressed a well attended meeting of Liberal women at Torquay, where he 'pointed out the important position which women occupied in the present contest. They must regard it as a duty to work and vote, because the election had been forced at a time when the men were still overseas... Although they had won, there was a danger that they might lose the peace.' Cooke was quoted as saying that 'you cannot put old wine into new bottles as the Unionists are trying to do today' adding that he wanted to go to Parliament to represent Democracy in its true form.[41] When criticised as too young compared to the other contenders, he replied that he was 'the only candidate who was old in these political matters of Liberalism'. Cooke spoke at the Brixham Town Hall where he told the crowd he had been 'brought up a Liberal, and believed in Liberal principles' and wanted to 'see every nation in the League of Nations' and 'see the war properly finished'.[42]

Cooke indeed was making an impression, as the following description of the candidate in the *Western Times* of December 1918 reveals:

> Captain Russell Cooke, the Liberal, and the youngest of the three aspirants to the seat, has undoubtedly made considerable headway, and won over many who would otherwise have supported the Labour ticket. Had this been an ordinary political election with Liberal, Unionist, and Labour candidates and longer time for preparation, Captain Cooke would have made a big show, but he has had to start with a goodly number of well-known Liberals supporting the Coalition candidate because he had the Lloyd George label... Captain Cooke's personality, his polished speeches showing considerable reading and thought, have made an excellent impression, and if he is a trifle academic in style, the fact that he takes his politics very seriously more than counter-balances this... Captain Cooke, coming as a complete stranger, has done well, and if he sticks to politics should do well.[43]

As with his mother's attempts in politics, in the end, Cooke did not do well – by a wide margin. He gained only 3,173 votes compared to Burns' 14,058 and Trestrail's 10,039, just 15 per cent of the poll.[44] Alex Potter, in *Torquay in the Great War* saw other forces at work: 'That a Labour candidate outpolled a Liberal in Torquay, even a Liberal running against the government, was a sign of the Liberal Party's deep crisis.'[45]

In a different contest altogether, Cooke had something of a winning streak. On 5 September 1919, he entered competition at the St Paul's Brotherhood Horticultural Show and despite a 'record success both in quantity and quality of the exhibits' and over 300 entries, he won first prize for his beetroot (turnip rooted), lettuce, turnips, cucumbers and pears, while placing second in the 'collection of vegetables' entry along with potatoes, cauliflowers, carrots, beans, melons and dessert apples. His cooking apples were a miserable fifth place.[46] It was quite an improvement on the previous year, when he had only one first prize with his French beans, peas, figs and melons, and a third with his spring onions.[47]

It is unlikely Cooke was directly involved. Later entries at flower and horticultural shows reveal that they were under the guidance of the head gardener at Bellecroft, but Cooke would have enjoyed taking the credit. His father had been a long-time benefactor at St Paul's, so he was following in a family tradition of supporting events in the local parish.[48]

While he had failed during his first official foray into politics in 1918, and was having moderate success at horticulture in 1919, he was about to be given a chance to succeed in something far more daring at the dawn of the decade: espionage.

Spying on the Russians

Cooke's career take a dramatic turn thanks in part to the marriage of his younger sister, Pattie (Margaret Dorothy) Russell Cooke. Prior to her marriage, they had been sharing accommodation whilst in London at 18 Portsea Place, near Hyde Park. On 26 October 1920, Pattie married Oswald Allen Harker (1886-1968) at St Mark's, North Audley Street, Mayfair (where Sidney would later marry Mel). In the absence of his late father, Cooke gave his sister away.[49] The event made the Isle of Wight press, who noted there were no bridesmaids, the bride wore 'a gown of cream broche crepe, draped on the left side, and caught up with orange blossoms, her chiffon veil edged with Brussels lace, which was fastened with a green wreath forming a train. She carried a sheaf of red roses.' A reception was held at John and Sybil Roskill's residence at 33a Montagu Square (Sybil was Sidney's older half-sister) and the couple honeymooned in the south of France.[50]

Harker, frequently nicknamed 'Jasper' (Figure 73) joined the MI5 security service in that year and was tasked with covering Soviet operations, including the possibility that the newspaper the *Daily Herald* was financially supported by the Soviet government.[51] According to the MI5 website biography on Brigadier Oswald Allen Harker, his background was with the Indian Police where he worked for fourteen years, becoming the deputy commissioner in Bombay before he was invalided home in 1919. He was soon head of the Service's 'B' division, a department that was charged with handling 'investigations and inquiries.'[52]

Harker had not only become Cooke's brother-in-law, he would now also be his boss. And they already had their first mission. Earlier in the summer of 1920, an English sculptor named Clare Sheridan (Figure 75),

Figure 73: A pencil sketch of Brigadier Oswald Allen Harker CBE, Sidney's brother-in-law who became a director of MI5. (Author's collection)

a cousin of Winston Churchill, met the chief Soviet negotiator, Lev Borisovich Kamenev, Trotsky's brother-in-law (Figure 74) purportedly to have a bust made. Harker and those at MI5 suspected more. As it happened, Cooke was a lifelong friend of Sheridan (through a mutual family acquaintance) and so Harker saw he could use Sidney to their advantage. In *Enemies Within: Communists, the Cambridge Spies and the Making of Modern Britain* author Richard Davenport-Hines explains what happened:

> MI5 resorted to family connections and social contacts in order to handle Kamenev and the *Daily Herald*. Jasper Harker had recently married Margaret Russell Cooke at a Mayfair church. She was the sister of Sidney ('Cookie') Russell Cooke, an intellectual stockbroker and Liberal parliamentary candidate, who had inherited a fine house on the Isle of Wight called Bellecroft. Russell Cooke had been a lover of Maynard Keynes, whose lifelong friend and business associate he remained, and was the son-in-law of the captain of the Titanic. Virginia Woolf called him 'a shoving young man, who wants to be smart, cultivated, go-ahead & all the rest of it'. Harker used his brother-in-law to compromise Kamenev.[53]

Davenport-Hines' source for the Woolf remark is possibly from the published history of Rowe & Pitman that references a dinner party in September 1928 attended by the Cookes, Virginia Woolf and Keynes.

Cookie

Figure 74: Lev Borisovich Kamenev (1883–1936), born Rozenfeld, was a Bolshevik revolutionary and a prominent Soviet politician (pictured right, with Ninoviev). Sidney was asked to spy on him. (Wikimedia Commons/Public Domain)

Woolf was quoted as above.[54] It is not surprising she knew of him. Keynes and Woolf were part of the 'Bloomsbury Group,' a collection of wealthy and influential British writers, philosophers, and artists of whom Keynes and Woolf were foremost, who regularly met in the Bloomsbury area of London. They were well known for promoting and nurturing young talent, were politically liberal and thrived on rebelling against society norms, especially those of a sexual nature; a code that fitted Cooke to a tee.

The situation with Sheridan Clare was a critical one, as Winston Churchill, then the Secretary of State for War in Lloyd George's Liberal government, was closely involved. Clare was Winston's only female cousin and despite their diametrically opposed political views, their mutual interest in art meant that, unbeknownst to Churchill, whilst he was visiting Clare in her London studio, only hours earlier Lev Kamenev had been there sitting for his bust. Churchill hated the Bolsheviks (he called them 'crocodiles') and wanted them expelled from the country.[55]

The first step was for Cooke to arrange a meeting with Kamenev, and Clare's studio was the obvious location. The following specifics of Cooke's mission are complete with dates and locations mostly provided by Clare Sheridan herself. Firstly, she wrote a book in 1921 entitled *Mayfair to Moscow – Clare Sheridan's Diary*, published with the intent of defending her interest in Bolshevik activities, which she claimed were more 'portrait work, not politics ... it is the psychology of people that interests me, not their politics.'[56] This was followed in 1936 by an exclusive article in the *Evening Standard* in which Sheridan revealed that

Titanic Legacy: The Captain, the Daughter and the Spy

Figure 75: Clare Sheridan pictured in 1922. *The Richmond Palladium and Sun-Telegram*, 18 April 1922. (Author's collection)

'Mr. Sidney Russell Cooke, a well-known City stockbroker and company director, enlisted her services on behalf of the British Intelligence Service to keep watch over Kameneff's [sic] movements – a mission which she accepted.'[57] But with reservations, as we shall see.

It all started on Thursday 26 August 1920 when Cooke visited Sheridan's London studio. Sheridan had just completed work on a bust of Russian Bolshevik Leonid Krasin, who had joined Kamenev in his visit to London for political negotiations. Then she wrote in her diary – without any explanation or suspicion: 'Sidney came to see me after dinner, and we talked fantastically about Russia, and what it might or might not lead to! He is terribly interested.'[58]

At this point, Sheridan would not have been aware of Cooke's ulterior motive – that he was 'terribly interested' in tracking Kamenev. He was certainly not wasting time. The very next day, Sheridan introduced Cooke to Kamenev on Friday 27 August during a lunch at Claridge's in Mayfair. The meeting must have gone well as Sheridan wrote in her diary that Sidney immediately invited Kamenev to visit his house on the Isle of Wight that weekend, along with Sheridan[59] The following day, Sheridan and Kamenev took a train from Waterloo to Portsmouth.

It was a daring suggestion. Perhaps Cooke had picked up on Kamenev's desire to visit the Isle of Wight as an irresistible opportunity. Or maybe the idea of visiting such a picturesque part of the country during summer had been planted earlier. Plans were hastily arranged, and Cooke met his guests in Portsmouth. Sheridan wrote:

> Kamenev picked me up at 12:15 and we caught a 12:50 from Waterloo to Portsmouth. Sidney met us at the Harbor, and escorted us to his house on the Isle of Wight, near Newport. A very attractive journey across, as it was warm and calm weather. A motor met us at Ryde and took us to his house, seven miles. On arrival we flung ourselves down in the sun on the grass of the tennis court.[60]

With the death of their mother in 1914, Cooke and his sister had inherited the family home of Bellecroft at 79, Staplers Road, a fine looking two-storey Georgian house built in 1805 that later (1953) became a Grade II listed building.[61] Positioned on a hill, it is constructed of yellow brick with a lead and slate roof and contained a hall, ballroom, three receptions, billiards room, fourteen bedrooms, three bathrooms, domestic offices and a servants' hall. The grounds had a four-room cottage, a stable for four horses, several gardens, an orchard and a farm.[62] Interestingly, according to property deeds, the 65-acre estate was purchased by Cooke from his younger sister Margaret in 1929 for £848.[63] So while Sidney and his sister Margaret jointly inherited the property (something that surely his mother would have pushed for, based on her life-long ambition for equality), Sidney later bought his sister's stake. The siblings had three employees based in the house, husband and wife team Charles and Rachel Morgan as the head gardener and caretaker, and Mary Ann Bashford, a 46-year-old cook.[64]

Today converted into flats, most of the estate was lost to redevelopment and it lacks the charm of a hundred years ago, although it still retains the large green lawns and views of the Solent from the roof.

Kamenev was duly impressed with the English scenery when he arrived on the Island. Sheridan later recalled that he was 'delighted with the smooth mown lawns and the roses. It was the England he had read in novels.'[65] If the idea was to relax the Russian, the plan was working. A friend of Sidney later observed that Kamanev 'brought no bodyguard or security men, but had a pistol in his suitcase'.[66] One of Cooke's primary tactics was to encourage Kamenev to talk – and this he certainly did according to Sheridan's diary account:

> After tea, as we lay full length on rugs, our heads leaning on the grassy bank, behind us, and the sun gradually sinking lower and lower, Kamenev for over an hour told us the history of the Russian Revolution.
>
> He told it to us haltingly, stumbling along in his bad French, wrestling with words and phrases, but always conveying his meaning and, above all, conjuring up the most graphic pictures – making us see with his eyes, live over the days with him, and know all the people concerned. He is amazingly forceful and eloquent. We sat silent and spell-bound.[67]

Kamenev's historical storytelling stretched back twenty years, with tales of revolution that included Lenin and Trotsky, secret organisations, their arrests and time in a Siberian prison. When they were called for dinner, he did not resume his talk of Bolshevik history, but he did continue to converse and according to Sheridan 'did most of the evening's talking'. She felt it was a 'great waste that his audience consisted only of us two, when so many might have been enthralled.' It was not wasted on Cooke. He was undoubtedly enthralled that his target was so free with conversation and information.

The following day, on the Sunday morning of 29 August, Cooke was up early in the morning to continue his surveillance. There was a slight hitch due to a cultural difference when the maid reported she had 'knocked on [Kamenev's] door in vain. It was locked.' When Kamanev later appeared, he commented that he thought it was strange a 'maid would want to bring him hot water before he was even out of bed!'[68]

When Sheridan awoke, she found Cooke and Kamenev talking over a fire and accused them of 'frousting' – meaning to lounge about in a hot, stuffy room – and ushered them out into the cold Bellecroft gardens. The air helped to restart Kamenev's talk of the Revolution, although

Figure 76: The Russell Cooke family estate, 'Bellecroft,' as it looked in 2023. (Photograph: Dan Parkes)

it was interrupted by the effect of an unusually cold summer, even by England's standards, and they were forced to return to the fire inside.[69]

Kamenev may have become more cautious about Russian political discussions after receiving a call in the morning from his secretary, who was concerned about his whereabouts:

> Later in the morning he was rung up by the delegation headquarters, who demanded to know where he had disappeared to. He laughed. His telephone number on the Island [sic] of Wight was all he knew. He had not yet mastered his host's name, the name of the house or of the village. 'But supposing something happens to you ... how shall we know?' asked the secretary in alarm, suspecting foul play.[70]

This was possibly the first time the name Sidney Russell Cooke came to the attention of the Russians and when they hurriedly began to cross-check his background and connections. In turn, Kamenev, likely warned by his delegation, kept conversation to that of a more banal nature. At 2:30 pm, he followed Cooke and Sheridan in an open top car to the south of the Island, where they stopped at a 'lonely' beach. As if Kamenev had been relegated to the role of a chaperone, he watched as Cooke and Sheridan paddled in the water and then sat on the beach. The beautiful scenery and the sight of the two enjoying the beach apparently made him happy and he was 'thoroughly laughing' and even wrote some romantically inclined verses to Sheridan on the back of a five-pound note. 'I don't know what happened to the bank note, but Kamenev wrote four lines, and Sidney the other four, in French. Kamenev likened me to Venus, but Sidney was flippant, and said that the part of me he liked best was my feet!'[71]

Returning to Bellecroft they stopped for a picnic on a common off a lonely road with the remainder of the day making politics recede like the tide. That was until Kamenov went to sign the Bellecroft visitors book before he left, in which he wrote: 'Workers of the world unit' inadvertently omitting the final 'e.' Sheridan was unfamiliar with the Communist slogan and wondered exactly what a 'workers unit' was.[72]

Moscow Mission

It was only a weekend jaunt and so by Monday, Sheridan was back in London and making plans to visit Russia as soon as the following weekend. Her ambition was to sculpt Lenin's head.[73] It was sometime between the weekend at Bellecroft and her journey to Moscow that

Cooke revealed his role in the Intelligence Service and their interest in Kamenev:

> Then one day [Sidney] explained to me that Kameneff [sic] had got to be watched, his every movement must be reported. He suggested that I should accept the mission, which would save my friend from the importunity of being followed by a detective. I accepted purely with a protective motive. 'Intelligence' should know just as much as I chose to them and no more. I was naively entertained by my new role. It gave me a feeling of importance. [74]

That Sheridan accepted an intelligence mission from Cooke is not mentioned at all in her diary, a matter too delicate to be committed to ink. She did write privately that an anonymous friend told her she was 'in great danger of being shot as a spy', to which she replied her sole motive for travelling to Russia was based on 'an artist's zeal'.[75] And in later diary entries while in Moscow, she continues the ruse, writing that 'if I had been a spy pretending not to understand Russian, I wonder whether I should have learnt interesting things.'[76]

On Friday 10 September 1920, Cooke travelled to London from Scotland, arriving at 5 pm and joining Sheridan at the studio by 10:30 pm. As Cooke was talking, Kamenev telephoned to tell her that he had an interview with none other than Lloyd George, the Prime Minister, and that as a result he had to immediately leave the country and could not return. He then invited Sheridan to join him. So it was that Cooke joined Sheridan and Kamenev as they boarded a train from St Pancras bound for Newcastle. There was a little hiccup with a handbag full of money that Cooke both caused and solved:

> Sidney, fulfilling his reputation as an organizer, discovered there were two trains going to Newcastle, and that the next one starting a little later had a restaurant car, so we transferred our luggage from the one to the other, and in the process I lost my handbag which had my hundred pounds in it in bank notes, all I possessed in the world! It caused me some agitation, but Kamenev was quite calm and seemed to think that money was not very important, and that I should not have much need of it in Russia. To my intense relief, however, Sidney found the case at Newcastle in the lost property office. It travelled ahead of us on the other train.

Author Davenport-Hines, rather than seeing this as an example of Cooke's organisational prowess, believes the handbag was 'doubtless searched' before it reappeared in the Newcastle lost luggage office.[77]

Cookie

In Newcastle, Sheridan boarded the SS *Jupiter* with Kamenev. Cooke was still there, ensuring that she went through with her travels to Moscow. She wrote, knowingly by this stage: 'I don't think he believed in the reality of my journey until he saw me safely past the passport officials!'[78]

Just over a month later, on Saturday 23 October, while Clare Sheridan was in Moscow – and only three days before Cooke's younger sister Pattie married MI5 agent Jasper Harker in Mayfair – Cooke's cover was blown. It was the day when Sheridan had just finished Trotsky's bust and was told, to her great relief, that it was a good likeness. She had already finished one of Lenin, and completing Trotsky's bust was something of a 'dream.' She wrote she had achieved her purpose. 'I have proved myself to these people.' It was not to be so.

A senior Russian diplomat named Maxim Litvinov, whom she had befriended, suddenly asked Sheridan probing questions about Cooke. She had great trust in Litvinov, and believed he was taking a protective role. She wrote in her diary the following exchange:

> To-day he gave me furiously to think. Suddenly, without any warning, he sat back in his chair and fixed me with his small eyes: 'Do you know a man called Russel [sic] Cooke?' he asked. It was rather a surprising question, and I admitted that I knew a very young man called Sidney Russel Cooke. Though why Litvinoff should have ever heard of him I couldn't imagine. He went on to say that Kamenev knows him. I said yes, that Kamenev had met him through me. Litvinoff said: 'He is in the British Intelligence Service, isn't he?' I confess to a slight shiver down my spine when he said this; but I refuted the statement. I said that so far as I knew (and it hadn't interested me very much) Sidney Cooke was working in the city awaiting a propitious moment to plunge into rather liberal politics. Litvinoff gave a sort of grunt, which denoted nothing at all, and refused to be drawn any further on the subject. But something seems to be in the air, and I cannot tell what it is.[79]

It is unlikely that Cooke, as he gave away his sister to Jasper Harker a few days later, had any idea that the Russians now knew his true intent – and how this had gravely endangered the life of his sculptor friend. She later conceded that it was 'the Russell Cooke friendship and that visit to the Isle of Wight that nearly landed me in trouble in Moscow'. Kamenev was not at all happy either when informed by the Cheka – the Russian secret police – that Cooke had been working for British intelligence. Sheridan wrote that 'it shattered his belief in me. There are certain things the Soviets take rather seriously, and they cannot admit that an individual should "play" with the I.D. or Intelligence Department.'[80]

Fortunately, her work on the busts of Lenin and Trotsky had endeared her to those in the Communist regime and she was able to return safely to England in November 1920. She was ruthlessly searched in Newcastle, pursued by the press and ostracised socially, but otherwise survived to tell the tale. Winston Churchill refused to meet her. She met with Cooke again, however, not long after, along with Irish playwright and fierce critic of Captain Smith, George Bernard Shaw. She wrote in January 1921: 'Bernard Shaw too I met at dinner at Sidney Cooke's, but Shaw with all his wit and genius has not the fierce flame that is characteristic of the Russian spirit.'[81]

Whether Sheridan ever told Cooke of what Maxim Litvinov had discovered is not known. Or whether Shaw ever realized he had dined with someone about to join the family of a Captain he had publicly criticised.

Regardless, Cooke would have soon discovered his ruse had been exposed with the publication of her diary later that year. In the meantime, he helped Sheridan travel to the United States. On 17 January 1921, she wrote that she 'sent my passport papers all filled up and signed to Sidney, to the Reform Club, and he is going to deal with the matter for me. There seem to be delays that one suspects of being deliberate – I feel none too easy just yet about that passport.' The Reform Club, located on Pall Mall in London, is a private gentlemen's club and mostly home to those with progressive political ideals, so well suited to Cooke. His membership is also referred to in his King's College entry.

Cooke's contacts at the Reform Club came through, as the following day, while Sheridan was having lunch at the Café Royal, Cooke turned up and returned her passport. The next day he accompanied Sheridan to the United States Consulate and by the weekend, she was aboard the Cunard *Aquitania* bound for New York.[82] Drama seemed to follow Sheridan wherever she went, including in the United States in the 1920s when she embarked on a speaking tour and published several books. By late 1921, she was involved in an affair with Charlie Chaplin, and then in April 1922 was allegedly revealing a shocking nude statue of 'King Jazz' in New York. She even returned to Moscow in 1923, where she discovered she was no longer welcome.

In late 1925 – after Cooke had been married for three years – he told MI5 that he was 'strongly of the opinion that [Sheridan] was in the pay of the Russians. [She was] free of debt for the first time in ten years, despite making no money from journalism or sculpture.' Though her cold reception there in 1923 did not support such a conclusion.[83]

There is one final reminder of Sheridan's dangerous excursion to Russia that likely cost Cooke his intelligence job: In 1929, with the rise of Joseph Stalin, Leon Trotsky was expelled from the Soviet Union and assassinated in his house in Coyocan, Mexico City, in August 1940. The study where he was murdered with an ice axe has been left exactly as it was found. In the corner, up high on a shelf, is a bust of Trotsky staring defiantly into the distance. This was the bust created by Clare Sheridan, the one she finished on the day Sidney Russell Cooke was exposed as a spy.

While Cooke was almost undoubtedly relieved of his MI5 duties after the failure of the Sheridan mission, his brother-in-law, Jasper Harker, eventually became the acting Director General of MI5 between June 1940 and 1941, and then stayed on as the Deputy Director General before retiring in 1946.[84] Sidney's school friend, Nicholas Davenport, offered Hinton Manor, his country house, to the war effort, and after the bombing of the MI5 war office, the manor was served a billeting order. This was a stroke of luck for Davenport, as Harker and his wife would bring him along with them every Friday night when they motored down to the manor.[85]

Harker is remembered for several not particularly endearing incidents, such as the time when Davenport, on receiving a call from a commanding officer telling him that the Germans were about to invade, went into the Brigadier's bedroom to warn him, and Harker responded with a curt 'Don't be a fool, MI5 hasn't telephoned,' and turned over and went back to sleep. Davenport later had to admit: 'We all looked pretty foolish when the dawn came with no order from headquarters.'[86] More seriously, Harker rejected vital intelligence about a Soviet spy and the British nuclear programme from Mona Maund, because he doubted her abilities as a woman spy. The consensus is that Maund's intelligence might have changed the direction of the Cold War, if Jasper Harker had not simply ignored it.[87]

8
'Ambitious and Adventurous'

In 1921, both Cooke and Keynes met women they would later marry. Keynes fell in love with Lydia Lopokova (1891-1981), a famous Russian ballerina whom he wed in 1925, much to the initial chagrin of his comrades in the Bloomsbury Group.

In early October 1921, Cooke took the law bar exam and passed with a Class III in Roman Law for the Inner Temple, one of the four Inns of Court (where Keynes had also been admitted in 1905).[1] Then in early December, it was announced that Cooke was engaged. A gossip column in a 9 December 1921 Liverpool evening newspaper could not resist making a *Titanic* connection, as well as commenting on Miss Melville Smith's beauty:

> Titanic Disaster Recalled.
> The announcement of the engagement between Stanley [sic] Russell Cooke, of 12, King's Bench-walk, Temple, and Helen Melville Smith, daughter of Mrs. Smith, of 41, Queen's Gate-gardens, is an echo of the Titanic tragedy. Her father, Captain F.J. Smith [sic], was in command of the White Star wonder vessel which sank during its maiden voyage, hundreds of people being drowned after a midnight collision with an iceberg.
>
> Miss Smith's father was one of the most respected seamen afloat, and his daughter more than inherits his good looks. Captain Smith was a hearty big man of the sea; his daughter is a very beautiful girl in the early twenties. Her fiancé is a relative by marriage of Sir Charles Dilke.[2]

While Mel is described as 'a very beautiful girl', Sidney was also similarly characterised, with a notable caveat by his friend Davenport: a 'good-looking young man with dark brown hair and brown eyes,

'Ambitious and Adventurous'

an aristocratic nose and the somewhat arrogant manner of the upper-class'.[3] A few days later, on the 13th, Cooke wrote a letter to Keynes in which he mentioned a new woman in his life, to be become his wife in little over a month's time. While he does not specifically name her, the timing of the letter after the engagement announcement and its offer of an introduction make it undoubtedly about Melville. The letterhead gives his new address, '12 King's Bench Walk, Temple, E.C.4', and likely in reply to an inquiry by Keynes, launches straight into an almost clinical description of his fiancée. Addressed to 'Maynard' it begins: 'She's certainly lovely, reasonably intelligent, some money (more in prospect), damn randy, & good-tempered. In addition she is ambitious & adventurous & anxious to help in all my wild schemes.'[4]

That she was 'reasonably intelligent' imputes condescendingly that she did not quite meet his own level of intelligence, perhaps reminding us of Virginia Woolf's earlier appraisal of Cooke as someone who 'wants to be smart' rather than someone who is. That he describes her as 'damn randy' – while considered an inappropriate disclosure of personal information, even to a friend – it does tell us that their relationship was sexually charged. When he mentioned that there is 'more money in prospect', he must be referring to Mel's mother, Eleanor, who had inherited Captain Smith's estate. His description of her as 'ambitious & adventurous' certainly tallies with what we know about Mel, particularly in her later life. As per earlier correspondence with Keynes, he once again refers to 'schemes' that likely indicate his various political agendas. As Sheridan had told Litvinov in Moscow, she thought Cooke was 'working in the city awaiting a propitious moment to plunge into rather liberal politics'. In the years following their marriage, he wrote several books about American politics. It is also possible that the expression 'wild schemes' also refers to his continued involvement in MI5.

Cooke finished the short letter to Keynes by suggesting he dine the following Monday at his place at 12 King's Bench Walk, when he could meet Mel in person. Or alternatively, he suggests 'a cocktail between five & seven any evening this week except Thursday. Ring up first to make sure. But come Monday if you can. S.R.C.'

We do not know if Keynes ever took up his offer to meet Mel. With so personal a description and Keynes' own affections now diverted elsewhere, he may well have simply been too busy or uninterested. All we do know is that this letter is the last of five from Cooke to Keynes found in the King's College, Cambridge archive.

Five days after Cooke's letter, three Banns were published on 18 and 25 December 1921 and 1 January 1922:

Titanic Legacy: The Captain, the Daughter and the Spy

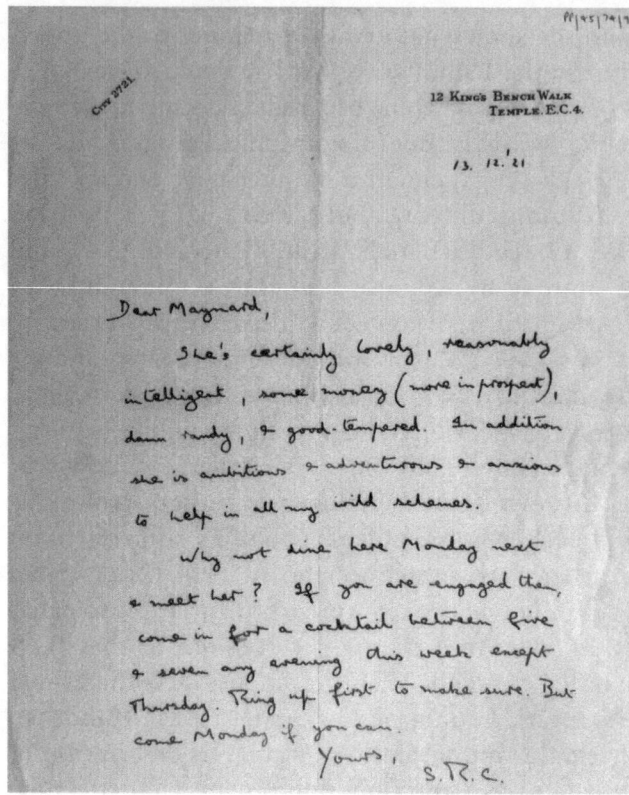

Figure 77: Sidney Russell Cooke's letter to Keynes in which he describes Mel as 'randy' as well as 'ambitious and adventurous.' (King's College Archive, Cambridge)

Mr. S.R. Cooke and Miss H.M. Smith

A marriage has been arranged between Sidney Russell Cooke, of Bellecroft, Newport, Isle of Wight, and 12, Kings Bench-walk, Temple, and Helen Melville, daughter of the late Captain E.J. Smith, R.N.R., R.D., and Mrs. Smith, of 41, Queen's Gate-gardens, S.W.7.[5]

On 31 December 1921, Sidney was reported to be briefly living in Holborn, occupying the flat of Stephen McKenna at 11 Stone Buildings, Lincoln's Inn (Holborn 553) while he was away visiting South America. If this was the same McKenna who was a prolific novelist (1888-1967) then there is a curious convergence of interest as McKenna worked in the War Trade Intelligence Department 1915-19, the same as Cooke.[6]

Sidney and Mel were married on Wednesday, 18 January 1922, in St Mark's Church, North Audley Street, Mayfair. The Anglican church had been built exactly one hundred years earlier in 1822, and later became known as the 'American Church' due to its proximity to the former United States embassy.

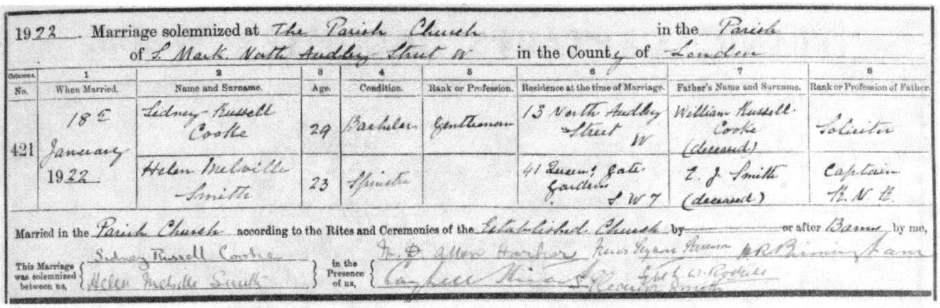

'Ambitious and Adventurous'

Figure 78: Sidney and Mel's marriage certificate, witnessed by her mother and Sidney's MI5 brother-in-law, Jasper Harker. (Courtesy of Paul Van Doodson)

The *Isle of Wight County Press* newspaper did not announce the wedding in its usual 'Births, Marriages, and Deaths' column on the front page, as it had with Sidney's younger sister's nuptials. On page eight, there is a short description of the event in the Newport local news column:

> MARRIAGE OF CAPT. S RUSSELL COOKE – The Bishop of Birmingham officiated on Wednesday … at the marriage of Captain Sidney Russell Cooke, son of the late Mr. and Mrs. W. Russell Cooke, of Bellecroft, and Miss Helen Melville Smith, daughter of the late Captain E.J. Smith, R.N.R., R.D., who died in the disaster to the Titanic, of which he was captain, and of Mrs. Smith, of 41 Queen's Gate-gardens, S.W. The bride, who was given away by her mother, wore a gown of her own design, in mediaeval style, of ivory velvet, the heavy Court train being lined with gold tissue and covered with a veil of gold tulle, and a headdress of pearl-embroidered gold lace. She carried a sheaf of daffodils, and daffodils were used in the decoration of the chancel. Sir Campbell Stuart was best man. There were no bridesmaids. During the signing of the register the choir sang Brahms's anthem 'How lovely is Thy dwelling place'.[7]

Mirroring what happened at Jasper and Pattie's wedding in 1920, when Sidney gave away his sister in place of their late father, Eleanor Smith gave away Mel in lieu of the late Captain Smith. The subsequent reception was once again held at 33a Montagu Square, the home of John and Sybil Roskill. The guest list was a veritable who's who, including Edith Lady Playfair, Lady Bonham-Carter, Lady Macmillan and Sir Edgar Chatfeild-Clarke. One name not included in the list was that of John Maynard Keynes. He may well have attended but avoided inclusion on the official guest list, or simply abstained from attendance altogether. The newspaper announcement finished by adding that the 'Captain and Mrs. Russell Cooke afterwards left for Paris.'

Titanic Legacy: The Captain, the Daughter and the Spy

Figure 79: *The Evening Express*, 19 January 1922, printed a wedding photograph with a caption that once again referred to the 'ill-fated Titanic'. (Author's collection)

The London *Times* added that 'the Rev. W.O. Pennyman, vicar of St. Mark's, assisted at the service, which was choral. Mr. F.S. Stevenson, Deputy-Lieutenant of Suffolk, escorted the bride to the church.'[8] This was the same Stevenson who wrote the poem about Captain Smith and was the secretary of the Captain Smith Memorial Committee.

The Liverpool *Evening Express* was the only newspaper to include a photograph of the couple leaving the church and could not resist the temptation to make a connection to the 'ill-fated Titanic' (Figure 79). While Sidney is beaming with happiness, it is not a particularly flattering photograph of Mel, an echo of how uncomfortable her father was in front of a camera.[9]

The marriage certificate helps fill in some of the gaps. Sidney is listed as a 29-year-old bachelor, a 'gentleman' residing at 13 North Audley Street.

This address is next door to the church, at the time 13 North Audley Street was the St Mark's vicarage. A wedding the following day also lists the groom as residing at '13 North Audley Street' revealing it was likely a custom of the day. Helen Melville Smith is listed as 23, a 'spinster' and her address 41 Queens Gate Gardens – the same address as the census the year before. There are five witness signatures, notably Mel's mother and Sidney's brother-in-law and MI5 colleague 'O. Allen Harker'.

Jasper was not the only spy connection at their wedding. Underneath Jasper's signature was the name of his best man: Sir Campbell Stuart, the Canadian-born deputy director of propaganda in enemy countries during the First World War and head of Electra House, 'which Ian [Fleming] came to know as Department EH, responsible for propaganda at the start of the Second World War'.[10] Stuart was the managing director of both *The Times* and the *Daily Mail* in 1921.[11] Sir Stuart was also gay. He was described as 'a very odd fish indeed' by novelist C. P. Snow.[12]

Leave the Noise Behind

The newlyweds made number 12 King's Bench Walk, Temple, their home in London during the weekdays and then Bellecroft on the Isle of Wight on the weekends.bThe district of Temple is sandwiched between the Royal Courts of Justice and the River Thames, a leafy, secluded legal quarter of the city. Not far from St Paul's Cathedral, vehicular access is today via barriers and tight security. Pedestrian access is primarily via Middle Temple Lane. The Oxbridge atmosphere is unmistakable. One reason for this seeming exclusivity is that the area is a 'royal peculiar' – a Church of England parish exempt from the jurisdiction of the diocese and subject directly to the monarch.

The unique nature of this legal oasis is described by Charles Dickens in *Barnaby Rudge*:

> There are, still, worse places than the Temple, on a sultry day, for basking in the sun, or resting idly in the shade. There is yet a drowsiness in its courts, and a dreamy dullness in its trees and gardens; those who pace its lanes and squares may yet hear the echoes of their footsteps on the sounding stones, and read upon its gates, in passing from the tumult of the Strand or Fleet Street, 'Who enters here leaves noise behind.' There is still the plash of falling water in fair Fountain Court, and there are yet nooks and corners where dun-haunted students may look down from their dusty garrets, on a vagrant ray of sunlight patching the shade of the tall houses, and seldom troubled to reflect a passing stranger's form. There is yet, in the Temple, something of a clerkly

monkish atmosphere, which public offices of law have not disturbed, and even legal firms have failed to scare away.[13]

The area is dominated by the Temple Church, built by the Knights Templar in the twelfth century. The church is presently owned by the Inner Temple and the Middle Temple, two of the four London Inns of Court that make up the English legal profession. The Temple Church might be one of the few reasons a tourist would venture into this exclusive part of London, but another could be the Inner Temple Gardens, that are only open between the hours of 12:30 and 3 pm, as a welcome refuge for those working in the area during their lunch break. Sidney and Mel's apartment at no. 12 overlooked the Temple Gardens, with views along the Thames. Located at the end of a secluded residential cul de sac, it was a uniquely private place considering its central London location. Numbers 12 and 13 stand out from the other buildings as the plain Regency style is faced with creamy white Bath stone, in contrast to the rest of King's Bench Walk that has the traditional red and brown brick exterior. Originally built in the early nineteenth century, the number 12 and 13 block was destroyed during the Blitz and has been faithfully rebuilt. Now a Grade II listed building, it is the home of a chamber of barristers who take the name of the firm from their address: 12 King's Bench Walk (or 12KBW).

The *Daily Herald* described the Russell Cooke's second floor residence of 1930 as a 'spacious and beautifully furnished flat ... overlooking the lawns and the Embankment.'[14] Mel would have quickly become accustomed to a range of different visitors, as there is evidence the apartment was used as a convenient 'safe house' for Sidney's MI5 acquaintances, certainly up until 1927. Author Davenport-Hines describes an occasion in that year when an MI5 spy 'disguised as a tramp' was in need of assistance and sent a 'panicky telegram' to Sidney's brother-in-law Harker, 'addressed to the chambers in the Temple of Harker's brother-in-law Sidney Russell Cooke, asking to be sent a revolver for self-defence'.[15] It is unclear if revolvers were routinely kept in the Temple flat.

Children, Books and the Firm

When he was not helping colleagues at MI5, Sidney was working at his day job, with his political aspirations never far from his mind. In 1923, Sidney became a member of the Stock Exchange and was regarded as one of the promising young men of the City – described as 'associated with the school of investment ideas generally labelled "The Keynes School". He served with his Cambridge friend Keynes, on the board

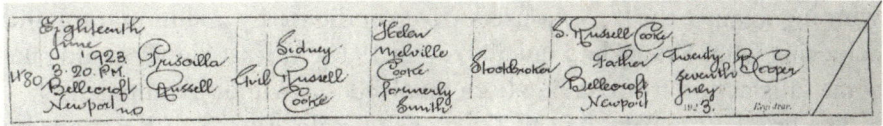

Figure 80: Birth certificate of Priscilla, 18 June 1923. (Courtesy of Paul Van Doodson)

of the National Mutual Life Assurance Society and was also a member of the Liberal Industrial Inquiry.'[16] In March 1923, in 'City News in Brief,' it was announced that Cooke had entered into partnership upon the retirement of a Mr E. Wightwick, with 'Messrs. Capel-Cure and Terry'.[17]

Sidney and Melville's twins, Simon Russell Cooke (1923-1944) and Priscilla Russell Cooke (1923-1947), were born at 3:20 pm on 18 June, and were non-identical twins (Figure 80). Sidney registered their births on 27 July and his occupation was noted as a 'stockbroker'. The baptism made the news in August 1923: 'Princess Beatrice attended the first christening at Carisbrooke Castle Chapel for a hundred and thirty years on Saturday, when the twin son and daughter of Mr. and Mrs. S Russell Cooke, Newport, were baptised.'[18] The Russell Cookes were certainly doing well, if the Governor of the Isle of Wight, Princess Beatrice, could arrange her affairs so as to be present at the christening of their children. Princess Beatrice had started to retire from public appearances after the death of her son, Prince Maurice of Battenberg, during the First World War, so it is surprising that she would bestow such an honour.

Shortly after the birth of the twins, Mel spoke at a public event for the first time. Mel appeared at the St Paul's (Barton) Horticultural Show held on 16 August 1923 to perform the opening ceremony. In a short speech, she told those gathered that it was the 'first occasion for her to speak from any public platform' and she was glad the event was being held at Barton, wishing the show every success and many happy returns.[19] Flower shows were later held in their home estate. In October that same year, she was once again called upon by St Paul's Church to perform an opening ceremony for an event to raise money for the restoration of the church.[20]

Work and family life certainly did not end Sidney's political interest, nor his involvement in espionage. In November 1923, he appeared once again in Torquay, giving a speech at the Town Hall in support of the Liberal candidate, Piers Gilchrist Thompson.[21] The Liberal party in Torquay had struggled to find another candidate after Sidney's crushing defeat during the 1918 election. Thompson suffered a similar fate in 1922 when the same Conservative candidate, Tory MP Colonel Burn, won again. When another election was called toward the end of 1923, Colonel Burns stepped down, allowing an opportunity for Thompson to make gains, eventually winning against the new Conservative candidate by a slim margin and achieving what Sidney had failed to do in 1918. At least Sidney could take some satisfaction from having been involved in a winning campaign.

The first edition of *The Oil Trusts and Anglo-American Relations* by E. H. Davenport (Ernest Harold Davenport, who used the pseudonym Nicholas Davenport) and Sidney Russell Cooke was published in 1923, with the Macmillan, New York edition released in 1924. This was not Sidney's first foray into print. Shortly before, he had been a contributor to a *Manchester Guardian* supplement on European finance edited by his former lover, Keynes.[22] As for Davenport, he was more than just a co-author. He had let 12 King's Bench Walk since 1916, the second-floor apartment that he subsequently sublet to Sidney soon after the war.[23] Cooke and Davenport had attended Cheltenham College together, and although Sidney went to Cambridge and Nicholas to Oxford, they came together after the war as part of a group of economists aligned with Keynes' post-war ideals.[24]

The idea for the book came from Davenport, not Cooke – and it had a White Star connection. Davenport had some years earlier taken a position with a new oil company formed by Lord Pirrie of Harland and Wolff (builders of White Star liners) and after an accusation that he had left some confidential papers in the squash court of a White Star ship, was fired by Lord Pirrie. Davenport began writing about oil in the *Manchester Guardian*, which brought him once again to the attention of Maynard Keynes. Davenport expressed a desire to write a full-length book about what he believed was an international oil war. 'Keynes approved my idea and the book was financed by my friend Sidney Russell Cooke on condition that his name appeared as co-author,' Davenport later recalled. 'I readily agreed and he was extremely helpful as a literary critic.'[25]

The book argues that government participation in the oil sector would jeopardise its development and that it is mistaken to consider that oil has the same political power as command of the sea. There was a generally positive review in *The Annals of the American Academy of Political and Social Science*: 'This book written by two British specialists deserves a reading by those who know both oil and politics; it is even more worth reading by those who know neither. In substance it is a non-technical discussion of oil concession ... though written by Englishmen the discussion is in no way prejudiced.'[26]

A December 1923 review from his local Isle of Wight newspaper evaluated the publication as a 'frank judgment of the rights and wrongs of the British and American positions... The book is cleverly written, and the name of the publishers is a sufficient guarantee for the excellence of its production.'[27]

The anti-imperialist leanings of the book made it of interest to the Soviet government and, despite having no permission to do so, they had the book translated into Russian and sold as a paperback by the War Ministry in Moscow. As there were still 'intellectual links between London and Moscow at that time, Sidney Russell Cooke took up the question with Kamenev to whom he had been introduced', although no royalties were ever paid.[28] The publication of his book the following year in the States prompted Sidney to make the journey across the pond and he arrived in New York on 28 April 1924, without Mel or Eleanor.

The book was instrumental in Sidney gaining employment at Rowe & Pitman in 1925. One of the most prominent stockbroking firms in the City, it would later be home to James Bond author Ian Fleming. There were several spy connections to the firm. Partner Lancelot Hugh Smith ('Lancey') had been involved in covert operations during the war and his brother Aubrey was ex-Naval Intelligence. According to author Andrew Lycett, 'Rowe and Pitman frequently provided a home for intelligence personnel ... even the unpublished official history of Rowe and Pitman concedes, "It is interesting to speculate whether R&P's Lancelot Hugh Smith was, by his own involvement and through the medium of his brother, a long term talent spotter for British Intelligence."'[29] In another account, Lycett notes that Lancey's links to espionage and to the Baltic meant that he probably encouraged Sidney to stay close to intelligence circles.[30]

Oliver Buckton also joins the dots from the book to Sidney's employment, and to the intelligence community:

> Most notoriously, Rowe & Pitman hired Sydney [sic] Russell Cooke in 1925 on the basis of his authorship (with Nicholas Davenport) of the book *The Oil Trust and Anglo-American Relations*. Cooke worked for MI5 during and after the war and is described by Andrew Lycett as a 'prototype James Bond'. Like Ian Fleming, Cooke took a keen interest in the development of the young Soviet Union after the Bolshevik revolution.[31]

When Lancey invited Sidney to join Rowe & Pitman, Sidney insisted on bringing Davenport with him. By October 1925, Sidney was a partner while 'Davenport was hired as a clerk to start up a long-overdue market intelligence section.' Davenport describes Cooke as making a favourable impression on Lancey due to his looks and upper-class manner: 'In a few days he was offered a partnership in Rowe and Pitman and had the magnanimity to tell the great man that although he was greatly flattered, he could not accept the offer unless he could bring with him a young friend called Davenport who wrote "all his economic stuff."'[32] Cooke's appointment was prominently displayed in the London *Times* to an extent that caused the Stock Exchange to ask questions, although George Rowe would later explain that the firm played no role in the *Times*' decision to feature it. There was another connection between the Cookes and the Rowe & Pitman firm. When the *Titanic* sank in the early hours of 15 April 1912, so did a number of Rowe & Pitman American share certificates, for which Lloyd's would later have to issue indemnity letters.[33]

Joining a busy firm such as Rowe & Pitman did not prevent Cooke from further writing. Buoyed by the success of their Anglo-American book, in October 1926 the co-authors published a controversial pamphlet delving into Australasian economics and 'the great question of Commonwealth finance' under the title of *Australian Finance*.

The book was in response to the 1926 Imperial Conference held in London from 19 October to 22 November 1926, which brought together the prime ministers of what was then known as the 'Dominions of the British Empire': Australia, Canada, India, Irish Free State, Newfoundland, New Zealand and South Africa. The conference was most remarkable for its Balfour Declaration that replaced the term 'Dominions' with the much less aggressive 'British Commonwealth'. The event is less well-known for the release of Cooke's book, although it was reviewed by the *Gloucester Journal*, who reported that 'Messrs. Sidney Russell Cooke and E.H. Davenport ... state that they have no prejudice against Colonial loans, but they fear that uneconomic borrowing must eventually lead to disaster. The pamphlet is published at one shilling by The Pelican Press, Carmelite-street, E.C.'[34]

The fault-finding intent of the pamphlet was plain to see from the very first page, which stated that in the 'whole British Empire there is no more voracious borrower than the Australian Commonwealth.' Australia was not happy with the criticism. In a confidential letter dated 14 December 1927, London-based Richard Casey, Australia's liaison officer for the Commonwealth Public Service, wrote to then Australian Prime Minister Stanley Bruce:

> I went last night to a small Group Meeting of the Royal Institute of International Affairs at which Cooke, of Davenport & Cooke, the authors of the pamphlet critical of Australian Finance, read a paper in which he reviewed the 'reforms' in Australian Finance since (and he rather implied consequent upon) their pamphlet of a year ago... Cooke does not propose to publish this paper but is to let me have a copy of it, which I will forward to you in due course.[35]

The insinuation is that Cooke and Davenport thought their work had influenced Australian practice. Among the notes that accompany the confidential letter, part of a release of 10,823 documents on Australian Foreign Policy between 15 May 1913 and 15 March 1983 by 'historian and hacker' Tim Sherratt of the University of Canberra,[36] were the following comments on Cooke:

> S.R. Cooke and E.H. Davenport, City of London brokers, had circulated at the 1926 Imperial Conference a pamphlet extremely critical of Australian loan raising behaviour. Explicit criticism was aimed at Australia's 'voracious' loans appetite but the authors probably reflected, too, British dissatisfaction with the degree to which Dominion borrowers were inhibiting domestic investment.[37]

The Wealthy Sporting Man

By 1926, Sidney was doing well, becoming a director for trusts with capital of £1,500,000. He was described as 'working on bold lines' and 'largely responsible for the success of the Grange and Ailsa Investment Trusts ... possessed of unusual enterprise and fertile and original ideas, he was always exceptionally temperamental... The Aika Investment Trust was formed in 1927 and the Grange Trust in 1926. Both have capitals of £750,000 and have been successful undertakings and have paid dividends.'[38]

Sidney was known as a 'wealthy man. He kept three motor-cars, and was interested in many sports.'[39] He played lawn tennis and made the news when he won two matches out of three for team 'Princes' during a March 1924 Cambridge tennis event.[40] He was 'summoned for driving a motor vehicle in a dangerous manner' on the evening of 28 August 1926 at Golders Green crossroads, after he mistakenly drove on the wrong side of the street thinking it was a one-way route. When a policeman said he would report it, Sidney was quoted as saying: 'If you had your returns, you would be prosecuted for causing a traffic nuisance.' It's an odd phrase, but essentially he was blaming the road layout or even the traffic officer's directions for his own error. He pleaded guilty to a technical offence and was fined the relatively minor amount of 20 shillings.[41]

Sidney was never too busy to forget his wedding anniversary – on 18 January. A society article in the January 1926 edition of *The Sketch* remarked that 'it is rather refreshing to hear of a couple continuing to celebrate the anniversary of their wedding day after the first year is past ... but a party of this description was given by Mr. and Mrs. Sydney [sic]

Russell Cooke the other day. He is half-brother to Sir Fisher Dilke, and Lady Dilke was among the guests.'[42] Their fourth anniversary was quite a celebrity affair – with politicians, popular singers and dancers in attendance.

Mel and the three-year-old twins were also newsworthy. Simon was recorded as appearing as one of the page boys and Priscilla a bridesmaid in a celebrity wedding on 17 June 1926 of Miss Rita Mew and Captain McGavin. Simon wore a delphinium blue silk suit with a white shirt and silver tie, while Priscilla was 'daintily dressed' in delphinium blue taffeta and a silver lace Dutch bonnet, carrying a silver basket of pin rosebuds. Sidney and Melville gave an electric lamp as a wedding gift.[43]

Mel began to flex her political muscles in October of 1926 when the president of the Newport Women's Liberal Association resigned, and putting herself forward she was successfully elected as her successor, following in the footsteps of Sidney's mother, who had also been president. On the occasion of her first meeting as president, the local newspaper printed an address by local Liberal politician Sir Godfrey Barling in which he placed more emphasis on Sidney's achievements than her suitability for the role, saying they were

> ... fortunate in securing Mrs. Russell Cooke's services, as she would also secure the interest for their Association of her distinguished husband who had long been an earnest and interested worker in the liberal cause. Capt. Sidney Russell Cooke put up a splendid fight for Liberalism in the Torquay division of Devonshire, and he had many times, at great inconvenience, come to the Island and made splendid speeches on behalf of Liberalism. They confidently predicted for Capt. Sidney Russell Cooke a very distinguished future, and they hoped that he would be elected for a Liberal constituency and perhaps, some day, become a Liberal Cabinet Minister.

The rest of Barling's speech made no reference to Mel at all. Only at the end of the meeting was there a reference to an invitation for members to visit Bellecroft next summer.[44] Melville had procured a political position, but only through her marriage to Sidney.

Sidney was widely known as a man who 'loved adventure and the unusual', if the papers were to be believed. During the total solar eclipse on 29 June 1927, more than 3 million people travelled north to stand under the path of totality as it passed over Lancashire and Yorkshire.[45] Sidney went one step further. This was the first total eclipse visible from British mainland soil in 203 years; there would not be another one until 1999. Weather conditions were predicted to be frustratingly poor for viewing. So, Sidney, never one to be outdone, chartered a plane, 'and from

MRS. RUSSELL COOKE, MISS ENID RAPHAEL, MRS. W. JOWITT AND MRS. FREDERICK LAWSON AS A KITCHEN STAFFORDSHIRE GROUP

Figure 81: An unrecognisable Mel Russell Cooke appeared in this 'tableau' on the far left. (*The Bystander* 7 December 1927. (Author's collection)

high above the clouds witnessed the phenomenon', afterwards describing his impressions in a newspaper article.[46]

It was perhaps this flight that inspired his wife Mel, if she was aboard, to consider obtaining her pilot's licence later. For the time being, she kept her focus on local spheres of interest. Mel opened the Wootton Horticultural Show on the Isle of Wight in August 1927. She told those gathered that she 'took a great interest in horticulture' and 'as to gardening being sometimes an exasperating occupation ... those who had lived in the north of England, where gardeners encountered great difficulties, were impressed with the much more favourable conditions of the Island for gardening.'[47]

At the end of 1927, an almost unrecognisable Mel appeared in an art 'tableau' that paid homage to her Staffordshire heritage. At the Empire Theatre, Nottingham, in aid of the Research Fund for Material Welfare, the china figures of a Staffordshire group were brought to life in an art installation that was described as 'uncannily like the originals'.[48]

Meanwhile, in 1928, Sidney served on the Liberal Industrial Inquiry[49] and also that year, on a hot day in July, he gave a well-received speech at a meeting of the Women Liberals in Newport, of which Mel was now president. In a 'thoughtful address' he criticised the Conservative Party as a threat to peace, as by nature they are 'reactionary and by inclination obstructive' and that unless Liberalism was maintained, 'they as women could not look forward with confidence to the future of their children.' He recommended armaments be reduced, and that they should reject an import tax on iron and steel, as it would gravely affect shipbuilding and other industries. In response, a vote of thanks was supported by Sir Godfrey Baring who said 'Captain Russell Cooke was carving out a great career for himself in the City, yet they hoped that he too, in the near future would be a Liberal candidate,' which earned a round of applause.[50]

In October 1928, it was reported in the *Daily Telegraph* that a 'Mr. Sidney Russell Cooke (Messrs. Rowe and Pitman)' was part of a 'new Marconi committee' formed to oversee a merger taking place that year and its effect on shareholders.[51] In the same year, he was also involved in the publication of a book entitled *Britain's Industrial Future* (commonly known as the 'Yellow Book') which was a report on the British Liberal Party's Industrial Inquiry of 1928. John Maynard Keynes was on the executive committee, while Sidney's name was listed under those who 'served on one or more of the Special Committees'.[52]

In 1929 another book, co-authored once more with E. H. Davenport, was released, entitled *Imperial Finance*. Like many aspects of Sidney's life, all was not as it seemed. Davenport remembered that he was brought by Cooke to meet the Governor of the Bank of England, Montagu Norman, who was worried by the inflationary nature of Australian government finance and wanted a critical pamphlet written, as long as it did not reveal he was its inspiration. Hence Davenport wrote the piece without ever divulging its instigation.[53]

The piece urged 'the adoption of a wise policy of overseas lending and the exercise of discrimination even in Imperial loans'.[54] Promoted by Sidney's employer Rowe & Pitman, it took another swipe at Australian finance, according to a letter dated 24 January 1929 by Richard Casey, Australia's liaison officer for the Commonwealth Public Service, to Australian Prime Minister Stanley Bruce: 'I attach a circular issued by Rowe & Pitman, a well-known Stock Exchange firm, with regard to Imperial Finance. As you will see, this is the latest form that Davenport & Cooke's attack on our Australian finance has taken. Cooke is a member of this firm.'[55]

In the 8 April 1929 'City Notes' in *The Times*, Sidney's book was discussed and its 'proposal to abolish the preference in the matter of stamp duty which Dominion and Colonial loans enjoy' was described as 'an unfortunate proposal, which, if adopted, would give serious offence in our Oversea[s] Dominions.'[56]

The 1929 'Alien Passengers for the United States' manifest reveals that 36-year-old Sidney and 31-year-old Mel took the SS *Aquitania* from Southampton on 27 April 1929 to the US. This was Mel's first trip to the country. Their visit was confirmed in a short announcement in the 'Court Circular' in the London *Times*: 'Mr. and Mrs. Sidney Russell Cooke are sailing in the Aquitania to-day, returning to London on June 10. (Address: Ambassadors Hotel, Park-avenue, N.Y.C.).'[57]

The Cookes were mixing both work and pleasure in the States:

> Sidney Russell Cooke visited the United States and Canada in May and June 1929. His diary recorded details of an exhausting social life as he rode, sailed, played tennis, and acquainted himself with the new talking pictures. He also managed to make contact with many of the leading financial firms including Dillon Read, Brown Brothers and Wood Gundy, as well as visit the Ford factory in Detroit where he witnessed 106,000 employees producing ninety-five cars an hour on a 'drive off' assembly line some 850 ft in length.[58]

Social Events and Sport

In April 1929, Simon and Priscilla, or the 'Russell Cooke twins' as they were often known, performed as part of a children's cabaret at The Palace, Freshwater, in the role of 'little worshippers' of a Peter Pan statue that 'at their behest ... comes to life and dances a joyful measure'. The six-year-old twins also took part in a 'pretty nursery rhyme number', helping raise £18 for the Freshwater and Totland War Memorial Nurses' Institute.[59]

Not long afterward, and in a rare photograph together, Sidney and Melville appeared at a social engagement in July 1929, a glamorous house party at West Wycombe Park (just northeast of London) to celebrate the christening of Sir John and Lady Dashwood's second son, John (Figure 82).[60] Sidney was one of John's five godparents at his christening the month before.[61]

They were photographed by *The Sketch* flanking the Countess of Seafield and a young Miss Sarah Dashwood. The 23-year-old Countess (Nina Caroline Studley-Herbert, 12th Countess of Seafield) was quite prestigious company for the Russell Cookes, a Scottish peeress who would marry the following year and by the 1950s was estimated to be the second richest woman in Britain after the Queen.[62]

Sidney looks noticeably uncomfortable on camera, with a forced smile, while Mel appears somewhat relaxed, holding the young Miss Dashwood's hand. Perhaps it is the lighting, or the fall of her dress, but one could be forgiven for thinking that she could soon be expecting another child.

Later that year, in November 1929, Mel was unanimously re-elected president of the Newport Women's Liberal Association – thanks to much

GUESTS AT THE CHRISTENING HOUSE-PARTY:
MR. RUSSELL COOKE, THE COUNTESS OF SEAFIELD, MISS SARAH DASHWOOD, AND MRS. RUSSELL COOKE.

Figure 82: Melville and Sidney in a rare photograph together at a prestigious event in High Wycombe. (*The Sketch* 24 July 1929. (Author's collection)

activity and increased membership, in addition to 'the great work for Liberalism rendered by the Russell Cooke family for many years'.[63]

Sidney was undoubtedly an all-round sporting man, described as a 'good shot, a fair golfer and also played squash rackets and lawn tennis'.[64] However, it was yachting for which he made the news. In 1928, he became a member of the Royal London Yacht Club (Cowes). He then had built 'a six-metre yacht of the international class, which was shipped to France for the international regatta at Cannes'. He would name the yacht after his daughter Priscilla.[65]

Sidney already had another yacht, the 16-ton Bermudian cutter *Nilda* built in 1911, an 'excellent vessel for cruising and racing, 48 feet in length'.[66] But it was the *Priscilla* that was catching everyone's attention: 'She is the first yacht of the rating to be built at Cowes. She was constructed by Messrs. H Gales and Co. from the design of Mr T.C. Letcher and Mr S. Russell Cooke, and as both designer and owner are new to class racing, the debut of *Priscilla* will be watched with interest... In comparison with older yachts *Priscilla* appears rather short, but her generous beam should enable her to carry her sail area of about 525 sq. ft. comfortably. The boat is equipped throughout with hollowspars made on the McGruer principle.'[67]

'Ambitious and Adventurous'

The new yacht made the local news at her launch.

> With an overall length of about 32 feet, she is a beautiful specimen of the marine architect's craft and her construction and finish are a great credit to her builders. With white bottom and green topsides Priscilla has a very attractive appearance. Built of yellow pine, with mahogany planking, and Marconi rigged, she is fitted with McGruer spars, and her sails are by the famous local firm of Ratsey and Lapthorne... Mrs Russel-Cooke [sic], the owner's wife, had christened her *Priscilla* by smashing a bottle of sparkling champagne on the bow.[68]

Whether Mel was aware of it or not, her father's company, the White Star Line, had a tradition of not christening their ships with champagne bottles. For example, the *Titanic* was launched to an estimated crowd of 100,000 with two simple rockets launched 15 minutes apart to announce the moment before it descended the slipway. No champagne bottles were ever broken.

Once the *Priscilla* was in the water, she was towed to a mooring up the Medina to be fitted out, then shipped on the SS *Morea* to Cannes for her debut. Sidney was described as a 'very enthusiastic yachtsman [who] will be making his debut in international racing'. He was 'evidently highly pleased with his boat [and] is a capable helmsman'.

Figure 83: The local newspaper printed a photograph of Sidney's new yacht named after his daughter Priscilla. *Isle of Wight County Press*, 16 March 1929. (Author's collection)

The *Priscilla* first raced at Cannes against sixteen boats in the Six-Metre Class in April 1929.⁶⁹ Her sail number was K26. She did not place. But, as he had earlier told the *County Press* reporter, the 'plan was to sail the *Priscilla* for about 10 days at the Cannes International regatta and then return to Cowes for the Solent regattas'.⁷⁰ This seemed to be the case, except that he made two important changes. He designed a new vessel (named the *Priscilla II*) to be even shorter, and sought the services of a helmsman. As with the gardens at Bellecroft, maybe Sidney was better as a manager.

Priscilla II was built in March 1930, in Fairlie, North Ayrshire, Scotland, at the Fife & Son boatyard, registered with the official number 341655 and described as a 'wood sailing vessel sloop'. Measuring 29.3 feet in length, 6.9 feet in breadth and having a depth of 4.1 feet, it was likely completed at Cowes.

As with his previous vessel, Sidney certainly intended to race her in the Solent. In the following months, the *Daily Telegraph* recorded many races that the *Priscilla II* competed in, describing how the '6-metre *Priscilla*, being painted green, looked just like a tiny Shamrock'.⁷¹ For example, on 29 May 1930, it was noted that in the 6 metre International Class 'Mrs. Russell Cooke's *Priscilla II* took second prize, and then on 30 May, third prize.'⁷² Although this is the only occasion the yacht was attached to Mel's name, it reveals she must have at times been involved in this particular maritime diversion.

The *Priscilla* did win elsewhere. In Plymouth it was recorded that the '6-metre international class was won by '*Priscilla* (S. Russell Cooke)' in early June 1930.⁷³ Shortly thereafter, in Southampton's Solent and as part of the Hythe Regatta, she won again with a time of '3h 3min 41sec' – just beating by one minute the *Prudence* on 18 June 1930.⁷⁴ The winning streak would not last. In the same Hythe Regatta, she was unplaced on 26 June 1930.⁷⁵ There was slight improvement the following week, when they returned to home waters and took part in the Island Sailing Club regatta for International and Solent classes in Cowes. On 30 July 1930, the *Priscilla* came second to *Prudence*, trailing by three minutes.⁷⁶

For these races, Sidney does not seem to have been at the wheel: '*Priscilla* was usually steered by Sir Ralph St G Gore, and had been fairly successful in Solent racing. She won first prize at Bembridge Regatta on Wednesday, and yesterday took second prize.'⁷⁷

Melville was more interested in hunting. At the end of November 1929, she attended the 'Pytchley Meet' at Naseby. Mel appeared in two striking photographs printed in separate publications. One has her perched on the rear open passenger door of a vehicle, attired in the traditional women's riding habit consisting of a bowler hat, stock tie and white gloves (Figure 84). She is peering into the distance, revealing a distinctive profile.

'Ambitious and Adventurous'

Even more impressive is the other photograph from the same event where she is atop her horse, riding just behind the most distinguished person in attendance, the Duke of York (Figure 85). Seven years later he would be King George VI. Mel was rubbing shoulders with royalty.

Right: Figure 84: Mel poised on the door of a vehicle at the Pytchley Meet, a fox hunting event, in her riding habit. (*The Sketch*, 4 December 1929)

Below: Figure 85: Mel (far left) riding with the Duke of York at the Pytchley hunt. Seven years later he was King George VI. (*Illustrated Sporting and Dramatic News*, 30 November 1929)

Sidney's co-author, Davenport, had also noted the Cooke's attendance at Pytchley Meet and saw it as an indication of 'fabulous income'. Unlike Sidney, Davenport was something of a left-leaning journalist, who held some disdain for the old-fashioned networks of privilege that were at the heart of the finance world. He described Rowe & Pitman as a 'snobbish upper-class firm' and wrote about the enormous profits the partners were earning:

> The Partners enjoyed fabulous incomes. Naturally they lived in great style with town and country houses, and many of them hunted in the shires. Sidney Russell Cooke and his wife Melville hunted with the Pytchley and looked magnificent on their splendid mounts.[78]

Prelude to Tragedy

Aside from sport, 1930 was a busy year for Sidney Russell Cooke. On 29 January 1930, it was reported in the *Daily Telegraph* that he was going to be appointed as a director of The National Mutual Life Assurance Society, a corporate pension fund based in London.[79] Nepotism was once again in play, as the chairman was none other than John Maynard Keynes (1921 to 1938). *The Times* reported the following day that Cooke's appointment as director was seconded by the Deputy Chairman and 'unanimously approved'.[80] He was also an honorary treasurer of the Queen's Institute of District Nursing.[81]

That same month, Sidney and Melville attended The Pytchley Hunt Ball where nearly five hundred guests danced until 5 in the morning. 'Mr. and Mrs. Russell Cooke brought Lady Seafield and Mr. Herbert.'[82] They were now regular fixtures at such hunting balls, having attended one the year before, the Beaufort Hunt Ball at Chippenham in January 1928.[83]

In the months before Sidney's death, Mel was pursuing interests other than yachting and hunting. She was still playing a role in local politics as the president of Newport Women's Liberal Association, while Sidney was vice-president of I.W. Liberal Association.[84] She also continued taking an active interest in art. She took part in a 'tableau at the Pageant of Italian Exhibition Pictures' of the artwork entitled 'Finding of Moses' by Giovanni Battista Tiepolo (Figure 86). In a grand *Daily Telegraph* photograph she was listed as 'Mrs. Sidney Russell Cooke', featuring prominently as Pharaoh's daughter, the tallest member of the group.[85] The tableau was part of a 'most imaginative tribute to the Italian Art Exhibition ... in the cause of charity at the Prince of Wales Theatre'.

'Ambitious and Adventurous'

Famous masterpieces in gold frames were revealed to a distinguished audience for half a minute each, 'living, breathing realities, in the persons of some of London's best known and most beautiful women ... a spectacle of loveliness'.[86]

Behind the scenes, something was wrong. By July 1930, Mel had an undisclosed health issue that resulted in her admission into a London nursing home for a minor operation. Sidney was also not well and had taken a 'health cruise to the West Indies' in February 1930. Davenport was quoted as saying that Sidney had suffered from 'overstrain':

> He was unable to sleep at night and was decidedly depressed. But upon the advice of his doctor in February he went on a health cruise to the West Indies... Although at the best of times not a robust type he came back a changed man, and so far as we know he had no recurrence of the trouble. He certainly had not complained of not being able to sleep.[87]

The Daily Telegraph added that according to his friends, as a result of his war experiences he was 'highly strung' and in January was 'on the

"FINDING OF MOSES," by Tiepolo—a tableau at the Pageant of Italian Exhibition Pictures. Left to right: Captain Cuthbert Orde, Mr. Francis Toye, Master George Murray-Smith, Miss Lucia Lawson, Mrs. Sidney Russell Cooke, Mrs. Lionel Cohen, Mrs. Bernard Freyberg, and Mrs. Fred Lawson.

Figure 86: Mel appeared in a leading role in this tableau in April 1930, playing Pharaoh's daughter (centre) the tallest of the group. *The Daily Telegraph* 10 April 1930. (Author's collection)

verge of a nervous breakdown and ordered to stop work and go for a six-weeks' cruise. He went to Panama, and on his return appeared to be completely recovered, and he at once resumed his business activities.'[88]

Privately, there was much more to this story, as revealed in Davenport's memoirs in 1974. Sidney was not 'on the verge of' but had suffered a nervous breakdown after he received what his co-author described as 'harsh treatment' by the 'powerful, pompous and unbending father-figure' at Rowe & Pitman, Lancelot ('Lancey') Hugh Smith, who had originally hired him:

> One day during the nerve-wracking bear market [Cooke] said to his senior partner: 'Lancey, the time is coming when you will go into the market and not find a bid in a hundred War Loans' (meaning £100,000). The great man replied: 'Sidney, I think you are losing your judgement.' Turning his back on Sidney he walked out of the room. The young man, who had been the 'blue-eyed' boy of the firm, now found himself cold-shouldered by his senior partner. It was more than he could bear. A nervous breakdown followed soon after. After nursing-home treatment Sidney went off on a voyage. He came back apparently restored to health.[89]

As serious as this might be, there was little outward indication of anything untoward. In fact, precisely a month before his death, a rather stunning photograph of Sidney was published in the 4 June 1930 edition of *The Tatler* magazine, under the heading 'Seafarers', where he is seen striding along the Cowes waterfront, seemingly oblivious to the photographer, wearing 'knickerbocker' short trousers, looking lost in thought (Figure 88). He is walking with Sir Fisher Dilke as they leave the R.Y.S. (Royal Yacht Squadron). Although the angle of the photograph does not help, Sir Dilke looks exceedingly tall, almost dwarfing his younger companion.

Sir Dilke was more than just a relative from his mother's side, he was actually Sidney's older half-brother, Sir Fisher Wentworth Dilke, 4th Baronet (1877-1944).[90] Dilke married Ethel Lucy Clifford in 1905. By 1911, he was a marine insurance underwriter at Lloyd's, living in Paddington. He saw service in the First World War, after which he became an avid yachtsman, later appointed a British observer on the US yacht the *Ranger* for the America's Cup races in 1937, about which he published a book.[91] So, it is not surprising that he is captured striding out of the Cowe's Royal Yacht Squadron with his younger half-brother. The caption below adds that 'Sir Fisher Dilke, who owns *Windrush* has a country house near Titchfield.'[92] It was a proud moment for Sidney as well. His yacht the *Priscilla* was coming second and occasionally first in races in Plymouth and Southampton.

'Ambitious and Adventurous'

The weekend before his death, Sidney and Melville spent time together at Bellecroft, where they entertained a house party: 'In Mr. Cooke's beautiful garden at Bellecroft, there was opened the annual exhibition of the Isle of Wight Rose Society and his little daughter Priscilla presented a bouquet to Lady Seely, who opened the show.'[93] With 108 entries, the event was described as a 'distinct advance on previous years. The King is patron, and gave a gold medal... Capt. and Mrs Russell Cooke were also specially thanked for placing their beautiful grounds at the disposal of the Society.'[94] The local newspaper described the event as having 'more than ordinary interest centred in the bouquet presentation by the charming little daughter... Pretty Priscilla, who so daintily discharged her first public duty, is one of twins – Simon and Priscilla.'[95] The moment was caught on camera, with the twins standing on either side of Lady Seely in a photograph that, in a bitter irony, was published in the same edition that would announce the death of their father (Figure 87).

Sidney personally steered his new yacht for the first time 'in a race at the Royal Corinthian Yacht Club regatta at Southsea on Saturday. *Priscilla II* is quartered at Cowes, and her skipper is Mr. Joe Oatley, of East Cowes.'[96]

Later, the couple 'spent a large part of Sunday playing with the children in the garden', which the *Daily Telegraph* said was 'illustrative of his domestic felicity'.[97] *The Times* reported that 'Priscilla (Mr. S. Russell Cooke)' finished second in the 6-metre International Class with a time of 4 hours, 22 minutes and 17 seconds – just three minutes behind *Prudence*.'[98]

Figure 87: The twins Priscilla (left) and Simon (right) wearing hats as they stand beside Lady Seely, presented a bouquet of flowers after she opened the Isle of Wight Rose Show at 'Bellecroft'. In a bitter irony, this photograph was published in the same newspaper edition that announced their father's death. *The Isle of Wight County Press*, Saturday 5 July 1930. (Author's collection)

Following their busy weekend, 'Mr and Mrs Russell Cooke left Newport on Monday for London.'[99] Sidney was back at work and looking well, according to a *News Chronicle* report: 'On Wednesday he attended a board meeting of the National Mutual Life Assurance Society, and appeared to be very bright and cheerful. Friends told him on Wednesday how well he was looking.'[100] On the same day, he met up with his colleague at National Mutual, John Maynard Keynes, for lunch.

Davenport remembered he was in a celebratory mood, 'noticeably cheerful'.[101] Davenport would later say that he had dinner with Cooke the night before his death and that Sidney's state of mind was *not* cheerful: 'He seemed calm, but a little distrait.'[102]

According to Mel's maid, Miss Ada May Violet Fancy, when Sidney visited Mel in the nursing home, 'he did not appear to be greatly worried about her condition.' The maid took the opportunity to vouch for Sidney. 'Mr. Cooke, who was tall and dark, was an especially kind and considerate man. He was extremely wealthy and had three cars.'[103] In another account, she said she 'saw her employer at 7 o'clock on Wednesday evening at the nursing home in Norfolk Square, where he was visiting his wife. He seemed very happy and in good health. He said he was dining with his wife and returning to his chambers for the night.'[104]

If you take a closer look at the photograph of Sidney walking along with his older half-brother, he appears lost in thought. Maybe something was troubling him or forces unknown were quietly plotting his downfall. Whatever the case, within the week, Sidney Russell Cooke would be dead.

SIR FISHER DILKE (left) AND MR. RUSSELL COOKE LEAVING THE R.Y.S.

Figure 88: Sidney Russell Cooke (right) walking with his older half-brother at Cowes, exactly a month before he died in mysterious circumstances. *Tatler* 4 June 1930. (Author's collection)

9

An 'Inexplicable' Shooting

Melville's day maid, a 23-year-old Miss Ada May Violet Fancy, made the grim discovery at around 8.15 am on the morning of Thursday, 3 July 1930, while taking a glass of orangeade to his bedroom.[1] The *Liverpool Echo* said that the maid 'saw a foot protruding from the doorway of the room'.[2] Sidney was found on his back in his King's Bench Walk sitting room with a fatal gunshot wound to the stomach and a double-barrelled sporting gun by his side. One of the most comprehensive reports on the shooting appeared in the *News Chronicle* the day after:

> The discovery was made by Miss Violet Fancy, of Perham Road, West Kensington, a daily maid who had been in the service of Mrs. Russell Cooke for a year. Mrs. Cooke is in a London nursing home, and her husband, after spending the day at his office in Bishopsgate, went to see her on Wednesday evening. He returned to his chambers, and when Miss Fancy went to Mr. Cooke's bedroom with tea shortly after 8 o'clock, she found it empty.
>
> MAID'S STORY: 'I went into the sitting-room and saw Mr. Cooke in his pyjamas lying on the floor with his sporting gun near him,' Miss Fancy told a News Chronicle reporter. 'There was no one in the building at the time, for the people who live on the floor above are away. All I remember is rushing down the stairs screaming for help, but no one heard me. Outside I stopped the first man I saw. He was a postman, and he fetched the police.
>
> 'Mr. and Mrs. Cooke usually spent their week-ends at their house in Newport, Isle of Wight, where their twin children are living. They always seemed most happy together.' Mr. Cooke was a keen shot, and often went away on shooting expeditions.[3]

Figure 89: The steps of no.12 King's Bench Walk, where maid Ada Fancy ran down and asked a postman to fetch the police. (Photograph: Dan Parkes)

The next day, further details were provided: 'Miss Ada May Violet Fancy, maid at Mr. Cooke's chambers, said that on Wednesday he slept there alone. On Thursday morning, when she went in she noticed the bedroom door was open and the bed empty. In the sitting room she found Mr. Cooke lying on his back on the floor. He was in his pyjamas and dressing gown.'[4]

On spotting the body, the maid 'ran down screaming to the courtyard, and told a postman, who fetched the police. Within minutes, detectives and police officers were in the rooms, and a doctor certified that Mr. Cooke was dead.' That nobody heard the shot was the first question on the minds of the detectives, according to the *Derby Daily Telegraph*, which printed the story on the day of the shooting. It was soon discovered that 'above Mr. Cooke's chamber are more residential chambers, but the occupiers of them are away this week. Below are many chambers which are used as offices by barristers, and these too, were empty during the night. Mr. Cooke, therefore, was alone in the building at the time of the tragedy.'[5]

Headlines

Sidney's death made headlines news, including the front page of the *Evening Standard* on Thursday, 3 July 1930, the day of the shooting,

An 'Inexplicable' Shooting

accompanied by a large photograph (Figure 91). The article noted that he was a 'stockbroker with a shotgun at his side' with the implication quite clear, and that the 'news [had been] kept from [his] wife all day. Daughter of Titanic Commander.'[6]

The local *Isle of Wight County Press* newspaper ran the announcement in its regular 'Births, Marriage, and Deaths' column on the front page of its Saturday, 5 July 1930 edition: 'Cooke – July 3, at 12 King's Bench walk, Temple, London, Sidney Russell Cooke of Bellecroft, Newport, aged 37'. On page 5 it ran the headline 'Tragic Death of Capt. S. Russell Cooke', along with the subheading, 'Verdict of Accidental Death' with a two-column article primarily based on the evidence given at the inquest. 'A painful shock and widespread and profound regret in the Island followed the startling announcement on Thursday morning of the death in tragic circumstances of Capt. Sidney Russell Cooke, of Bellecroft.'[7] For any reader, it must have been especially poignant to have made the connection between the death of Sidney and the photograph of his twins at the Rose Show on page 3.

Another local newspaper, the *Southern Daily Echo*, ran with the headline on the front page 'Tragic End of City Director' and noted the Island connection: 'Mr. Russell-Cooke was a member of a family which

Mr. S. Russell Cooke, a member of the Stock Exchange, who was found shot dead in his chambers at King's Bench Walk, Temple, yesterday.

Figure 90: *The Daily Mirror of* 4 July 1930 included a photograph of Sidney.

has been connected with the Isle of Wight for generations. He inherited Bell Croft [sic], a beautiful old country house, standing in an old-world garden, just outside Newport. During the last General Election Mr. Russell-Cooke spoke several times at political meetings on behalf of the Liberal candidate, Mr. St John Hutchinson, who was recently appointed Record of Hastings.' The *Daily Echo* failed to make the *Titanic* connection, ending simply with 'Mr. Russell-Cooke leaves a widow and twin children.'[8]

The *Hampshire Advertiser* carried the by-line 'Associations with Isle of Wight and Southampton' and wrote that 'Captain Russell-Cooke was a speaker of great power, and able to deal with figures in a fascinating manner, as was proved on more than one occasion during political campaigns in the Isle of Wight, when he spoke on behalf of the Liberal candidate. The family of Russell-Cooke is one of the oldest in the Island, and its members are greatly respected.'[9]

Some regional newspapers added some unverified details absent in the standard syndicated accounts. For example, the *Yorkshire Evening Post* added that Sidney was found 'on the floor of the sitting-room with his head against the wall near the fireplace... Mr. Cooke's bed had been slept in. The bedroom door was wide open. The flat is on the second floor. Mr. Cooke was alone last night, as his wife was away.'[10]

The twins were seven years old when they heard the shocking news. They were by all accounts in the family home of Bellecroft when it happened. Melville heard the news from Miss Sinclair, the matron of the nursing home in Norfolk Square, Westminster, where Mel was a patient (contrary to reports that she was 'in the country'). Mel, who was described as a 'wife bereaved for second time by tragedy' was in the nursing home 'where she is undergoing a slight operation, and [Sidney] was feeling reassured and happy about her progress ... it was stated that she had been told of the tragedy during the afternoon.'[11]

Their reactions are unrecorded, other than a curious note from the *News Chronicle* reporter that there was 'no need for any anxiety as to the condition of Mrs. Cooke in the nursing home'. The *Evening Standard* reported that she was 'as well as can be expected'.[12] A *Daily Mirror* account stated that it was the maid, Miss Fancy, who 'broke the news to her yesterday afternoon, and then broke down'.[13] With implications of suicide, Mel could have only reminded her of the rumours swirling around the press about her father shooting himself on the bridge of the *Titanic*. It was as if history was repeating itself.

On 7 July, only four days after the death, Mel did make a short public statement: 'Mrs. Sidney Russell Cooke wishes to thank all her friends for their sympathy, letters, and flowers, which she hopes to acknowledge personally in due course.'¹⁴ The following day in the London *Times* there was a similar message, in the Court Circular column.¹⁵

Nicholas Davenport, described as one of his closest friends, expressed his thoughts on behalf of the family to a *News Chronicle* reporter: 'It is an inexplicable mystery to all who knew him... Although like most people at present, he was not too happy about business, he had no personal financial worries. His domestic affairs were of the happiest.'¹⁶

The magazine *The Bystander* placed Sidney's death alongside an 'appalling record' of young people who had died that year – a 'sign of the times': 'The death of Mr. Russell Cooke has come as a great shock to his many friends. He frequently used to entertain parties at the Isle of Wight, and he was considered a very clever young business man.'¹⁷

There was another tribute, from Sidney's colleague, Mr C. T. D. Burchell, deputy chairman of the National Mutual Life Assurance Company: 'Mr. Russell Cooke was a man of great ability. He was a charming fellow, a sportsman in the fullest sense of the word. To those of us who were with him on Wednesday he seemed his usual cheerful self, and the news of his death comes as a great shock. Mr. Burchell also referred to the fact, already mentioned, that during the war Mr. Russell Cooke sustained severe shell shock.'¹⁸

There was one tribute of particular note, published anonymously the day after his death in the *Evening Standard*:

> The tragedy of Mr. Russell Cooke's sudden death leaves one with an almost angered sense of wastage. The war has already taken full toll of Mr. Cooke's generation, and he was himself the type of man which we can ill afford to lose.
>
> Ardent, imaginative, and withal strictly practical, Mr. Russell Cooke was one of the few among our younger financiers who seemed to combine the caution of the old fashioned City methods with the vision and initiative necessary to face altered conditions.
>
> Mr. Cooke, above all, was a man who was always learning. I remember years ago accompanying him on a short visit of inspection abroad. He spent his time asking all manner of questions and acquiring all manner of information. His handsome, vivid face was actually aflame with curiosity.¹⁹

Were these the words of Keynes, perhaps? Sidney's local Isle of Wight newspaper paid tribute to 'a man of outstanding ability, he was a charming companion and a sportsman in the best sense of the term. He was possessed of exceptional intellectual and literary ability, and some of his writings on financial and economic subjects have attracted

Titanic Legacy: The Captain, the Daughter and the Spy

Figure 91: The shooting was headline news in the late edition of the *Evening Standard*, 3 July 1930. (Author's collection)

attention, not the least being a pamphlet which he wrote on Australian finance.'[20] The newspaper ignored the fact that most of the Australian attention to his pamphlet was distinctly negative.

The *County Press* also quoted the 'Peterborough' gossip column in the *Daily Telegraph*. It reads as though it was someone close – perhaps a family member:

> He had a wonderful capacity for being interested in a great variety of subjects, and was possessed of an impish sense of humour, which at times would give place to fits of acute depression, only to reassert itself as quickly as it passed. Well read beyond the average, he is keenly interested in art in all its forms, though in latter years after dinner conversations round his table would most usually turn to pure economics. He had a gift for friendship with intelligent people and of acquiring knowledge on subjects of every-day interest.
>
> On the other side he was a keen sportsman with a ruling passion for yachting, to which hunting ran a close second as his favourite pastime. In the forthcoming races in Long Island Sound for the England-America cup he had high hopes of success with a new 6-metre with which he had been winning races in the Solent during the past few weeks. In games,

though he was a sound golfer, his aptitude was for the moving ball, and this natural quickness of eye made him a good sporting shot.

The anonymous 'Peterborough' writer rounds off his tribute with some words about Mel and her famous father:

> His wife, a well-known figure with the Pytchley, at the opera, and in artistic, literary, and social circles generally, is tall and fair, and bears a striking family likeness to her father, who went down as captain of the ill-fated Titanic. Scarcely a week passes without bringing to Mrs. Russell Cooke some tribute to the high esteem in which Capt. Smith was held by regular Atlantic voyagers. To this day she is constantly meeting new friends who, on learning her father's name, tell her how they would delay their trip if necessary in order to sail on whatever ship Capt. Smith was then commanding.[21]

The Inquest

There was clearly some uncertainty as to exactly how Sidney died, resulting in a City Coroner inquest that took place on the afternoon of Friday, 4 July 1930, the day after the shooting, presided over by Dr F. J. Waldo, who sat with a jury. W. T. Monckton K.C. attended on behalf of the family. Mel was too ill to attend, remaining in the nursing home. The *Evening Standard* observed that a double-barreled sporting gun and 'what appeared to be a bottle of oil and other apparatus for gun cleaning were brought into the court by a police sergeant and placed with a leather gun-case near Dr. Waldo.'[22]

It was first established that 'Mr. Cooke had recently made arrangements for a holiday to shoot grouse in Scotland,' providing an apparent motive for him to be cleaning his gun. This information came from Frederick Archibald Hugo Pitman, of Mulberry Walk, Chelsea, who told Dr Waldo that Sidney 'wanted to go on his holidays on a certain date, as he was anxious to do some shooting. He had an invitation to shoot grouse in Scotland.' Pitman himself was a keen sportsman and had excelled in the Oxford boat races, won medals in the Olympics and joined his father's business after the war. He was also a colleague of Ian Fleming.[23] He last saw Sidney alive on Wednesday evening in the Rowe & Pitman office at 43 Bishopsgate:

> I have known Mr. Russell Cooke as a partner and friend for a considerable time and I know nothing that might worry him. A question arose on Wednesday evening as to when some of us should take our

holidays. He particularly wished to go on a certain date, which was not altogether convenient to the rest of us. He said he wanted to go on a date mentioned, as he was anxious to do some shooting.'[24]

Another witness at the inquest, cousin Oliver Paget-Cooke, said that 'Mr Cooke had no financial worries at all, and was happily married. He was rather overworked but had nothing else to trouble him.'[25] The London *Times* phrased this differently: 'He had no financial worry, but absolutely the reverse, and was extremely happily married.'[26] Paget-Cooke, a solicitor at Rowe & Pitman, noted in a separate report that 'the previous evening he dined with his wife at the nursing home.'[27]

An interesting observation was made by Paget-Cooke in the *Daily Telegraph* under a subheading of 'Horror of Blood'. Sidney was apparently 'affected at the sight of blood, and some years ago, when he crushed his finger in a hatchway, he nearly fainted at the sight. He was not morose, nor had he ever threatened to take his life.'[28] In response, the Coroner made a peculiar observation: 'Even the bravest men will sometimes faint at the sight of blood, and it has been known for V.C.s to break down in that way.'[29]

Dr A. Westerman, a divisional surgeon of the City Police, was an eyewitness to the scene of the shooting and from the outset expressed his view that the death was a terrible accident. He described the victim as a 'slender, healthy, well-nourished man'[30] and gave the following detailed statement:

> There was a gunshot wound about an inch in diameter on the left side of the abdomen, and another small wound two inches below. Death was due to heart failure following shock and hemorrhage. The end of the barrel must have been within two and six inches from the skin when the shot was fired... My first impression when I got there was that it was a case of accident and not suicide. Further examination strengthened that. The gun was not on the floor, but on the sofa, and in no case in my experience where a person tried to commit suicide had he shot himself in the abdomen with the wound pointing downwards. I suggest that he was sitting down on the sofa cleaning the gun and was leaning over when the gun went off. The opening in the pyjamas and dress gown bear that out.[31]

Another newspaper reported more details on the injuries sustained:

> There was a gunshot wound on the left side of the abdomen, below the ribs. There was also a slight wound in the same region. The skin in the neighbourhood was blackened and there was some superficial

An 'Inexplicable' Shooting

scorching, which rather indicated that the gun might have been no more than 2in – certainly not more than 6in – from the skin. In the muscle of the abdomen were found two cartridge wads and a quantity of pellets. The cause of death was heart failure, due to shock and haemorrhage, following a gunshot wound to the abdomen.[32]

Dr. Westerman admitted to the Coroner that there was a possibility it was self-inflicted, but he reiterated that this death, after further examination, was accidental: 'My reason is the position of the gun... Where suicide has been intended the shot has been directed to other parts of the body and not to the abdomen. It is nearly always directed towards the heart, and very rarely has the abdomen been chosen.'[33]

A juryman questioned the doctor on exactly how Sidney would have shot himself and Westerman explained that he was likely sitting on the sofa cleaning the gun, and pushing it, when it accidentally fired as the safety catch was not on. But if he was sitting on the sofa, why did he end up on his back on the floor? A juror asked: 'Would not he have fallen on his face instead of his back?' to which the police surgeon answered: 'He may have got to his feet for a moment.'[34]

Police Sergeant Bruty, who also produced a plan of the chambers at 12 King's Bench Walk as an exhibit, said that there was a rod left in one barrel of the gun, leaving the other barrel free for use.[35] Then followed 'dramatic tests with a gun' to establish a possible cause of death:

Half-brother's test
Ernest George Daw, gunmaker for a New Bond-street firm, advanced the theory that Mr. Cooke was sitting on the sofa cleaning his gun, holding the gun with his left hand and the rod with his right, the barrel being towards him. He made a grab at the gun to prevent it slipping and, in doing so, touched the trigger. Mr. Daw illustrated his theory, using Mr. Cooke's gun. A juryman about the same height as Mr. Cooke, who was 6ft, 1 in., then took the gun to test Mr Daw's theory.

Mr. Cooke's half-brother then came forward and tested the theory. 'I can do it with the greatest ease,' he said. Dr. Beddart, of St. Bartholomew's Hospital, who was in court for another inquest, said that he often cleaned his own gun holding it with his two hands and pushing the rod through against his stomach. He suggested that this would account for the nature of the wound. The jury returned a verdict of 'accidental death'.

The coroner joined with the jury in expressing sympathy with the widow and family and business associates. Mrs. Russell Cooke, who had been informed of the death of her husband, was yesterday reported to be 'as well as can be expected.' She is in a West end nursing home.[36]

The unidentified 'half-brother' mentioned was, of course, Sir Fisher Dilke, the man who was pictured in the last known photograph of Sidney, walking in Cowes a month before (Figure 88). The very tall Sir Dilke was able to hold the gun facing against his stomach with the 'greatest ease'. Whether six-foot-one-inch-tall Sidney could have done the same was in part shown by the juror of similar height who tested the theory – although the article is ambiguous as to that particular outcome. The implication is that it was feasible.

Once all the evidence had been considered on the afternoon of Friday, 4 July, the jury was satisfied it was physically possible and returned an 'accidental death' verdict. The following day, newspaper headlines announced that the stockbroker's death was a 'cleaning mishap'. But not everyone was buying it.

Suspicions

When Sidney's body was first discovered, the circumstances of his death were considered, in the words of E. H. Davenport, an 'inexplicable mystery'. A few days later, Sir Arthur Conan Doyle died, on 7 July 1930, which subsequently dominated the daily newspapers the day before Sidney's funeral. In analysing the facts surrounding the mysterious death of the city stockbroker, it is applicable to use an approach advocated by Sherlock Holmes: 'When you have eliminated all which is impossible then whatever remains, however improbable, must be the truth.' There were three ways in which Sidney could have met his end: through an accident, murder, or suicide. While the latter two possibilities were ruled out at the inquest, suspicion remained.

Death from an unintentional shooting is more frequent than many would think. On average about 500 people a year die in the United States through accidents with firearms, an alarming number under the age of 25.[37] Specific deaths involving the cleaning of a gun are not unheard of. In Thailand in 2021, a 42-year-old man shot himself in the chest while cleaning a gun that he had forgotten to check was unloaded.[38]

The key question in the case of Sidney is why he was cleaning not only a loaded gun, without the safety catch on, faced towards him, but at such an early hour on a Thursday morning. Was it his practice to do so? Was a shooting expedition imminent? Had he become overfamiliar with such a weapon during his traumatic time with the Post Office Rifles?

Although at the inquest the maid testified that Sidney had never mentioned to her his intention to go out shooting, his colleague Pitman testified that they discussed a shooting holiday the day before his death, as he was 'anxious to do some shooting', but they could not agree on dates. The anonymous tribute by 'Peterborough' said that shooting was his second favourite sport.[39] Which begs the question: Did he not have much experience cleaning guns? His unorthodox approach to cleaning indicates either inexperience or overconfidence. Double barrel shotguns do need to be cleaned regularly. However, the most common practice is to detach the wooden stock end of the gun from the barrel, so that it splits open and allows easy access to both ends of the barrels when cleaning with a rod. Why was Sidney cleaning with the stock still engaged, the safety off and the gun loaded? Either he was new to the task or had developed bad habits. Or something happened to cause him to take an unnecessary risk.

Then there is the possibility of suicide. With the Wall Street Crash of 1929 still fresh in reporter's minds, it is unsurprising some wanted to draw a connection. The myth of 'the jumpers of 1929' – an increase of financiers jumping off buildings or putting guns to their heads – has developed steadily ever since the Great Depression took its toll on the world economy in the 1930s, in a false memory phenomenon sometimes referred to as the Mandela Effect.[40] In reality, the suicide rate in New York was actually lower in in the weeks following the Crash.[41]

In his 1997 film, James Cameron included a reference to fictional villain Caledon Hockley shooting himself after financial ruin during the Stock Market Crash. The love interest, Rose, while telling her story about Hockley, says 'The Crash of '29 hit his interests hard, and he put a pistol in his mouth that year. Or so I read.' Some have even drawn a connection between this line of dialogue and the mysterious death of Sidney Russell Cooke.

Author Jonathan Piles in his book *Churchill's Secret Enemy* concludes that Cooke committed suicide.[42] Economic historian Robert Skidelsky in his biography of John Maynard Keynes specifically states that Cooke 'shot himself dead' as a 'victim of the financial reversals he and his firm, Rowe and Pitman, suffered in the long bear market which started with the Wall Street Crash.'[43]

Coverage of Sidney's death was often alongside articles about the financial downturn. For example, the *News Chronicle* ran a photograph of Sidney 'the City stockbroker' next to the headline 'Wall Street Blow to Europe', which detailed a loss of over ten million pounds to the French tourist economy due to the Wall Street disaster.[44]

During the inquest, the question of his character was discussed, and Sidney was described by his cousin, Oliver Paget-Cooke, as 'rather excitable and a little bit highly strung'.[45] He had experienced a severe form of post-traumatic stress (PTSD), then known as shell shock, during the war, which had resulted in hospitalisation. Was his mental health fragile? Was he experiencing disturbing flashbacks?

As pointed out by the police doctor, there is the matter of the angle of the weapon – that he shot himself in the stomach. Most suicide victims choose either the head or the heart. It seems improbable that someone known for an aversion to the sight of blood would shoot himself in the abdomen. The scene does not align with suicide either. A cleaning rod was found in one of the two barrels of the gun, an unlikely option for a suicide victim – unless he was deliberately wanting to obscure his self-destructive intent from family and friends.

The final issue is motive. It could not have been financial. Under the headline 'Riddle of Rich Man's Fate' the *Daily Herald* noted that 'according to his business associates, [he] appeared to have no financial worries, was not affected by any of the 'crashes' or Stock Exchange troubles, and was in perfect health.' The paper quoted an unnamed 'intimate friend and business associate' (most likely Davenport, or possibly Hugo Pitman) who said: 'The last thing which Mr. Cooke said on leaving the office last night was that he was going to get a hair-cut. He seemed perfectly easy about everything… He always impressed everyone by his great zest for life. He was a wealthy man.'[46]

Miss Fancy described her employer as a 'tall, dark and handsome man. He and his wife and I got on very well together. Mr. Cook [sic] was a very wealthy man and I know of nothing that was worrying him or depressing him.'[47]

During the inquest, cousin Paget-Cooke, when asked by the coroner if Sidney had any financial worries, responded: 'None. As a matter of fact it was absolutely the reverse.'[48] Was there an issue of having *too much* money? Paget-Cooke added: 'It is true, I should say that he was hard worked; but there was nothing else, no financial worry of any kind.' Paget-Cooke also spoke about his married life, saying that he 'was happily married and was absolutely devoted to his wife and family. Before the night of the tragedy [he] dined with his wife at Norfolk Square, where she had gone into a nursing home.'[49] He also vouched that he was a sober, temperate man who did not take drugs. The maid said that Sidney got on well with his wife and said she had never heard of any troubles in the twelve months she had worked there.[50]

If family life was happy, and he was experiencing success in both his work and sporting life, an obvious motive for suicide seems rather unclear. That is, until the publication of his co-author's memoirs in 1974 revealed that Cooke's PTSD, while perhaps exacerbated by his war experiences, actually had its origin in the 'harsh treatment of a highly intelligent and over-wrought young man'. Davenport described his schoolfriend as 'a

An 'Inexplicable' Shooting

highly sensitive young man beneath his acquired panache – he was in fact, an intellectual manqué – and I could see that partnership worries were breaking his nerves.' Davenport's use of the French term 'manqué' may refer to Sidney's unsuccessful political aspirations. More pointedly, the partnership worries were due to the conversation previously mentioned that Davenport witnessed, in which Hugh 'Lancey' Smith had said, in response to Cooke's financial projections: 'Sidney, I think you are losing your judgement.' It was a serious comment from a senior partner who had originally hired him and made more acute by Smith turning his back on Cooke and walking out of the room, a physical manifestation of receiving the proverbial 'cold shoulder'. Sidney, as a sensitive man who Davenport framed as the 'blue-eyed boy of the firm,' took it badly:

> It was more than he could bear. A nervous breakdown followed soon after. After nursing-home treatment Sidney went off on a voyage. He came back apparently restored to health.

The time spent recuperating in Panama was not entirely successful, if Davenport's final moments with his friend are accurate: 'I went to dine with him alone in my flat in the Inner Temple which he then rented from me. He seemed calm, but a little distrait. We played bézique in silence. The next morning, 3 July 1930, he was discovered dead with his sporting gun beside him. I had lost my best friend, and Rowe and Pitman their most intelligent partner.'[51]

'Bézique' is a French card playing game that only requires two players. There is an issue with this 1974 account, however. Contemporary reports were all unanimous that Sidney spent the evening with his wife at the nursing home in Paddington, with this confirmed by the Cooke's maid. It also does not align with Davenport's own public comments, in which he described the shooting as an 'inexplicable mystery,' or such as published in the *News Chronicle* in which he described his friend in a celebratory mood:

> This week he was noticeably cheerful. He had steered his own yacht to victory in a race off the Isle of Wight, and came in the office on Monday morning as proud of his achievement as a schoolboy. The mood remained with him on Wednesday. The last we saw of him was shortly after 5 o'clock, when he left the office to get his hair cut. During the evening he went to see his wife at the nursing home. What happened after that nobody knows.[52]

Are Davenport's 1974 memoirs a confession of sorts, or simply a hazy recollection of events, or an attempt to fix blame on the 'upper-class Establishment' he railed against? More critically, why did he not mention

Cooke's falling out with Lancey, and his own meal the night before, at the inquest? Davenport's description of Cooke as 'a little distrait' (or distracted) could well have helped explain why he was so cavalier with the cleaning of the gun so as to risk doing so with it loaded and the barrels still engaged. His 1974 account does not reference the inquest's conclusion of an accidental death, a notable omission considering his alternative explanation. Is it possible that there is no contradiction, as the card game took place after Sidney visited Mel?

No matter the apparent discrepancy, what is sure is that Davenport blamed the tragedy on the 'insensitivity' of the 'Establishment' and the event changed his career path. He wrote: 'The shock of Sidney's death turned me sharply against the hard upper crust of City life. I wanted to get out as quickly as possible.'[53] He admitted he was 'feeling depressed over the tragedy of Sidney Russell Cooke' and that while he expected to be offered a partnership with Rowe & Pitman, he was disinclined to take it as 'Sidney's death had made their office feel like a morgue.' Due to the 'distress' he was experiencing, Davenport soon after left the firm to join Chase Henderson and Tennant, a decision he regretted. He also took over Sidney's role as a director of the National Mutual Life Assurance Society, along with Keynes as chairman, which provided a 'great lift' to his career and a foot on the City ladder of promotion, later becoming a well-respected economist, journalist and sociologist.

There is yet another angle on the suicide scenario and an additional meeting that took place the day prior to the shooting that also contradicts Davenport's appraisal of a distracted man still grappling with the effects of a nervous breakdown. Author Davenport-Hines who, in the course of reconstructing John Maynard Keynes' love life for his book, *Universal Man*, discovered that the two men had met for lunch the day before, while Mel was recovering in a nursing home. On 6 July, just two days after Sidney's death, Keynes wrote a letter from Tilton House, in Firle, East Sussex, to Jack Sheppard, a longtime colleague at King's College, telling him that he 'had lunched with him [Sidney] a few hours before and he seemed in absolutely good spirits.' Although the paragraph about 'Cookie' is at the end of a two-page letter, there is evidence he was greatly affected by his death. He wrote: 'I've been most upset by poor Cookie's death. It's difficult in such a case to believe in an accident, but I really think it is the more probable explanation.'[54] Davenport-Hines goes one step further in his conclusions: 'His happy lunch, hours before his death, with an ex-lover who continued to matter to him, raises the possibility that he shot himself in a lonely paroxysm of miserable regrets at married life.'[55] While a possibility, what is not discussed by Davenport-Hines is that Sidney's family life was by all accounts happy – and the unavoidable fact that a cleaning rod was still in one of the barrels of the gun. As Keynes wrote, an accident is the 'more probable explanation.'

A cause that was never raised during the inquest, except perhaps in hushed and unrecorded conversations, was that something far more sinister had occurred. It was not revealed in the press or coroners reports – for rather obvious reasons – that Sidney worked for MI5 and the apartment in which he was found dead had been used as a 'safe house', along with reports of spies sending messages to 12 King's Bench Walk requesting a 'revolver for self-defence'.[56] Guns were indeed kept in the flat during the last twelve months the Russell Cookes lived there. During the inquest, the maid confirmed that she had 'seen the shot gun in the hall, on the top of a cupboard'.[57]

The spy connections in Sidney's life have led modern-day authors to speculate foul play was afoot. Author Oliver Buckton in *The World Is Not Enough, A Biography of Ian Fleming*, observed: 'While the inquest recorded an accidental death, Hugo Pitman – later to become senior partner at Rowe & Pitman – told a colleague of his conviction that Cooke had been shot by Russians.'[58] Hugo Pitman was the nephew of Frederick Pitman, the eponymous founder of Rowe & Pitman and likely not given to flights of fancy.

Buckton's conclusions are probably based on Andrew Lycett's history of the Rowe & Pitman firm. In his 1996 Ian Fleming biography, Lycett firstly wrote that 'Sidney Russell Cooke, who died in mysterious circumstances, [was] possibly murdered by the Russians.'[59] Lycett expanded further on this in 1998: 'An inquest recorded that Cooke had shot himself accidentally while cleaning his gun, but rumours of Soviet involvement persisted. Hugo Pitman, who was not a great fabricator of tales, told a young colleague specifically that Cooke had been shot by the Russians.'[60]

Others suspected that Harker was involved. Richard Davenport-Hines, in his book *Enemies Within: Communists, the Cambridge Spies and the Making of Modern Britain*, made the following observation:

> Another puzzle is the fate of Sidney Russell Cooke. In July 1930 he was found in the dining-room [sic] of his chambers in Temple dead of an oddly angled gunshot wound to the abdomen. It was unlikely that the wound was accidental; hard to believe that 'Cookie' had killed himself; but the possibility that he died as the result of his association with Harker has never been aired.'[61]

Due to Sidney's failure with the Sheridan mission and his identity subsequently exposed by the Russians in late 1920, there is a case to be made for Russian involvement. The man he was tasked with tracking, Lev Kamenev, fell out of favour with Stalin, was arrested in 1935 and executed by firing squad in 1936. Leon Trotsky was assassinated with a pickaxe in 1940. While in 1930, the man who unmasked Sidney's identity, Maxim Litvinov, was appointed by Stalin to the People's Commissar for Foreign Affairs and did not oppose the removal of Kamenev and Trotsky. Litvinov, too, eventually fell out of favour with Stalin and was killed in 1951. Sheridan Clare later lamented, 'horrible Stalin killed all my friends.'[62] Was Sidney one of those friends?

There are some unanswered questions. For example, the precise model of the weapon Sidney used was never revealed by the coroner or the press, its identity something of a mystery. Would deposits have formed in this particular model of gun that would require cleaning? What was Sidney's level of experience with this hunting rifle? Was he known to clean guns in the early hours of the morning? Were there traces of alcohol or drugs in his blood? Why did Sidney clean it with the barrels facing toward his stomach, while loaded, with no safety catch and without that stock and barrels separated? Would a rod placed in a barrel remain there if the other barrel had been fired? What was the exact time of death?

It is tantalising to imagine a scenario in which a Russian operative is tasked to remove an opposing agent by concocting a piece of clever theatre that creates an illusion that Sidney was simply cleaning a gun. When all evidence is considered, it is an unlikely option. As Keynes wisely opined in his private letter and aligned with detective Holmes' advice about removing the improbable: 'It's difficult in such a case to believe in an accident, but I really think it is the more probable explanation.'[63]

Funeral

Events moved hastily. In less than a week, Sidney had been buried. His body was discovered on the Thursday, an inquest on the Friday, and then his funeral took place on the Tuesday, on 8 July. The service had been announced in the London *Times* the day after his death, on 4 July when even before the inquest it was listed 'as the result of an accident' and that the funeral would be held at 'Brookwood Cemetery on Monday next, July 7 [sic], train leaving the Necropolis Station, 121, Westminster Bridge-road, at 11.40 a.m. Flowers may be sent to the Necropolis Station.'[64]

The funeral took place in the family plot at Brookwood Cemetery, also known as the London Necropolis, the largest cemetery in the UK. It was officiated by the Rev. Francis Helm. Sidney was buried in plot number 32 (Figure 92). There were some familiar names among those who attended:

his older half-brother, Sir Fisher Dilke, brother-in-law, Mr Harker, the Paget-Cookes, the Roskills, Sir John and Lady Dashwood, and Mr S. Pitman.[65] The Isle of Wight local newspaper added some extra details: that the Bellecroft head gardener, Mr Blaney, also attended, and the Isle of Wight Liberal Association – of whom Sidney was vice-president – was represented by a Mr Fred Baker, as the president Sir Godfrey Baring had been 'unavoidably prevented from attending'. It noted that 'there were many floral tributes, those from the Island including one from the president and officials of the I.W. Liberal Association and another from the Newport brand of the league of Young Liberals, of which the deceased was president.'[66]

This was followed by a memorial service held at 12:30 pm on Thursday 10 July at St Helen's Bishopsgate, officiated by the Rev. S. T. H. Saunders, the rector. Among the congregation at this event there were again some notable names – the Pitmans, the Dashwoods, Sidney's co-author E. H. Davenport and 'many members of staff of Messrs. Rowe and Pitman, of which Mr. Cooke was a partner'.[67] St Helen's Church is just a few minutes' walk from the Rowe & Pitman office, so was a logical choice, especially for colleagues unable to attend at the Necropolis on the Tuesday.

Figure 92: The grave of Sidney Russell Cooke, at Brookwood Cemetery, Woking. (Photograph: Dan Parkes)

Tributes continued during the week. An Isle of Wight newspaper quoted *The Times*:

> The City has lost one of the most brilliant and promising of the younger generation of business men. Intensely enthusiastic over any cause on behalf of which his services were enlisted he never failed to inspire his colleagues with a sense of his energy, courage, and resourcefulness. At the same time, he was a most loyal and devoted friend, ever ready to sympathise with and assist those who came to him for help and advice.'[68]

When the National Mutual Life Assurance Society held a General Meeting on Wednesday 28 January 1931, its chairman, Keynes, made a rare public statement about his 'Cookie':

> Gentlemen – Before proceeding to our ordinary business I have to record with the deepest personal sorrow the death during the year of our youngest director, Mr. Sidney Russell Cooke. Mr. Russell Cooke was fast making for himself a position of great esteem in the City. The premature loss of his brilliant and engaging personality will be a source of lasting regret to those who knew him well.[69]

Part Three
The Daughter

Figure 93: Helen Melville Russell Cooke, the daughter of Captain Smith and wife of Sidney Russell Cooke. (Artwork courtesy of Paul Van Doodson)

10

A Penalty, a Fire and a Collision

In another curious twist to the 'inexplicable' shooting story, the *News Chronicle* ran an article on 22 July 1930, following up on the 'Shot Stockbroker' and published that Sidney left £120,098. In modern terms this would be equivalent to £5,480,0000 (about $US6.6 million) according to the Bank of England Consumer Price Index (CPI) inflation data. A 're-marriage penalty' dictated that if Melville should remarry, the estate transferred to the two children. It was the same addendum Captain Smith had put in his will in 1903.

Two days later, a *Western Morning News* article provided further details, including a breakdown on what each family member received:

YACHTSMAN'S WILL
FORMER CANDIDATE FOR TORQUAY
Mr Sidney Russell Cooke, of Bellecroft, Newport, Isle of Wight, former unsuccessful candidate for Torquay Division, who died under tragic circumstances at the age of 37 on July 3, left estate of the value of £120,098 gross and £91,369 net... Probate of his will has been granted to his widow, Mrs Helen Melville Cooke, of the same address; Oliver Daysell Paget Paget-Cooke, solicitor, of Old Square, Lincoln's Inn, W.C.: and Reginald Franks, insurance broker, of 4 Albion-street, Hyde Park, W. He left £5,000 to his wife, £5,000 upon trust for his son Simon Russell Cooke, £10,000 upon trust for his daughter Priscilla Russell Cooke, £1000 to his sister Margert Dorothy Russell Harker, and £4000 upon trust for her benefit for life with remainder to his residuary estate, and the residue of his property upon trust for his wife during widowhood, with remainder to his said son or his issue, whom failing, to his said daughter or her issue.[1]

Mel's inheritance of £5000 would equal £228,000 ($US277,000) in today's money, while the £10,000 trust for Priscilla would amount to £456,000 ($US555,000).[2]

For a woman in the 1930s, Mel now had some financial security, safe in the knowledge that the twins would also be cared for. It was little consolation for such an 'inexplicable' tragedy. Yet further family misfortune lay around the corner.

Mel had to move on with her life and one of her first public indications of this was the sale of Sidney's precious award-winning racing yacht named after their daughter, the *Priscilla II*. There were undoubtedly sentimental connections, but it was also a financial liability. Although it had been 'hauled up at Messrs. W. White and Son's Vectis yard', by September 1930 it was sold.[3] 'The Fife-designed 6-metre racing yacht Priscilla II, which the late Capt. S. Russell Cooke had built this year, has been acquired by Mr. R.M. Teacher, a well-known Clyde yachtsman.'[4] By 1935, the yacht's name had been changed to *Alana*, and was still being raced by Teacher in 1947.[5]

The yacht spent the 1950s and 1960s on the West Coast of Canada, competing in championships until the 1990s when her journey came to a disappointing end in a Vancouver Island junkyard. It seemed that would be the tragic finale for the racing yacht, until the dilapidated remains were rescued in 2000 by a Maine yachtsman, Toby Rodes, and she was fitted with a new keel, mast and boom and, by consulting the original plans, the deck and cockpit layout were restored. Under the sail 'KC 11' she appeared prominently in the summers of 2003 and 2004, and in 2008 was listed for winning a Newport race.[6] She remains across the Atlantic, still racing as of 2019 under the sail number 'US 52'.[7] Sidney's legacy lives on in the yacht he named after his daughter.

The Tragedy of the Roskill Fire

Melville was hoping to start the new year afresh and, continuing a family tradition, entered Bellecroft into the Isle of Wight Horticultural competition in January 1931 – a notoriously difficult time of year for even the most ardent gardener. It must have been welcome news to learn that she had won first place in the 'Two flowering plants' category.[8] The moment of good tidings was fleeting.

Just before 6 am on 14 February – Valentine's Day – 1931, a terrible fire broke out on the second floor of Judge John Roskill's house at 33a Upper Montagu Street, Marylebone, that resulted in further tragedy for the Russell Cooke family. The residence had many memories; Jasper and Pattie Harker had their wedding reception there in 1920, as did Sidney and Mel in 1922. Mrs Sybil Roskill was Sidney's 51-year-old half-sister, the elder daughter of Ashton Dilke and Margaret Russell Cooke, the suffragette. Married in 1901, Sybil had four sons with John Roskill – Ashton, Stephen, Oliver and Eustace. Stephen was in the Navy and some years before had heroically saved his ship from disaster after it broke its moorings, by diving into the water and somehow managing to get a line to the harbour pier.[9] It was a similar kind of gallantry that would cost Sybil Roskill her life, two days after the thirtieth anniversary of their marriage.

The oldest son, 29-year-old Ashton, was the first to alert his family a fire had broken out, one that had quickly engulfed the upper floors. Instinctively, Sybil did not think of herself but of 25-year-old Oliver, who was lying ill with pneumonia in an adjacent room. Instead of trying to seek help, Sybil attempted to reach the bedside of her son. While she managed to rescue Oliver, her attempt to save the family nurse did not succeed and overcome by smoke, she was badly burned. As the firemen arrived on the scene they saw John Roskill at the bedroom window furiously pointing to the room beside him, where his wife and son were. Climbing a fire escape, the firemen entered the room and rescued the son who was still alive and wrapped in blankets.

Sybil was not as fortunate. She was brought out of the house unconscious and rushed to hospital in an ambulance, succumbing to her injuries on the way. She was not the only life lost. Miss Weir, the family nurse, also died. The severity of the blaze was such that three firemen were injured when a staircase collapsed during the rescue. Ashton seriously injured himself when he jumped from the second floor and missed the fireman's sheet. While the servants on the top floor were all saved, a 20-year-old Doris Gorman was in severe shock from the fatal events of the morning.[10]

Sybil's death made the news of the Monday papers, with one even printing her photograph (Figure 94). The *Aberdeen Press and Journal* ran a headline with the words 'Heroism and Sacrifice of K.C.'s wife. LIFE GIVEN FOR HER SON.' Other newspapers drew a connection with the events that had happened only six months earlier: 'It was only last summer that the late Mrs. Russell-Cooke's brilliant youngest son, Captain Sidney Russell-Cooke, lost his life as the result of a shooting accident at his London flat.'[11]

An inquest began on 17 February 1931 and was not completed until April, adjourned to wait for the recovery of Ashton Roskill. The source of the fire was established early in the proceedings: alterations to a fireplace next door.[12]

A Penalty, a Fire and a Collision

Figure 94: Mrs Sybil Roskill, Sidney's half-sister who died in a fire as she tried to save her son. (*Illustrated London News*, 21 February 1931)

During 1931, Mel had taken up lodgings elsewhere in London, rather than be based in Temple, which more so than Woodhead was now a source of much sorrow. The electoral register for 1931 shows that she had returned to Paddington, residing at number 10 Somers Place, near Hyde Park.[13] Such an address does not exist today, as Somers Place in the W2 postcode was renamed Somers Crescent in 1938.[14]

Eleanor's Death

Only a few months later, tragedy was to strike again – just under a year since Mel had lost her husband – when her mother, Captain Smith's widow, died in tragic circumstances. 69-year-old Eleanor was still living at 41 Queens Gate Gardens in South Kensington and reportedly suffering from deteriorating health. 'In recent years Mrs. Smith, who was 70 [sic], had not enjoyed the best of health, although she had been greatly benefited by a prolonged trip to Switzerland during the past winter in company with her daughter. But her sight was fast failing.'[15]

Titanic Legacy: The Captain, the Daughter and the Spy

Figure 95: An oil painting of Captain Smith's widow, Sarah Eleanor Pennington Smith. (Courtesy of Smith family descendant Norma Williamson, retouched by Paul Van Doodson)

On the afternoon of Sunday 26 April 1931, it was raining hard, and Eleanor was attempting to cross Cromwell Road in Kensington. The busy main road intersects with Queens Gate Gardens where she lived, and she must have made the journey on foot many times. A combination of the weather and her failing health was to be her downfall. Holding up an umbrella in her hand against the rain momentarily obscured her vision and she was struck by a London taxicab. It was not travelling fast, no more than five miles an hour, but the fall caused a serious blow to the head leaving her unconscious. She died in St Mary Abbot's Hospital in Kensington two days later on Tuesday 28 April from a fractured skull, having never regained consciousness.

Several newspapers covered the loss.

On the 29 April there was an announcement in the Death column of the London *Times*:

SMITH – On April 28, 1931, in London, as the result of an accident, SARAH ELEANOR, widow of CAPT. E.J. SMITH of S.S. Titanic, in her 70th year. Funeral on Friday, May 1. Train leaves Necropolis Station 11.40.[16]

In the *Daily Telegraph*, the 'Peterborough' column headlined it with 'A Link with the Titanic', stating that it brought back 'memories of the tragic disaster just nineteen years ago'.[17] The death was even covered by Captain Smith's hometown of Hanley, which ran the headline 'Death of the 'Titanic' Captain's Widow', although the article gave no details of the accident and instead focused its copy on her husband's life and 'heroism'.[18] In Southampton, the local *Southern Daily Echo* announced her death: 'Mrs. Sarah Eleanor Smith, widow of Captain E.J. Smith, commander of the Titanic, has died in London as the result of an accident. Each year since the loss of the Titanic Mrs. Smith has sent, on St. George's Day, a button-hole of red and white roses to the Mayor of Southampton in memory of her husband. It is only a week ago that the Mayor received the last gift.'[19]

St George's Day, when Eleanor would have sent the Mayor of Southampton her annual red and white roses, was three days before her fatal collision with a London cab. Despite the length of time since the tragedy, and the constantly changing face of the Mayor concerned (there were 16 different mayors between 1912 and 1931),[20] Eleanor continued the tradition honouring her husband right up until her death.

As with Sidney's mysterious demise, Mel had to endure yet another inquest, this time held in Paddington two days later on Thursday, 30 April. The taxi driver, Robert Smith of Fulham, gave evidence in which he 'estimated his speed at four to five miles an hour. He said that Mrs Smith was crossing with her back partly turned towards him, and although he sounded his horn and shouted, she crossed in front of his cab and was struck by the front wheel.' It was stated by 'a solicitor representing the family that Mrs Smith was practically blind in the left eye'.[21]

There was also an eyewitness, a 'Mrs. Anne Giidea, of Stanhope gardens, South Kensington, said she saw the accident. Mrs. Smith seemed to walk into the taxi, which was coming along the road at a slow pace.'[22]

Returning a verdict of accidental death, the jury exonerated the driver from blame. The *Evening Standard* summarised in its headline that the 'umbrella hid view' and there was simply no chance for the driver Robert Smith to have avoided the accident.[23]

On Friday 1 May 1931, Eleanor was buried in Brookwood Cemetery (Figure 96). It was the same cemetery where her son-in-law Sidney was laid to rest. She is buried in the Russell Cooke family plot number 32, two graves from her son-in-law.

Only a few weeks prior and just a short distance away, in plot number 25, someone with another *Titanic* connection was also buried – Sir Cosmo Duff Gordon (1862-1931).[24] He and his wife had survived the sinking aboard emergency lifeboat no. 1 that, although designed for an occupancy of 40, had only 12 people aboard. There was also a

Figure 96: A close-up on Eleanor's grave reveals the extra inscription 'Widow of Captain Edward John Smith S. S. Titanic'. (Photograph: Dan Parkes)

cloud cast over their escape when it transpired that Duff Gordon had offered the lifeboat crew £5 each, with an insinuation of bribery, which, while rejected as 'unfounded' by the Board of Trade inquiry, dented his reputation. He died of natural causes on 20 April 1931, eight days before Eleanor. His wife, Lady Duff Gordon, died precisely four years after her husband and they are both buried in Brookwood, within sight of the Eleanor and the Russell Cooke family plot.

On 2 July, Eleanor's probate was given to 'Helen Melville Cooke widow. Effects £12084'. It was quite a substantial sum considering that the probate amount she inherited from the death of her Teddy was a quarter of that – £3,186. In modern terms, it would equal over half a million pounds. As Sidney had written to Maynard Keynes in December 1922, this was the 'more money in prospect' he had likely referred to, although it pales in comparison to the total of £120,098 he left.

Flowers and Some Modelling

Melville continued to live at Bellecroft. London now held too many unpleasant memories and the Island with its beaches and gardens offered much needed respite. Indeed, Davenport sold 12 King's Bench Walk very quickly after his tenant's death, on 17 July 1930.[25] It is understandable that Mel would not want to return there. Instead, she took part in competitions at the Summer Show of the I.W. Horticultural Association in Newport where she won a cup for her carnations.[26] And she reappeared in autumn to take first prize in the 'open air cut flowers' section of the Isle of Wight Horticultural Association autumn exhibition'[27] and in 'open classes' at the all-Island Show of Chrysanthemums at the Drill Hall in Newport.[28]

The following year, she exhibited 'wonderful carnations' at the I.W. Horticultural Association in July 1932, although it was attributed to the 'gardener, P. Blaney,'[29] the work described as 'alone worth a visit' and winning first prize in the 'display of perpetual flowering carnations' section. Mel was presented with the 'Mrs. Millard challenge cup.'[30]

For a change of scenery, she appeared in the guest list of several London weddings in 1932, Mr Sebag-Montefiore and Miss Nathan in September, and Commander Hall and Miss Ritchie in October.[31]

The children's health and education were on her mind. She was encouraging them to flourish. Three years after the death of her father, 10-year-old Priscilla had her photograph published as part of an article, 'A Portfolio of Fashion for the Younger Generation', in the August edition of *The Bystander*, a British tabloid magazine (Figure 97). The article was compiled by Madge Garland, an influential journalist in British fashion, and Priscilla's photograph was credited to 'Lemare.' This was the French photographer Jacques Lemare, who was developing his photography in 1933. He was actually cutting his teeth for what he would eventually become, a director of photography in French cinema.

The portrait of Priscilla must have been all in a day's work for the aspiring cinematographer. She is seated on a lawn and looking off camera wistfully to her right, in a very similar manner to her grandmother's photograph when her mother was only a few years old. It is hard to tell if the garden trellis, with hints of what could be Bellecroft award-winning flowers behind her, is for real or in a studio – the lighting indicates the latter. The photographic series was displaying 'Summer Fashions for Smart Young People,' and the caption tells us that Priscilla 'has chosen from the White House a green linen dress which ties in a bow on either shoulder'. The page is shared by a photograph of four-year-old John Duff Cooper, the son of Lady Diana Cooper, a well-known actress and aristocrat, indicating Priscilla was in illustrious company. She was described as 'the ten-year old daughter of Mrs Sydney [sic] Russell Cooke' who 'has a twin brother, Simon'.[32]

The news reports of flower shows and children did not quite live up to Mel's reputation as 'ambitious and adventurous'. That was until 1934.

Figure 97: Ten-year-old Priscilla was selected for a fashion shoot in the popular magazine *The Bystander*, 2 August 1933. (Author's collection)

An article published in April that year revealed that 'recently Mrs. Cooke was thrown from her horse when the animal put its hoof in a rabbit hole. She suffered a broken collar bone from which she is recovering.'[33] Despite the injuries incurred, only months later Mel was about to stretch her wings ever further.

11

Aviatrix and a Twin Tragedy

One night in August 1934, the subdued animal noises on a farm in Tilford, Surrey were suddenly interrupted by that of a spluttering engine. There was a moment of silence and then from above, a sudden crash of metal as a Gipsy Moth biplane fell out of the sky and bounced along the uneven field. Designed without any brakes and just a skid on the tail, the plane snaked along the field, the pilot wrestling to regain control. The field was crossed and the forward momentum of the aircraft catapulted it through the fence of a chicken run. With panicked fowl squawking and scattering in fear of the large metal bird that had burst into their midst in the middle of the night, the biplane came to a halt as its wings were caught in the fencing, crashing into the perimeter hedge. As the noise of the terrified chickens slowly subsided, the two pilots checked on each other to discover they both, thankfully, had relatively minor injuries. In the dark it was hard to tell exactly what had happened. The damage seemed minimal. It certainly could have been much worse. Then there was the flash of car headlights from a passing motorist who quickly spotted the unusual sight of a Gipsy Moth biplane poking its head through the hedge. Help was soon at hand.

One of the occupants who gingerly stepped out of the damaged aircraft was Mrs Russell Cooke. She was not just a passenger. Less than a fortnight later, she received her flying certificate.

Airwork Flying School

Melville showed her adventurous side that Sidney found so attractive when in 1934 she decided to become a pilot, her training commencing at Heston Airport. Heston Aerodrome was home to Airwork Flying School and became a centre of private flying as well as a convenient commercial route between London and the Isle of Wight. The ease of travel from Bellecroft must have appealed to Mel. Maybe she spotted advertising in 1930 that touted the school as 'the most up-to-date school in the world', where students could learn to fly in a Gipsy Moth.

Most likely Mel was inspired by a crop of aviatrix pioneers of the 1930s, such as the young Yorkshirewoman Amy Johnson who flew solo from England to Australia in May 1930, in a Gipsy Moth, taking 19 days. She was only 27. The feat gained her a CBE. This was followed by New Zealander Jean Batten who also flew a Gipsy Moth from England to Australia single-handedly in 1934, taking just 15 days. She was just 25 and was known for her aviation achievements and her glamorous appearance.[1]

Pushing the limits of record-breaking technology is inherently risky. As with the infamous disappearance of Amelia Earheart in 1939, Amy Johnson likewise vanished without a trace when her plane crashed into the Thames Estuary in 1941.

Mel was to experience her own brush with death, although at a much earlier stage in her aviation career. On the night of Friday, 3 August 1934, there were reports that a plane had crashed into a chicken run near Tilford, Farnham in Surrey, although the occupants escaped with only minor injuries.

The pilot was Flight Lieutenant Christopher Clarkson of London, flying from Heston to Shanklin on the Isle of Wight. Tilford is almost exactly half-way between London and the Island, and midway, 'difficulty was experienced, owing, it is believed, to a choked petrol feed'.[2] The local Isle of Wight news also ran a short article the following Saturday, identifying the other occupant, no doubt to Mel's mortification: 'A Newport woman escaped with only minor injuries after she was involved in a plane crash in Surrey. Mrs. Russell-Cooke was flying from the Island to Heston, near London, when a fault developed with the aircraft's petrol feed, causing the pilot to crash land in a chicken run near Tilford. The pilot, Flight-Lieutenant Clarkson, from London, was unhurt.'[3]

32-year-old Flight Lieutenant Christopher Clarkson (1902-1994), a Royal Air Force instructor at the Central Flying School since 1924, was known for winning competitions in his Gipsy Moth by performing various aerobatics, including landing without use of an engine or brakes in 1931 – something which may well have made the emergency landing in a farm a more feasible option. The following year, he made the news with an 'exhibition of inverted flying on a Gipsy 2 Moth.'[4] Flying upside down in those early days was not for the faint-hearted. Described in 1933 as 'one of the finest aerobatic pilots in England',[5] the Clarkson Trophy was named after him. Starting in 1935, the Central Flying School presented this award for aerobatics from 1935 to the best all-round pilot. The trophy is impressive in its own right, with a model of a bi-plane atop four thick plinths, with the names of the winners inscribed.[6]

In a more detailed account printed in the *Citizen* newspaper in Gloucestershire, the 'passenger' was listed as

> ... Mrs. Russell Cooke, of Somers-place, London ... who occupied the front cockpit [and] had cuts on the nose and the pilot cuts on the left wrist... The pilot was trying to land in a field when the machine crashed into a chicken run, finishing up with the nose poking through a hedge at the side of the road. Chickens were scattered but none was killed ... both [were] taken to Farnham by a passing motorist.[7]

Melville was quite likely more than simply a passenger. Sitting in the front cockpit seat she was almost undoubtedly learning, too. Twelve days later, on 15 August 1934, Mel received her certificate from the Airwork School of Flying rated for operating an 'Avro Club Cadet on a Genet 7 cyl.'

The certificate included an identity photograph that reveals any injuries to her nose must have been purely superficial, as there is no indication in the photograph – unless the picture was taken prior to her close call with a chicken run (Figure 98).

The Avro Club Cadet was a 1930s single-engine British biplane trainer aircraft, designed with folding wings and with an Armstrong Siddeley Genet Major 1 7-cylinder air-cooled radial piston engine, capable of 135 horsepower (101 kW).[8]

Figure 98: Mel's photograph ID for her Airwork certification. (Courtesy of Paul Van Doodson)

With her newly granted 'wings', Mel was perhaps inclined to travel more. A few months later, in October 1934, she was photographed sitting with golfers at North Berwick, Scotland, with the caption noting that visitors were from 'even such remote places as Belgrave Square and the club reserves of "Pell Mell" and Piccadilly' (Figure 99).[9]

The following year she was using her own aircraft to go holidaying. Photographed proudly standing with her plane, a Gipsy Moth 3 (Figure 100), *The Tatler* of 31 July 1935 wrote: 'At Heston: The roving camera-man finds Mrs. Russell Cooke just after her arrival at our leading airport, on her return from a holiday in which bathing, both the sun and sea variety, has played a prominent part. Her machine is a Moth Gipsy 3.'[10] The Gipsy Moth 3 was actually a de Havilland DH.60 Moth, an upgrade model with the engine inverted that was released in 1931.[11] The photograph was part of a spread on activities at Heston Aerodrome, an airfield located to the west of London that the *Tatler* reporter notes was 'particularly busy at this time of the year, when everybody is either just departing for their holiday or just returning from it'.

It remains to be seen whether Mel's involvement in a minor plane crash with a dashing and equally adventurous Flight Lieutenant was a hint there was something more going on. In addition to a flying lesson, they were maybe intending to spend the weekend at Bellecroft (the incident did take place on a Friday night after all).

Figure 99: Mel (far right) on a trip to North Berwick for a game of golf. (*The Tatler* 10 October 1934, author's collection)

Figure 100: Mel with her own private aircraft, a Gipsy Moth 3, in July 1935. *The Tatler*, 31 July 1935. (Author's collection)

Not that Mel was averse to travelling by sea. In August 1935, she took the P&O ship the *Chitral* on a voyage to Gibraltar, noted on the passenger list as a 37-year-old of '10, Somers Place' of 'nil' occupation. Not obvious to the casual reader, ten lines below her entry was a Christopher Clarkson, aged 34, of '128 Piccadilly' and in 'aviation sales'.[12] He was the only other passenger with the destination of Gibraltar. Mel was still travelling with her Flight Lieutenant – for pleasure, rather than business it would appear.[13]

Clarkson was three years younger than Mel. And one of her more well-known love interests was even younger – 18 years younger.

David Rolt and Leafield

David Rolt was born in Yorkshire in 1915 and became a sought-after British portrait and landscape painter during the 1940s and 1950s, although his real love was painting trees (Figure 101). Despite a forceps delivery that damaged his skull at birth, leaving him with a lifelong disability in his right arm and leg, he was socially well connected and painted portraits for a living. While in his early 20s, during the mid-to-late 1930s, Mel met Rolt and formed a relationship that would last until her death. They had both lost a parent at a young age (Mel was 14 and David 10) and had a reputation for kindness and creativity, qualities that likely drew them to each other. He painted portraits of her at least three times (Figure 102). Art collector Robert Eagle, who owns a

Figure 101: A self-portrait by David Rolt, 1941. (Courtesy of Toby Rolt/Robert Eagle Fine Art)

gallery devoted to the work of twentieth-century British and Irish artists, describes Mel as

> ... a vivacious woman who drove fast cars and held a pilot's licence, she was 18 years older than him and already married, but their relationship continued until the artist was in his 40s, when Rolt married Minnie Bradford, a girl 20 years younger than himself. That marriage lasted just ten years. Minnie re-married, but Rolt never did. His friendship with Mel continued until her death in 1973 ... she remained Rolt's friend and confidante for the rest of her life.[14]

In a memoir to mark the posthumous exhibition of David Rolt's work held in 1986, Alistair Forbes described Rolt as having 'curiously elongated features'. It was his conversation, 'an amalgam of curiosity, sympathy, wide even erudite reading and an elegant lack of disdain for gossip that made David such an enchanting companion.'[15] In this, Rolt personified qualities that had made Melville's father so popular with his passengers. Rolt lived and painted at no. 115 Ebury street, London, at the beginning of the Second World War and this was where Forbes himself was painted. 'Whatever the result on the canvas, to be in the company of this artist was time superbly spent as he went about his business ... to watch David's dot-and-carry-one sashaying back and forth to the easel, with much sucking and relighting of his pipe, was as good as a Stanislavsky-directed play.'

Forbes does not mention Melville but does describe in 1940 a time when he 'crossed over to visit David in the pretty house in the Isle of Wight in which he was then briefly residing', which sounds a good match for Bellecroft. Forbes also recalled when Rolt was 'installed in the Cotswold village he always called "sunny Leafield"' and that he was 'often lucky enough to stay with him, and many blacked-out evenings in those agreeable pre-TV days were enjoyably spent listening to David reading aloud from the stories of Saki, something he did most admirably.' He must, of course, be referring to Pratts House, in Leafield, where Mel would eventually reside. David and Mel also spent some time together in Ireland, so it is not surprising that Forbes mentioned visiting Rolt 'for another wartime week ... on the glorious blue-green Co. Mayo coast'.

Rolt painted several portraits of Mel, including one of her leaning pensively against a wall with a bright orange head band (Figure 102). Signed, it is an unframed and undated work of oil on canvas, measuring 20 x 24 in. (50.8 x 61 cm.) and was sold at auction in 2012.[16] Another undated work, labelled as 'lady wearing a blue jacket', is a portrait of Mel, looking down as if she is perhaps reading, her hair tightly curled

Figure 102: A younger Mel wearing a bright head band, in a painting by David Rolt. (Courtesy of Toby Rolt/Robert Eagle Fine Art)

(Figure 117). Paintings hang on the wall behind her, hinting at her love of art as she was an avid art collector.[17]

Mel visited Canada aboard the *Empress of Britain* departing from Southampton for Quebec on 3 October 1936. But her home was still the Isle of Wight; the 1939 registration notes a 'Helen M R Cooke,' described as 'widowed' and her occupation of 'private means' residing at Bellecroft. By this stage, the house was numbered 19 and according to the census, there were twelve people residing there, including a boys schoolmaster, a kitchen maid, parlour maid and cook.[18] Mel was still socialising locally. Her name appeared on the list of attendees at Lady Baring's Charity Ball in August 1939, an annual event held at Northwood House, in Cowes.[19]

Rolt painted Mel in her new home in the village of Leafield in Oxfordshire. She is seen reclining gracefully on a settee, a dark coat on her shoulders and a book on her lap (Figure 103). Not that life in the quiet village was all about relaxing. During the war years, she enlisted with the local police and ambulance service.[20]

The twins Priscilla and Simon were also subjects of David Rolt's artistic eye. Priscilla was painted sporting dark hair with a scarf around her neck and seated, leaning on one elbow. It is a natura, yet dignified pose, very

Aviatrix and a Twin Tragedy

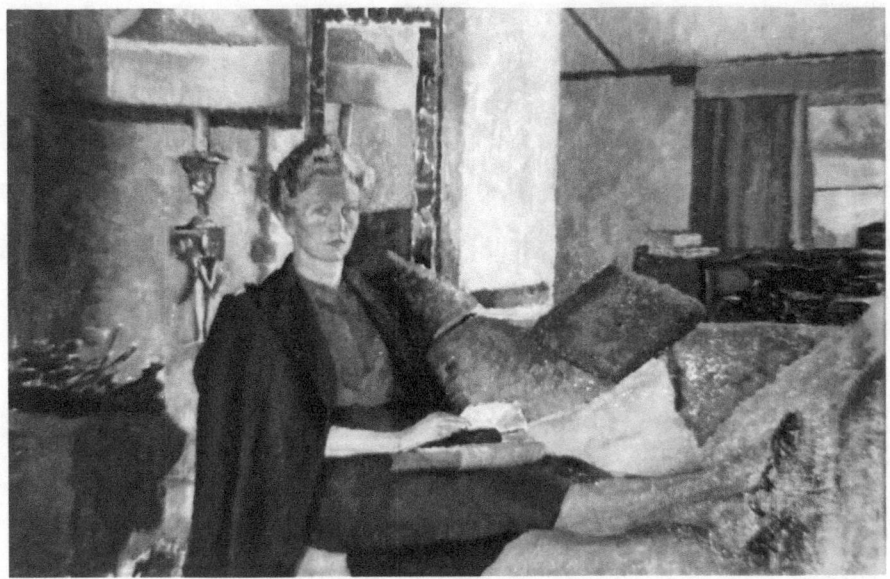

Figure 103: Mel reclining in her home, most likely at Pratts House in Leafield, in a painting by her partner David Rolt. (Photograph: John Pladdys)

similar in style to her mother (Figure 114). As a sign of world events at that increasingly perilous time, Simon was painted in his RAF uniform, in a chair placed next to a window, bathing him in the warmth of natural sunlight (Figure 110). He looks a little apprehensive. Leafield had become a place of refuge from the threat of war for the Russell Cookes. Sadly, Simon would be unable to escape from the coming onslaught for long.

Simon, RAF Flying Officer

While Melville was flying her Gipsy Moth and posing as the muse of a renowned painter, her son Simon was a 'Wykehamist', studying at Winchester College. In September 1936, at 13 years of age, Simon joined the college, having previously studied at Ashdown House preparatory school in East Sussex (now closed, it once counted Boris Johnson among its alumni). On joining Winchester, Simon was placed in 'E House, Morshead's' or 'Freddie's'. Following both his mother and father, he was, according to a college biography, 'from the start largely absorbed in his two main interests – the aeroplanes which he was later to fly, and boats and the sailing of them. He was never happier than when building a model aeroplane, for which he had a considerable flair, or when sailing a boat at which he spent most of his holidays in the Isle of Wight.'[21] Simon both rowed and coxed for his house IV and was actively involved

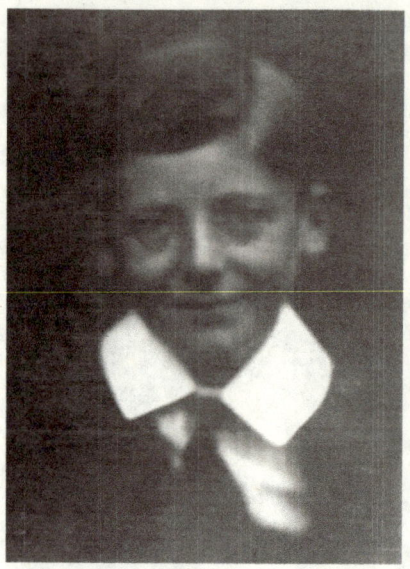 

Figure 104: Simon at a 'somewhat unexpected tea-party', Sunday, 11 July 1936. (Warden and Scholars of Winchester College)

Figure 105: Mel, her son Simon and what is probably the family dog. (Courtesy of John Pladdys)

in supporting social and sporting occasions such as the Eton Match, where a photograph reveals he helped lick 1100 stamps in 40 minutes for sending out the invitations (Figure 106).[22]

During his time at the college, the family moved from Bellecroft to Pratts House in Leafield.[23] In a family photograph taken in the rear garden of their new house in the Oxfordshire village (Figure 105) Simon is smartly dressed in a suit with a pin on his collar, while his mother Mel has her arm through his, her other arm around the family dog. They are both grinning widely. It is a happy, spontaneous moment in the sun.

In 1940, Simon was formally photographed with the Morshead boys, the group neatly attired in dress suits and arranged behind trophies the house had won (Figure 107). By December that year, at the age of just 17, he began working in an aircraft factory. And as soon as he turned 18 the following year, he joined the Royal Air Force to play his role in the national effort to confront the Nazi threat. He would have heard how his father was involved in action during the First World War.

For initial training he joined the RAF Short Course at Oxford, most likely as part of the Oxford University Air Squadron, in which up to 300 trainees were taken on six-month courses.[24] In the same year, just before the US entered the war, Simon continued his instruction in the US as part of the Arnold Scheme that began in June 1941, fast-tracking

Aviatrix and a Twin Tragedy

Figure 106: Simon (far left) helped lick 1,100 stamps for invitations to an Eton Match, Sunday, 8 May 1938. (Photograph courtesy of the Warden and Scholars of Winchester College)

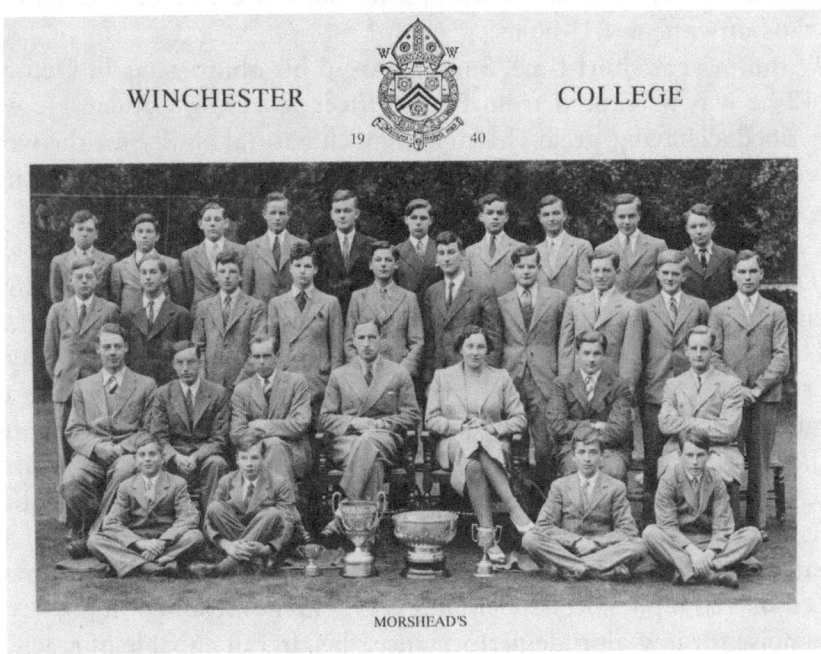

Figure 107: Morshead's House at Winchester College. Captain Smith's grandson, Simon, is standing in the third row from the front, fifth boy from the left. (Photograph courtesy Warden and Scholars of Winchester College)

Figure 108: A close-up of Simon from the 1940 college photograph. (Warden and Scholars of Winchester College)

pilots on an extensive training programme that was so demanding that of the 7,885 RAF personnel who entered the scheme, almost half (3,392) failed and 81 were killed.[25] Simon managed to pass and returned to the UK in 1942 as a fighter pilot. He was posted to the RAF Coastal Command which was tasked with protecting Allied conveys from attack by the Luftwaffe and U-boats.

Within a very short time, Simon proved his abilities, as in October 1942 he was promoted from Pilot Officer to Flying Officer. He was described as having 'great charm and much natural ability for the work in connection with flying, whether as pilot or designer, which he had always intended to do'.

The Wykehamist War Service Roll of Honour records that he was 'P/O [Pilot Officer] June 42, F/O. [Flight Officer] Oct 42, F/Lt. [Flight Lieutenant] Oct. 43'.[26] These dates are confirmed in the *London Gazette*.

He eventually joined 144 Squadron an operational unit that played a crucial role in the battle above Britain, motto 'Who shall stop us' (Figure 109). The Squadron had been equipped with Bristol Beaufighters in January 1943 and by April Simon was flying the Beaufighter TF Mk.X aircraft, a variation that was known as the 'Torbeau' or torpedo fighter, as it was equipped with torpedoes or RP-3 (60 lb) rockets capable of all-weather as well as night attacks.[27] With a crew of two, it had a maximum speed of 320 mph, and its Hercules XVII engines resulted in improved low-noise for low-altitude performance, the aircraft capable of reaching 29,000 feet.[28] Simon served with 144 Squadron in Algeria from June to August 1943, where he was involved in carrying out anti-shipping strikes in the Mediterranean, and then returned to Scotland where he was based

Aviatrix and a Twin Tragedy

Figure 109: The RAF heraldic badge of 144 Bomber Squadron (courtesy of the RAF Heraldry Trust, with permission of the Ministry of Defence, UK)

at Tain and then Wick. Throughout his time with the 144 Squadron, Simon continued to prove himself, as evidenced in a testimonial from his Wing Commander to his mother:

> Your son since he joined the Squadron has gradually established himself to be one of the best and most reliable pilots and at the same time he has never allowed his work to finish in the air, but has shown himself to be very capable in carrying out the various ground duties associated with the work of the Squadron. On and off duty he was always popular with all ranks.[29]

Situated in the very north of Scotland, RAF Wick was an ideal strategic location for anti-shipping operations over the North Sea and off the coast of Norway. The downside was that it was also a 'dry town,' with no pubs, and it was very cold; John O'Groats was a freezing 12-mile bicycle ride away. A sense of the danger during the sorties they flew is given by one of Simon's fellow airmen at Wick, navigator F.S. Holly from Deganwy, Gwynedd:

> I served as a navigator on 144 Squadron which flew Beaufighters (crew of 2) and which was stationed at Wick from October 1943 to May 1944. I had joined it at Tain in August 1943, just after my 22nd birthday. The crews of 144 were trained to drop torpedoes and on early operations from Wick these were carried. Later, we flew in

Figure 110: A painting of Simon Russell Cooke in RAF uniform, likely at home in Pratts House, by the artist David Rolt. (Photograph: John Pladdys)

conjunction with 404 (Canadian) Squadron, which was armed with rockets – the aircraft of both squadrons had four 20mm cannons mounted inside the fuselage. The early sorties usually consisted of 4 aircraft. When we reached the Norwegian coast we turned south and did a patrol. If we met a suitable ship, we would attack it. Otherwise we would fly back to Wick with the torpedoes – they were too expensive to jettison. Sometimes on reaching Norway we would split into two pairs – one patrolling North and the other South. These patrols were called 'Rovers'. When we went with 404 squadron the formations were bigger. Rockets could be used in places that were inaccessible to torpedoes and some attacks were made against ships in harbour. Sometimes, if we were going further north than usual, we would land at Sumburgh on the way out and take on more fuel. All our flying was at low level and in stormy weather the aircraft often returned to Wick covered with salt... Flying at 50 to 150 feet above the sea in the dark with anti-aircraft fire from 20 ships concentrated on you, is an unforgettable experience.[30]

Flying Officer Oliver Philport, like Simon, had trained at the Oxford University Air Squadron, and was flying a Beaufort in January 1941 when he was shot down by German anti-aircraft fire off Norway. The crew ditched into the North Sea and were picked up by a German naval vessel.

Aviatrix and a Twin Tragedy

It was his involvement in the successful 'Wooden Horse' plot, in which he was one of three who managed to escape, that made him famous.

Simon was not going to be so lucky.

On 23 March 1944, Simon, the 20-year-old Flying Officer of the Royal Air Force Volunteer Reserve, (Service Number 124429) was the pilot aboard a Beaufighter TFX aircraft, serial number NE473, with 21-year-old Flight Sergeant John Edward Beaman, navigator (Service Number 1335845), from West Ham, Essex. Their mission was to attack a shipping convoy off Bremangerlandet, South of Maloy, Norway. They came under fire, an engine was hit and their plane crashed into the sea. Unlike Philport, or his mother Mel, Simon did not survive the crash,

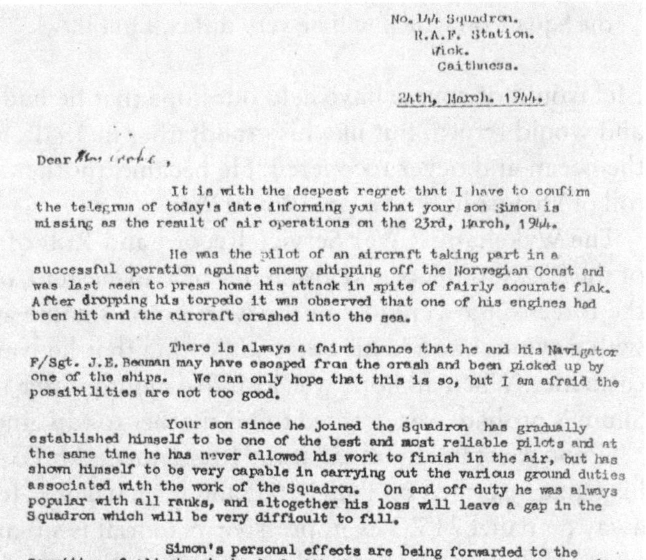

Figure 111: The letter Melville was dreading to receive, informing her that Simon was lost in action. (Photograph courtesy of John Pladdys)

reported 'believed killed'.³¹ In a report by the Wing Commander, sent the following day from Wick, he described what happened (Figure 111):

> He was the pilot of an aircraft taking part in a successful operation against enemy shipping off the Norwegian Coast and was last seen to press home his attack in spite of fairly accurate flack. After dropping his torpedo it was observed that one of his engines had been hit and the aircraft crashed into the sea.
>
> There is always a faint chance that he and his Navigator F/Sgt J.E. Beaman may have escaped from the crash and been picked up by one of the ships. We can only hope that this is so, but I am afraid the possibilities are not too good ... altogether his loss will leave a gap in the Squadron which will be very difficult to fill.

Mel would of course have held out hope that he had somehow survived and would return. But like his grandfather in 1912, his body was lost to the ocean and never recovered. He became another statistic in the huge toll of life lost in the Second World War.

The Wykehamist War Service Record and Roll of Honour notes that of the 2370 students and graduates of Winchester College who served in the forces, 269 were lost in the war. Simon's name appears on page 97, with a symbol beside his entry indicating that he was one of the college casualties. When all hope was lost, five months later, on 23 August 1944, Simon's probate was granted to his mother for an amount of £360 8s 6d.

Simon is commemorated at the Runnymede Air Forces Memorial, with his name inscribed on Panel 205, and his navigator John Beaman not far away on panel 215. The impressive memorial is situated on a hill not far from Heathrow Airport, so has a constant flow of air traffic flying over it, a reminder that the site is in memory of more than 20,000 members of air forces of the British Empire who were lost in air and other operations during the War who have no known grave, many lost without trace. In the village of Leafield, Simon's name is etched into the wooden lychgate at the entrance of St Michael & All Angels Church. His name also appears inside the church, in the 1939-1945 roll of honour. The church is located just around the corner from Pratts House, so would have been a constant reminder to Mel of the son she had lost.

Priscilla and Polio

Mel was not the only person connected to the *Titanic* to suffer such loss. The *Titanic*'s senior surviving officer, Charles Lightoller, lost his youngest son, 21-year-old RAF pilot Herbert Brian, who was killed in action on the first night of Britain's entry into the war (4 September 1939). Closer still, her partner at the time, David Rolt, lost his younger brother Cecil, whom he adored, in April 1945. Simon's nonidentical twin, Priscilla, must have also suffered greatly from the loss of a sibling who was dear to her.

The following year Priscilla fell in love and married John Phipps. He is not to be confused, as some have, with Oswald Constantine John Phipps, the Marquess and 12th Lord of Normandy (married to Grania Guinness in 1951).[32] John Arneal Constantine Phipps was born in 1910, so was 13 years older than Priscilla, not dissimilar to the 11-year difference between the ages of her grandparents, Edward and Eleanor. When the couple married in September 1945 in Westminster, Priscilla was 22 and John 35.

There is a glimpse of the single Priscilla in two photographs. Not unlike the picture of her mother taken in the gardens of Winn Road, Southampton (when Mel had a small dog on her lap, Figure 27), Priscilla is smartly dressed and poses with two canine friends, one of whom she appears to be feeding, with her mother grinning widely beside her (Figure 112).

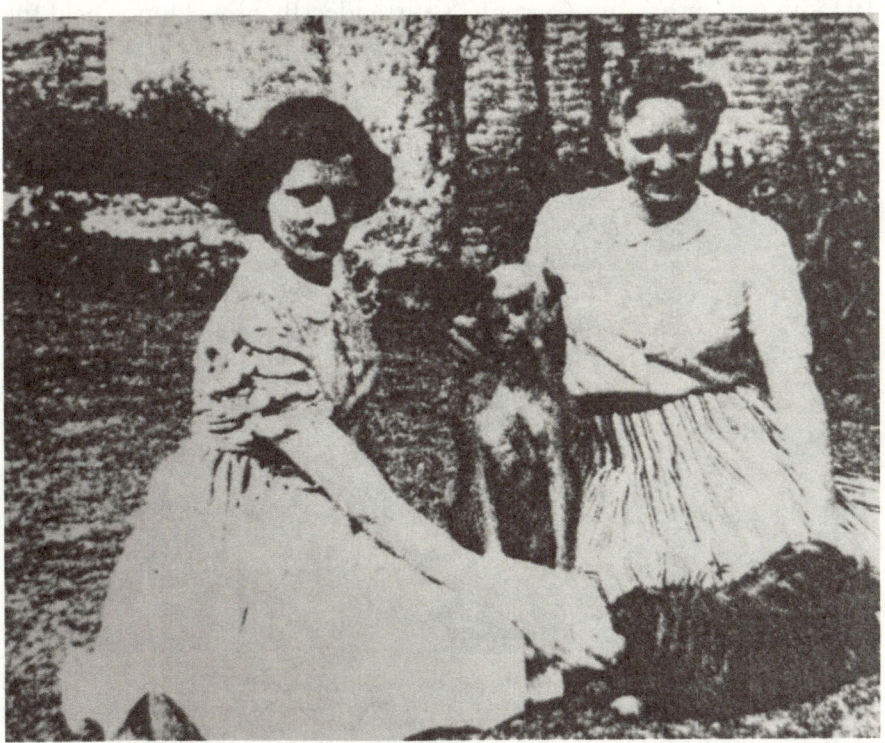

Figure 112: Another family photograph with a dog – in this case two. Priscilla poses with her mother in the backyard of Pratts House in Leafield, at a similar time to the picture taken of Simon, Figure 105. (Photograph courtesy of John Pladdys)

Titanic Legacy: The Captain, the Daughter and the Spy

Some years later, she is wearing a not dissimilar dress and socialising with RAF captains and pilot officers at a 'Queen Charlotte's Christmas Leave Ball' in late December 1941. Over 1,000 people were present at the charity evening, the ball an occasion for presenting debutantes – young upper-class women entering the social circuit to meet eligible bachelors. In among photographs of lords and ladies in their finest evening wear at dining tables chatting with men in uniform, is picture of a table (Figure 113) headed by 'Brigadier Portman' – almost undoubtedly Brigadier Guy Maurice Berkeley Portman, born in 1890 so then aged 51. In 1941, he was Commanding Officer of the 168th Infantry Brigade and Aide-de-Camp to King George VI. Sitting quietly to his left is 18-year-old 'Miss Russell Cooke' politely listening in as Brigadier Portman is engaged in conversation with Lady Jowitt opposite. Priscilla looks a little apprehensive, as if somewhat out of her depth in the conversation.[33] At the time, her brother Simon was in the US training to be a RAF pilot, while her uncle, Brigadier Jasper Harker was acting Director General of MI5. This was quite likely her moment as a debutante, in the middle of a world war.

It was a lawyer from Chelsea she would be courted by and marry in 1945, two months after Germany's surrender. By now, Phipps held the title of 'Major.' Their impending nuptials were announced in the London *Times* on 25 June 1945:

Brigadier Portman, Miss Russell Cooke, Captain P. B. L. Matthews, Miss Penelope Jowitt, Lieut. M. R. K. Garnett, Miss Judith Anderson and Lady Jowitt were together

Figure 113: Priscilla as a debutante at 'Queen Charlotte's Christmas Leave Ball'. She would soon marry a Major. *The Tatler and Bystander*, 31 December 1941. (Author's collection)

Aviatrix and a Twin Tragedy

MAJOR J. C. PHIPPS AND MISS RUSSELL COOKE. The engagement is announced of John, elder son of Sir Edmund Phipps, C.B., of 21, Carlyle Square, Chelsea, and of the late Lady Phipps, and Priscilla. daughter of the late Sidney Russell Cooke and Mrs. Russell Cooke, of Pratts, Leafield, Oxfordshire.[34]

They were married at St. Martin-in-the-Fields on Thursday 6 September 1945, Priscilla given away by her uncle Jasper, with a reception at the Savoy Hotel: 'Mr. Nicholas Phipps (brother of the bridegroom) was best man.'[35]

The couple settled at 19 Archery Close, in St George's Fields, London, a neighbourhood near Hyde Park that was very familiar to the Russell Cookes. Sidney and his sister Pattie had lived just around the corner at 18 Portsea Place before their marriages.

John had been educated at Winchester and Trinity College, Oxford, and was working as a barrister in Middle Temple in 1933.[36] He was admitted to the Middle Temple Inn on 31 December 1930, at the age of 20, while living at 21 Carlyle Square in Chelsea with his father, Sir Edmund Bampfylde Phipps, a retired civil servant. Phipps was recommended by the President of Trinity College: 'I believe him to be a gentleman of respectability and a proper person to be admitted as a student of the Honourable Society of Middle Temple with a view to being called to the Bar.'[37]

Figure 114: A painting of Priscilla, likely posed in Pratts House, Leafield, by the artist David Rolt. (Photograph: John Pladdys)

Both his education and his work obviously have connections to the Russell Cooke family: Priscilla's brother Simon studied at Winchester and her father Sidney Russell Cooke lived in Temple. Whether either of these connections resulted in the couple meeting is unclear. Priscilla's marriage and the end of the war surely provided a much needed injection of optimism to Mel and the family; even if it was to be temporary.

After only two years of marriage, Priscilla died on 7 October 1947, at Galashiels, Selkirkshire in Scotland, after a 'short illness'.[38] She was only 24. The illness was later confirmed to be acute paralytic polio.

The World Health Organisation (WHO) defines polio as a highly infectious disease that 'invades the nervous system and can cause total paralysis in a matter of hours ... one in 200 infections leads to irreversible paralysis (usually in the legs). Among those paralysed, 5–10% die when their breathing muscles become immobilized.'[39] During the 1940s, there had been severe outbreaks of poliomyelitis (shortened to 'polio' by the media), with as many as 7,800 cases per year in the UK and up to 750 deaths. A vaccine was introduced in the 1950s that by the 1980s had all but eradicated the infectious disease.[40]

Such progress was too late for Priscilla. Ten days after her death, at noon on Friday, 17 October 1947, a memorial service was held for her at the Parish Church of St. Luke, Sidney Street in Chelsea.[41] The London *Times* reported on the memorial service, noting that 'Mrs. Melville Russel Cooke (mother)' was present along with 'other members of the family' and an impressive list of attendees including a Lord Chancellor, a Viscountess and a number of Honorable and Lady guests. Rev W. G. Arrowsmith officiated, assisted by the Rev J. S. Martin, while the Lesson was read by Lord Oaksey.[42]

Why Priscilla died in southeast Scotland is something of a mystery. Had she contracted the disease while visiting, or had she been admitted to a hospice when her condition was judged to be serious? Whatever the case, she was nearer to where her twin Simon had been based during the war.

It was a terrible year for her husband John. He also lost his father Edmund Phipps C.B., according to *Kelly's Handbook to the Titled, Landed and Official Classes* (1960). In a rather bizarre coincidence, the handbook notes that John remarried two years later to a woman named Sheila Seeds who was herself previously married to another John – Sir John Wentworth Dilke. He was the son of Sir Fisher Wentworth Dilke – Sidney's older half-brother. Sheila divorced Sir John in 1949, the same year she married barrister John Phipps. That they were distant family members means the couple may well have met at some family event over the years – even at Priscilla's memorial service.

John prospered in his job after the remarriage. The short biography in *Kelly's Handbook* states: 'barr. Middle Temple 1933, junior counsel for the Crown in appeals to London sessions 1953, recorder of Gravesend 1957, prosecuting counsel to the Crown, North London sessions 1958, a metropolitan magis, from 1959.'[43]

John had a brother, Nicholas Phipps (1913-1980) who had been his best man at Priscilla's wedding and was a prolific light-comedy British actor and screenwriter and appeared in more than thirty films between 1940 and 1970, known for being tall and dark-haired, and taking on caddish roles.[44]

He and Sheila went on to have two daughters (Elizabeth and Susan). They divorced in 1964 and he remarried in 1965 to Hermione Deedes and lived to the age of 76, dying on 30 July 1986.[45] In October, his probate was released which indicates he had retired to Etchingham in East Sussex: 'Phipps, John Constantine of St Giles Burwash Etchingham E Sx died 30 July 1986 Probate London 14 October £574,575.'[46]

As for his first wife, it is uncertain where Priscilla was buried or cremated. Just as the final resting place of her legendary grandfather and her twin brother is a mystery so, sadly, is the present location of Priscilla's grave.

In an unpleasant twist of fate, 53-year-old Margaret Harker, Sidney's younger sister, also died just two days before Priscilla, on 5 October 1947, after a short, undisclosed illness.[47] Unlike Priscilla, whose grave is unknown, Margaret has her own headstone in the Russell Cooke family plot, situated prominently between her brother and Eleanor Smith.

There is no record of how Mel responded to the loss of both her children between 1944 and 1947 – other than a moment when she confided to one of her few intimate friends that she was afraid of forming close relationships because they seemed destined to end in tragedy.[48] Unless Mel remarried or had children, her death would be the end of Captain Smith's family line.

12
Leafield Life

Melville was 49 years old when Priscilla died. Before turning 50, she had lost her father, mother, husband, son and daughter. It was an unbearable weight to carry at such an age, but Mel was already moving on and starting a new life in the Oxfordshire countryside.

Bellecroft, the large estate of 65 acres and the grade listed building perched on a hill on the Isle of Wight, was much too large and too far away. During the early war years, it would also become a dangerous location, with the Island frequently bombed by the Luftwaffe en route to Portsmouth and Southampton. In July 1941, Mel signed off the property for use by the State of War Department, reimbursed with £175 plus £52 per annum.

Having settled in the small village of Leafield in the early 1940s, in April 1944 she finally put Bellecroft on the market, with advertisements appearing in *The Sunday Times* in London from April through to November 1944. It listed a 'farm (let on a yearly tenancy at £180 per annum)' and the estate with an income of 'about £355 per annum' (Figure 115).[1]

She eventually sold Bellecroft in 1945 for £6,000 to the Newport Borough Council. In 1959, the council used the land to set up two police houses, and the house itself was sold to a television hire company Radio Rentals. The estate was divided up to form private residential housing. The grand house was later redeveloped into 12 flats.

From one hill to another, Mel escaped to the small village of Leafield, four miles northwest of Witney. With a population that has regularly sat just shy of a thousand, the hilltop village is nestled in the Cotswolds Hills in an area designated as one of outstanding natural beauty. Long before Mel arrived, Leafield was coincidentally once a centre for pottery production, just as her father's hometown still is.[2]

Figure 115: 'Bellecroft' for sale in 1940, revealing how it used to look, with an entrance to the side of the property. (Courtesy of Keith Prowse)

Figure 116: Undated photograph of Pratts House, Leafield. (Oxfordshire County Council – Oxfordshire History Centre, Reference: POX0194196)

St Michael & All Angels Church dominates the area, its spire conspicuous for miles. Just across the village green and around the corner from the church, a small seventeenth-century house became Mel's home. Originally, it was called 'Ivy Dene' and was owned by a Mr and Mrs Pratt. Mel subsequently renamed it 'Pratts House,' in tribute to its former occupants, a building that was Grade II listed in 1989. The listing describes the two-storey house as constructed of stone coursed rubble and having a stone slate roof and featuring a six-panel part glazed door.[3] When Simon died in 1944, he was recorded as a 'native' of Leafield, so it seems the twins had moved with their mother into the countryside and resided at Pratts.

What drew Mel to this quiet and isolated village, where everyone knows everyone else? When she arrived during the war, it consisted of just a few families. She would have been the odd one out. Some locals said that she mostly kept to herself, while others thought she was at least occasionally active in local events. She was always referred to as 'Mrs Russell Cooke' and many were not familiar with her past, which would have been one attraction. Another draw could well have been the Akeman Street airfield at the end of Witney Lane that was used during the war years primarily for training.[4] The grass airfield would have been convenient for her private plane and could also facilitate visits by her son Simon.

That the war drove her to Leafield is indicated in the recollection of a student visitor who remembered that she told them she had been 'living on a channel island' (actually, the Isle of Wight) 'when the Nazi invasion loomed, and not knowing England well they took a map and found the spot furthest from any seacoast, namely Leafield. I have no idea whether she was serious (or indeed whether Leafield really fits that description), but it matters little.'[5]

The house itself was split in two – Pratts House and Pratts Cottage. Originally workers' houses, the cottage next door housed Derek and Mary Moss, with Mary employed as Mel's housekeeper and cook. A servant's bell was used to call Mrs Moss on Mel's whim, and according to a local, Mary Lougheed, the requests became so frequent that Mary Moss put in a request to get a council house to escape the constant demands of Mrs Russell Cooke. Mel had a tight spiral staircase taken out and replaced with a more manageable flight of stairs. Mary Lougheed remembers that the redesign was prompted by concerns over Mel's heart. Mary still has a piece of Mel's staircase in her house today.

Gardening was one of Mel's hobbies, carried over from her time at Bellecroft, and since Pratts had large grounds, she was able to indulge her interest, spending much of her time in her garden. Standing in the corner of the yard is a wonderful specimen of a Dawn Redwood tree, which, until a discovery in China in 1946, was thought to have been extinct for five million years. Three seedlings somehow made their way into the botanic gardens at Cambridge University and, more surprisingly, Mel's backyard. It was perhaps inspired by David Rolt's love of painting trees that they decided to plant what is now judged one of the 50 'Great British Trees'.[6]

While it is a much smaller abode than Bellecroft, she could still enjoy socialising. John Pladdys explains that 'in spite of her love of solitude,

Figure 117: An oil on canvas portrait of Mel by David Rolt labelled a 'Lady wearing a blue jacket', probably painted at Pratts House. It captures not only Mel's fashion sense, but a contemplative moment. (Toby Rolt/Robert Eagle Fine Art)

she thrived on social events, and there were many parties at Pratts, often attended by well-known personalities. For example, the renowned Bomber Harris ... was a frequent visitor at weekends.'[7] Bomber Harris was painted by David Rolt, an oil portrait of him sitting at a table in 1942.

Embroidery was another of Mel's hobbies – several examples still adorned the house during the 1990s, including a bird pattern and a more modern creation entitled 'Hands' that shows an outstretched hand with long sleeves, possibly inspired by a work of art.

Mel was developing quite an art collection, much of which adorned the walls of Pratts House. In 1946, she acquired a painting directly from the Irish artist J. B. Yeats (Jack Butler Yeats, 1871-1957) entitled 'Nearing Dublin'. It was painted in 1924 and shows a train moving its way through the Irish countryside. It realised a price of £69,300 at auction in 2022. Despite the valuable artwork and expensive furniture, according to Pladdys, Mel often slept alone in the large house and always refused to lock the door. She was also not entirely precious about her collection. Some of the fine furniture had to be retouched because she had a habit of chaining her dogs to it.[8]

During the 1950s, Mel spent time with Rolt in County Mayo, Ireland, where she bought a house named 'Seaview' on the southern shore of Clew

Bay near Old Head Beach, overlooked by Croagh Patrick Mountain. The location no doubt inspired Rolt's work.

In 1953, Mel purchased the three works of another Irish artist, Evie Hone (1894-1955), who often worked in stained glass, from a contemporary gallery in Dublin that was exhibiting her work. A devout Catholic, much of Hone's art was centred on religious themes, and the paintings Mel bought feature Saint Cecilia and a stained-glass window triptych. The third is of an island. Mel and David's presence together was even listed publicly in an article in the *Dublin Evening Mail*, under the title a 'Notable Gathering' where it described 'people of distinction in many walks of life were among those who went to the opening of Miss Hone's exhibition. Among them I noticed ... Mrs Russell-Cooke, Mr David Rolt.'[9] In November 1954 Mel added to the three works by Hone with the purchase of a fourth entitled 'Archangel with Lute' signed and dated 'Evie S Hone/1954' and purchased from the Dawson Gallery in Dublin.[10]

Mel maintained at least one residence in London, in Somers Place (Crescent), Paddington, and was still travelling. There is a 1953 record of her departing for New York on 20 November aboard the *Britannic*, with her residence listed as 7 Astell House, Astell Street, London. The *Britannic* was a White Star ship launched in 1929 (not to be confused with the *Titanic*'s sister ship lost in 1916). By the time Mel was aboard her, she was now a Cunard ship, the rival companies having merged in 1934. The sailing was delayed by 24 hours when a small leak was discovered that required repair.[11] The 27,666-ton liner with 480 passengers aboard had to be moved into West Gladstone Dock to allow divers to mend an underwater valve.[12] Did anyone know that Captain Smith's daughter was aboard?

The transatlantic journey may have been more than just a holiday. In 1953, something else happened of note. A film based on the *Titanic* tragedy was released in that year, beginning a resurgence of interest in the disaster.

Smith on Screen

Some years earlier, in July 1925, a seven-year-old boy made a trip from New York to Southampton with his mother and sister aboard the White Star ship the RMS *Olympic*, the older sister ship to the *Titanic*. The young boy, named Walter Lord, was entranced by the decks that 'seemed to go on for miles; the public rooms seemed like a palace, the four funnels seemed big beyond belief.'[13] The young Lord had further connections to the ship. His grandfather would never travel with any captain other than Smith, insisting on sailing aboard the *Baltic* or later the *Adriatic*, because Smith was Master.[14] Imagining that a ship of such grandeur could sink within a few hours inspired him to start reading, drawing, and collecting everything he could find about the *Titanic*. This was during a time when the human tragedy of international conflict and economic depression had muted any interest in the pre-war maritime disaster. That was about to change.

In 1953, the Hollywood studio Twentieth Century-Fox released the film *Titanic*, a big budget vehicle for popular character actor Clifton Webb, who was then under contract to the studio. The quite substantial role of Captain Smith was played by Brian Aherne, an Academy Award-nominated British actor who was working in the States. He was aged 50 at the time and, despite the requisite beard, bore little resemblance to the Captain.

As the first big budget Hollywood treatment of the story, it was not surprising that its release registered among family members, including distant relatives of Captain Smith. Under the headline of 'Relatives of Titanic Commander Visit Film' a news item reported that a showing of the 1953 epic at the Odeon cinema Hanley, Stoke-on-Trent, was attended by Sarah Harris, 'the only living first cousin of Commander Smith, who is in her 94th year' and was the guest of honour (Figure 118). It was clearly an event for the town, as the Mayor and Mayoress also attended, along

Relatives of Commander W. T. Smith, R.D., R.N.R., visited the film "Titanic" at the Odeon, Hanley, on Tuesday. Left to right in this picture are Mr. M. Yardley, Mrs. W. Smith, the Lady Mayoress (Mrs. Bennett), Mr. William Smith, Midshipman W. Russell-Smith, the Lord Mayor (Alderman A. E. Bennett), and Mrs. Sarah Harris, of Hanley (the only living first cousin of Commander Smith, who is in her 94th year).

Figure 118: The Friday, 28 August 1953 edition *The Staffordshire Weekly Sentinel* that incorrectly refers to commander 'W.T. Smith'. (Courtesy of Norma Williamson, great granddaughter of Mrs Sarah Harris)

Figure 119: Group photograph taken by the *Staffordshire Sentinel* and given to the Harris family at the Hanley film showing of the *Titanic* film in August 1953. In the middle of the group is the 94-year-old cousin of Captain Smith, Sarah Harris. Back row: M. Yardley, Olive Stubbs (née Harris), her husband (with koala tie) William Stubbs, Frederick Harris, William Smith, Mary Jane Heaton Harris. Second row: Emily Kaill. (née Harris). Front row: Lord Mayor (Alderman A. E. Bennett) Sarah (née Smith) Harris, Midshipman 'W. Russell-Smith', Lady Mayoress Mrs Bennett. (Photograph and identifications courtesy of Norma Williamson)

with 18-year-old midshipman 'W.R. Russell-Smith,' suitably attired in Royal Navy uniform.[15]

In another photograph at the same event, they are all seated around the 94-year-old cousin of Captain Smith, flanked by midshipman 'Russell-Smith' and the Mayor and Mayoress, and the rest of the Harris family including Sarah Harris' children Olive, Mary Florence and Frederick (Figure 119). Sarah Harris was the Captain's cousin through her father George, who was brother to E.J.'s father Edward.[16]

The Mystery of the Missing Midshipman

The inclusion of midshipman 'Russell-Smith' at the 1953 cinematic event in Hanley was curious, as his genealogical connection to the legendary captain was not established. Copy in the accompanying *Staffordshire*

Leafield Life

Sentinel would only clarify that rather than 'Russell-Smith' his actual name was 'W.R. Smith' and that he was in the Royal Fleet Auxiliary, formerly of the HMS *Conway* Training Ship, and he attended with his parents Mr and Mrs William Smith of Cobridge, Staffordshire. No doubt his Navy uniform was an attraction, explaining why in two photographs he was positioned next to Captain Smith's closest living relative, first cousin Sarah Harris.

It transpires that 'W.R. Smith' was William Russell Smith, born in 1936 to William Henry Smith, son of George Thomas Smith, so clearly no discernible relation to E.J. Smith, except in name only.[17] If they were related it was very distantly. As explained by the uniform, he was an HMS *Conway* cadet from 1951 to 1953 (Figure 120) and by 1956 was Third Officer aboard the Admiralty tanker the RFA *Wave Commander* (8,141 tons). It was at this point the mystery of the midshipman suddenly deepened.

On 10 April 1956, while the *Wave Commander* was sailing through the English Channel bound for Bahrein, Egypt, 19-year-old William Russell Smith disappeared sometime after 7 pm and despite an all-night search was never seen again. He had been reported missing at 7:50 pm when he failed to appear for his watch, while the vessel was 12 miles off Beachy Head near Eastbourne, south of the Royal Sovereign lightship that was stationed in the middle of the Channel.[18] At the time of his

Figure 120: Midshipman William Russell Smith, photographed at the time of the 1953 screening of *Titanic* in Stoke-on-Trent, looking at the memorial tablet to Captain Smith. On 10 April 1956 he would disappear from a vessel on the English Channel and never be seen again. (From *The Man Who Sank the Titanic* by Gary Cooper)

disappearance the sea was calm, and after a thorough search conducted by the Eastbourne lifeboat, the Fisheries protection vessel *Squirrel*, and an RAF rescue launch, the search was called off at dawn.[19] His body was never recovered and two Admiralty inquiries concluded he was lost overboard. News articles reported that the missing man was the eldest son of Mr and Mrs Smith of Bedford House, Bromley-street Cobridge, in Stoke-on-Trent, but did not reference any connection to the legendary captain, even though in an interesting coincidence the Third Officer had gone missing 44 years almost to the day that Captain Smith was lost at sea. The Admiralty gave the family a death certificate stating he was presumed drowned. However, they also added it was feasible he had been picked up by a passing ship.

Things took a sinister turn when nine days later Commander 'Buster' Crabb, a Royal Navy frogman and diver, vanished while spying for MI6 on a Soviet cruiser docked in Portsmouth Harbour. Unlike William Russell Smith's disappearance, Crabb's failed covert operation on 19 April 1956 made front page news due to the diplomatic crisis it caused. The British press, suspicious of the official cover story, speculated that the Russians had captured Crabb. William Smith took note of this theory, especially after it was published in a 1960 book, and went to the press claiming the disappearance of his son was connected.[20] 54-year-old 'Bill' Smith was quoted in the *Daily Herald* of June 1960 as believing that his missing son was now on the same Russian ship that Commander Crabb was allegedly aboard, after seeing a photograph in a newspaper article covering the publication of a book claiming Crabb was captured by the Russians. The photograph had been discovered by his younger son Donald, who had immediately recognised his older brother among a group of Russian sailors. So certain was Bill Smith that he wrote to the Soviet Embassy in London asking to be immediately put in touch with his son.[21] Just as the Crabb case remains a mystery, so does the disappearance of Third Officer Smith. Donald Smith believed the loss of his brother caused the death of his mother and that a secret contact in MI6 was assigned to watching his own movements.

38 years later, in 1994, Donald was himself in the press, under the bold headline 'Did lost sailor son defect to the Russians?' Based on a book published in 1968, it was claimed that Soviet informants had admitted that the Third Officer was now a second lieutenant in the Russian Navy and had adopted the name 'Rodion Vladimirovich Smirnov'.[22] There was a notable difference: this article mentioned Captain Smith was from the 'same family'. A caption under a photograph of William Russell Smith states that the young man is standing next to his 'great uncle' Captain Smith's memorial tablet.[23] Although never mentioned in the 1950 press coverage,

the midshipman was now a 'great nephew'. Unsurprisingly, during the 1990s, Donald Smith would subsequently appear at *Titanic* events and in the media as Captain Smith's 'great-nephew' (see Chapter 13).

An 'Infuriating' Film

When Mel watched the 1953 film, would she be frustrated by the portrayal of her father as a contrasting mix of aloof overconfidence followed by decisive action during the evacuation? While her assessment was far from complimentary, it was a finer point that drew her particular ire, that in the 'infuriating film' he was shown smoking a pipe rather than a cigar (Figure 121). Mel was not the only one who questioned Aherne's portrayal. Third class survivor Eugene Daly thought the resemblance between Captain Smith and Brian Aherne 'was not sufficiently striking. Capt. Smith was a tall, white-haired man'.[24]

The young boy named Walter Lord, who had taken a keen interest in *Titanic* after his trip aboard the *Olympic*, was now a writer with one book published, and he now turned his attention to a retelling of the *Titanic* story. Between 1954 and 1955, he began contacting more than 60 survivors. One of these was a 'Mrs Cooke' – the daughter of Captain Smith. Their correspondence is now part of the Lord-MacQuitty Collection at the National Maritime Museum in Greenwich, London.

Mel was informed that Lord had written to the *Manchester Guardian* requesting survivors from the *Titanic* or *Carpathia* to help with his book. She took the initiative and wrote directly to Lord, to his New York address, on 4 June 1955 (Figure 121). It provides a unique insight into her feelings about the cinematic portrayal of her father:

7/105 Onslow Square – London S.W.7,
Knightsbridge 4834
4th June 1955

Dear Mr. Lord
Some time recently, I am told, you wrote to the Manchester Guardian to ask for any survivors of Titanic or Carpathia.
 I am not a survivor in the strict sense but I am the daughter of Captain E.J. Smith. I am of course most interested in the fact that you are writing about the disaster.
 I did in fact this spring read through all the old Times (London) of that year in the London Library and quite a few interesting things turned up. I should be only too glad to help you with any facts – though

what I know is mostly about my father personally of which my mother told me both at the time (when it made not much impression as I was quite a small child) and subsequently when I found it quite fantastic – it's the things that weren't done which seem so unbelievable – specially after having re-read those files.

Do write to me when you have time and tell me what approach you are taking in your book – I don't know if it's a legal aspect or maritime or what. There was an infuriating film about 2 years ago – when my father was shown coming in to the 1st class saloon in his over coat and smoking a PIPE – I almost exploded and I should think, though it sounds flippant I don't mean it that way, he turned in his grave. Cigars were his pleasure – and one was only allowed to be in the room if one was absolutely still, so that the blue cloud over his head never moved!

Yours very sincerely
(Mrs.) Melville Russell Cooke[25]

Walter Lord replied almost immediately, with a carefully typed letter on 26 June 1955, a copy of which he retained for reference, also in the Lord-MacQuitty Collection. He described Mel's letter as 'wonderful ... you can't imagine how pleased I am to hear from Captain Smith's daughter – the only other trace of you I've ever seen is a charming picture of you sitting on your Mother's knees.' He then described his editorial approach and how much he enjoyed the 'delightful little sketch of your Father and his cigars', and that any more 'little vignettes' of that nature would be most welcome. He notes from his research he has established that Smith was 'so gallant and brave, and so worshipped by the men who sailed

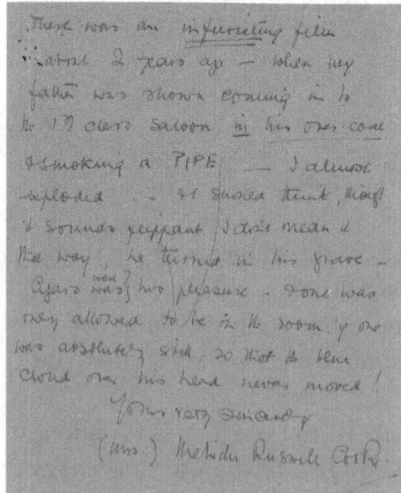

Figure 121: The last page from a letter to author Walter Lord from Mrs Russell Cooke in which she offers assistance with his research and describes the 1953 *Titanic* film portrayal of her father as 'infuriating'. (© National Maritime Museum, Greenwich, London / Lord-MacQuitty Collection)

under him... I know what a strong personality he had... That spirit and loyalty could be imbedded so deep in the crew of a ship so long since gone is perhaps the finest tribute of all to their Captain.'[26]

If there was further correspondence, it is not recorded. It is likely that Mel did not feel there was a huge amount she could offer, especially if he was taking a 'maritime' angle. She was only 14 when her father died, and he was mostly away at sea, and as later acknowledged, she would always regret that she was never really close to him.[27]

The book, published in November 1955, was *A Night to Remember* and the most notable reference to what author Walter Lord gained from his contact with Mel was the quote about her father, that 'cigars were his pleasure.' In the book's acknowledgements, Lord specifically addresses her input: 'Especially, I want to thank Captain Smith's daughter, Mrs M.R. Cooke, for the charming recollection of her gallant father.'[28]

Released just before Christmas 1955, Lord's book was an instant success, selling 60,000 copies within two months of publication and remaining on the best-seller list for six months, with a paperback edition released in 1956. It formed the basis for the British cinema version that entered production in 1957. 50-year-old Laurence Naismith was an obvious choice for the role of Captain Smith. He was a merchant marine seaman before becoming an actor and served nine years in the Royal Artillery, with the final rank of Acting Battery Commander.

Naismith's portrayal of Captain Smith would become one of his most memorable roles, unique in that it also received the approval of the Captain's daughter herself. While MacQuitty's production diary mentions the visits of survivors and their families to the sets once shooting commenced in October 1957, it sadly neglects to detail Mel's visit, but it was quite likely either in late December 1957 or early January 1958, during the night filming in Pinewood Studios. According to a 13 December 1957 article in the *Middlesex Independent* under the headline 'She once stood on the bridge of Titanic,' Mel told the reporter that she had been invited to visit the set to watch Naismith at work. She was described as a '57-year-old London woman' living in Onslow Square, Knightsbridge:

> She was invited to Pinewood Studios to talk about her father with producer William MacQuitty and director Roy Baker for their new film 'A Night to Remember'... thanks to Mrs. Russell Cooke's help, producer MacQuitty has been able to ensure absolute accuracy in the characterisation of Captain Smith in his film. The part will be played by actor Laurence Naismith, and Mrs. Russell Cooke has already been invited to watch him at work. 'I am looking forward to that,' she

says. 'In fact I am looking forward to the whole film. It is about time someone told the true story of the Titanic.'[29]

Mel was actually aged 59, not 57, at the time. Captain Smith signed on aboard *Titanic* as 59 when he was 62, a case of 'like father, like daughter'. When she visited the set, author Jeffrey Richards said she 'was overcome with emotion' on meeting Laurence Naismith, the actor who was playing her father and who was said to 'resemble him closely'.[30] William MacQuitty wrote that Mel was 'shocked by the remarkable likeness'.[31]

There is a single photograph of Mel meeting Naismith, caught in mid conversation, appropriately standing on the ship's bridge set in Pinewood Studios, with an engine telegraph just in front of them. Mel is listening as she gestures slightly toward the telegraph, with a cigarette almost falling from between her fingers. Naismith is also motioning with his hand toward the telegraph, as if he is explaining how it works – or that it is simply a prop. An interesting detail spotted by author Dr Paul Lee is that if you look closely, the telegraph has a 'Close watertight doors' indicator – a fictional addition.[32]

In anticipation of the release of the film, there is one only known reference to Mel attending a *Titanic* reunion of sorts, on the night of 14 April 1958 in a London hotel, marking the 46th anniversary of the sinking. The press would print photographs of four survivors sitting

Figure 122: Mel visits the bridge set of the film *A Night to Remember* and meets the actor playing her father, Laurence Naismith. (From the collection of Edward Kamuda, courtesy of Karen Kamuda and the Titanic Historical Society)

at a dinner table holding a large *Titanic* deck diagram: Lawrence Beesley (second class passenger), Marjorie (Collyer) Dutton (second class passenger), Gus Cohen (third class passenger) and Violet Jessop (stewardess). In doing so, the press (such as *The Illustrated London News* of 26 April 1958) inadvertently cropped out a fifth attendee at the event, the person sitting on the far left, holding the other end of the long deck plan: the Captain's daughter, in a dark dress and wearing a large pearl necklace, her eyes avoiding the press and fixed in conversation with the survivors (Figures 123 and 124). One wonders at the conversation at the dinner table. Did Beesely tell Mel about his 1912 efforts to rebalance the narrative on her father's culpability? Did Dutton talk about her mother Charlotte Collyer's story of how Smith possibly died? All that we presently know is that that the event was in response to the filming of *A Night to Remember* and in an effort to widen the scope of the Titanic Relief Fund, which in 1958 stood at £100,000.[33]

The film premiered on Thursday 3 July 1958, at the Odeon Cinema in Leicester Square, with newsreels stating that ten survivors were in attendance, plus the Second Officer's widow Sylvia Lightoller, who was filmed receiving a kiss from the film's star Kenneth More, who played her

Figure 123: Mel, far left, sitting at a table with *Titanic* survivors on 14 April 1958, on the 46th anniversary of the sinking. The survivors, from left: Lawrence Beesley (second class passenger), Marjorie (Collyer) Dutton (second class passenger), Gus Cohen (third class passenger) and Violet Jessop (stewardess). (Photograph courtesy of Stephen Raffield)

Figure 124: For many years there was no information about this image of Mel. The recent discovery of an uncropped photograph dated 14 April 1958 revealed she was attending a London event with *Titanic* survivors, which explains the deck plan behind her. (Shutterstock)

husband. There is no mention of Mel, or an indication as to her response to the production – or that she even saw the film. Compared to Aherne's 'infuriating' take on her father, she likely found Naismith's portrayal measured and dignified.

Village Life

Sometime during the late 1950s or early 1960s, Melville settled permanently into her new home in Leafield. Spending more time in the quieter realm of the countryside was likely in part motivated by another tragedy that took place on Mel's doorstep in 1959. On 13 July, the police were arresting a German-born petty thief, Guenther Podola, at South Kensington Tube station, when the criminal escaped their grasp and sought refuge behind a pillar in the hall of nearby 105 Onslow Square. Once the police found him, he pulled out a semi-automatic pistol and shot 43-year-old Detective Sergeant Raymond Purdy through the heart, fatally wounding him. Podola was later apprehended, tried, found guilty and hanged – the last man to be hanged for killing a police officer in the UK. In 2019, a memorial plaque was installed in the portico at 105 Onslow Square, a constant reminder of the murder of a policeman in the line of duty.[34] For Mel, it was probably another tragedy too close to home, making the peaceful village of Leafield an even more attractive prospect.

Local villager Mary Lougheed described Mel as 'very secretive and very smart. She was tall, with a military bearing and always dressed in black, with a peak hard hat.' The costume Mary described is not far removed from the photograph of Mel poised on the door of a vehicle in her riding habit at the Pytchley Meet (Figure 84).

Mel was known for her cars; one resident, whose father owned the local Wychwood Garage that serviced her vehicle, remembered Mrs Russell Cooke as a 'lovely, elegant lady' who drove a smart 'powder blue' Peugeot 404 (although it could also have been a Mercedes) that had the registration plate 'MEL 108'. Equally, there is a recollection that there was 'sadness in her life'.[35] John Pladdys also discovered during his research in the 1990s that she loved fast cars, having a sports car herself and was heard 'boasting about the time it had taken her to drive the 70-odd miles from her London flat'. Local people still remembered 'The Titanic captain's daughter' as she was often referred to. John Pladdys interviewed several villagers and neighbours during the early 1990s and discovered that as an active member of the community, she did not hide from her maritime connection:

> Throughout her time at Leafield she took a leading part in all village activities. She made no secret of her family and its tragic past played by her father in the *Titanic* disaster. One or two villagers had some very forthright views, particularly a retired admiral who always steadfastly maintained that Captain Smith had been to blame.[36]

She also became well known for her generosity and hospitality. She once gave a personalised pocketknife owned by her father to a local friend that later ended up sold at auction in April 2023. The steel-bladed 8.2cm long gold pocketknife is engraved with the initials 'EJS' on one side and '1906' on the other, dating it to the year when Captain Smith sent a letter from the *Baltic* to his eight-year-old daughter. It was also the last year in Liverpool before the family moved to Southampton. Nevertheless, Mel disregarded the sentiment and gave it to her village friend, Alice Dore.[37]

Or take, for example, the case of two students in the early 1970s studying at Oxford University who were renting a cottage on the other side of a field from Mel. They described her as

> ... terribly kind to us and used to have us over on Sundays for some of her wonderful sherry and a simple lunch... Despite the inhuman

number of tragedies she had borne, she was full of joy and charm and a kind of class that one does not find anymore; the sort of person who could mix real (and substantial) jewels with fantasy ones, and carry it off, as she did for her 74th birthday which we attended. One of those persons who leave the world a poorer place.[38]

The Matchmaker

Melville's relationship with the artist David Rolt changed in 1960 when he married Penelope Minnie Bradford, who was more than 20 years his junior. In 1959, the actress Valerie Hobson (married to the soon-to-be-disgraced politician John Profumo) introduced Rolt to 19-year-old Minnie and, on Thursday 21 April 1960 they were married at Westminster Abbey. *The Daily Mirror* ran an article on the couple, with the headline 'Penelope, 19, weds artist, 46' accompanied by photographs of the young bride bursting with joy.[39]

The marriage ended in divorce after ten years and two children. Minnie remarried twice while Rolt never married again, and his friendship with Mel continued. He lived just 20 miles away from Leafield village in Freseden, a hamlet north of Swindon.[40] In another curious *Titanic* connection, Minne remarried to Honourable John Astor V, a member of the prominent Astor family that included John Jacob Astor IV, who was lost in the sinking.[41] Rolt died in 1985, aged 70, while undergoing surgery to correct the damage sustained at birth that had been causing him much pain.

It was shortly after Rolt's marriage to a teenager that Mel met a young woman from Spain, a Marietta Gordillo Martin, possibly from the same Gordillo family that has been described as a 'well-known family of artists and art dealers in Spain'.[42] In 1962, Marietta travelled from Spain to England and met Mel at a house party in Lancashire and 'the pair soon formed a close bond and deep friendship with Mel taking the young Marietta under her wing.'[43] Mel became something of a 'second mother' to Marietta. In 1963, Mel and Marietta were staying with Lord and Lady Burnham at Hall Barn, an historic country house in Beaconsfield, Buckinghamshire, when Marietta was introduced to William Anthony Coleridge. Better known to many as Tony, he was a passionate art and ceramics collector but with a particular focus on English furniture.[44] In 1962, Tony had just joined Christie's. As both Mel and Tony were art collectors, it is reasonable to infer that conversation was free and easy between the two during their time at Hall Barn. But Tony's eye was on the woman who had just arrived from Spain, Marietta, and who shared his enthusiasm for art. They were married on 26 June 1967, embarking on a shared journey of collecting, forming what would later be known as the 'Marietta and Anthony Coleridge Collection'.

A year after their marriage, Tony published a book that would be a great influence in the field of furniture collectors entitled *Chippendale Furniture: The Work of Thomas Chippendale and his Contemporaries in the Rococo Style*. The publication of this seminal book cemented his reputation as a leading furniture historian. He was appointed a director of Christie's in 1966 and by 1970 he had risen to become head of the furniture department.[45]

When Mel was looking to raise some finance, it is not surprising that she turned to Christie's and sold some of her jewellery in a London auction in October 1967 and then later some of her art collection in further Christie's auctions in June and July 1968.[46]

No doubt fuelled by their mutual interest in art, Mel remained an integral part of the newlyweds' life, but in a way that would be wholly unexpected.

13

The 'Remarkable Lady'

In one of her last known pieces of correspondence about her *Titanic* connection, Mel wrote a very short note to Edward Kamuda (1939-2014) of Indian Orchard, Massachusetts. Kamuda was a *Titanic* enthusiast inspired by the 1953 *Titanic* film and using a survivor's contact list that accompanied the 1958 release of *A Night to Remember*, had begun collecting accounts and memorabilia. Of the 87 survivors listed, 75 responded.[1] In 1963, he co-founded the 'Titanic Enthusiasts of America', which was later renamed the 'Titanic Historical Society', an organisation that is still in existence today.[2]

In 1971, Edward Kamuda wrote to Mel with an inquiry as to Captain Smith's family, asking whether her father had any brother or sisters – perhaps wanting to confirm stories from those who claimed to be a descendant. Her curt response, dated 22 June 1971, was 'Edward John

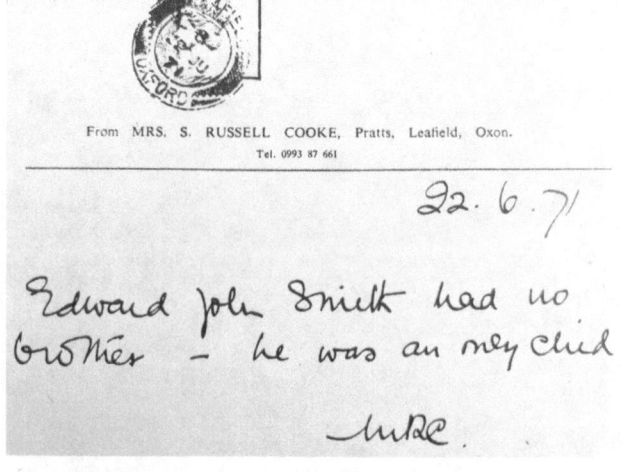

Figure 125: A short note Mel wrote to Edward Kamuda of the Titanic Historical Society in the United States, explaining that her father was an 'only child'. (Courtesy of the Edward Kamuda collection and Karen Kamuda of the Titanic Historical Society)

The 'Remarkable Lady'

Smith had no brother – he was an only child.' The postcard had a Pratts House letterhead, and was signed with her initials M.R.C. It was not entirely helpful, as her father did have an older half-brother, from whom the Hancock family in the US descended. Maybe Kamuda had specifically referred to those with the name Smith and who had claimed they were bloodline descendants – in which case Mel pointedly explained it was not possible.

Brookwood Burial

On Saturday, 18 August 1973, Melville Russell Cooke suddenly died. She was 75 years old. 'A neighbour called at the house and found her collapsed on the bed, having been preparing for a bath. She was rushed to the Radcliffe Infirmary in Oxford but was found to be dead on arrival.'[3]

Mel's passing caused some commotion in the village. Mary Lougheed remembers that in the evening the nearby Witney police visited and fetched resident Peter MacGregor from the middle of a council meeting, which caused considerable consternation on his part. MacGregor and housekeeper Mary Moss were then interviewed by the police about the circumstances of her death.

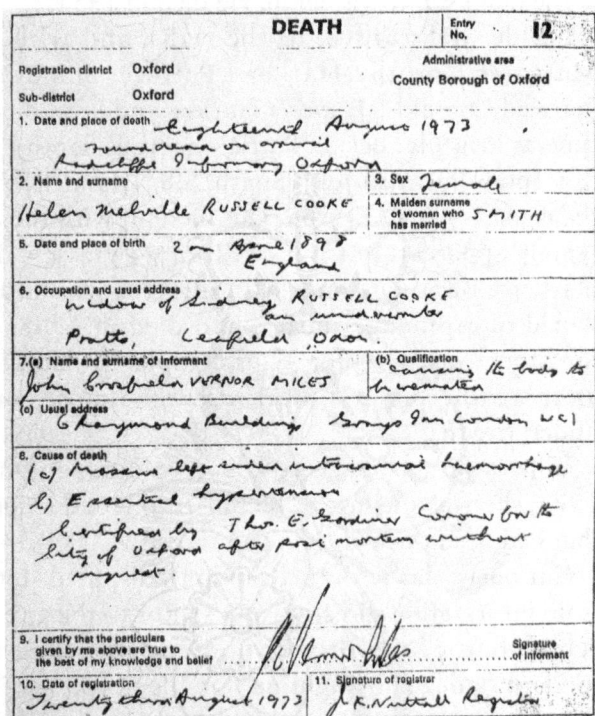

Figure 126: A copy of Helen Melville Russell Cooke's death certificate. (Author's collection)

The cause of death was a 'massive left-sided intracranial haemorrhage and essential hypertension', the certificate registered on 23 August 1973 (Figure 126). Hypertension is more commonly known as high blood pressure and can be caused by smoking. The bad heart that had warranted a redesign of the staircase was her ultimate undoing.

The London *Times* death notice was printed on 21 August 1973: 'RUSSELL COOKE, HELEN MELVILLE, widow of Sidney, suddenly on 18th August, at Leafield, Oxfordshire. Cremation at Headington Crematorium, Oxford, Thursday 23rd August, 11am.'[4]

Her ashes were later buried in her husband's grave at Brookwood, in the Russell Cooke family plot number 32. Strangely, the headstone simply states, 'And Melville his wife,' and does not include any dates of either her birth or death (Figure 127).

The plot, now overgrown, is still dominated by a large cross indicating William Russell Cooke's grave (Sidney's father) with the inscription 'of Bellecroft, Isle of Wight'. It seems fitting that the family patriarch would have such a prominent position and is joined by his suffragette wife Margaret. The remaining graves are a veritable directory of Mel's life. Buried in the same grave as her is Sidney's cousin Oliver Paget-Cooke, who had been a colleague of Sidney's at Rowe & Pitman and had testified at the inquest into his death. He died in 1954.

Beside Mel's grave, to the right, and with a grave to herself, is Margaret Dorothy Harker ('Pattie'), Sidney's younger sister who married Oswald ('Jasper') Harker and who died in 1947 at the same time as Priscilla. Beside Pattie's grave is Sarah Eleanor Smith: 'Widow of Captain Edward John Smith, S.S. Titanic'. To the casual observer at the cemetery, it seems the odd one out, with the connection to Mel not readily apparent. In front of Eleanor's grave is that of Oswald 'Jasper' Harker CBE, the former MI5 director who introduced Sidney to the world of espionage. Jasper had died in 1968, and his grave, unlike the other graves in plot 32, is completely flat, the words barely legible after weathering and until recently almost completely obscured by undergrowth.

When Mel's ashes were added to the family plot in the summer of 1973, she was the last to be buried there, the denouement for a family that had been through so much tragedy.

Curiously – as with the Captain's disputed statue in Lichfield – there is no information directing any visitor to the graves. Despite a complete rebranding of the Brookwood cemetery and the addition of large modern signage highlighting notable people buried in each section, the panel covering plot 32 makes no reference to the Russell Cooke family

The 'Remarkable Lady'

or the Captain's widow. It does mention one notable person, buried in neighbouring plot 35, also referred to as 'The Ring', that is characterised mostly by the burials of the wealthy: John Sargent – the artist who painted Sidney's suffragette mother Margaret in 1895 (Figure 71).

Figure 127: Sidney and Mel's grave. There are no dates for Mel's birth and death. It simply reads: 'And Melville his wife'. (Photograph: Dan Parkes)

Figure 128: The Russell Cooke plot as it looks today. The two large crosses on the left are for William and Margaret Russell Cooke, and Sir Henry Paget-Cooke (the shorter cross). The three similar looking graves toward the back are those of Sidney and Mel Russell Cooke and Oliver Paget-Cooke; Margaret Harker (Sidney's sister); and Eleanor Smith (Captain Smith's widow). The flat grave in the foreground is Oswald Harker's, the MI5 director. (Photograph: Dan Parkes)

Surprise Inheritance

Mel's probate record was released the month following her death: 'Cooke, Helen Melville Russell otherwise Helen Melville of Pratts Leafield Oxfordshire died 18 August 1973 probate London 21 September £101216.'

What is absent is the identity of the individual who inherited her property, and especially her art collection. To their great surprise, it was Anthony and Marietta Coleridge. Marietta had indeed become something of a daughter to Mel, to the extent Mel had changed her will. The Christie's auction notes in 2022 made mention of the Coleridge's astonishment:

> Mel remained an integral part of the newlyweds' life, however, following Mel's sudden death in 1973, they were astonished to find that she had left them her house, Pratt's, at Leafield near Burford and the notable collection within.[5]

In Anthony Coleridge's memoirs, he wrote about the sudden acquisition of that substantial art collection: 'Its contents form a major portion of our collection. [Mel] had great taste and we shall forever be in her debt. She was a remarkable lady and a great beauty.'[6]

The Coleridges clearly held Mel in high esteem, as they retained both the house and her art collection for many years. Anthony was Christie's principal auctioneer in their House Sales team for over 20 years, becoming the Director, Chairman and later President of Christie's South Kensington. Marietta opened her own antique shop 'Presantiques' in November 1979, located at 11a William Street in London. A review in the London *Times* described it as a very unique gallery, with almost all items small or portable and most importantly, of Marietta's personal choice. For ethical reasons, the review pointed out, Anthony was not involved, although his experience had unavoidably influenced her; in fact, it was he who made her want to study antiques in the first place.[7]

In the early 1990s, John Pladdys visited Pratts House in Leafield while researching an article he was writing for the Titanic Historical Society's *Commutator* journal. The Coleridges kindly allowed him access to the property, and he discovered Rolt's artwork on the walls and the letter Captain Smith wrote to his daughter. The Coleridges later sent Pladdys low-quality photocopies of the early family photographs of Mel, including one in which Sidney had been deliberately cut from the image (the full image can be seen in Figure 82). Did this indicate a reluctance on Mel's part to include any reference to her husband, with the assumption that some may have thought his death was a suicide?

The 'Remarkable Lady'

To commemorate the twentieth anniversary of Mel's death, on the evening of 18 August 1993 the bells in the tower of St Michael & All Angels Church, Leafield, rang a full peal of 5040 changes in 2 hours and 47 minutes. The event was arranged by John Pladdys, who is also an experienced bell ringer, and he performed the peal with the assistance of five others. On 30 January 1994, the team of ringers visited Leafield once more to attend a dedication of a commemorative black and gold board in the church, arranged by the ringers, friends from the village and the Titanic Historical Society (U.S.A.).[8] The board states: 'In memory of Helen Melville Russell-Cooke, the daughter of Commander Edward John Smith of R.M.S. Titanic, who died on August 18th, 1973, much respected during her 40 years in this village.'

The ceremony was attended by local villagers who had known Mel, the Coleridges, author Pat Lacey, and many were afterwards invited to Pratts House, just around the corner, for refreshments and a viewing of items belonging to Mel. It is presently unknown what happened to most of these items, although when the 'Marietta and Anthony Coleridge Collection' was put up for auction in July 2022, several notable pieces were from Mel's collection, including an oil painting by David Rolt.

Pratts House still exists today, the name on the gate, its extensive gardens with a variety of trees that are reminiscent of Mel and her tree-painting partner. As a listed building, little has changed since Mel and family lived there, the staircase specially built for her still providing

Figure 129: Pratts House as it looked in August 2023. (Photographs: Dan Parkes)

easy access to the rooms on the first floor, multiple bathrooms, and windows the length of the house supplying ample natural light to the low ceiling quarters. There are hints of the eccentric previous occupants: an intimidatingly ornate door knocker and a religious crest on the wall with the Latin phrase 'in principio erat verbum' – 'In the beginning was the word.' (John 1:1.)

The Night Lives On

Not long after Melville passed away and the Coleridges inherited Pratts House, *Titanic* author Walter Lord made contact and formed a friendship with the couple. He wrote to Anthony and Marietta on 1 October 1978 in his own hand from a London address, expressing gratitude for their 'hospitality, kindness, and help' when he was in London 'doing research on Dunkirk'. His *The Miracle of Dunkirk: The True Story of Operation Dynamo* would not be published until 1982, and in line with his previous works, it would become a *New York Times* best seller. Lord enclosed with his letter a 'photo of Mrs. E.J. Smith and her baby daughter (Mel didn't you call her?) copied for you from a magazine published at the time of the disaster' along with a 'copy of a letter from Mrs. Cooke to me at the time I was doing research on the Titanic. I thought you might enjoy the little vignette of her father smoking his cigar ... and her indignation that the 20th Century-Fox film had him coming into the First Class lounge wearing his overcoat and smoking a pipe!' Lord signed off the letter with hopes for a 'chance we can get together for some evening. It could be so much fun to see you both again.'[9]

Marietta wrote a convivial reply the following month, She told Walter he was 'absolutely SWEET to have taken so much trouble to have Mel's photograph reproduced' describing it as 'adorable and I am putting it in a little frame somewhere in the house. We also enjoyed Mel's letter to you and indeed, yours to us.' As for meeting again, she wrote that she did not want to 'bully you or to make you feel that you must see us when we suggest it so ... but please don't dare to leave London without getting in touch as we'd love seeing you... Perhaps you might enjoy a quiet weekend here where you could work in the room at the top which overlooks miles and miles of Wiltshire Downs (or is it something else?).'

Despite having contacted those who had inherited Mel's legacy of correspondence and artwork, it is noteworthy that Lord does not include any reference to the couple in the sequel to his bestselling book *A Night to Remember* that was published in 1986 entitled *The Night Lives On: Thoughts, Theories and Revelations about the Titanic*. Released in

The 'Remarkable Lady'

August 1986, within a year of the discovery of the wreck, its timing was clearly not coincidental, and the discovery may have expedited its writing. It certainly covers matters concerning Captain Smith in far greater detail than its predecessor, for example examining the Captain's career, his handling of ice 'warnings' and a discussion of possible negligence. Did he ever explore what the Coleridges had in their possession, or had he dismissed its relevance to the sequel's intent to examine the various myths that had developed in the aftermath of the sinking? Or had Lord formed a negative attitude toward the *Titanic*'s master that made the topic overly sensitive? He does describe Smith as having a casual approach to lifeboat drills (which is unfair) although in his scrutiny of the various inquiries and legal action to secure 'blame' he remains uncharacteristically muted as to his final opinion.[10] It seemed like a missed opportunity to explore further. *The Night Lives On* was the last book he ever published, having authored twelve historical works before his death in 2002.

Relative Connections

The discovery of the *Titanic* wreck in 1985 created a new wave of fascination for the legendary shipwreck, and along with it those claiming to be relatives, many with quite tenuous connections. As we have seen, in the early 1990s a Donald Smith from Stoke-on-Trent appeared in television documentaries, newspaper reports and at *Titanic* conventions claiming to be Captain Smith's 'great-nephew'. He had in his collection artifacts he said his great uncle had once owned, including a telescope, a cigar holder, a pair of epaulettes, two pocket watches and a sextant. Most of the items were inscribed with the Captain's name or initials. As to their provenance, Don explained to a BBC reporter in 2002 that the items were 'handed down to him as a teenager by his own grandfather who himself received them from the late Captain Smith's wife in 1912 shortly after the tragedy'.[11] He began signing autographs at conventions, then designing a stamp that read: 'Personally autographed by Donald Smith, Great Nephew to Captain E.J. Smith, Master of the *Titanic*.'

As Mel had explained to Edward Kamuda in 1971, Edward John Smith was an only child. His older half-brother, Joseph Hancock, was from Edward's mother's previous marriage. It was technically impossible for Don Smith to be Captain Smith's 'great-nephew'. There were rumours in *Titanic* circles and on internet forums of unpleasant encounters, of Don storming out of conventions when the Captain was criticised or when his family history was questioned, responding that he did not have to prove his lineage to anyone. By 2004, he had completely disappeared from the *Titanic* scene. The only statement came via a friend, Donald J. A. Smith (apparently not a relation of either the Captain or Don Smith), on 12 May 2004, in which he explained that with 'both innocence and intelligence – [Don] continued to believe what had been told him, with assurances and material proofs, from earliest childhood... Mr Smith remains intent upon never again – even privately – discussing his being or his not being the "great-nephew of Captain Smith of the Titanic". Not even if he is.'[12]

Nothing more about Don Smith and his claim to be the Captain's great-nephew was ever heard again. When Don died in 2017 and the details of his family tree were analysed, no connection could be found to any immediate or even distant relative of Captain Smith. The artifacts engraved with the Captain's name have since disappeared. If they were ever to appear at auction and have their provenance vindicated by specialists, they would prove to be of considerable monetary value. Recent research has discovered that Don was the younger brother of Midshipman William Russell Smith who appeared in uniform at the 1953 film screening beside the Captain's first cousin Sarah Harris and then disappeared, presumed drowned, in the English Channel in 1956. During that time, Don's older brother was simply described as a 'relative' and never touted as a 'great-nephew', a moniker Don seems to have first adopted in the 1990s.[13]

In 1996, a book was published entitled *Master of the Titanic* by Pat McLernon (née Lacey, 1922-2016) who had already established herself as a novelist before embarking on writing something a little closer to home: a dramatisation of the life of Captain Smith. At the beginning of her book, she is described as the 'great-great-niece of Captain E.J. Smith descended from his half-sister Thirza [sic]. She grew up in Abergavenny and took early retirement from the Civil Service to write ... the author of eight previous novels and countless articles and short stories.'[14]

The writing process began in 1991 with twelve months of research that involved visiting Well Street, Hanley, and Smith's old school in Etruria, as well as Liverpool and Southampton. In January 1992, McLernon used an article in a local Staffordshire newspaper to disclose that she had 'so far covered his life up to 1880 and the end of his period under sail' and requested help in tracing ancestors of two branches of the Captain's family – the Harringtons and Hancocks. She also said that the story would 'probably be published in two parts and will be in the form of a historical novel under her pen-name, which is Pat Lacey'.[15] By April 1992 she gave an update, stating that she had spent 18 months researching and writing and was about to launch into the last 32 years of his life. 'When I think about Captain Smith I feel proud. But I'm not looking forward to

The 'Remarkable Lady'

writing about the Titanic. In fact I'm almost dreading it because it's so terribly sad.'[16]

The book was finally completed and released in a single volume in 1996. The epilogue explains that she once owned a slim volume of verse that was inscribed with 'To Edward J. Smith from his mother, on his 10th birthday', which she was 'foolish enough to lend out' and was forever lost, much to her deep regret. She also admitted that her mother, Annie or 'Queenie,' never met 'Uncle Edward' nor 'Uncle Joseph' but recalls 'being told by her mother … that Edward was more like a friendly brother to her than an uncle, and that both he and Joseph were happy, laughing men.' With such tenuous connections and recollections, 74-year-old McLernon's book about her great-grand-uncle takes the form of a fictional re-imagining of his life – with an emphasis on the romance, including several sex scenes, perhaps not surprising for an author who had written romantic short stories for Harlequin. A disclaimer on the copyright page provides a necessary caveat that 'although based on fact, Captain Smith's biography has been enhanced with imaginary characters and incidents.' While intelligently written and an engaging read, it has no usefulness as biography.

In a 1998 *Birmingham Post* article, McLernon admitted that she did not know how Ted and Eleanor met: 'Eleanor's family are supposed to have bred horses. I got him going there to buy a horse to learn to ride in the book, but I don't know how they met. Captain Smith knew my grandmother and mother used to say he was a very jovial, gay in the

Figure 130: Pat McLernon (Lacey) at the Lichfield Statue. *Birmingham Evening Mail*, Friday, 17 July 1998. (Author's collection)

old-fashioned sense of the word, man.'[17] She did offer her opinion of the man himself:

> He was a conscientious, brave man. Perhaps he was too relaxed on Titanic but he certainly wouldn't have anticipated all the coincidences that happened... It was the custom of a captain when they got near ice on this route to go fast in order to get out of trouble as long as the visibility was good. When he turned in around about nine o'clock, the visibility was good and stayed good... He was a really nice man. He didn't try to save himself. His widow in a letter said it was quite true he swam to a lifeboat with a child and then returned to go down with his ship.

People magazine quoted her as a 'distant relative' and in reference to the Captain contemplating retirement after *Titanic*, McLernon said that given what happened, 'it's a jolly good job he went down with her instead.'[18]

When she visited Smith's Lichfield statue for the first time on 16 July 1998, the *Lichfield Mercury* printed a dramatic photograph of her standing 'in the shadow of Capt Smith' looking up at the memorial under the headline 'Facing up to an infamous forefather'.[19] The *Birmingham Daily Post* ran the same story with the less provocative headline, 'Face to face with a famous relative' and noted that the 'great-great-niece' had not visited the statue before, or seen the James Cameron film, feeling it might be a 'harrowing experience... I actually hated killing [Smith] off and drowning him at the end of my book. I don't think I could watch it.'[20]

When Don Smith disappeared in the early 2000s, McLernon became something of a spokesperson for the Captain, appearing on the ITV *Daybreak* talk show in London on 13 April 2012 in the lead-up to the hundredth anniversary of the sinking. She sat alongside Irish actress Ruth Bradley, who was starring in the Julian Fellowes' 2012 *Titanic* miniseries as Mary Maloney, a fictional third class passenger.

The following year, when Clive Palmer's Titanic II concept hit the news, ITV once again fielded a response from McLernon. In the short interview, the 91-year-old said she thought the Titanic II idea was in 'poor taste' but conceded that interest in the disaster 'just doesn't sink'.[21] Palmer's ambitious idea of a full-scale recreation of the legendary liner seems to have done just that.

Pat McLernon died on 10 May 2016 in Milton Keynes at the age of 94.[22] There is some irony that the last descendant with any direct link to Smith was a romantic fiction author who wrote a book about a Captain who once proclaimed he was 'not very good material for a story'.

EPILOGUE

The Legacy of Captain Smith

Polish-born maritime artist Marek Sarba created what is one of the most impressive oil paintings of *Titanic* ever created – with a catch. The 34ft x 48ft oil on canvas entitled 'And the Band Played On...', completed in the early 2000s, took years to paint and portrays in detail 57 passengers and crew assembled on the steps of *Titanic*'s grand staircase. Captain Smith is depicted at a notable distance from the group, standing alone on the right of frame, with what remains of the bridge helm telemotor as it looks on the wreck. This was an intentional decision by the artist, who says Smith is a man who did not do his job, by attempting to set a 'speed record'. 'Captain Smith, you do not deserve to stand between the people ... he is alone.'[1]

In fairness, Sarba's artistic interpretation and reaction to Captain Smith is certainly not unique. Since 1912, Captain Smith has been the subject of many cinematic, television and musical portrayals that varyingly depict him as a seadog hero, a scapegoat, or simply senile.[2]

The mood in Smith's hometown of Hanley has always been mixed. On 1 October 1985, exactly a month after the discovery of the wreck, local pub landlord John Pazio began brewing his own ale, with a label on the bottle featuring Captain Smith. The 'Titanic Brewery' which started as a seven-barrel microbrewery has now expanded to eight pubs and eight cafe bars with more than 200 staff, producing four million pints every year. The award-winning brewery itself does not shy away from its local connection. It funded the plaque that sits – albeit erroneously – at 51 Well Street in Hanley, identifying the street as the home of Captain Smith.[3]

Titanic Legacy: The Captain, the Daughter and the Spy

In 1987, Gary Cooper published his first biography on Smith with the evocative title of *The Man Who Sank the Titanic?* later updated and expanded in his 2011 book *Titanic Captain.* Despite such a balanced and detailed analysis, local appraisal remains mostly critical. During the 2012 centenary, the Potteries Museum & Art Gallery installed a 'Titanic Trail' exhibition in which a visitor survey revealed most still believe Captain Smith was to blame for the disaster. Even as recently as September 2023, when a large mural appeared in Hope Street, Hanley, it featured the curious phrase 'Fail we may, sail we must.' The word 'fail' lies conspicuously across the famous arms-crossed *Olympic* photograph of the Captain, a reflection of how many of the locals feel about the man from Hanley who became the internationally renowned 'Millionaires' Captain'.

The tragic nature of what happened to his family is sometimes attributed to a 'curse'. Such a sensational suggestion ignores who his daughter really was – a woman who had inherited her father's happy disposition, a passionate art collector, an enthusiastic sportswoman and aviator, an elegant lady with a reputation for generosity and hospitality. Where the real curse may lay is how Captain's Smith legacy has been remembered, in most cases unfairly and inaccurately, in parallel to rumours about and judgment pronounced on his son-in-law, Sidney.

To those in the small Oxfordshire village where 'Mrs Russell Cooke' spent her final days, she was also known by a title that she may well have felt uncomfortable bearing, for reasons that were arbitrary and loaded with judgment. It is a title that in retrospect, after closely examining Edward Smith's actions on the night of the disaster and the further tragedy his descendants endured, should not have been such a heavy burden to bear. In fact, it seems quite apparent she had every right to be proud to carry such a moniker, despite the associated insinuations with which it is encumbered.

Helen Melville was indeed, 'The *Titanic* Captain's Daughter'; a title sadly missing from the grave that marked the end of the *Titanic* family legacy.

Recommended Reading

Cooper, G. J., *The Man Who Sank the Titanic? The Life and Times of Captain Edward J. Smith* (Witan Books, 1992)

Cooper, G. J., *Titanic Captain: The Life of Edward John Smith* (The History Press, 2011)

Layton, J. Kent and Fitch, Tad and Wormstedt, Bill, *On a Sea of Glass: The Life & Loss of the RMS Titanic* (Amberley Publishing, 2012)

Behe, George, *On Board RMS Titanic: Memories of the Maiden Voyage* (The History Press, 2012)

Pladdys, John, 'The Captain's Daughter, Helen Melville Russell-Cooke,' *The Titanic Commutator* (Volume 17, Number 2, Titanic Historical Society, 1993)

Sheil, Inger, *Titanic Valour: The Life of Fifth Officer Harold Lowe* (The History Press, 2012)

Lord, Walter, *A Night to Remember* (R & W Holt, 1955)

Lord, Walter, *The Night Lives On: New Thoughts, Theories, and Revelations About the 'Titanic'* (William Morrow and Company, Inc., 1986)

Eaton, John P. and Haas, Charles A., *Titanic: Triumph and Tragedy* (W.W. Norton & Company, 1995)

The 1912 United States Senate Hearings into the sinking of the RMS Titanic and the British Wreck Commissioner's Inquiry on behalf of the Board of Trade: www.titanicinquiry.org

Biographies of the *Titanic* officers and associated articles: www.titanicofficers.com

Acknowledgements

This book is not intended to compete with Stoke-on-Trent historian Gary Cooper's excellent *Titanic Captain* biography, instead I hope it compliments it. It is a sequel of sorts. A highlight of the writing process has been corresponding with Gary every step of the way, sharing and commenting on the new research as it came along. He even assisted in the transcription of some documents when I realised his museum background made him far more proficient at deciphering illegible handwriting and barely readable newspaper copy. I am hugely indebted to him for his help, friendship and generosity, and especially for writing the foreword.

Another unexpected friendship came via an excellent article Cornwall researcher John Pladdys wrote for the Titanic Historical Society's *Commutator* magazine in 1993, 'The Captain's Daughter, Helen Melville Russell-Cooke'. Pladdys has been very generous with his help and permission to use his research and reprint his photographs. Karen Kamuda of the Titanic Historical Society also kindly assisted along with granting permission to reprint her late husband Ed's photographs that were used in the Pladdys article.

A person's life story can be a series of residences, of places that they once called home. The story of Captain Smith and his family is no exception. I feel privileged to have met and befriended many of those living in the homes that make up this story, in some cases unintentional custodians of history. You will have indirectly met many of them in the course of this book and it would be remiss of me not to express my sincere gratitude to them for allowing me access, in particular Tim Cook (Alexandra Road), Rose Gallagher (Marine Cres), Duncan and Sarita Bradley (Winn Road), Keith and Yvonne Prowse along with Valerie Dyer (Bellecroft), and Charmaine Cole (Pratts House). Also, John Staunton,

Acknowledgements

of 'Seaview' in Clew Bay, County Mayo, Ireland and Janice Cooper of Woodhead house and farm in Winwick.

Gary Cooper and I are most thankful to Dave Middlemore, from Stoke-on-Trent council who took us on a personal tour of Hanley Town Hall in 2023, which is presently not accessible to the public. The visit was facilitated by Stoke-on-Trent councillor Lorraine Beardmore, as well as council staff David Harris and Sam Holdcroft. I am grateful to David Glenwright, Head of Marketing at Titanic Brewery Co Ltd, for taking us on a tour of the brewery. Another important visit, to meet 94-year-old Mary Lougheed, who remembered Mel's time in Leafield village, was thanks to Deborah Triff and Middletown Grange care home.

It is also a story of letters. In this book, you will have discovered much about the lives of Captain Smith's family from the letters he wrote, as well as those of his wife, daughter, and son-in-law. This is primarily due to the unexpected generosity of Paul O'Pecko of G.W. Blunt White Library, at the Mystic Seaport Museum, for allowing me to reprint the private letters in their collection, especially that of Eleanor, his widow, for the first time in their entirety.

Comprehensive archives also played an important role in confirming dates, locations and people, and access to newspapers and documents. Jo Wren, Archives, Maritime and Local Studies Assistant for Southampton City Council, was particularly helpful in allowing access to the Brian Ticehurst collection, as well as to the collection of local newspapers, much of which has yet to be digitised. She was very patient re-training me on the ancient art of loading microfilm cartridges. Tom Davies at King's College, Cambridge, was especially helpful, as was Celia Pilkington at the Inner Temple archive, along with Francesca Tate at the Middle Temple archive, Lesa Davies, a research assistant for the Isle of Wight Heritage Service and Stefan Dreisbach-Williams, Seamen's Church Institute; and not forgetting the staff of the British Library. Suzanne Foster, the College Archivist at Winchester College, surprised me with some wonderful photographs and information about Simon Russell Cooke's time there.

Another delight has been the visual story told via some outstanding photographs. I am particularly indebted to Paul Van Doodson and Norma Williamson, both distant descendants of the Smith family, who kindly gave me permission to use photographs from their collections. As well as the invaluable photographs of Smith from the collections of Kevin Saucier (Titanic Items Collection) and Spencer Knarr; I feel privileged to be able to present these in this book. Access to the paintings of David Rolt and information on the artist is thanks to Robert Eagle, of Robert Eagle Fine Art (roberteaglefineart.co.uk) as well as David's son, Toby Rolt, whom it has been a pleasure to meet. He has kindly allowed me to include several of his father's paintings. There were many who also assisted in the identification of photographs, in particular Randy Bryan Bigham whose knowledge of fashion is extraordinary and helped with the dating of the Smith family photographs.

There are many more who have assisted in various ways, and to whom I am indebted. In no particular order: Mike Poirier, Charles Haas, Mike Beatty, George Behe, Dr Paul Lee, Phillip Hind, Mark Pendery, Marc Waddington, Donald J.A. Smith, Allen Guille, Chris Humby, Stephen Raffield, J. Kent Layton, Monika Simon, Heather Blackman, Richard Davenport-Hines, Christopher Walker, Tatiana Yamshanova, Karen Louise, Pat Holloway, 'WhispyBlink' (Findagrave), Gavin Krom, Petra Feyahn, Mi Elfverson, Peter 'Art' Lewry and Penelope Tull, Geoff Whitfield, Clive Sweetingham (British Titanic Society) and Danielle Tarento. If I have omitted someone I am truly sorry.

I take copyright very seriously and have spent several months contacting as many as possible to get permission for inclusion or quotation, with more than 200 such interactions. Some items are from sources who have been difficult to trace or possibly ceased to exist. If I have inadvertently infringed anyone's rights, please do accept my sincere apology in advance and notify me accordingly. The publishers will endeavour to provide correct credits on reprint. I am hugely grateful to the authors, collectors, editors, archives and publishers who said yes.

Mia Fernandez both inspired me to set up the 'Titanic Officers' website in the first place and kindly offered to check a near final draft and has been a source of much advice and encouragement. A special thanks to Gregg Jasper, who embarked on what must have been the daunting and headache-inducing task of checking and editing the manuscript. I am truly thankful for his patient and unrivalled attention to detail. On that point, it must be noted that all opinions, omissions, and errors remain entirely my own and do not necessarily reflect those referenced in the citations, sources, end notes or acknowledgements.

The most important thanks go to my wife, Itsuka, for her endless support and for putting up with my obsessive research. It was also her keen eye that spotted Titanic Beer in Stoke-on-Trent, for which we are both grateful. I never thought it was possible that drinking in a local pub could qualify as serious research.

Endnotes

Chapter One: Cities of the Sea

1. *Liverpool Weekly Courier*, 9 April 1898, courtesy of Timothy Cook
2. 'The Captain's Daughter, Helen Melville Russell-Cooke' John Pladdys, *The Titanic Commutator*, Volume 17, Number 2, 1993
3. *Master of the Titanic: The Career of Captain Ted Smith*, by Pat Lacey (1996), Book Guild
4. A letter written by the Captain's widow, Eleanor Smith, to Frank Hancock, shortly after the *Titanic* tragedy. It can be read in full in Chapter 4 under the subheading 'Eleanor's Letter'. Reprinted with kind permission by the Mystic Seaport Museum: VFM 194, Manuscripts Collection, G.W. Blunt White Library, Mystic Seaport Museum.
5. 'Captain E. J. Smith Memorial – A souvenir of the unveiling of the memorial, July 29th, 1914' (1914)
6. *Oakland Tribune*, 19 April 1912 (courtesy of Mike Poirer)
7. *Staffordshire Sentinel* 16 April 1912, also, *The Man Who Sank the Titanic? The Life and Times of Captain Edward J. Smith* by Gary Cooper (1992), Witan Books, p.22
8. 'Captain E. J. Smith Memorial – A souvenir of the unveiling of the memorial, July 29th, 1914' (1914)
9. The story was in the form of a long letter sent to London's *Daily Telegraph* in 1912 and reprinted in *The Daily News* (Perth, Australia) on 12 June 1912, p.6 courtesy of Gary Cooper, ('Voyage,' The Official Journal of Titanic International Society, issue 94, Winter 2015-16)
10. 'The Titanic and Waterloo, An Introduction to the Titanic history in Waterloo,' Seafront Resident's Action Group (SRAG) booklet
11. *Titanic Captain: The Life of Edward John Smith*, by G.J. Cooper (2011), The History Press.
12. Dave Gittens, 'Could you make it to Extra Master?' *Encyclopedia Titanica* https://www.encyclopedia-titanica.org/extra-master.html
13. *Recollections and Reflections* by Henry Martyn Hart (1917), J.W. Hart, p.105–106, courtesy of Gavin Thom, and George Behe. It must be noted that Hart

(1838-1920) seems to be referring to being aboard the *Britannic* in the late 1870s, while Smith did not command the *Britannic* (launched in 1874) until 1888, so he could be confusing E.J. with someone else. Or it could be when Smith was Second Officer aboard the *Britannic* (1884-1885), or later Chief Officer (1887).

14. *Liverpool Echo*, 8 March 2012 'Family showcase former home of Titanic captain Edward Smith'
15. *The Press* (Christchurch), 20 February 1890, Volume xlvii, Issue 7480, pages 4 and 6, courtesy of the Papers Past archive https://paperspast.natlib.govt.nz/ In an article published on 14 April 2012 on the *Stuff* website, it possibly identified the man who bowled Captain Smith for a duck as Harvey Hawkins, according to his great-grandson Bryce Hawkins. Harvey Hawkins is known locally for building Godley House in nearby Diamond Harbour in 1880. https://www.stuff.co.nz/the-press/news/6741594/Canterbury-links-to-Titanic
16. This clarification is thanks to research by Mark Baber in his article 'E. J. Smith, Coptic Aground and Rio – Two out of three ain't bad?' *Encyclopedia Titanica*, https://www.encyclopedia-titanica.org/e-j-smith-coptic-aground-and-rio---two-out-of-three-aint-bad-11534.html
17. National Archives, record number GBC_1891_2982_0065
18. *Warrington Guardian*, Gareth Dunning, 'Titanic captain Edward Smith was married in Warrington' 29 August 2022
19. In the wake of the Titanic disaster, some have claimed Roberston was a psychic or a prophet, writing about an event that would not take place until 14 years later. However, there are also many key differences. For example, Robertson's ship has a paddlewheel and was on its third (not maiden) voyage. 'Titan' was also a popular name at the time, and Robertson clearly knew shipbuilding trends and made some reasonable assumptions. In another book about submarines, he wrote about the early use of a 'periscope' which shows he was keenly interested in new maritime technology. He changed some details in the book post-*Titanic* disaster, realising that there was profitability in the similarity.
20. *Titanic Captain*, by G.J. Cooper, (2011) The History Press p93
21. From paperwork provided by Timothy Cook, its original owner was a Richard Kelsall, a wholesale fish salesman whose family were also steamship owners under the name the Kelsall Brothers. In 1893 Richard Kelsall gave 20 Alexandra Road to Louisa Cooper to mark her wedding to his nephew Joseph Kelsall at Christ Church on the same road. (The Kelsall One-Name Study, a web-site for Kelsall Genealogy, https://kelsall.one-name.net/trees/staffordshire-trees/kelsall-brothers-fish-merchants-sons-of-richard-kelsall-and-ann-kettle/)
22. 'The Gores Street Directory of 1901,' courtesy of Timothy Cook
23. British Listed Buildings, '17 Marine Crescent, A Grade II Listed Building in Crosby, Sefton' www. britishlistedbuildings.co.uk
24. *Midweek Visitor* (Southport, Formby & Crosby), 29 March 2016
25. *The Captain, Titanic & Me*, by Rose Gallagher (2012) YouCaxton
26. National Archives, London, UK record GBC_1901_3443-3444_0619
27. National Archives, London, UK record GBC_1901_3333-3335_0704
28. 'Edward John Smith, Captain on the Titanic,' by Linda D Wilding, The Family History Society of Cheshire, https://www.fhsc.org.uk/
29. *Titanic Captain*, by G.J. Cooper, (2011) The History Press.
30. *Titanic Captain*, by G.J. Cooper, (2011) The History Press. p.106
31. *The New York Times*, 9 July 1904
32. *Titanic Captain*, by G.J. Cooper, (2011) The History Press. p.62
33. VFM 194, Manuscripts Collection, G.W. Blunt White Library, Mystic Seaport Museum, Inc., Mystic Connecticut, USA

34. *Titanic Captain*, by G.J. Cooper, (2011) The History Press. p.114
35. *Master of the Titanic: The Career of Captain Ted Smith*, by Pat Lacey (1996), Book Guild
36. *Titanic Captain*, by G.J. Cooper, (2011) The History Press. p.54
37. J. Rush, *The Daily Mail*, 9 April 2013
38. 'Captain E. J. Smith Memorial – A souvenir of the unveiling of the memorial, July 29th, 1914' (1914)
39. *The Toronto Daily Star*, 18 April 1912 'Did Loose Rivets Sink the Titanic?'
40. Sotonopedia, the online A–Z of Southampton's history www.sotonopedia.wikidot.com
41. 'New plaque will mark the birthplace of Captain Edward Smith 100 years on from the Titanic disaster' https://public-relations-consultants.co.uk/new-plaque-will-mark-the-birthplace-of-captain-edward-smith-100-years-on-from-the-titanic-disaster/
42. *Southern Daily Echo*, Dan Kerins, 10 January 2012
43. *The Southern Daily Echo*, Southampton, 18 April 1942.

Chapter Two: Playing on *Titanic*'s Bridge

1. *The New York Times*, 7 January 1907
2. *The New York Times* 16 April 1912
3. *The Boy's Own Paper* 8 August 1908
4. *The Poverty Bay Herald*, 27 July 1907 (courtesy of Paul Lee)
5. Originally published in *The World's Work*, December 1909, courtesy of Paul Lee, but also quoted in the *New York Times*, 16 April 1912 and *Washington Times*, 17 April 1912. The other newspaper accounts place Smith's words during the *Adriatic*'s maiden voyage in 1907, which is possible.
6. *Washington Times*, 17 April 1912
7. *The New York Times*, 5 July 1920, *On a Sea of Glass* (2012) by J. Kent Layton, Tad Fitch and Bill Wormstedt, page 48, courtesy of Gregg Jasper.
8. The captain was the only member of the deck department to earn a yearly salary.
9. Article 90 of the King's Regulations gave Smith the authority to display the Blue Ensign. He held a Blue Ensign Warrant, No. 690, according to the book *Titanic: Triumph and Tragedy* by John P Eaton and Charles A. Haas (1995), W.W. Norton & Company. See also 'Spark's Titanic FAQs,' Parks Stephenson, http://titanic.marconigraph.com/mgy_faqs.html
10. *The New York Times*, 9 September 1907, courtesy of Mark Baber. The account spells Lanier's name incorrectly as 'Lander.'
11. *Sunday Magazine* of the *New-York Tribune*, courtesy of Gary Cooper/Mark Baber, 'A few glimpses of Captain Smith' (*Voyage*, The Official Journal of Titanic International Society, issue 94, Winter 2015-16)
12. A letter written onboard the Cunard RMS *Aquitania*, June 1914, reprinted in 'Captain E. J. Smith Memorial – A souvenir of the unveiling of the memorial, July 29th, 1914' (1914)
13. G.W. Blunt White Library, Mystic Seaport, Mystic Connecticut, USA
14. *Titanic Captain*, by G.J. Cooper, (2011) The History Press p.132
15. *Titanic Captain*, by G.J. Cooper, (2011) The History Press. p.133
16. 'Bill Sauder's Titanic' Facebook page, 24 July 2023 post: https://www.facebook.com/billsauderstitanic
17. Borzio, Breed Standards, The Kennel Club (https://www.thekennelclub.org.uk/breed-standards/hound/borzoi/)
18. 'The priceless Peggy Guggenheim,' *The Independent*, 21 October 2009
19. *Titanic Captain*, by G.J. Cooper, (2011) The History Press. p.81, 82
20. *Belfast Telegraph*, 24 March 2012

21. For more information on the 'Rigel' dog legend, 'Did Murdoch have a heroic dog named Rigel?' on the website www.williammurdoch.net
22. *I'll See You In New York, Titanic, The Courage of a Survivor* by David Haisman (1999), Boolarong Press
23. *On a Sea of Glass: The Life & Loss of the RMS Titanic*, by Bill Wormstedt, J. Kent Layton, Tad Fitch (2012), Amberley Publishing
24. *The New York Times*, 17 August 1909
25. *The Colorado Statesman*, 20 August 1910, for more information see Sam Brannigan's article 'The Fearless Mrs Givens – Purser accused of discrimination, overruled by Captain Smith' https://www.encyclopedia-titanica.org/the-fearless-mrs-givens.html
26. *The 'Big Four' of the White Star Fleet: Celtic, Cedric, Baltic & Adriatic*, by Mark Chirnside (2016), History Press
27. *Birmingham Evening Dispatch*, 16 April 1912
28. *Staffordshire Sentinel*, 16 April 1912
29. *The New York Times*, 11 June 1911
30. *The New York Times*, 20 June 1911
31. *RMS Olympic: Titanic's Sister*, by Mark Chirnside (2015), The History Press
32. *The New York Times*, 21 June 1911
33. *The New York Times*, 22 June 1911
34. *The New York Times*, 29 June 1911
35. *San Francisco Call* 29 August 1911
36. 'Titanic Facts – The Life & Loss of the RMS Titanic in Numbers' https://titanicfacts.net/
37. 'Titanic's Captain in Kinemacolor,' *Moving Picture News*, 1912.
38. *The Daily Telegraph* (London) 30 April 1931 p. 12. A 1934 article on Eleanor and Mel after the disaster also described the Captain as 'blue-eyed'; (*Daily News* (New York) 15 April 1934)
39. Research courtesy of João Gonçalves and Boris Mileski. The 'Catalogue of Kinemacolor film subjects: animated scenes in their actual colors' by Natural Color Kinematograph Co., Ltd was published in 1913 and listed an item numbered '291' titled 'The Leviathan of the Deep. The S.S. Olympic at Southampton June 11th. 1911'. The description includes 'a group of the ship's officers, with Captain Smith, who went down with the *Titanic*, to which ship he was appointed in 1912, is of special interest.' the film was not shot in colour, but converted afterward by means of a colorisation process. The book can be accessed here: https://archive.org/details/McGillLibrary-rbsc_catalogue-kinemacolor_ColgateIXNaturalColor-17612
40. *The Brooklyn Daily Eagle*, 17 April 1912
41. *The World, Evening Edition* (New York), 21 September 1911
42. According to the Merchant Shipping (Exemption from Pilotage) Act, 1897, shipowners were exempt from liability when under compulsory pilotage. However, this changed on 1 January 1918 when the Pilotage Act, 1913 came into force, aligning with international convention that the made the shipowner or master liable for any loss or damage even if under compulsory pilotage.
43. *The Sting of the Hawke* by Samuel Halpern and Mark Chirnside (2015)
44. *Home From The Sea* by Arthur Rostron (1931)
45. *Lively Ahoy: Reminiscences of 58 Years in the Trinity House Pilotage Service* by George W. Bowyer (1930) p 37 (Published by H.B. Broadbere, Southampton, now out of print)
46. *Washington Times*, 16 April 1912
47. *The New York Times* of 8 February 1903 ran an article on the new White Star liner the *Cedric*, that was described under the headline of 'The Largest Ship

Endnotes

Afloat' as 'built on the cellular double bottom principle, and has numerous water-tight compartments that make her practically unsinkable' (quote courtesy of Mark Baber/*Encyclopedia Titanica*). Cunard's *Mauretania* was also called 'unsinkable' in 1906 (*The Shipbuilder*, Autumn 1906, 'The Cunard Liner Mauretania'). Claims that Captain Smith was 'overconfident' when describing *Titanic* as 'unsinkable' need to be viewed in the context that most large ships of that time were similarly designed and advertised as 'practically unsinkable'. Courtesy of Mark Baber/*Encyclopedia Titanica*.

48. G.W. Blunt White Library, Mystic Seaport, Mystic Connecticut, USA
49. *New York Post*, 19 April 1912
50. G.W. Blunt White Library, Mystic Seaport, Mystic Connecticut, USA
51. *Aberdeen Journal*, 22 September 1911
52. *New-York Tribune*, 30 November 1911
53. *Washington Times*, 17 April 1912
54. 'Sea Kelpie' is a mythical sea creature of bad luck and the article in the *Ledger-Dispatch* 17 April 1912 counted five incidents that convinced them 'Sea Kelpie' was 'active with Capt. Smith': 1. Hawke collision, 2. Losing a propeller in February 1912, 3. Damage on exit from Belfast after repairs, 4. SS *New York* near collision 5. Iceberg.
55. 'British Wreck Commissioner's Inquiry on Behalf of the Board of Trade' (1912), Day 17, 5 June 1912, testimony of Harold A. Sanderson
56. *The Hawaiian Gazette* (Honolulu, Oahu, Hawaii), 23 April 1912. From the University of Hawaii at Manoa. Chronicling America: Historic American Newspapers. Lib. of Congress. https://chroniclingamerica.loc.gov/lccn/sn83025121/1912-04-23/ed-1/seq-1/
57. *The Brooklyn Daily Eagle*, 17 April 1912
58. VFM 194, Manuscripts Collection, G.W. Blunt White Library, Mystic Seaport Museum, Inc., Mystic Connecticut, USA
59. *The Examiner*, Launceston, Tasmania, 26 April 1912
60. *On a Sea of Glass* by Bill Wormstedt, J. Kent Layton, Tad Fitch (2012), Amberley Publishing
61. *On a Sea of Glass* by Bill Wormstedt, J. Kent Layton, Tad Fitch (2012), Amberley Publishing p.37
62. *When the Ships Came In*, by Jack Lawrence, 1940, Farrar & Rinehart, p256 (courtesy of Mike Poirier)
63. *New York Post*, 19 April 1912
64. *The Illustrated London News*, 27 April 1912
65. Lawrence Beesley's letter to the *New York Times*, 29 April 1912, *On Board RMS Titanic – Memories of the Maiden Voyage* by George Behe (2012), The History Press
66. 'Titanic's Lifeboats: An Increased Capacity' Mark Chirnside, *Atlantic Daily Bulletin*, March 2018: Pages 28-29 (www.markchirnside.co.uk)
67. *New York Post*, 19 April 1912
68. 'British Wreck Commissioner's Inquiry on Behalf of the Board of Trade' (1912), Day 17, 5 June 1912, during the testimony of Harold A. Sanderson
69. *The Evening Journal*, 19 April 1912 (courtesy of Mike Poirier)
70. *New-York Tribune*, 2 December 1910
71. James Moody's letter to Margaret Moody, 4 April 1912, courtesy of the website 'Bridge Duty, Officers of the RMS Titanic,' Inger Sheil & Kerri Sundberg 1999
72. *The New York Times*, 6 June 1911
73. *Halifax Morning Chronicle*, 9 April, 1912
74. *Titanic Captain*, by G.J. Cooper, (2011) The History Press
75. *The Titanic – Everything Was Against Us* by Simon Angel (2012)

76. A 2015 UK government report on 'English Life Tables No.17: 2010 to 2012' noted that 'for males, life expectancy at birth increased from 51 years in 1910-1912 to 79 years in 2010-12, while for females it increased from 55 to 83 years... People aged 60 could expect to live around 9 years longer in 2010-2012 than 100 years earlier.' (https://www.ons.gov.uk/peoplepopulationandcommunity/birthsdeathsandmarriages/lifeexpectancies/bulletins/englishlifetablesno17/2015-09-01)
77. A recollection of Dr Beaumont, from *Titanic Voices: Memories from the Fateful Voyage* (1994) quoted in *On a Sea of Glass* by Bill Wormstedt, J. Kent Layton, Tad Fitch (2012), Amberley Publishing, p.47
78. *When the Ships Came In*, by Jack Lawrence (1940) Farrar & Rinehart p.257 (courtesy of Mike Poirier)
79. *Amsterdam Evening Recorder*, 23 April 1912, courtesy of Mike Poirer and quoted in *On a Sea of Glass* by Bill Wormstedt, J. Kent Layton, Tad Fitch (2012), Amberley Publishing, p.69
80. Letter written by Walter Lord to Mrs Russell Cooke, National Maritime Museum, Greenwich, London, Lord-MacQuitty Collection, LMQ/7/1/18
81. The story that Wyckoff Van der hoef was the only paying first class passenger on *Titanic*'s delivery ship has been found to be unlikely in Brandon Whited's article "A Quay Question": https://www.encyclopedia-titanica.org/a-quay-question-titanic-belfast-southampton-passenger.html
82. 'She once stood on bridge of Titanic,' *Middlesex Independent, W. London Star*, 13 December 1957.
83. *William McMaster Murdoch, A Career at Sea: The Complete and Documented Version*, by Susanne Störmer (2002)
84. *Sincerely Harry – The Letters of Henry Wilde, Titanic's Chief Officer*, by Michael Beatty (2017), Lulu
85. *William McMaster Murdoch, A Career at Sea: The Complete and Documented Version*, by Susanne Störmer (2002)
86. *Titanic and Other Ships*, by Charles Herbert Lightoller (1935), Ivor, Nicholson and Watson
87. *Sincerely Harry – The Letters of Henry Wilde, Titanic's Chief Officer*, by Michael Beatty (2017), Lulu
88. *William McMaster Murdoch. A Career at Sea: The Complete and Documented Version*, by Susanne Störmer (2002)
89. A quote from an unnamed source from *The Bystander*, printed in *The Western Guardian*, 8 May 1912. Courtesy of Paul Lee.
90. G.W. Blunt White Library, Mystic Seaport, Mystic Connecticut, USA
91. *Titanic Captain*, by G.J. Cooper (2011), The History Press.
92. 'She once stood on bridge of Titanic,' *Middlesex Independent, W. London Star*, 13 December 1957.
93. Lee Raymond collection of the Southampton Maritime Museum, quoted in *Titanic Voices: Memories from the Fateful Voyage* (1994) by Alastair Forsyth, Donald Hyslop, Sheila Jemima p.92
94. 'A few glimpses of Captain Smith,' by Gary Cooper, *Voyage* edition 94, Titanic International Society, Winter 2015 – 2016
95. *Titanic in Photographs*, by Daniel Klistorner, Bruce Beveridge, Scott Andrews, Steve Hall, Art Braunschweiger (2011), The History Press
96. *A Brush with Life*, by Norman Wilkinson (1969) quoted in *Titanic Voices: Memories from the Fateful Voyage* (1994) by Alastair Forsyth, Donald Hyslop, Sheila Jemima p. 94
97. Recollection of Roy Diaper (Southampton City Heritage Oral History) quoted in *Titanic Voices* (1994) by Alastair Forsyth, Donald Hyslop, Sheila Jemima p. 94

Endnotes

98. In recent years, more emphasis has been put on the coal bunker fire, with exaggerated claims of its influence on the disaster, although in reality it played a very minor role as it was put out on Saturday 13 April, a full day prior to the iceberg collision. For more information see *Titanic: Solving The Mysteries* by J. Kent Layton, et. al, or check www.titanicswitch.com/coalbunker_fire.html
99. 'British Wreck Commissioner's Inquiry' (1912), Day 17, 5 June 1912, testimony of Harold A. Sanderson, also quoted in *Titanic: Triumph and Tragedy* by John P Eaton and Charles A. Haas (1995), W.W. Norton & Company, p.72
100. 'Titanic: She sailed only half full?' Mark Chirnside, *Titanic Commutator*, April 2019, (www.markchirnside.co.uk)
101. *The Loss of the SS. Titanic*, by Lawrence Beesley (1912)
102. Ibid.
103. Ibid.
104. This rare story is thanks to Tiphaine Hirou, from a May 1912 account in Les Cahiers de l'Ecole Nationale de Rouen, released in 17 April 2012, http://seabird.over-blog.com/article-titanic-la-derniere-escale-103575443.html
105. *Encyclopedia Titanica* (2022) James Arthur Paintin URL: https://www.encyclopedia-titanica.org/titanic-victim/james-arthur-paintin.html
106. *Titanic in Photographs*, by Daniel Klistorner, Bruce Beveridge, Scott Andrews, Steve Hall, Art Braunschweiger (2011), The History Press, p.120
107. *Titanic in Photographs*, p.129
108. *The Paterson Morning Call*, 3 May 1912, courtesy of Michael Poirier
109. Ibid.
110. *Discretions and Indiscretions* (British edition) by Lady Duff Gordon (1932) pp. 149-150
111. *The Man Who Sank the Titanic? The Life and Times of Captain Edward J. Smith*, by Gary Cooper (1992) Witan Books, p.76
112. Transcription from an audio interview with Marion Kenyon, 6 April 1957, courtesy of Michael Poirier
113. *The Man Who Sank the Titanic?* p.76
114. BBC radio interview, broadcast 11 April 1987, interviewed by Roger Clark (https://www.bbc.co.uk/archive/the-way-it-was--eva-hart/zns2cqt)
115. 'Over to You' 1987, 3-part interview with Eva Hart, Youtube video, https://www.youtube.com/watch?v=M0akUzKVKKs
116. Eva Hart's autobiography is a 1994 book entitled *Shadow of the Titanic A Survivor's Story: Biography of Miss Eva Hart, MBE, JP* by Eva Hart, Ronald C. Denney, later reprinted as *A Girl Aboard the Titanic: A Survivor's Story* in 2000 and 2012. The later edition also contains her mother Esther Hart's account that was published in the *Ilford Graphic*, 12 May 1912. Neither of these accounts mention her meeting Captain Smith.
117. *I'll See You In New York, Titanic, The Courage of a Survivor*, by David Haisman (1999), Boolarong Press
118. Other accounts by Edith Haisman have not included the story about meeting Captain Smith. Researcher and author Paul Lee has commented on some inaccuracies between the 1912 account from her mother and her later accounts in the 1980s, as discussed here: https://www.paullee.com/titanic/EHaisman.php
119. *Victoria Daily Times*, 25 April 1912 (courtesy of Mike Poirer). Andrew Grieve mentions Smith as captain on the *Runic*'s maiden voyage from Liverpool to Australia in 1901, but this does not align with Smith's records. Grieve may be referring to Smith's command of the *Coptic* to Australasia in 1890.
120. *When the Ships Came In*, by Jack Lawrence, (1940), Farrar & Rinehart p.257 (courtesy of Mike Poirier)

121. Limitation of Liability Hearings, Deposition of Mrs Elizabeth L. Lines, Titanic Inquiry Project, titanicinquiry.org
122. *Berkshire Evening Eagle*, 22 April 1912, *On Board RMS Titanic – Memories of the Maiden Voyage*, by George Behe (2012), The History Press.
123. 'United States Senate Hearings into the Sinking of the RMS Titanic' (1912), Day 11, 30 April 1912, testimony of Joseph B. Ismay
124. *The Truth about the Titanic*, Colonel Archibald Gracie, (1913), p.3
125. A letter Ruth Becker wrote to the *St Nicholas Magazine* in 1913, 'On Board RMS Titanic – Memories of the Maiden Voyage' by George Behe (2012), The History Press
126. White Star Line letter to captains, *On Board RMS Titanic – Memories of the Maiden Voyage*, by George Behe (2012), The History Press p.29
127. 'The Truth about the Titanic,' Colonel Archibald Gracie, (1913)
128. Cunard website accessed in 2023: https://www.cunard.com/en-gb/activity-types/daytime/interdenominational-church-service
129. *Death of a Purser: Hugh Richard Walter McElroy Chief Purser of the RMS Titanic Biography* (2011) by Frank McElroy, with thanks to Mike Poirier and his article 'Piecing together a Titanic puzzle, The Complex case of Mrs Cassebeer,' Voyage (#87), the Titanic International Society.
130. *The Titanic on Film: Myth versus Truth*, Linda Maria Koldau, (2014), McFarland & Co. Beesley's letter to the *New York Times* published 29 April 1912 also describes 'For Those in Peril on the Sea' as sung in the second class evening service, and that many of the hymns at the informal event dealt with 'safety at sea' no more than two hours before the *Titanic* struck ice.
131. 'British Wreck Commissioner's Inquiry' (1912), Day 2, 2 May 1912, testimony of Archie Jewell
132. https://www.encyclopedia-titanica.org/the-forgotten-drills-aboard-titanic.html
133. All indicated clock times henceforth are *Titanic* time (not GMT) and based upon 'Chronology of Events with References and Notes' (revised 7 January 2024) by Samuel Halpern. See also 'Failure To Act: The Titanic and the Ice Warnings,' by Paul Lee http://www.paullee.com/titanic/icewarnings.php.
134. *Rhode Island Sunday Magazine*, 15 April 1962, *On Board RMS Titanic – Memories of the Maiden Voyage* by George Behe (2012), The History Press
135. 'British Wreck Commissioner's Inquiry' (1912), Day 11, 20 May 1912, testimony of Charles H. Lightoller
136. For more information on the exact text of each message and the reply, *Titanic – Signals of Disaster*, by John Booth and Sean Coughlan (1993), White Star Publications
137. Statement issued by J. Bruce Ismay to *The Times* 21 April 1912, and reprinted in *The Ismay Line*, Wilton J. Oldham (1961), Journal of Commerce & Shipping Telegraph
138. 'United States Senate Hearings into the Sinking of the RMS Titanic' (1912), Report – Ice warnings
139. *Encyclopedia Titanica* (2013) 'Acquitting the Iceberg,' by Peter Elverhøi
140. *Encyclopedia Titanica* (2003) 'Marconigrams sent and received by Captain Smith on the Titanic,' Brian J. Ticehurst, UK
141. *Titanic Myths, Titanic Truths*, by Capt. David G. Brown, (2012), self-published under the CreateSpace Independent Publishing Platform
142. 'United States Senate Hearings into the Sinking of the RMS Titanic' (1912), testimony of Imanita Shelley, in the form of an affidavit
143. *Discretions and Indiscretions* (British edition) by Lady Duff Gordon (1932) pp.149-150

Endnotes

144. Failure To Act: The Titanic and the Ice Warnings, by Paul Lee http://www.paullee.com/titanic/icewarnings.php.
145. *Titanic and Other Ships* by Charles Herbert Lightoller (1935), Ivor, Nicholson and Watson
146. For more information on Bride defending his colleague against Lightoller's accusations involving the *Mesaba*, www.titanicofficers.com/article_16.html
147. The Third Titanic Inquiry, Ryan v. OSNC, Transcript of Precis Law Report, by Senan Molony, *Encyclopedia Titanica* https://www.encyclopedia-titanica.org/ryan-v-osnc.html
148. Researcher and author Sam Halpern has calculated that the story of Smith turning 'The Corner' late was the result of an erroneous SOS position. See 'Pitman's Corner' at https://titanicology.com/Titanica/PitmansCorner.html
149. 'British Wreck Commissioner's Inquiry' (1912), Day 11, 20 May 1912, testimony of Sir Cosmo Duff-Gordon
150. *The Kansas City Star*, 1 February 1937 (Courtesy of Mike Poirer)
151. 'United States Senate Hearings into the Sinking of the RMS Titanic' (1912), Marian Thayer, Affidavit
152. Elmer Taylor, private account, courtesy of George Behe
153. *The New York Times*, 22 April, 1912
154. 'United States Senate Hearings into the Sinking of the RMS Titanic' (1912), Day 9, 27 April 1912, testimony of Charles Lightoller, recalled
155. *The New York Times*, 22 May 1912
156. *On a Sea of Glass*, by Bill Wormstedt, J. Kent Layton, Tad Fitch (2012), Amberley Publishing
157. 'United States Senate Hearings into the Sinking of the RMS Titanic' (1912), Affidavit by Eleanor Widener.
158. *On a Sea of Glass* (2012), Amberley Publishing
159. *Daily Mail*, 9 March 2012
160. *On Board RMS Titanic – Memories of the Maiden Voyage*, by George Behe (2012), The History Press
161. 'Her Husband Went Down with the Titanic' by René Harris, *Liberty* magazine, 23 April 1932, courtesy of Randy Bryan Bigham and Gregg Jasper.
162. 'United States Senate Hearings into the Sinking of the RMS Titanic' (1912), Affidavit of Daisy Minahan
163. *Los Angeles Times*, 21 April 1912, *Eugene Morning Register* (Oregon), 28 April 1912, courtesy of Gavin Thom and George Behe. Minahan's accounts need to be treated with some caution as she generally painted the officers in a bad light, including insinuations during the Senate Inquiry that Fifth Officer Lowe was drinking, for which Lowe (an abstainer) demanded a retraction.
164. 'British Wreck Commissioner's Inquiry' (1912), Day 11, 20 May 1912, testimony of Charles H. Lightoller
165. The Third Titanic Inquiry – Ryan v. OSNC, Transcript of Precis Law Report, by Senan Molony, *Encyclopedia Titanica* https://www.encyclopedia-titanica.org/ryan-v-osnc.html
166. 'British Wreck Commissioner's Inquiry' (1912), Day 11, 20 May 1912, testimony of Charles H. Lightoller
167. The Third Titanic Inquiry – Ryan v. OSNC, Transcript of Precis Law Report, by Senan Molony, *Encyclopedia Titanica* https://www.encyclopedia-titanica.org/ryan-v-osnc.html
168. British Wreck Commissioner's Inquiry, Day 13, 22 May 1912, testimony of Joseph Boxhall
169. BBC radio, 22 October 1962, radio broadcast by Commander Joseph Boxhall

Chapter Three: The Convergence of the Twain

1. *The Southern Daily Echo,* 15 April 1912 (courtesy of the Southampton Local History archive)
2. *Western Times,* 16 April 1912
3. *The Southern Daily Echo,* 16 April, (courtesy of the Southampton Local History archive)
4. *The Southern Daily Echo,* 17 April, (courtesy of the Southampton Local History archive)
5. *Daily Sketch,* 17 April 1912
6. *Southampton Times and Hampshire Press,* 20 April 1912
7. *The Hampshire Advertiser County Newspaper,* 20 April 1912 (courtesy of the Southampton Local History Archive)
8. *The Southern Daily Echo,* 18 April 1912 (courtesy of the Southampton Local History archive)
9. *The Daily Mirror,* 22 April 1912
10. *The Titanic and the City of Widows it left Behind,* by Julie Cook, (2020), Pen & Sword Ltd.
11. *Titanic Captain,* by G.J. Cooper (2011), The History Press.
12. 'British Wreck Commissioner's Inquiry' (1912), Day 11, 20 May 1912, testimony of Charles Herbert Lightoller
13. *St. Joseph News-Press,* 17 April 1912
14. *On a Sea of Glass* (2012), Amberley Publishing, p.361
15. 'United States Senate Hearings into the Sinking of the RMS Titanic' (1912), Day 5, 24 April 1912, testimony of Robert Hichens
16. For example, the research of *Titanic* author Samuel Halpbern, in his book *Prelude to an Allision: Titanic's Fatal Encounter Revisited.*
17. British Wreck Commissioner's Inquiry on behalf of the Board of Trade, May–July 1912. Day 13, Boxhall testimony
18. BBC radio, 22 October 1962, radio broadcast by Commander Joseph Boxhall
19. 'United States Senate Hearings into the Sinking of the RMS Titanic' (1912), Day 7, 25 April 1912, testimony of Alfred Olliver
20. 'British Wreck Commissioner's Inquiry' (1912), Day 5, 9 May 1912, testimony of Thomas P Dillon
21. *The Loss of the SS. Titanic,* by Lawrence Beesley (1912)
22. *The Guardian,* 22 September 2010 'Titanic rescue scuppered by officers' "criminal" decision, claims author' – Courtesy of Guardian News & Media Ltd
23. 'United States Senate Hearings into the Sinking of the RMS Titanic' (1912), Day 7, 25 April, testimony of Alfred Olliver,
24. 'United States Senate Hearings into the Sinking of the RMS Titanic' (1912), Day 3, 22 April, testimony of Joseph G Boxhall,
25. 'British Wreck Commissioner's Inquiry' (1912), Day 13, 22 May 1912, testimony of Joseph G Boxhall
26. 'The Post Office Aboard the Titanic,' The Postal Museum, https://www.postalmuseum.org/blog/post-office-aboard-titanic/
27. 'United States Senate Hearings into the Sinking of the RMS Titanic' (1912), Day 7, 25 April 1912, testimony of Alfred Olliver
28. 'United States Senate Hearings into the Sinking of the RMS Titanic' (1912), Day 7, 25 April 1912, testimony of Albert Haines
29. 'United States Senate Hearings into the Sinking of the RMS Titanic' (1912), Day 1, 19 April 1912, testimony of Joseph Bruce Ismay
30. 'British Wreck Commissioner's Inquiry' (1912), Day 13, 22 May 1912, testimony of Joseph G Boxhall

Endnotes

31. 'United States Senate Hearings into the Sinking of the RMS Titanic' (1912), Day 3, 22 April 1912, testimony of Joseph G Boxhall
32. *On a Sea of Glass* (2012), Amberley Publishing, pp.162-163
33. 'British Wreck Commissioner's Inquiry' (1912), Day 13, 22 May 1912, testimony of Joseph G Boxhall
34. 'United States Senate Hearings into the Sinking of the RMS Titanic' (1912), Day 5, 24 April 1912, testimony of Harold G Lowe
35. 'United States Senate Hearings into the Sinking of the RMS Titanic' (1912), Day 4, 23 April 1912, testimony of Herbert J Pitman,
36. 'I Was There – The Sinking of the Titanic by Commander Lightoller,' BBC radio, 1 November 1936
37. *On a Sea of Glass* (2012), Amberley Publishing, p.163
38. *The Man Who Sank the Titanic?* by Gary Cooper, (1992), Witan Books, p.103
39. *The New York Times*, 19 April 1912 statement by Harold Bride
40. 'British Wreck Commissioner's Inquiry' (1912), Day 4, 8 May 1912, testimony of James Johnson
41. *Rhode Island Sunday Magazine*, 15 April 1962, *On Board RMS Titanic – Memories of the Maiden Voyage*, by George Behe (2012), The History Press
42. 'British Wreck Commissioner's Inquiry' (1912), Day 11, 20 May 1912, testimony of Annie Robinson
43. *Thomas Andrew Shipbuilder* (1912) by Shan F. Bullock
44. *A Night to Remember*, by Walter Lord (1955), R & W Holt
45. *The Washington Herald*, 19 April 1912, courtesy of Mike Poirer and quoted in *On a Sea of Glass* (2012), Amberley Publishing, p.159
46. 'British Wreck Commissioner's Inquiry' (1912), Day 9, 16 May 1912, testimony of Charles Mackay
47. 'British Wreck Commissioner's Inquiry' (1912), Day 19, 7 June 1912, testimony of Paul Maugé
48. *Daily Telegraph*, 29 April 1912, courtesy of *Titanic: The Homecoming, Tales from The Lapland* by Dr Paul Lee (2020)
49. 'United States Senate Hearings into the Sinking of the RMS Titanic' (1912), Day 11, 30 April 1912, testimony of Charles Stengel,
50. 'British Wreck Commissioner's Inquiry' (1912), Day 11, 20 May 1912, testimony of Walter Wynn
51. 'United States Senate Hearings into the Sinking of the RMS Titanic' (1912), Day 3 22 April, testimony of Joseph G Boxhall
52. 'I Was There – The Sinking of the Titanic by Commander Lightoller,' BBC radio, 1 November 1936
53. 'British Wreck Commissioner's Inquiry' (1912), Day 3, 7 May 1912, testimony of Robert Hichens
54. 'United States Senate Hearings into the Sinking of the RMS Titanic' (1912), Day 5, 24 April 1912, testimony of Robert Hichens
55. 'British Wreck Commissioner's Inquiry' (1912), Day 13, 22 May 1912, testimony of Joseph G Boxhall
56. 'A Talk by the Fourth Officer of the Titanic,' by William Sandrey, May (1959), *Nautical Magazine*, pp. 262–264, courtesy of Brown, Son and Ferguson (Glasgow) and Nigel Brown.
57. BBC radio, 22 October 1962, radio broadcast by Commander Joseph Boxhall
58. *The New York Times*, 19 April 1912 statement by Harold Bride
59. *The Man Who Sank the Titanic?* by Gary Cooper, (1992) Witan Books, p.96
60. BBC radio, 22 October 1962, radio broadcast by Commander Joseph Boxhall
61. *The New York Times*, 19 April 1912, statement by Harold Bride

62. 'United States Senate Hearings into the Sinking of the RMS Titanic' (1912), Day 3, 22 April 1912, testimony of Joseph G Boxhall
63. This interesting point indicating Captain Smith may have been more competent than he is given credit for was discovered by *Titanic* researcher and author Jim Currie and posted on the 'RMS Titanic Facts, History and Biography – Encyclopedia Titanica' Facebook group. Currie notes that the position Smith calculated was Latitude 41°44' North, Longitude 50°24' West and calculating 20 miles backward on the reverse Titanic course places Titanic at 41°45.7' North, Longitude 49° 57.2' West. The wreck lies at Latitude 41°43' 32' N Longitude 49°56' W and that is at distance of 1 mile south and 0.5 miles west of where Smith would have placed her had he been given more accurate information.
64. 'British Wreck Commissioner's Inquiry' (1912), Day 12, 21 May 1912, testimony of Charles H. Lightoller
65. *Titanic and Other Ships* by Charles Herbert Lightoller (1935), Ivor, Nicholson and Watson
66. 'United States Senate Hearings into the Sinking of the RMS Titanic' (1912), Day 4, 23 April 1912, testimony of Herbert J Pitman
67. 'British Wreck Commissioner's Inquiry' (1912), Day 19, 7 June 1912, testimony of Paul Mauge
68. *The New York Times*, 19 April 1912, statement by Harold Bride
69. 'United States Senate Hearings into the Sinking of the RMS Titanic' (1912), Day 14, 4 May 1912, testimony of Harold S Bride
70. 'British Wreck Commissioner's Inquiry' (1912), Day 14, 23 May 1912, testimony of Harold S. Bride
71. Harold Bride's letter to Mr W Cross, Marconi Co, 27 April 1912, *On Board RMS Titanic – Memories of the Maiden Voyage*, by George Behe (2012), The History Press
72. 'British Wreck Commissioner's Inquiry' (1912), Day 15, 24 May 1912, testimony of Samuel Hemming
73. 'British Wreck Commissioner's Inquiry' (1912), Day 3, 7 May 1912, testimony of Robert Hichens p
74. 'British Wreck Commissioner's Inquiry' (1912), Day 4, 8 May 1912, testimony of John Poingdestre
75. *Newark Evening News*, 19 April 1912
76. *The Times*, 20 April 1912
77. From a letter Gladys Cherry wrote on 17 April 1912 aboard the *Carpathia*. *On Board RMS Titanic – Memories of the Maiden Voyage*, by George Behe (2012), The History Press
78. From a letter Marie Young wrote on 18 April 1912 aboard the *Carpathia*. *On Board RMS Titanic – Memories of the Maiden Voyage*, by George Behe (2012), The History Press
79. *The Globe Democrat*, 19 April 1912, courtesy of Michael Poirier
80. *The Paterson Morning Call*, 20 April 1912, courtesy of Michael Poirier
81. 'United States Senate Hearings into the Sinking of the RMS Titanic' (1912), Day 11, 30 April 1912, testimony Helen Bishop
82. *Boston Daily Globe*, 21 April 1912
83. *Hull Daily Mail*, 18 May 1912
84. *The New York Herald*, 20 April 1912, quoted in 'Thomas Andrews Shipbuilder' by Shan F. Bullock (1912)
85. *Washington Post* 19 April 1912, *On Board RMS Titanic – Memories of the Maiden Voyage*, by George Behe (2012), The History Press
86. *Washington Post*, courtesy of the *Encyclopedia Titanica* article 'A Titanic Mystery: Exploring the Escape of Robert W. Daniel, The rescue of one of the Titanic

Endnotes

disaster's most prominent first-class survivors' by Randy Bryan Bigham, Richard Edwards and Brandon Whited (https://www.encyclopedia-titanica.org/titanic-mystery-exploring-escape-robert-daniel.html)

87. *The New York Herald*, 19 April 1912
88. *The Truth About the Titanic*, by Archibald Gracie IV (1913) pp.125, 126
89. *The Truth About the Titanic*, by Archibald Gracie IV (1913) pp.128-9, 132
90. 'United States Senate Hearings into the Sinking of the RMS Titanic' (1912), Day 1, 19 April 1912, testimony of Charles Ligtoller
91. 24 April 1912 account, unknown newspaper, by Mrs Chambers courtesy of Mike Poirer and quoted in *On a Sea of Glass* (2012), Amberley Publishing, p. 191
92. 'United States Senate Hearings into the Sinking of the RMS Titanic' (1912), Day 10, 29 April 1912, testimony of Hugh Woolner
93. 'United States Senate Hearings into the Sinking of the RMS Titanic' (1912), Day 1, 19 April 1912, testimony of Charles H. Lightoller,
94. 'British Wreck Commissioner's Inquiry' (1912), Day 12, 21 May 1912, testimony of Charles H. Lightoller
95. *The New York Times*, 22 April 1912
96. 'British Wreck Commissioner's Inquiry' (1912), Day 12, 21 May 1912, testimony of Charles H. Lightoller
97. 'United States Senate Hearings into the Sinking of the RMS Titanic' (1912), Day 7, 25 April 1912, testimony of Frank O. Evans,
98. 'United States Senate Hearings into the Sinking of the RMS Titanic' (1912), Day 9, 27 April 1912, testimony of William Burke
99. 'British Wreck Commissioner's Inquiry' (1912), Day 13, 22 May 1912, testimony of Joseph G Boxhall
100. Letter written by George Rowe to Walter Lord June 1955, http://www.paullee.com/titanic/gtrowe.php
101. BBC radio, 22 October 1962, radio broadcast by Commander Joseph Boxhall
102. 'British Wreck Commissioner's Inquiry' (1912), Day 13, 22 May 1912, testimony of Joseph G Boxhall
103. 'United States Senate Hearings into the Sinking of the RMS Titanic' (1912), Day 3, 22 April 1912, testimony of Joseph G Boxhall
104. 'British Wreck Commissioner's Inquiry' (1912), Day 13, 22 May 1912, testimony of Joseph G Boxhall
105. Letter written by George Rowe to Walter Lord June 1955, http://www.paullee.com/titanic/gtrowe.php
106. Account via Richard Faber, courtesy of Don Lynch, *On Board RMS Titanic – Memories of the Maiden Voyage*, by George Behe (2012), The History Press
107. 'United States Senate Hearings into the Sinking of the RMS Titanic' (1912), Day 1, 19 April 1912, testimony of Alfred Crawford
108. *The New York Herald*, 19 April 1912
109. 'United States Senate Hearings into the Sinking of the RMS Titanic' (1912), Day 7, 25 April 1912, testimony of Thomas Jones
110. From a letter Marie Young wrote on the 18 April 1912 aboard the *Carpathia*. *On Board RMS Titanic – Memories of the Maiden Voyage*, by George Behe (2012), The History Press
111. Transcription from an audio interview with Marion Kenyon, 6 April 1957, courtesy of Michael Poirier
112. *Philiadelphia Inquirer*, 20 April 1912
113. 'Lady Rothes Describes the Horror Of Survivors' Chase Of Phantom Light' *New York Herald*, 21 April 1912
114. Transcription from a handwritten letter, August 1955, http://www.paullee.com/titanic/Rothes.php

115. 'My Maiden Voyage,' by Roberta Maioni, *Daily Express*, 1926 typed account, Encyclopedia Titanica, https://www.encyclopedia-titanica.org/roberta-maioni-titanic-account.html
116. Martha Stone dictated her account to Evelyn Campbell after arriving in New York, *Cincinnati Enquirer*, 20 April 1912, *On Board RMS Titanic – Memories of the Maiden Voyage*, by George Behe (2012), The History Press
117. 'United States Senate Hearings into the Sinking of the RMS Titanic' (1912), Day 4, 23 April 1912, testimony of Arthur G. Peuchen
118. *New York Times*, 22 April 1912
119. 'United States Senate Hearings into the Sinking of the RMS Titanic' (1912), Day 4, 23 April 1912, testimony of Arthur G. Peuchen
120. 'United States Senate Hearings into the Sinking of the RMS Titanic' (1912), Day 18, 25 May 1912, statement of Mrs Lucian P. Smith
121. *Washington Evening Star*, 20 April, 1912
122. 'The Titanic: Our Story' by Elizabeth Mussey Eustis and Martha Stephenson (6-page booklet published in 1912)
123. 'The Loss of the Titanic', An address by Washington Dodge to San Francisco's Commonwealth Club, *On Board RMS Titanic – Memories of the Maiden Voyage*, by George Behe (2012), The History Press
124. *The Truth About the Titanic*, by Colonel Archibald Gracie IV (1913) p.84
125. 'British Wreck Commissioner's Inquiry' (1912), Day 12, 21 May 1912, testimony of Charles H. Lightoller
126. *101 Things You Thought You Knew About The Titanic... But Didn't!* by Tim Maltin (2010)
127. 'United States Senate Hearings into the Sinking of the RMS Titanic' (1912), Day 7, 25 April 1912, testimony of William Ward
128. *Manitoba Free Press*, 29 April 1912, *On Board RMS Titanic – Memories of the Maiden Voyage*, by George Behe (2012), The History Press
129. *Titanic and Other Ships*, by Charles Herbert Lightoller (1935), Ivor, Nicholson and Watson
130. *New York Times*, 19 April 1912
131. 'United States Senate Hearings into the Sinking of the RMS Titanic' (1912), Day 5, 24 April 1912, testimony of Charles H Lightoller
132. 'United States Senate Hearings into the Sinking of the RMS Titanic' (1912), Day 7, 25 April 1912, testimony of George T. Rowe
133. *The Paterson Morning Call*, 3 May 1912, courtesy of Michael Poirier
134. 'United States Senate Hearings into the Sinking of the RMS Titanic' (1912), Day 3, 22 April 1912, testimony of Joseph G. Boxhall
135. BBC radio, 22 October 1962, broadcast by Commander Joseph Boxhall
136. Ibid
137. *Atlantic City Daily Press* 23 April 1912, courtesy of George Behe
138. 'United States Senate Hearings into the Sinking of the RMS Titanic' (1912), Day 7, 25 April 1912, testimony of John Hardy
139. 'United States Senate Hearings into the Sinking of the RMS Titanic' (1912), Day 15, 9 May 1912, affidavit of Mahala Douglas
140. 'Her Husband Went Down with the Titanic' by René Harris, *Liberty* magazine, 23 April 1932, courtesy of Randy Bryan Bigham and Gregg Jasper. As with other articles written many decades post-disaster, this story needs to be treated with caution as it contains details that Harris did not include in other accounts and may be prone to exaggeration. For more information see 'A Night to Forget: Renée Harris and the Titanic Disaster' https://www.encyclopedia-titanica.org/a-night-to-forget-rene-harris-and-the-titanic-disaster.html
141. *On a Sea of Glass* (2012), Amberley Publishing, p.163

Endnotes

142. *Bureau County Republican*, 2 May 1912
143. *Daily Herald*, 29 April 1912, courtesy of *Titanic: The Homecoming: Tales From The Lapland*, by Dr Paul Lee (2020)
144. 'United States Senate Hearings into the Sinking of the RMS Titanic' (1912), Day 14, 4 May 1912, testimony of Harold Bride
145. *The New York Times*, 19 April 1912, statement by Harold Bride
146. *Somerset County Gazette*, 16 April 2012
147. *Hampshire Independent*, 4 May 1912, courtesy of *Titanic: The Homecoming: Tales From The Lapland*, by Dr Paul Lee (2020).
148. *Sinking of the Titanic Memorial Edition Thrilling Stories Told By Survivors*, by Jay Henry Mowbray, The Minter Company, Harrisburg, Pa, (1912)
149. 'The Loss of the Titanic' – An address by Washington Dodge to San Francisco's Commonwealth Club, *On Board RMS Titanic – Memories of the Maiden Voyage*, by George Behe (2012), The History Press
150. 'United States Senate Hearings into the Sinking of the RMS Titanic' (1912), Day 7, April 25 1912, testimony of Samuel Hemming
151. *Daily Mail*, 30 April 1912, courtesy of 'Titanic: The Homecoming: Tales From The Lapland' by Dr Paul Lee (2020)
152. *The New York Herald*, 19 April 1912
153. *Western Daily Mercury*, 29 April 1912 courtesy of 'Titanic: The Homecoming: Tales From The Lapland' by Dr Paul Lee (2020)
154. 'British Wreck Commissioner's Inquiry' (1912), Day 9, 16 May 1912, testimony of Edward Brown
155. *Daily Sketch*, 29 April 1912 quoted in *On a Sea of Glass* (2012), Amberley Publishing, p.325
156. British Board of Trade Inquiry disposition, quoted in *On a Sea of Glass* (2012), Amberley Publishing, p.326
157. *Express and Echo* (Exeter) 29 April 1912, courtesy of *Titanic: The Homecoming: Tales From The Lapland*, by Dr Paul Lee (2020). Lee's book also notes that the *Daily Chronicle* of the same date described this unidentified steward as 'in attendance on the millionaires all the time', which would make him a first class steward.
158. *Daily Express*, 29 April 1912, courtesy of *Titanic: The Homecoming: Tales From The Lapland*, by Dr Paul Lee (2020)
159. *The Man Who Sank the Titanic?* by Gary Cooper, Witan Books, (1992) pp.136, 138
160. *National Magazine*, October 1912 *On Board RMS Titanic – Memories of the Maiden Voyage*, by George Behe (2012), The History Press
161. *The Titanic: End of a Dream*, by Wyn Craig Wade (1992), Penguin
162. 'How the Wireless Call Came,' *The New York Times*, 19 April 1912
163. For a detailed examination of the history of ship captains going down with their ships and in some cases committing suicide prior to the *Titanic* disaster, 'The Captain Goes Down with the Ship' https://titanicofficers.com/article_40.html
164. *The Southern Daily Echo*, 19 April 1912 (courtesy of the Southampton Local History archive)
165. 'When *Titanic* sank in 1912, P-D reporter Carlos Hurd landed the story of a lifetime,' by Tim O'Neil *St. Louis Post-Dispatch* 15 April 2023 https://www.stltoday.com/news/archives/when-titanic-sank-in-1912-p-d-reporter-carlos-hurd-landed-the-story-of-a/article_d9c85a14-ffef-5b71-924f-c3b2e32bff95.html
166. *New York Morning World*, 18 April 1912, quoted in *On a Sea of Glass* (2012), Amberley Publishing, p. 305. *The New York World*, with its morning and

evening editions, was owned by Joseph Pulitzer, who was also the owner of the *St. Louis Post-Dispatch* where Hurd worked.
167. *New York Herald*, 19 April 1912
168. *The New York Times*, 18 April 1912
169. *The New York Times*, 19 April 1912, page 4
170. *The Courier – The Freeman Courier*, Freeman, South Dakota, 2 May 1912, courtesy of George Jacub
171. *Brooklyn Daily Eagle*, 19 April 1912
172. Ibid.
173. *Worcester Evening Gazette*, 20 April 1912
174. *Washington Times*, 19 April 1912
175. *On a Sea of Glass* (2012), Amberley Publishing, p. 330
176. *New York Herald*, 19 April 1912
177. *Discretions and Indiscretions* by Lady Duff Gordon (1932) references Captain Smith being drunk, the first officer shooting himself and a stampede of first class passengers trampling women and children and then added: 'I need not say how false these rumours were ... the memory of Captain Smith has been too abundantly established as a sailor and a gentleman to need any comment by me.' (pp. 167-168). Courtesy of Gregg Jasper.
178. Personal account published in the 11 May 1997 edition of *Main Line Life* (excerpts also appeared in Paul Quinn's book *Dusk to Dawn*), and also partly quoted in Bill Wormstedt's website: https://www.wormstedt.com/Titanic/shots/shots.htm
179. *The Daily Mirror*, 19 April 1912, page 2
180. *Chicago Daily Journal*, 24 April 1912
181. For a list of these accounts: https://www.williammurdoch.net/mystery02_witnesses_overview.html – Also: https://www.wormstedt.com/Titanic/shots/shots.htm
182. '107 #82: 'First Officer Murdoch shot one or two passengers before shooting himself' https://timmaltin.com/2019/05/03/murdoch-shot-himself/
183. *The Daily Mirror*, 20 April 1912
184. *Daily Mirror*, 20 April 1912 as quoted in 'Titanic from Rare Historical Reports' by Peter Boyd-Smith (1998), Steamship Publications
185. 'The End of the Titanic' *Daily Mirror*, 20 April 1912, 'How the Titanic Heroes Went to their Doom' *Daily Sketch*, 20 April 1912.
186. *The New York Times*, 20 April 1912 quoted in *On a Sea of Glass* (2012), Amberley Publishing, p. 324
187. *The Times* (London) 20 April 1912
188. *The Daily Mail*, 20 April 1912 and quoted in 'Titanic from Rare Historical Reports' by Peter Boyd-Smith (1998), Steamship Publications
189. *Chicago Examiner*, 19 April 1912
190. *The New York Times*, 20 April 1912
191. *Aberdeen Daily Journal*, 29 April 1912 (courtesy of Gavin Krom)
192. *A Night to Remember*, by Walter Lord (1955), R & W Holt
193. *The New York Times*, 21 April 1912
194. 'Women and Children First!' by Ben Johnson https://www.historic-uk.com/CultureUK/Women-Children-First/
195. *Staffordshire Sentinel* 24 April 1913
196. *Chicago Tribune*, 18 April 1912, p. 4
197. The story was in the form of a long letter sent to London's *Daily Telegraph* in 1912 and reprinted in *The Daily News* (Perth, Australia) 12 June 1912, p.6, courtesy of Gary Cooper, ('Voyage,' The Official Journal of Titanic International Society, issue 94, winter 2015–16)

198. *The Evening Journal*, 19 April 1912, courtesy of Mike Poirier
199. 'The Transatlantic Captains', *Harper's Monthly Magazine*, London, 1886. First Edition.
200. *The Chicago Daily Tribue*, 19 April 1912 quoted in *On a Sea of Glass* (2012), Amberley Publishing, p. 327
201. *The Springfield Union*, 20 April 1912, courtesy of Mike Poirier
202. *Peterson Morning Call*, 23 April 1912
203. *The Truth About The Titanic* by Archibald Gracie IV (1913), p. 206
204. 'United States Senate Hearings into the Sinking of the RMS Titanic' (1912), Day 9, 27 April 1912, testimony of Frederick D. Ray
205. James Arthur Paintin biography, *Encyclopedia Titanica*, https://www.encyclopedia-titanica.org/titanic-victim/james-arthur-paintin.html
206. *The New York Herald*, 19 April 1912
207. *Washington Times*, April 19, 1912, quoted in *On a Sea of Glass* (2012), Amberley Publishing, p. 315
208. For more information on Robert Daniel's account, *Encyclopedia Titanica* article 'A Titanic Mystery: Exploring the Escape of Robert W. Daniel...', by Randy Bryan Bigham, Richard Edwards and Brandon Whited (https://www.encyclopedia-titanica.org/titanic-mystery-exploring-escape-robert-daniel.html)
209. 1912 Titanic memorial book, Mellors and Bankworth, courtesy of Robert L.Bracken/*Encyclopedia Titanica* https://www.encyclopedia-titanica.org/william-mellors.html
210. *Somerset County Gazette*, 16 April 2012
211. *New York Times*, 20 April, 1912:
212. 'United States Senate Hearings into the Sinking of the RMS Titanic' (1912), Day 14, 4 May 1912, testimony of Harold S. Bride
213. 'United States Senate Hearings into the Sinking of the RMS Titanic' (1912), Day 10, 29 April 1912, testimony of Harold S. Bride
214. *The Truth About the Titanic*, by Colonel Archibald Gracie IV (1913) p.60
215. *The Daily Sketch*, 20 April 1912
216. From a quote by steward Alexander Littlejohn, a friend of Browns, in *The Weekley Telegraph*, May 10, 1912, referenced in *On a Sea of Glass* (2012), Amberley Publishing, p.325
217. *Chicago Examiner*, 19 April 1912
218. *The Globe*, 29 April 1912
219. *The Man Who Sank the Titanic?* by Gary Cooper (1992) Witan Books p.135
220. *Brooklyn Daily Eagle*, 19 April 1912
221. *The Daily Sketch*, 20 April 1912, also *The Daily Mirror* 20 April 1912
222. *The Man Who Sank the Titanic?* by Gary Cooper (1992) Witan Books p.135
223. *Daily Enterprise*, 20 April 1912
224. *Western Daily Mercury*, April 29 1912, courtesy of Ioannis Georgiou and Gavin Krom
225. '*On a Sea of Glass* Fitch (2012), Amberley Publishing, p.323, also courtesy of 'Belfast's Own' by Stephen Cameron.
226. *Atlantic City Daily Press*, 23 April, 1912, courtesy of George Behe
227. *Gosport and County Journal*, 16 May 1912, courtesy of Titanic: The Homecoming: Tales From The Lapland by Dr Paul Lee (2020)
228. *Chicago Daily Tribune*, 19 April 1912, quoted in *On a Sea of Glass* (2012), Amberley Publishing, p.333
229. *The Globe*, 29 April 1912
230. *Hampshire Independent*, 2 May 1912 courtesy of Gavin Krom, also quoted in *Titanic: The Homecoming: Tales From The Lapland* by Dr Paul Lee (2020)

231. *The Truth About The Titanic* by Archibald Gracie IV (1913), pp. 89-90
232. There are several other accounts that could refer to Smith but cannot definitely be identified as him. For example, third class passengers Edward Dorking and Eugene Daly spoke of an unidentified man at collapsible B who died. Dorking said he wore an officer's uniform, while Daly said that when they refused a man entry as they would all go down, his reply was 'God Bless You. Goodbye.' For more information on these accounts, *On a Sea of Glass* (2012), Amberley Publishing, p. 334
233. Undated letter to Walter Lord, courtesy of Paul Lee, http://www.paullee.com/titanic/whurst.html
234. *A Night to Remember* by Walter Lord (1955), R & W Holt, pp. 117-118
235. 'Miscellaneous Southampton Council interviews with relatives of survivors' courtesy of Paul Lee, http://www.paullee.com/titanic/index.php
236. *Daily Telegraph* 29 April 1912, courtesy of *Titanic: The Homecoming: Tales from The Lapland* by Dr Paul Lee (2020)
237. *The Sinking of the SS Titanic April 14–15, 1912*, by Jack Thayer
238. *The New York Evening World*, 20 April 1912
239. *Oxfordshire Weekly News*, 1 May 1912, also *Daily Mail*, 29 April 1912
240. *Washington Post Semi-Monthly Magazine*, 26 May 1912, *On Board RMS Titanic – Memories of the Maiden Voyage*, by George Behe (2012), The History Press
241. *New York Herald*, 20 April 1912 quoted in *On a Sea of Glass* (2012), Amberley Publishing, p. 332
242. *Chicago Examiner*, 19 April 1912
243. *Chicago Tribune*, 20 April 1912
244. *The Times* (London) 29 April 1912 (courtesy of Gavin Krom).
245. *The New York Times*, 19 April 1912 quoted in '*On a Sea of Glass* (2012), Amberley Publishing, p. 332
246. *The Times* (London), 29 April 1912
247. *Elmira Star Gazette*, 20 April 1912
248. *Yorkshire Post*, 23 April 1912
249. *The Western Daily Mercury* 29 April 1912 (courtesy of Tad Fitch and Bill Wormstedt, 'Shots in the Dark' https://www.wormstedt.com/Titanic/shots/shots.htm)
250. *The Daily Sketch*, 30 April 1912 (courtesy of Tad Fitch and Bill Wormstedt, 'Shots in the Dark' https://www.wormstedt.com/Titanic/shots/shots.htm)
251. *Brooklyn Daily Eagle*, 19 April 1912
252. 'Captain's Last Act' *Daily Express*, 20 April 1912
253. *Sheffield Evening Telegraph*, 22 April 1912
254. *Washington Herald*, 21 April 1912
255. *New York Herald* 19 April 1912, quoted in *On a Sea of Glass* (2012), Amberley Publishing, p. 331
256. *Western Morning News*, 29 April 1912 (courtesy of Gavin Krom)
257. Letter written by Elizabeth Nye on board the *Carpathia* to her parents dated 16 April 1912, *On Board RMS Titanic – Memories of the Maiden Voyage*, by George Behe (2012), The History Press
258. *Folkestone Herald*, 4 May 1912
259. *New York Herald* 20 April 1912, quoted in *On a Sea of Glass* (2012), Amberley Publishing, p.333
260. *Western Times*, 30 April, 1912
261. *Western Morning News*, 29 April 1912
262. The details of 'Steward Charles Collins' and also 'Cyril Handy''s account do not align with what other eyewitnesses stated. This is discussed in further detail in *On a Sea of Glass* (2012), Amberley Publishing, p.333

Endnotes

263. *Titanic, 100th Anniversary Edition, A Night Remembered*, 2011, by Stephanie Barczewski, p171
264. *The New York Times*, 19 April 1912
265. For example, this reference can be found in the *Encyclopedia Titanica* online biography (https://www.encyclopedia-titanica.org/titanic-victim/alma-cornelia-palsson.html)
266. *The Culver Citizen*, Indiana, 13 March 1913, (courtesy of Mike Poirer)
267. *The Sheffield Daily Telegraph*, 30 April 1912
268. *The Truth About The Titanic* by Archibald Gracie IV (1913) p.95
269. *On a Sea of Glass* (2012), Amberley Publishing, p.335
270. *Titanic Captain*, by G.J. Cooper (2011), The History Press
271. *The Deathless Story of the Titanic: Complete Narrative With Many Illustrations* (1912) by Philip Gibb

Chapter Four: 'In the Hands of the Evil One'

1. *Washington Times*, 17 April 1912
2. *The New York Times*, 19 April 1912
3. *Star Tribune*, 17 April 1912
4. *Chorley Guardian*, 18 July, 1958
5. *The Daily Record*, 24 April, 1912 (courtesy of Paul Lee)
6. *The Southern Daily Echo*, 18 April 1912, courtesy of the Southampton Local History archive
7. *The Daily Record*, 24 April, 1912 (courtesy of Paul Lee)
8. *The Southern Daily Echo*, 19 April 1912, courtesy of the Southampton Local History archive. Incidentally, Mayor Henry Bowyer was the brother of Trinity House harbour pilot George Bowyer, who was at the helm during both the *Olympic-Hawke* collision and the *Titanic* near collision with the *New York*.
9. All figures based on the Purchasing Power Calculator at measuringworth.com dated July 2023.
10. G.W. Blunt White Library, Mystic Seaport, Mystic Connecticut, USA
11. *The New York Times*, 19 April 1912
12. 'Captains of Atlantic Liners' by Alfred T. Story, *Strand Magazine*, London Vol. 14, Iss. 80 (Aug 1897), 201–208
13. G.W. Blunt White Library, Mystic Seaport, Mystic Connecticut, USA
14. Lawrence Beesley's letter to the editor, *The New York Times*, 29 April 1912
15. *The Titanic Disaster of a Century*, by Wyn Craig Wade (2012), Skyhorse
16. *Titanic Lives: Migrants and Millionaires, Conmen and Crew*, by Richard Davenport-Hines (2012), Harper Press, p.343
17. 'United States Senate Hearings into the Sinking of the RMS Titanic' (1912), testimony of Imanita Shelley, in the form of an affidavit
18. *Titanic and Other Ships*, by Charles Herbert Lightoller (1935), Ivor, Nicholson and Watson
19. 'United States Senate Hearings into the Sinking of the RMS Titanic' (1912), Day 5, 24 April 1912, testimony of Charles H. Lightoller
20. *Berkshire Evening Eagle*, 22 April, 1912 'On Board RMS Titanic – Memories of the Maiden Voyage' by George Behe (2012), The History Press
21. *Washington Times*, 24 April 1912.
22. 'United States Senate Hearings into the Sinking of the RMS Titanic' (1912), Day 4, 23 April 1912, testimony of Herbert J. Pitman also 23 April 1912 newspaper account 'Third Officer and Look Out of Titanic Tell of Sinking of the Great Ship,' https://strangeago.com/2017/07/14/third-officer-look-titanic-tell-sinking-great-ship/

23. 'United States Senate Hearings into the Sinking of the RMS Titanic' (1912), Day 5, 24 April 1912, testimony of Harold G. Lowe
24. 'United States Senate Hearings into the Sinking of the RMS Titanic' (1912), Day 15, 9 May 1912, testimony of Harold G. Lowe
25. 'United States Senate Hearings into the Sinking of the RMS Titanic' (1912), speech of Senator William Alden Smith
26. Reprinted by the *Evening Star* (Washington, DC) on 23 April 1912, and the *Washington Post* on 24 April 1912. Quoted in *Titanic: Triumph and Tragedy* by John P Eaton and Charles A. Haas (1995), W.W. Norton & Company, p.223.
27. *Shipping Gazette and Lloyd's List*, 7 August 1912.
28. *Titanic and Other Ships*, by Charles Herbert Lightoller (1935), Ivor, Nicholson and Watson
29. British Inquiry, The Official Transcript of the British Inquiry into the sinking of the RMS Titanic May 2-July 3, 1912 p. 786
30. 'British Wreck Commissioner's Inquiry' (1912), Day 12, 21 May 1912, testimony of Charles H. Lightoller
31. *The Other Side of the Night, The Carpathia, the Californian, and the Night the Titanic Was Lost*, by Daniel Allen Butler, (2009), p.187
32. A special thanks to Gary Cooper and his friend Ernie Luck for correcting my initial transcription error in which I thought Eleanor was referring to Captain 'Gates' and concluded she was likely referencing Horatio Gates (1728–1806), a British-born American general whose victory in the War of Independence later became a matter of debate and even a board of inquiry, although charges were never pressed. Smith's waxwork in Madame Tussauds was placed next to Robert Scott, in a nod to the heroic nature of their deaths.
33. 'British Wreck Commissioner's Inquiry' (1912), Final Report
34. 'British Wreck Commissioner's Inquiry' (1912), Day 21, 11 June 1912, testimony of Sir Walter J. Howell
35. 'British Wreck Commissioner's Inquiry' (1912), Final Report
36. 'British Wreck Commissioner's Inquiry' (1912), p.1658
37. 'British Wreck Commissioner's Inquiry' (1912), Day 27, 19 June 1912, testimony of John Pritchard
38. 'British Wreck Commissioner's Inquiry' (1912), Day 27, 19 June 1912, testimony of Hugh Young
39. 'British Wreck Commissioner's Inquiry' (1912), Day 27, 19 June 1912, testimony of William Stewart
40. 'British Wreck Commissioner's Inquiry' (1912), Day 27, 19 June 1912, testimony of John A. Fairfull
41. 'British Wreck Commissioner's Inquiry' (1912), Day 27, 19 June 1912, testimony of Andrew Braes
42. 'British Wreck Commissioner's Inquiry' (1912), Day 21, 11 June 1912, testimony of Frederick Passow
43. 'British Wreck Commissioner's Inquiry' (1912), Day 21, 11 June 1912, testimony of Betram F. Hayes
44. 'British Wreck Commissioner's Inquiry' (1912), Day 21, 11 June 1912, testimony of Benjamin Steele p
45. 'British Wreck Commissioner's Inquiry' (1912), Day 24, 14 June 1912, testimony of Richard O. Jones
46. 'British Wreck Commissioner's Inquiry' (1912), Day 24, 14 June 1912, testimony of Edwin G. Cannons
47. 'British Wreck Commissioner's Inquiry' (1912), Day 24, 14 June 1912, testimony of John B. Ranson

48. 'Ryan versus The White Star Line,' 18 April 2012, BBC News https://www.bbc.co.uk/news/uk-northern-ireland-17612629
49. The Third Titanic Inquiry – Ryan v. OSNC, Transcript of Precis Law Report, by Senan Molony, *Encyclopedia Titanica* https://www.encyclopedia-titanica.org/ryan-v-osnc.html
50. It is worth noting that the conclusion included criticism regarding the alleged lack of binoculars, despite rather detailed clarification that binoculars would not have been used aboard *Titanic* to spot an iceberg. This reveals that rather than focusing on actual causes, the case was more intent on supplying a guilty verdict to satisfy the issue of ticket conditions and subsequent damages.
51. *Daily News*, 14 May 1912
52. *Daily News*, 20 May 1912
53. *Daily News*, 22 May 1912
54. *Daily News*, 25 May 1912
55. Limitation of Liability Hearings, testimony of William T. Turner

Chapter Five: 'A Deathless Crown at Duty's Post'

1. Fatality report for body 157, Records of the Medical Examiner for the City of Halifax and Town of Dartmouth, RG 41, Series C, Vols. 75, 76 & 76A, held at the Nova Scotia Archives
2. *Press Democrat*, Santa Rosa, California, Volume XXXIX, Number 170, Sunday Morning, 21 July 1912
3. *The Honolulu Star-Bulletin* 3 August 1912, p. 3
4. *The Washington Herald*, 23 July 1912
5. *The Honolulu Star-Bulletin* 3 August 1912, p. 3
6. *The Mahoning Dispatch* 23 January 1914, p. 5
7. 1 August 1912, Library of Congress, *Encyclopedia Titanica*, https://www.encyclopedia-titanica.org/doubt-story-of-captain-pryal-19138.html
8. *There Are No Dead*, Sophie Radford de Meissner (1912)
9. *The Man Who Sank the Titanic?* by Gary Cooper (1992) Witan Books p. 137
10. *Life* magazine, 12 February 1940, p. 95, by Charles Wilson, New York
11. *The Weekly World News*, 10 September 1991
12. The accounts of Captain Smith's ghost appeared in the article 'Ghostly Tales from the Titanic' by Jason D. Tiller on Encyclopedia Titanica, published 27 May 2023 (https://www.encyclopedia-titanica.org/ghostly-tales-from-the-titanic.html). Tiller's reference for the story is an account contained in an article by Jo Harrington on Wizzley, a writer's community, entitled 'Titanic Ghosts, Curses and Premonitions'. Harrington, who describes herself as a 'historian, pagan, gamer and geek' supplies no sources in the account of Eleanor seeing her husband's 'ghost'. https://wizzley.com/titanic-ghosts/
13. *The Mirror*, 18 November 2018, https://www.mirror.co.uk/news/weird-news/haunted-mirror-possessed-ghost-titanic-13608741
14. *Skeptical Inquirer*, A Closer Look: The Provenance of Captain Smith's 'Haunted' Mirror 11 February 2019, by Kenny Biddle, https://skepticalinquirer.org/exclusive/the-provenance-of-captain-smithrsquos-lsquohauntedrsquo-mirror/
15. *The Evening Standard*, Ogden City, Utah, 28 August 1912, courtesy *Encyclopedia Titanica* https://www.encyclopedia-titanica.org/indifferent-to-fate-since-fathers-death-19149.html
16. *Staffordshire Sentinel*, 22 April 1912, courtesy of Clive Sweetingham/British Titanic Society
17. *The Southern Daily Echo*, 20 April 1912 (courtesy of the Southampton Local History archive).
18. *Hampshire Advertiser*, 20 April 1912.

19. 'Titanic Memorial Window' British Titanic Society, https://www.britishtitanicsociety.com/titanic-memorial-window/
20. 'Captain E. J. Smith Memorial – A souvenir of the unveiling of the memorial, July 29th, 1914' (1914)
21. *The Sunday Times*, 21 April 1912
22. *The Daily Record*, 24 April 1912 (courtesy of Paul Lee)
23. *Larne Times*, 4 May 1912
24. https://api.parliament.uk/historic-hansard/commons/1912/oct/07/lord-merseys-report (Contains Parliamentary information licensed under the Open Parliament Licence v3.0.)
25. *The Brooklyn Daily Eagle*, 17 April 1912
26. *The Southern Daily Echo*, 19 April 1912 (courtesy of the Southampton Local History archive)
27. *The Man Who Sank the Titanic?* by Gary Cooper (1992) Witan Books p.39
28. *The Southern Daily Echo*, 20 April 1912 (courtesy of the Southampton Local History archive); transcription assistance Gary Cooper, Joe Baldwin and Gregg Jasper.
29. *The Southern Daily Echo*, 22 April 1912 (courtesy of the Southampton Local History archive, with transcription assistance from Joe Baldwin, Archives and Local Studies Assistant).
30. *The Southern Daily Echo*, 23 April 1912 (courtesy of the Southampton Local History archive)
31. *The Times* (London) 23 April 1912
32. The Titanic Crew Memorial was originally a drinking fountain unveiled in 1915 in the Southampton Common, not far from the former Smith house in Winn Road. It was later moved to within the grounds of the city's Holyrood Church in 1972, obscuring it even further from public view.
33. *The Southern Daily Echo*, 15 April 1913 (courtesy of the Southampton Local History archive). The excerpt is from the book *In Memoriam – The Titanic Disaster* by H. Rea Woodman, dated February 1913 and which can be read in full online at https://openlibrary.org/works/OL1521484W/In_Memoriam
34. In a letter written on board the Cunard RMS *Aquitania*, June 1914, reprinted in 'Captain E. J. Smith Memorial – A souvenir of the unveiling of the memorial, July 29th, 1914' (1914).
35. *The Hawaiian Gazette*, 23 April 1912, page 5
36. *British Weekly*, reprinted in 'Captain E. J. Smith Memorial – A souvenir of the unveiling of the memorial, July 29th, 1914' (1914)
37. *Oakland Tribune*, 19 April 1912 (courtesy of Mike Poirer).
38. *The Daily Sketch*, 25 April 1912
39. 'Captain E. J. Smith Memorial – A souvenir of the unveiling of the memorial, July 29th, 1914' (1914)
40. *Staffordshire Sentinel* 16 April 1912
41. *Chicago Daily Tribune*, 17 April 1912 (courtesy of Mike Poirer). Mullet's account needs to be treated with caution as it contains details that do not align with what we know about Captain Smith. For example, Mullet states that he was first mate and Smith third mate on a ship named the *Black Ball*, for which there is no record. He also says that Smith was made captain of the *Oceanic*, for which there is also no record.
42. *Brisbane Courier*, 24 April 1912 (courtesy of Clive Sweetingham, British Titanic Society)
43. *Oakland Tribune*, 19 April 1912 (courtesy of Mike Poirer)
44. *The Examiner* (Launceston, Tasmania) 26 April 1912 courtesy https://www.encyclopedia-titanica.org/officers-of-the-titanic-19334.html
45. 'Captain E. J. Smith – Some Characteristics' *Darling Downs Gazette*, 1 May 1912 (courtesy of Clive Sweetingham, British Titanic Society).

Endnotes

46. Ibid.
47. 'The Man Who Sank the Titanic? by Gary Cooper (1992) Witan Books p.39
48. *Titanic and Other Ships*, by Charles Herbert Lightoller (1935), Ivor, Nicholson and Watson
49. Third Officer Henry Cater is frequently misidentified as Second Officer Lightoller in the *Olympic* group photograph with Captain Smith, and that is often mislabelled as *Titanic*. Cater is standing second from the left, next to Purser McElroy.
50. *Manawatu Times*, 20 April 1912, courtesy of Inger Sheil
51. *Nelson Evening Mail*, 20 April 1912, courtesy of Inger Sheil
52. *Western Daily Mercury*, 30 April 1912
53. *The Southern Daily Echo*, 29 April 1931 (courtesy of the Southampton Local History archive).
54. *The Daily Record*, 24 April 1912 (courtesy of Paul Lee)
55. *Staffordshire Sentinel*, 2 May 1912
56. *Staffordshire Sentinel*, 6 May 1912
57. *The Times* (London)v 30 April 1912
58. *Pittsburgh Daily Post*, 29 April 1912
59. *The Times* (London), 7 May 1912
60. *Daily Sketch*, 7 May 1912
61. *London Evening Standard* 6 – 7 May 1912
62. *Lloyd's Weekly Newspaper* 12 May 1912
63. *The Times* (London) 27 May, 1912
64. *The Times* (London) 28 May, 1912
65. "Captain smith was Tussauds Exhibit" *Encyclopedia Titanica* https://www.encyclopedia-titanica.org/captain- smith-was-tussauds-exhibit.html
66. *Manchester Guardian*, 19 March 1925
67. For more information on the fire check this article: "The Day Madame Tussauds Caught Fire And Most Of The Waxworks Melted" Londonist https://londonist.com/london/history/the-day-madame-tussauds-caught-fire-and- most-of-the-statues-melted
68. *Staffordshire Sentinel* 17 April 1912
69. *Titanic Captain*, by G.J. Cooper (2011), The History Press. p. 222
70. Using the retail price index calculator on measuringworth.com. The Bank of England inflation calculator estimates £21 in 1912 as £1985 in 2023 (www.bankofengland.co.uk/monetary-policy/inflation/inflation-calculator)
71. *Staffordshire Advertiser*, 1 February 1913
72. *Staffordshire Sentinel*, 16 April 1913
73. *Staffordshire Sentinel*, 29 May 1913
74. *Staffordshire Sentinel*, 24 April 1913
75. Ibid.
76. Ibid.
77. Ibid.
78. Ibid.
79. *Titanic Captain*, by G.J. Cooper (2011), The History Press. p. 223
80. *Master of the Titanic: The Career of Captain Ted Smith*, by Pat Lacey (1996), Book Guild. The anecdote was told to Steve Rigby of the British Titanic Society after giving a talk at a senior citizens association in Warrington.
81. 'Lichfield researchers debunk "myth" of city's Titanic captain statue' BusinessLive, 30 May 2013 https://www.business-live.co.uk/economic-development/lichfield-researchers-debunk-myth-citys-3912833
82. 'Captain E. J. Smith Memorial – A souvenir of the unveiling of the memorial, July 29th, 1914' (1914).
83. *Titanic Captain*, by G.J. Cooper (2011), The History Press. p.248, end note 10

84. 'Captain E. J. Smith Memorial – A souvenir of the unveiling of the memorial, July 29th, 1914' (1914).
85. Letter to the Editor, *Lichfield Mercury*, 5 June 1914
86. Letter to the Editor, *Lichfield Mercury*, 8 June 1914
87. *Lichfield Mercury*, 19 June 1914
88. *Titanic Captain*, by G.J. Cooper (2011), The History Press. p.226
89. *Lichfield Mercury*, 19 June 1914
90. Titanic Memorials https://www.titanic.memorial/post/memorial/captain+smith+statue+lichfield/
91. *Birmingham Weekly Mercury*, 8 April 1990
92. *Birmingham Weekly Mercury* 31 July 1977 and 29 July 1984
93. *Titanic Captain*, by G.J. Cooper (2011), The History Press. p.233
94. *Staffordshire Advertiser* 1 August 1914
95. 'Captain E. J. Smith Memorial – A souvenir of the unveiling of the memorial, July 29th, 1914' (1914)
96. Ibid.
97. *Staffordshire Advertiser* 1 August 1914
98. 'Captain E. J. Smith Memorial – A souvenir of the unveiling of the memorial, July 29th, 1914' (1914).
99. *The Walsall Advertiser* 1 August 1914
100. David J. Woodnall, 'A Lichfield Memorial to the *Titanic* Captain' *Lichfield Mercury*, 7 November 1958, courtesy of *'Titanic, 100th Anniversary Edition, A Night Remembered*, by Stephanie Barczewski (2011)
101. *The Lichfield Mercury*, 1 November, 1985
102. *The Tamworth Herald*, 31 March 1989
103. *The Lichfield Mercury*, 31 March 1989
104. *The Lichfield Mercury*, 7 April 1989
105. BBC news, 'Statue of Captain Smith of the Titanic is restored,' 28 July 2010, http://news.bbc.co.uk/local/stoke/hi/people_and_places/history/newsid_8864000/8864652.stm
106. BBC news 'Titanic Captain Smith statue Hanley move campaign' 26 August 2011 https://www.bbc.co.uk/news/uk-england-stoke-staffordshire-14678152
107. 'Titanic battle rages over statue', *The Guardian* 15 October 1985
108. *Titanic, 100th Anniversary Edition, A Night Remembered*, by Stephanie Barczewski, (2011) pp. 181-182
109. *Business Live*, 'Lichfield researchers debunk 'myth' of city's Titanic captain statue,' 6 April 2012 https://www.business-live.co.uk/economic-development/lichfield-researchers-debunk-myth-citys-3912833
110. *Birmingham Mail*, 16 April 2012 https://www.birminghammail.co.uk/news/local-news/a-staffordshire-park-fell-silent-in-a-moving-183229
111. Lichfield Live, 19 April 2012 https://lichfieldlive.co.uk/2012/04/19/lichfield-service-rounds-off-a-week-of-events-to-mark-100th-anniversary-of-titanics-sinking/
112. *Southern Evening Echo*, 14 April 1962, thanks to 'Titanic Victims and Survivors Remembered: A new index of death notices and in memoriams in Southampton local newspapers' by Veronica Green, Southampton Central Library (2016)

Chapter Six: London Life
1. *Southampton Times and Hampshire Press*, 20 April 1912
2. *The Worlds and I* by Ella Wheeler Wilcox (1918), courtesy of Mike Poirier
3. BBC news, 'Southampton's lost Titanic generation', 10 April 2012, https://www.bbc.co.uk/news/uk-england-hampshire-17535757

Endnotes

4. VFM 194, Manuscripts Collection, G.W. Blunt White Library, Mystic Seaport Museum, Inc., Mystic Connecticut, USA
5. Courtesy of *The Titanic and the City of Widows it left Behind*, Julie Cook, (2020), Pen & Sword Ltd, and *Titanic from Rare Historical Reports* by Peter Boyd-Smith (1998), Steamship Publications
6. According to calculators on https://measuringworth.com/
7. *The Daily Telegraph* 30 April 1931
8. Sotonopedia, the online A–Z of Southampton's history http://sotonopedia.wikidot.com/page-browse:winn-road
9. *Daily News* (New York) 15 April 1934
10. *Encyclopedia Titanica*, 'Letter re Officer Wilde' from Brian Ticehurst, https://www.encyclopedia-titanica.org/letter-re-officer-wilde.html
11. 'Edward John Smith, Captain on the Titanic' by Linda D Wilding, The Family History Society of Cheshire, https://www.fhsc.org.uk/
12. *Master of the Titanic: The Career of Captain Ted Smith*, by Pat Lacey (1996), Book Guild
13. *The Staffordshire Sentinel*, 24 April 1913
14. Originally it was a house with royal connections. Built circa 1857-1870, its first owner was the Earl of Strathmore and Kinghorne, the father of the Queen Mother and the grandfather of Queen Elizabeth II. In 1909, the house was sold and converted into a hotel.
15. A History of Strathmore Hotel 41 Queen's Gate Gardens, London SW7 5NB https://www.gemhotels.com/hotels-london/strathmore-hotel-history
16. Index Of Ships Listed In 'British Merchant Vessels Lost 1914-1918' Naval-history.net, by Dr Graham Watson, https://www.naval-history.net/WW1NavyBritishShips-Locations10AttackedMNDate.htm
17. 'Captain Edward John Smith of the Titanic' by Kathleen Alice Evans https://www.yumpu.com/en/document/view/56696158/captain-edward-john-smith-of-the-titanic
18. *Daily News* (New York) 15 April 1934 – it states that 'after years, Mrs Smith brought Melville to London, where she met Sidney Russell Cooke, a popular figure in the yachting and hunting worlds and a well known business man.'

Chapter Seven: Cookie

1. Sidney's father, William Russell Cooke, founded Russell-Cooke Solicitors in 1880 along with his brother Sir Henry Paget-Cooke. The firm is still in existence today, listed in the UK top 100 London-based law firms (www.russell-cooke.co.uk).
2. *Women's Suffrage* by Margaret Mary Smith Cook, 1885, Publisher S. Sonnenschein https://openlibrary.org/books/OL7027827M/Women%27s_suffrage
3. *The Isle of Wight County Press*, 31 January 1903.
4. *The Times of London* 23 May 1914
5. *The Times*, 23 May 1914
6. *The Isle of Wight County Press*, 22 February 1913
7. *The Isle of Wight County Press*, 13 September 1913
8. *The Isle of Wight County Press*, 11 October 1913
9. *The Isle of Wight County Press*, 15 November 1913
10. Ibid.
11. *The Isle of Wight County Press*, 23 November 1914
12. *The Isle of Wight County Press*, 18 July 1914
13. *The Isle of Wight County Press*, 11 July 1914
14. That Sidney and Pattie became joint owners is documented in *The county families of the United Kingdom; or, Royal manual of the titled and untitled aristocracy of England, Wales, Scotland, and Ireland* (1920)

15. *Cheltenham Chronicle and Gloucestershire Graphic*, 23 May 1914
16. *The county families of the United Kingdom; or, Royal manual of the titled and untitled aristocracy of England, Wales, Scotland, and Ireland*, 1920
17. *The Western Times*, 27 November 1918
18. *Isle of Wight Observer*, 17 August 1912
19. *The Isle of Wight County Press*, 17 August 1912
20. *The Western Times*, 27 November 1918
21. 'The Post Office Rifles' The Postal Museum, https://www.postalmuseum.org/collections/post-office-rifles/
22. Commonwealth War Graves Commission, Post Office Rifles Cemetery, Festubert https://www.cwgc.org/visit-us/find-cemeteries-memorials/cemetery-details/19101/post-office-rifles-cemetery-festubert/
23. *Gloucestershire Echo*, 5 June 1915
24. *The Isle of Wight County Press*, 5 July 1930
25. *News Chronicle*, 4 July 1930
26. King's College, Register 1797–1925, p. 447 courtesy of Tom Davies, Assistant Archivist, King's College, Cambridge
27. *The county families of the United Kingdom; or, Royal manual of the titled and untitled aristocracy of England, Wales, Scotland, and Ireland* (1920)
28. *The Western Times*, 27 November 1918
29. *Maynard Keynes: An Economist's Biography*, by Donald Moggridge (1992), Routledge
30. National Portrait Gallery, 1916: The Trial of Roger Casement https://www.npg.org.uk/whatson/display/20031/1916-the-trial-of-roger-casement.php
31. *Maynard Keynes: An Economist's Biography*, by Donald Moggridge (1992), Routledge
32. *Memoirs of a City Radical*, by Nicholas Davenport (1974), Willmer Brothers
33. University of Cambridge, Archive Centre, King's College, Cambridge Reference Code: GBR/0272/JMK/PP/45/74, Correspondence from Sydney Russell Cooke to J.M. Keynes, 1913 – 1921, https://archivesearch.lib.cam.ac.uk/repositories/7/archival_objects/286222
34. Ibid.
35. Ibid.
36. Ibid.
37. *Universal Man – The Seven Lives of John Maynard Keynes*, by Richard Davenport-Hines (2015), William Collins, pp. 270, 227, 229
38. *Torquay in the Great War*, by Alex Potter (2015), Pen & Sword Ltd.
39. *The Western Times*, 27 November 1918
40. *The Western Times*, 14 December 1918
41. *The Western Times*, 3 December 1918
42. *The Western Times*, 10 December 1918
43. *The Western Times* 16 December, 1918
44. 'British Parliamentary Election Results, 1918 – 1949' F.W.S Craig, Political Reference Publications, Glasgow, 1949 p. 332
45. *Torquay in the Great War*, by Alex Potter (2015), Pen & Sword Ltd.
46. *The Isle of White Country Press*, 6 September 1919
47. *The Isle of White Country Press*, 7 September 1918
48. *The Isle of White Country Press*, 31 January 1903
49. *The Times* 27 October 1920
50. *The Isle of White Country Press*, 30 October 1920
51. *Maxim Litvinov: A Biography*, by John Holroyd-Doveton (2013). Woodland Publications. p. 200

Endnotes

52. 'Brigadier Oswald Allen Harker (Director 1940-41)' MI5 Security Service website 'Who We Are' https://www.mi5.gov.uk/brigadier-oswald-allen-harker
53. *Enemies Within: Communists, the Cambridge Spies and the Making of Modern Britain*, by Richard Davenport-Hines (2018), William Collins
54. *From Diamond Sculls to Golden Handcuffs*, by Andrew Lycett, (1998), Robert Hale.
55. 'Clare Sheridan: "The nearest thing to a sister that Winston ever had"' by David Stafford, 23 March, 2020, *The Churchill Project*, Hillsdale College https://winstonchurchill.hillsdale.edu/clare-sheridan/
56. *Mayfair to Moscow – Clare Sheridan's Diary* (1921) Boni and Liverlight Publishers
57. 'I Shadowed Kameneff by Clare Sheridan' *Evening Standard*, 25 August 1936
58. *Mayfair to Moscow – Clare Sheridan's Diary* (1921) Boni and Liverlight Publishers, p.33
59. *Mayfair to Moscow – Clare Sheridan's Diary* (1921) p.34
60. *Mayfair to Moscow – Clare Sheridan's Diary* (1921) p.35
61. British Listed Buildings https://britishlistedbuildings.co.uk/101233835-bellcroft-house-newport-and-carisbrooke)
62. Advertisement in *The Sunday Times* (London) 5 November 1944
63. Property deeds information courtesy of Keith Prowse, present owner of 'Bellecroft' and Ian George, whose father lived in Stapler's Road.
64. National Archives, record GBC/1921/RG15/05406/0503/01
65. 'I Shadowed Kameneff by Clare Sheridan' *Evening Standard*, 25 August 1936
66. *Memoirs of a City Radical* by Nicholas Davenport (1974), Willmer Brothers, p.14
67. *Mayfair to Moscow – Clare Sheridan's Diary* (1921) Boni and Liverlight Publishers, p.36
68. 'I Shadowed Kameneff by Clare Sheridan' *Evening Standard*, 25 August 1936
69. *Mayfair to Moscow – Clare Sheridan's Diary* (1921) pp. 37-38
70. 'I Shadowed Kameneff by Clare Sheridan' *Evening Standard*, 25 August 1936
71. *Mayfair to Moscow – Clare Sheridan's Diary* (1921) p.38
72. 'I Shadowed Kameneff by Clare Sheridan' *Evening Standard*, 25 August 1936
73. *Mayfair to Moscow – Clare Sheridan's Diary* (1921 p.39, 44
74. 'I Shadowed Kameneff by Clare Sheridan' *Evening Standard*, 25 August 1936
75. *Mayfair to Moscow – Clare Sheridan's Diary* (1921) p.44
76. *Mayfair to Moscow – Clare Sheridan's Diary* (1921) p.120
77. *Enemies Within: Communists, the Cambridge Spies and the Making of Modern Britain*, by Richard Davenport-Hines (2018), William Collins
78. 'Mayfair to Moscow – Clare Sheridan's Diary' (1921) p. 50
79. *Mayfair to Moscow – Clare Sheridan's Diary* (1921) p. 159
80. 'I Shadowed Kameneff by Clare Sheridan' *Evening Standard*, 25 August 1936
81. *Mayfair to Moscow – Clare Sheridan's Diary* (1921) p. 211
82. *Mayfair to Moscow – Clare Sheridan's Diary* (1921) pp. 214-226
83. 'Clare Sheridan: "The nearest thing to a sister that Winston ever had."' by David Stafford, 23 March 2020, *The Churchill Project*, Hillsdale College https://winstonchurchill.hillsdale.edu/clare-sheridan
84. MI5 Security Service 'Brigadier Oswald Allen Harker (Director 1940-41)' https://www.mi5.gov.uk/brigadier-oswald-allen-harker
85. *Memoirs of a City Radical*, by Nicholas Davenport (1974), Willmer Brothers, p. 128
86. *Memoirs of a City Radical* by Nicholas Davenport (1974), Willmer Brothers, p. 130
87. 'Lillian 'Mona' Maund – A Forgotten MI5 Agent' Stamford Schools, https://www.stamfordschools.org.uk/about-stamford/news/lillian-mona-maund-a-forgotten-mi5-agent/

Chapter Eight: Ambitious and Adventurous

1. *The Times* (London), 28 October 1921 – Bar examination results.
2. *Evening Express* (Liverpool), 9 December 1921
3. *Memoirs of a City Radical*, by Nicholas Davenport (1974), Willmer Brothers, p.15
4. University of Cambridge, Archive Centre, King's College, Cambridge Reference Code: GBR/0272/JMK/PP/45/74, Correspondence from Sydney Russell Cooke to J.M. Keynes, 1913–1921, https://archivesearch.lib.cam.ac.uk/repositories/7/archival_objects/286222
5. *The Times* (London), 8 December 1921
6. Stephen McKenna (novelist) https://en.wikipedia.org/wiki/Stephen_McKenna_(novelist)
7. *The Isle of Wight County Press* 21 January 1922. Transcription assistance provided by Gary Cooper, Inger Sheil and Randy Byran Bigham.
8. *The Times* (London) 19 January 1922
9. *The Evening Express*, 19 January 1922
10. *Ian Fleming: The Man Who Created James Bond*, by Andrew Lycett, (1996), W&N
11. 'Stuart, Sir Campbell Arthur (1885–1972), newspaper manager', Oxford Dictionary of National Biography. Oxford University Press. 2004)
12. *Universal Man – The Seven Lives of John Maynard Keynes*, by Richard Davenport-Hines (2015), William Collins, p.237
13. *Barnaby Rudge*, Chapter 15, by Charles Dickens (1841)
14. *Daily Herald*, 4 July 1930
15. *Enemies Within* by Richard Davenport-Hines (2018), William Collins
16. *Evening Standard*, 3 July 1930
17. *The Times* (London) 29 March 1923
18. *Cheltenham Chronicle and Gloucestershire Graphic*, 4 August 1923
19. *The Isle of White County Press*, 18 August 1923
20. *The Isle of White County Press*, 20 October 1923
21. *Western Morning News*, Plymouth, Devon, 1 December 1923
22. *Universal Man – The Seven Lives of John Maynard Keynes*, by Richard Davenport-Hines (2015), William Collins, p.145
23. Thanks to Celia Pilkington at the Inner Temple archive for helping establish ownership. 12 King's Bench Walk is listed as let by 'E.H. Davenport' 1916–1930. Davenport mentions witnessing the dramatic destruction of a Zeppelin in 1916 above North London, from a view in the Temple Gardens, indicating he was originally living there and sometime later – certainly by the early 1920s – was sub-letting it to Sidney.
24. *From Diamond Sculls to Golden Handcuffs*, by Andrew Lycett, (1998), Robert Hale
25. *Memoirs of a City Radical*, by Nicholas Davenport (1974), Willmer Brothers, pp. 13-14
26. *The Annals of the American Academy of Political and Social Science* Volume 115 Issue 1 (1924)
27. *The Isle of White County Press*, 29 December 1923
28. *Memoirs of a City Radical* by Nicholas Davenport (1974), Willmer Brothers, p. 14
29. *Ian Fleming: The Man Who Created James Bond*, by Andrew Lycett, (1996), W&N
30. *From Diamond Sculls to Golden Handcuffs*, by Andrew Lycett, (1998), Robert Hale.
31. *The World Is Not Enough – A Biography of Ian Fleming*, by Oliver Buckton (2021), Rowman & Littlefield
32. *Memoirs of a City Radical* by Nicholas Davenport (1974), Willmer Brothers, p.15

Endnotes

33. *From Diamond Sculls to Golden Handcuffs*, by Andrew Lycett, (1998), Robert Hale.
34. *The Gloucester Journal*, 16 October 1926.
35. Documents on Australian Foreign Policy, Volume 17: My Dear P.M. – R.G. Casey's Letters to S.M. Bruce, 1924–1929, 76, Wednesday, 14 December 1927, https://wragge.github.io/dfat-documents-web/volumes/volume-17-1923-1929-letters-from-s-m-bruce-to-r-g-casey/76/
36. https://timsherratt.org/
37. Documents on Australian Foreign Policy, Volume 17: 'My Dear P.M. – R.G. Casey's Letters to S.M. Bruce, 1924–1929', 76, Wednesday, 14th December 1927, https://wragge.github.io/dfat-documents-web/volumes/volume-17-1923-1929-letters-from-s-m-bruce-to-r-g-casey/76/ -footnote no.16
38. *Evening Standard*, 3 July 1930
39. *News Chronicle*, 4 July 1930
40. *The Sunday Times* (London), 9 March 924
41. *Hendon & Finchley Times*, 1 October 1926
42. *The Sketch*, 27 January 1926
43. *The Isle of Wight County Press*, 19 June 1926
44. *The Isle of Wight County Press*, 23 October 1926
45. *The Independent*, 6 August 1999
46. *News Chronicle*, 4 July 1930
47. *The Isle of Wight County Press*, 6 August 1927
48. *The Bystander*, 7 December 1927
49. *The Times* (London) 5 July 1930
50. *The Isle of Wight County Press*, 28 July 1928
51. *The Daily Telegraph*, 10 October 1928
52. 'Britain's industrial future: being the report of the Liberal Industrial Inquiry of 1928' by the Liberal Industrial Inquiry
53. *Memoirs of a City Radical* by Nicholas Davenport (1974), Willmer Brothers, p.18
54. *The Isle of Wight County Press*, 23 March 1929
55. Documents on Australian Foreign Policy, Volume 17: 'My Dear P.M. – R.G. Casey's Letters to S.M. Bruce, 1924–1929', 169, Thursday, 24 January 1929, https://wragge.github.io/dfat-documents-web/volumes/volume-17-1923-1929-letters-from-s-m-bruce-to-r-g-casey/169/
56. *The Times* (London) 8 April 1929
57. *The Times* (London) 27 April 1929
58. *From Diamond Sculls to Golden Handcuffs*, by Andrew Lycett, (1998), Robert Hale
59. *The Isle of Wight County Press*, 27 April 1929
60. *The Sketch*, 24 July 1929
61. *Bucks Herald*, 28 June 1929
62. 'The Londoner's Diary' *Evening Standard*, 16 March 1957
63. *The Isle of Wight County Press*, 16 November 1929
64. *The Daily Telegraph*, 4 July 1930
65. *News Chronicle*, 4 July 1930
66. *Hampshire Telegraph*, 15 May 1931
67. *The Observer*, 21 April 1929
68. *The Isle of Wight County Press*, 16 March 1929
69. *The Daily Telegraph*, 9 April 1929
70. *The Isle of Wight County Press*, 16 March 1929
71. *The Daily Telegraph*, 7 May 1930
72. *Daily Telegraph*, 29 May 1930, 30 May 1930.
73. *Western Morning News*, 10 June 1930

74. *The Daily Telegraph*, 19 June 1930
75. *The Daily Telegraph*, 27 June 1930
76. *The Daily Telegraph*, 1 July 1930
77. *The Daily Telegraph*, 4 July 1930
78. Quoted from *Memoirs of a City Radical* (1974) by Nicholas Davenport.
79. *The Daily Telegraph*, 16 January 1930
80. *The Times* (London), 30 January 1930
81. *The Times* (London), 18 July 1930
82. *Northampton Chronicle and Echo*, 10 January 1930
83. *Wiltshire Times and Trowbridge Advertiser*, 7 January 1928
84. *The Courier and Advertiser*, 4 July 1930
85. *The Daily Telegraph*, 10 April 1930
86. *The Daily Telegraph*, 12 April 1930
87. *News Chronicle*, 4 July 1930
88. *The Daily Telegraph*, 4 July 1930
89. *Memoirs of a City Radical* by Nicholas Davenport (1974), Willmer Brothers, pp. 35-36
90. Sir Fisher Wentworth 5th Baronet Dilke's mother was Margaret Mary Smith, who remarried and became Margaret Russell Cooke, Sidney's mother.
91. *Observer On Ranger: During The Races for The America's Cup 1937*.
92. *The Tatler*, 4 June 1930
93. *Evening Standard*, 3 July 1930
94. *Hampshire Advertiser*, 5 July 1930
95. *The Isle of Wight County Press*, 29 June 1930
96. *The Isle of Wight County Press*, 5 July 1930
97. *The Daily Telegraph*, 4 July 1930
98. *The Times* (London), 1 July 1930
99. *Cheltenham Chronicle and Gloucestershire Graphic*, 5 July 1930
100. *News Chronicle*, 4 July 1930
101. *News Chronicle*, 4 July 1930
102. 'Memoirs of a City Radical' by Nicholas Davenport (1974), Willmer Brothers, p. 36
103. *Evening Standard*, 3 July 1930
104. *The Isle of Wight County Press*, 5 July 1930

Chapter Nine: An 'Inexplicable' Shooting

1. Ada May Violet Fancy married Leslie James Hacquoil in 1934, at St Helier. The 1997 death certificate for Ada May Hacquoil states a birth date of 24 November 1906, making her 23 in July 1930.
2. *Liverpool Echo*, 3 July 1930
3. *News Chronicle*, 4 July 1930
4. *The Daily Telegraph*, 5 July 1930
5. *Derby Daily Telegraph*, 3 July 1930
6. *Evening Standard*, 3 July 1930
7. *The Isle of Wight County Press*, 5 July 1930
8. *The Southern Daily Echo*, 3 July 1930 (courtesy of the Southampton Local History archive)
9. *Hampshire Advertiser* 12 July 1930
10. *Yorkshire Evening Post* 3 July 1930
11. *Daily Herald*, 4 July 1930
12. *Evening Standard*, 4 July 1930
13. *Daily Mirror*, 4 July 1930
14. *The Daily Telegraph*, 7 July 1930

Endnotes

15. *The Times* (London), 8 July 1930
16. *News Chronicle*, 4 July 1930
17. *The Bystander*, 9 July 1930
18. *News Chronicle*, 4 July 1930
19. *Evening Standard*, 4 July 1930
20. *The Isle of Wight County Press*, 5 July 1930
21. *The Isle of Wight County Press*, 5 July 1930
22. *Evening Standard*, 4 July 1930
23. *Olympedia*, Hugo Pitman biographical information, https://www.olympedia.org/athletes/37429
24. *The Times* (London) 5 July 1930
25. *Daily Herald*, 5 July 1930
26. *The Times* (London), 5 July 1930
27. *Evening Standard*, 4 July 1930
28. *The Daily Telegraph*, 5 July 1930
29. *The Isle of Wight County Press*, 5 July 1930
30. Ibid.
31. *The Daily Telegraph*, 5 July 1930
32. *The Isle of Wight County Press*, 5 July 1930
33. Ibid.
34. *News Chronicle*, 5 July 1930
35. *The Daily Telegraph*, 5 July 1930
36. *News Chronicle*, 5 July 1930
37. Aftermath, 2021 Accidental Gun Death Statistics in the US, https://www.aftermath.com/content/accidental-shooting-deaths-statistics/
38. *Bangkok Post*, 21 April 2021 https://www.bangkokpost.com/thailand/general/2103143/man-shoots-himself-while-cleaning-rifle
39. *The Isle of Wight County Press*, 5 July 1930
40. The Mandela Effect is a false memory phenomenon in which a large portion of the population remember an event that did not actually happen, named after Fiona Broome, a paranormal researcher who coined the term after discovering a significant number of people at a conference in 2010 shared her false memory that Nelson Mandela had died in prison during the 1980s. (https://www.techtarget.com/whatis/definition/Mandela-effect)
41. 'The Jumpers of '29' by Bennet Lowenthal, *The Washington Post*, 25 October 1927, https://www.washingtonpost.com/archive/opinions/1987/10/25/the-jumpers-of-29/
42. *Churchill's Secret Enemy: MI5 and the Plot to Stop Winston Churchill*, by J.W. Pile (2012)
43. *John Maynard Keynes, 1883–1946*, by Robert Skidelsky, courtesy of Peter 'Art' Lewry and Penny Tull.
44. *News Chronicle/Daily News*, 4 July 1930
45. *The Isle of Wight County Press*, 5 July 1930
46. *Daily Herald*, 4 July 1930
47. *Daily Mirror*, 4 July 1930
48. *The Isle of Wight County Press*, 5 July 1930
49. Ibid.
50. Ibid.
51. *Memoirs of a City Radical* by Nicholas Davenport (1974), Willmer Brothers p.35, 36
52. *News Chronicle*, 4 July 1930
53. *Memoirs of a City Radical* by Nicholas Davenport (1974), Willmer Brothers p.37
54. King's College archive, JMK to Jack Sheppard GBR/0272/JTS/2/112, with special thanks to archivist Tom Davies for assistance with transcription.

55. *Universal Man – The Seven Lives of John Maynard Keynes*, by Richard Davenport-Hines (2015), William Collins, p.238
56. *Enemies Within: Communists, the Cambridge Spies and the Making of Modern Britain*, by Richard Davenport-Hines (2018), William Collins
57. *The Isle of Wight County Press*, 5 July 1930
58. *The World Is Not Enough – A Biography of Ian Fleming*, by Oliver Buckton (2021), Rowman & Littlefield
59. *Ian Fleming: The Man Who Created James Bond*, by Andrew Lycett, (1996), W&N
60. *From Diamond Sculls to Golden Handcuffs*, by Andrew Lycett, (1998), Robert Hale.
61. *Enemies Within: Communists, the Cambridge Spies and the Making of Modern Britain*, by Richard Davenport-Hines (2018), William Collins
62. 'Clare Sheridan: "The nearest thing to a sister that Winston ever had."' by David Stafford, 23 March 2020, *The Churchill Project*, Hillsdale College https://winstonchurchill.hillsdale.edu/clare-sheridan/
63. *Universal Man – The Seven Lives of John Maynard Keynes*, by Richard Davenport-Hines (2015), William Collins, p.238
64. *The Times* (London), 4 July 1930
65. *The Daily Telegraph*, 9 July 1930
66. *The Isle of Wight County Press*, 12 July 1930
67. *The Daily Telegraph*, 10 July 1930 and 11 July 1930
68. *The Isle of Wight County Press*, 12 July 1930, from *The Times* (London), 5 July 1930 obituary.
69. *The Times* (London), 29 January 1931

Chapter Ten: A Penalty, a Fire and a Collision

1. *Western Morning News*, 24 July 1930
2. Bank of England Inflation Calculator https://www.bankofengland.co.uk/monetary-policy/inflation/inflation-calculator
3. *The Isle of Wight County Press*, 13 September 1930
4. *The Daily Telegraph*, 16 September 1930
5. 6 metre Archive, https://6metrearchive.org/boat/priscilla-ii/
6. Classic Six-Metre Newsletter No.10, 26 November 2004, https://6metrearchive.org/, KOLLEGEWIDGWOK YACHT CLUB Blue Hill, Maine, April 2009
7. North American 6 Metre Association http://www.6mrnorthamerica.com/alana.html, 2019 New York Yacht Club Annual Regatta - Classics season kicks off by Bill Lynn 14 Jun 2019 https://www.sail-world.com/news/218618/New-York-Yacht-Club-Annual-Regatta-classics-fleet, https://www.rieffboats.com/alana
8. *The Isle of Wight County Press* 10 January 1931
9. *The Daily Telegraph*, 'London Day By Day' 16 February 1931
10. *Aberdeen Press and Journal* 16 February 1931
11. *The Isle of Wight County Press*, 21 February 1931
12. *The Times* (London), 15 April 1931
13. Electoral Registers 1832–1965, Westminster, Paddington, 1931, courtesy of Norma Williamson.
14. PostalareaW2,www.theundergroundmap.com/article.html?id=1302&item=800
15. *The Daily Telegraph*, 30 April 1931
16. *The Times* (London) 29 April 1931
17. *The Daily Telegraph*, 30 April 1931 p.12
18. *Evening Sentinel*, Stoke-on-Trent, Staffordshire, England, 29 April 1931

Endnotes

19. *The Southern Daily Echo*, 29 April 1931 (courtesy of the Southampton Local History Archive)
20. For a list of all Southampton Mayors: https://www.southampton.gov.uk/media/keglagmp/list-of-current-mayors-at-2022.pdf
21. *The Kensington News and West London Times*, 1 May 1931, *The Scotsman*, 1 May 1931
22. *The Kensington News and West London Times*, 1 May 1931
23. *Evening Standard*, 30 April 1931
24. Brookwood Cemetery, Notable Graves, https://brookwoodcemetery.com/2020/12/02/sir-cosmo-edmund-duff-gordon/
25. The tenancy records for 12 King's Bench Walk show it was subsequently let to a Mr J.A. White on '17/7/30' only a few weeks after Sidney's death. The records also note that Mr White gave notice to quit in May 1931 but died in that same month.
26. *West Sussex Gazette*, 16 July 1931
27. *Portsmouth Evening News*, 3 October 1931
28. *Portsmouth Evening News*, 7 November 1931
29. *Hampshire Advertiser*, 23 July 1932
30. *The Isle Of Wight County Press*, 16 July 1932
31. *The Times* (London), 29 September 1932 and 24 October 1932
32. *The Bystander*, 2 August 1933
33. *Daily News* (New York), 15 April 1934

Chapter Eleven: Aviatrix and a Twin Tragedy

1. Of the 30,000 pilots in the UK in 2023, fewer than five per cent were women. (https://www.bbc.co.uk/news/uk-england-66201917)
2. *The Gloucestershire Echo*, 4 August 1934
3. *The Isle of Wight County Press*, 11 August 1934
4. *Boston Guardian*, 21 May 1932
5. *The Bystander*, 22 March 1933 p.530
6. Trophies Awarded at CFS And Command Competitions http://www.centralflyingschool.org.uk/CFSTrophies1.htm
7. *Citizen*, Gloucestershire, 4 August 1934
8. https://en.wikipedia.org/wiki/Avro_Club_Cadet
9. *The Tatler*, 10 October 1934, had the headline '"Gowfin" at North Berwick'.
10. *The Tatler*, 31 July 1935
11. https://en.wikipedia.org/wiki/De_Havilland_DH.60_Moth
12. Passenger Lists Leaving UK 1890-1960, BT27, National Archives, Britain
13. Christopher Clarkson had a long career in aviation that eventually took him to the US. According to his *New York Times* obituary, he had been educated at Lancing College in Sussex, after which he joined the Royal Air Force in 1924 and became an instructor at the Central Flying School. At some point afterward, and likely around the time he met Mel, he returned to civilian life as a test pilot, winning trophies for aerobatic and cross-Channel air races. During the Second World War he was sent to the US to test aircraft where he received the Air Force Cross. He remained in the States working for the British Embassy, Vickers-Armstrong and British Aircraft Corporation, until retiring in 1965. He died in 1994 aged 92, survived by his wife Evelyn Clark Clarkson and three daughters. https://www.nytimes.com/1994/06/23/obituaries/christopher-clarkson-92-ex-raf-pilot.html)
14. Robert Eagle Fine Art, https://www.roberteaglefineart.co.uk/
15. David Rolt by Alastair Forbes, a memoir accompanying a posthumous exhibition of David Rolt's work in 1986, courtesy of Robert Eagle of Robert Eagle Fine Art.

16. Invaluable, https://www.invaluable.com/auction-lot/david-rolt-1916-1985-527-c-82f7699490
17. Robert Eagle Fine Art, https://www.roberteaglefineart2.co.uk/paintings/0090-lady-wearing-a-blue-jacket-(mel)-rolt-david.html
18. 1939 registration of Bellecroft, 19 Stalpers Road, courtesy of Norma Williamson.
19. *The Isle of Wight County Press*, 5 August 1939
20. 'The Captain's Daughter, Helen Melville Russell-Cooke' by John Pladdys, *The Titanic Commutator*, Volume 17, Number 2, 2nd Quarter, August – October 1993
21. 'Wykehamist War Service Record and Roll of Honour' May 1947, p.182
22. With thanks to the College Archivist, Suzanne Foster, and the Warden and Scholars of Winchester College.
23. John Pladdys, in his article 'The Captain's Daughter, Helen Melville Russell-Cooke' (*The Titanic Commutator*, Volume 17, Number 2, 2nd Quarter, August–October 1993) dated Mel's move to Leafield as the year 1934, the year she obtained her pilot's licence, which is quite feasible. However, she continued to own Bellecroft until 1945 and had a London residence at least until the late 1950s.
24. https://en.wikipedia.org/wiki/Oxford_University_Air_Squadron
25. https://en.wikipedia.org/wiki/Arnold_Scheme
26. 'Wykehamist War Service Record and Roll of Honour' May 1947, p.182
27. Wikipedia entry: https://en.wikipedia.org/wiki/Bristol_Beaufighter
28. *The Bristol Beaufighter, a Comprehensive Guide for the Modeller* by Richard A. Franks, Bedford, UK: SAM Publications, 2002.
29. Letter from Wing Commander to Mrs Cooke dated 24 March 1944.
30. Wings Over Wick, 1939–1945, Torpedo Squadrons, Mr F S Holly, Deganwy, Gwynedd, This was a 1996 project of Hillhead Primary and published in a booklet. Used with permission, thanks to Bill Fernie of caithness.org. http://www.caithness.org/wings/torpedosquadrons/fsholly.htm
31. Winchester College at War https://www.winchestercollegeatwar.com/RollofHonour.aspx?RecID=200&TableName=ta_wwiifactfile&fromSearchPage=true
32. *The Independent*, 3 February 1994, Obituary: The Marquess of Normanby, https://www.independent.co.uk/news/people/obituary-the-marquess-of-normanby-1391556.html
33. *The Tatler and Bystander*, No. 2114, 31 December 1941
34. *The Times* (London), 25 June 1945
35. *The Times* (London), 7 September 1945
36. *Kelly's Handbook to the Titled, Landed and Official Classes*, (1960), p.1595
37. John Phipps Call Papers, admission forms and admission record courtesy of Francesca Tate, Middle Temple Archivist
38. *The Daily Telegraph*, 8 October 1947
39. World Health Organisation, Poliomyelitis https://www.who.int/en/news-room/fact-sheets/detail/poliomyelitis
40. University of Oxford, Vaccine Knowledge, Polio (Poliomyelitis) https://vk.ovg.ox.ac.uk/polio#Key-disease-facts
41. *The Daily Telegraph*, 14t and 15 October 1947, pages 10 & 6
42. *The Times* (London), 18 October 1947
43. *Kelly's Handbook to the Titled, Landed and Official Classes*, 1960, p.1595
44. Internet Movie Database (IMDB) https://www.imdb.com/name/nm0681043
45. *The Times* (London), 1 August 1986
46. Probate courtesy of Norma Williamson
47. *The Times* (London), 6 October 1947

48. 'The Captain's Daughter, Helen Melville Russell-Cooke' by John Pladdys, *The Titanic Commutator*, Volume 17, Number 2, 2nd Quarter, August – October 1993

Chapter Twelve: Leafield Life

1. Advertisement, *The Sunday Times*, 2 April 1944
2. Cotswolds https://www.cotswolds.com/plan-your-trip/towns-and-villages/leafield-p2082513
3. HistoricEnglandhttps://historicengland.org.uk/listing/the-list/list-entry/1053457
4. Local history of Leafield – https://leafieldparishcouncil.org/the-parish/parish-history/
5. From the 1970s Oxford student the late Ted Gorton, posted on *Encyclopedia Titanic* (https://www.encyclopedia-titanica.org/community/threads/helen-russell-cooke.8577/#post-369336).
6. Dawn Redwood, Metasequoia glyptostroboides Taxodiaceae (Redwood family), Cambridge University Botanic Garden, https://www.botanic.cam.ac.uk/the-garden/gardens-plantings/trees/dawn-redwood/
7. 'The Captain's Daughter, Helen Melville Russell-Cooke' by John Pladdys, *The Titanic Commutator*, Volume 17, Number 2, 2nd Quarter, August – October 1993
8. Ibid.
9. *Dublin Evening Mail*, 8 May 1953
10. Christie's Online auction 21044, July 2022, 'Five Private Collections, Lots 179, 224–227, https://onlineonly.christies.com/s/five-private-collections/
11. 'Britannic repairs speeded', *The New York Times*. 22 November 1953. p. 239
12. *The Times* (London), 21 November 1953
13. 'Memories of the Olympic,' by Walter Lord, 1967, *The Titanic Commutator*, Titanic Historical Society,
14. Letter from Walter Lord to Mrs Russell Cooke, 26 June 1955, courtesy of the National Maritime Museum, Greenwich, London, Lord/Maquitty Collection, LMQ/7/1/18
15. 28 August 1953, edition *The Staffordshire Weekly Sentinel*, courtesy of Norma Willamson.
16. *The Staffordshire Weekly Sentinel* photograph, courtesy of Norma Willamson.
17. Genealogical information courtesy of Gary Cooper. There are several family trees on genealogical websites for the midshipman's family, but none presently connect with the established tree of E.J. Smith.
18. *The Times*, 12 April 1956
19. *Staffordshire Sentinel*, 12 April 1956 courtesy of Gary Cooper.
20. The book is most likely *Frogman Extraordinary: The Commander Crabb Case*, by J. Bernard Hutton, 1960
21. *Daily Herald*, 10 June 1960, courtesy of Gary Cooper.
22. It is likely that the book is *Commander Crabb is Alive*, by J. Bernard Hutton, 1968
23. *Staffordshire Sentinel*, 7 February 1994, courtesy of Gary Cooper
24. *Connacht Sentinel*, 12 October 1954
25. National Maritime Museum, Greenwich, London, Lord-MacQuitty Collection, Ref: LMQ/7/1/18
26. Ibid.
27. 'The Captain's Daughter, Helen Melville Russell-Cooke' by John Pladdys, *The Titanic Commutator*, Volume 17, Number 2, 2nd Quarter, August – October 1993
28. *A Night to Remember* by Walter Lord (1955), R & W Holt
29. 'She once stood on bridge of Titanic' – *Middlesex Independent*, W. *London Star*, 13 December 1957, p. 2

30. *A Night to Remember: The Definitive 'Titanic' Film* (British Film Guides) by Jeffrey Richards (2003), I.B. Tauris
31. *Titanic Memories, The Making of A Night to Remember*, by William MacQuitty (2000), National Maritime Museum, p. 20
32. 'The Goofs of A Night To Remember' (1958, Rank Pictures), by Dr Paul Lee http://www.paullee.com/titanic/antr1958goofs.php
33. *The Illustrated London News*, 26 April 1958
34. 'D S Raymond Purdy' https://thepolicememorialtrust.org/ds-raymond-purdy/
35. Memories courtesy of Heather and Christine Blackman.
36. 'The Captain's Daughter, Helen Melville Russell-Cooke' by John Pladdys, *The Titanic Commutator*, Volume 17, Number 2, 2nd Quarter, August – October 1993
37. Auctioned on 22 April 2023 by Henry Aldridge & Son Limited, the pocketknife was listed with the following provenance: 'Capt. Smith's daughter, Mrs. Melville Russell Cooke, to a local friend, Alice Dore, and thence by descent, Christies London 1999'.
38. From the late Ted Gorton and his wife, posted on *Encyclopedia Titanic* (https://www.encyclopedia-titanica.org/community/threads/helen-russell-cooke.8577/#post-369336).
39. *The Daily Mirror*, 22 April 1960, p.17
40. Courtesy of the David Rolt biography, Robert Eagle Fine Art https://www.roberteaglefineart.co.uk/
41. The Hon. John Astor (1923-1987) was the great-great grandson of William Backhouse Astor (1792-1875), who was John Jacob Astor IV's grandfather.
42. 'Meet the crypto evangelist who's going to shoot a movie with Ridley Scott' 12 May 2022, *El Pais*, https://english.elpais.com/economy-and-business/2022-05-12/ethereum-the-movie.html
43. Christie's https://onlineonly.christies.com/s/five-private-collections/david-rolt-1916-1985-177/156869
44. Bellmans Fine Art auctioneers, 'The Anthony & Marietta Coleridge Collection | Worcester Ceramics & Works of Art' 30 August 2022 https://www.bellmans.co.uk/story/bellmans-the-anthony-mariette-coleridge-collection
45. *The Times* (London), 31 March 1966
46. *The Times* (London) 26 September 1967, 18 June 1968, 16 July 1968

Chapter Thirteen: The 'Remarkable Lady'
1. https://titanichistoricalsociety.org/
2. Edward Kamuda https://en.wikipedia.org/wiki/Edward_Kamuda
3. 'The Captain's Daughter, Helen Melville Russell-Cooke' by John Pladdys, *The Titanic Commutator*, Volume 17, Number 2, 2nd Quarter, August – October 1993
4. *The Times* (London), 21 August 1973
5. Christie's https://onlineonly.christies.com/s/five-private-collections/david-rolt-1916-1985-177/156869
6. Bellmans Fine Art auctioneers, 'The Anthony & Marietta Coleridge Collection | Worcester Ceramics & Works of Art' 30 August 2022 https://www.bellmans.co.uk/story/bellmans-the-anthony-mariette-coleridge-collection
7. *The Times* (London), 15 December 1979
8. 'Tribute to Captain Smith's Daughter, Helen Melville Russell-Cooke,' by John Pladdys, *The Titanic Commutator*, Volume 18, Number 1, 1st Quarter – May 1994 to July 1994
9. National Maritime Museum, Greenwich, London, Lord-MacQuitty Collection, Ref: LMQ/7/1/18

Endnotes

10. *The Night Lives On: Thoughts, Theories and Revelations about the Titanic*, by Walter Lord (1986), HarperCollins Publishers
11. BBC Scotland, 'Titanic collection on display,' 12 August 2002, http://news.bbc.co.uk/1/hi/scotland/2186944.stm
12. *Encyclopedia Titanic* discussion forum, 12 May, 2004.
13. For a more detailed discussion of Don Smith's claims and his family tree, see 'Don Smith – Was he really Captain Smith's Great Nephew?' https://www.titanicofficers.com/article_29.html
14. *Master of the Titanic: The Career of Captain Ted Smith*, by Pat Lacey (1996), Book Guild. After some research on Ancestry.co.uk it was established that the connection is through Patricia's mother, Annie Norah Isabel Lacey (née Meadowcroft also known as 'Queenie') who was the daughter of Annie Mary Catherine Harrington, the child of Thyrza Hancock, Captain Smith's half-sister.
15. *Staffordshire Sentinel*, 3 January 1992
16. *Staffordshire Sentinel*, 15 April 1992
17. 'Old Sea Dog Who Sailed into History' *Birmingham Daily Post* 14 March 1998
18. 'Sunken Dreams: Tales of Life and Death from a Night to Remember' People, 16 March 1998, https://people.com/human-interest/110th-anniversary-of-titanic-sinking-tales-of-life-and-death-from-people-archives/
19. *Lichfield Mercury*, 23 July 1998
20. *Birmingham Daily Post*, 17 July 1998
21. ITV 26 February 2013, https://www.itv.com/news/meridian/update/2013-02-26/titanic-ii-in-poor-taste-ship-masters-relative-tells-meridian/
22. Patricia Jeanne Lacey was born in Frome, Somerset, on 2 May 1922 and was married in 1974 to Henry George McLernon. She died in Milton Keynes on 10 May 2016. Thanks to Geoff Whitfield.

Epilogue: The Legacy of Captain Smith

1. Marek Sarb's explanation is contained in a video entitled 'A Conversation with Artist Marek Sarba at the United Theatre in Westerly, RI on February 16, 2023' posted by the J. Russell Jinishian Gallery, https://www.youtube.com/watch?v=baqrrabCW48
2. For a complete analysis of each cinematic, television and musical portrayal: titanicofficers.com under Captain Smith and the section 'Film Portrayals' (https://titanicofficers.com/titanic_01_smith_16.html)
3. For more information on the Titanic Brewery see article on titanicofficers.com

Index

A Night to Remember (film) 347-350, 354
Adler, Julius (New York harbour pilot) 54
Afric (ship) and officers 66, 203, 204
Aherne, Brian (actor) 341, 345
Airwork Flying School 315, 316, 317
Aldridge, Henry and Andrew (auctioneers) 34, 98, 406
Allen, Mr (Public Trustee Office) 236
Anderson, Harry 98
Andrews, Thomas (Harland & Wolff managing director) 115, 116, 117, 153
Angel, Simon (author) 72
Anning, Captain (White Star) 203
Apfeld, Captain Gerhard Christopher 186, 187
Aquitania (ship) 260, 276, 277, 373
Armstrong, Emma 23
Armstrong, John Sinclair 226
Arnold Scheme (United States) 324
Arrowsmith, Rev W. G. 334
Ashdown House preparatory school 322
Aspinall, (Admiralty counsel) 183
Astor, Colonel John Jacob and Lady Astor 98, 122, 123, 211, 221, 352, 406
Athinai (ship) 93, 94
Avro Club Cadet 317
Bagshaw, William 206
Bailhache, Justice 186
Ball, Phil 229
Bamford, Reverend F. J. 243, 244
Barczewski, Stephanie (author) 161
Baring, Sir Godfrey and Lady 276, 303, 322

Barker, Reginald (Assistant Purser) 86
Barker, Thomas (photographer) 86
Barkworth, Algernon 123
Barling, Sir Godfrey (Liberal politician) 274, 276
Bashford, Mary Ann (Bellecroft cook) 255
Batten, Jean 316
Battle of Festubert 246
Baxter, T., Sheriff of Lichfield 227
Beachler, Fred (*Carpathia* passenger) 160
Beaman, John Edward, Flight Sergeant 329, 330
Beaumont, J. C. H. 72
Becker, Ruth 91
Beddart, Dr (St Bartholomew's Hospital) 295
Beesley, Lawrence 68, 82, 83, 88, 89, 92, 111, 152, 169–171, 349
Behe, George (author) 30, 99
Bell, Joseph Chief Engineer 22, 86, 113, 116
Bellecroft house, Isle of Wight 243, 244, 245, 248, 249, 250, 255–257, 264, 265, 274, 285, 289, 290, 307, 313, 316, 321, 322, 336, 356, 395, 404
Benham, Albert 'Ben' 77
Bereford, Lord Charles 227
Beresford, Lord Charles, MP 225
Bird, Vivian (columnist) 225
Birkenhead (ship) 149
Birkhead, May 140
Bishop of Winchester 194
Bishop, Helen 122, 123
Blair, David 74

Index

Blaney, Mr (Bellecroft head gardener) 303, 313
Blewitt, Bob, Lichfield councillor 230
Bloomsbury Group 253, 262
Blunt, Commander W. F. 59, 64, 65
Boer War 28
Bonbright, Mr 226
Bowyer, George W. (harbour pilot) 59, 60, 61, 79, 82, 85, 389
Bowyer, Henry (Mayor) 168, 206, 389
Boxhall, Joseph 19, 86, 95, 97, 101, 104, 106, 109, 112, 114, 115, 117, 118, 119, 126, 127, 134, 135, 166, 168, 173, 178
Brabazon Employment Society 243
Bradford, Minnie 320, 352
Braes, Captain Andrew 184
Brereton, George (also Boden, Brayton or Braden) 152, 153, 159
Brett, Anne 27, 37, 224
Bride, Harold (junior wireless operator) 96, 104, 115, 118, 121, 136, 137, 152
Bristol Beaufighters 326–329
Britannic (ship) 340
British Board of Trade Inquiry into the *Titanic* disaster 175–178
British Commonwealth (Dominion) 272
British Titanic Society 231
Broadbere, Rosina 155
Brookwood Cemetery 245, 302, 311, 312, 356, 357
Brown, Caroline 123
Brown, David (author) 95
Brown, Edith 89, 90, 164
Brown, Edward (steward) 138, 152
Brown, Margaret (Molly) 124
Brown, Mrs (Bellecroft housekeeper) 245
Brown, Thomas and Elizabeth 89, 90
Browne, Francis (photographer) 83, 84
Bruce, Stanley, Australian Prime Minister 272
Bruty, Police Sergeant 295
Bucknall, Henry W. J. 57, 196
Bucknell, Emma 129
Buckton, Oliver (author) 271, 301
Burchell, C. T. D. 291
Burke, William (dining room steward) 126
Burnham, Lord and Lady 352
Burns, Colonel (Conservative-Unionist Party) 249, 250, 269
Butler, Daniel Allen (author) 178
Butt, Major Archibald 97, 99, 135, 150

Calfornian (ship) 96
Cameron, James 230, 231, 297
Campbell, Captain Charles 167
Candee, Helen 123, 124
Cannons, Captain Edwin Galton 185, 187
Capel-Cure and Terry 269
Capen, G. A. 17
Carpathia (ship) 68, 139, 140
Carter, William and Lucile 97
Casement, Roger 247
Casey, Richard (Australia Commonwealth Public Service) 272, 276
Cassebeer, Eleanor Genevieve 92
Cater, Henry (White Star officer) 205, 206, 393
Central Flying School 316, 317, 403
Chamberlain, Austen 248
Chambers, Bertha 124
Chambers, Kate 27
Chambers, Norman 116
Chaplin, Charlie 260
Cheltenham College 245
Cherry, Gladys 122
Chevré, Paul 122, 142
Chitral (ship) 320
Christchurch, New Zealand 22
Christie's (auctioneers) 352, 353, 358
Churchill, Winston 33, 252, 253, 260
Clarke, Captain Arthur Wellesley 176
Clarke, Captain Maurice 82
Clarkson, Flight Lieutenant Christopher 316, 317, 318, 320, 403
Cohen, Gus 349
Coleridge, William Anthony and Marietta Gordillo 34, 352, 353, 358–360
Collins, John (also possibly Charles Collins) 161, 388
Collyer, Charlotte 156
Compton, Mary Eliza 122
Conservative Party 248, 275
Cook, David 29, 235–237
Cook, Julie (author) 106
Cook, Timothy 25, 372
Cooper, Gary (author) 7–9, 18, 32, 33, 47, 78, 106, 139, 164, 222, 224, 366
Crabb, Commander 'Buster' 344
Crawford, Alfred 128
Crosby 20, 22, 25, 26
Crosby, Captain Edward 92
Curry, Florence May 37
Curry, Phillip (White Star Line manager, Southampton) 103, 104

Dahl, Charles 133
Daly, Eugene 345
Daly, Peter Dennis 126
Daniel, Robert Williams 123, 138, 148, 151
Dashwood, Sir John and Lady, John and Sarah 277, 303
Daunt's Rock 35
Davenport, Ernest Harold (Nicholas) 261, 262, 270, 276, 282–285, 290, 296, 298, 299, 300, 303, 312, 398
Davenport-Hines, Richard (author) 172, 249, 252, 258, 268, 300
Davy, Captain George 25
Daw, Ernest George (gunmaker) 295
Deedes, Hermione 335
Deutschland (ship) 94
Diaper, Roy 80
Dick, Albert and Vera 123
Dickens, Charles 267
Dilke, Ashton 241, 308
Dilke, Charles 241, 262
Dilke, Sir Fisher Wentworth and Lady Ethel Lucy 274, 284, 303, 334, 400
Dilke, Sir John Wentworth 334
Dillon, Thomas (engine room trimmer) 110
Dodge, Ruth 143
Dodge, Washington 132, 138
Dominy, George (JP) 195
Dore, Alice 351
Dorking, Edward 136
Douglas, Mahala 135
Douglas-Wiggin, Kate 45
Dowager Countess of Arran 226
Doxrud, Captain H. D. 168, 169
Doyle, Sir Arthur Conan (author) 188–190, 296
Duff Cooper, John and Lady Diana 313
Duff Gordon, Lady 87, 95, 143, 311, 386
Duff Gordon, Sir Cosmo 95, 97, 159, 311
Dutton, Marjorie (Collyer) 349
Eagle, Robert 320
Earheart, Amelia 316
Elliot, Alderman 218
Empress of Britain (ship) 322
English, E. J. 47
Ennis, Barbara 166
Etruria British School 213, 215, 216, 217, 362
Eustis, Elizabeth 132
Evans, Frank (seaman) 126
Evans, Kathleen Alice 239

Evans, Joseph 47
Extra Master certificate 19, 20
Fairfull, Captain John A. 184
Fancy, Ada May Violet 286, 287, 288, 290, 298, 301, 395
First World War 67, 221, 240, 246, 249, 267, 269, 284, 324
Fitzpatrick, Cecil (mess steward) 153
Fleet, Frederick (lookout) 107
Fleming, Ian 267, 271, 293
Forbes, Alistair 321
Frauenthal, Isaac 87, 122
Freseden 352
Fuller, Reverend Wilfrid 223
Futility (book) 24
G. W. Blunt White Library 30, 32
Gallagher, Rose 26
Galloway, David 153
Garland, Madge 313
Geen, Mayor Alderman and Mayoress 207, 215
George, David Lloyd (Prime Minister) 258
Gibbs, Phillip (author) 164
Giidea, Anne 311
Gilbertson, Captain John 239
Gipsy Moth biplane 315, 316, 318
Gittens, Dave 19
Givens, Fanny 52
Gordon, Colonel William Washington 32
Gordon, Rev. Percy 207
Gore, Sir Ralph St G 280
Gorman, Doris 308
Gracie, Colonel Archibald 91, 92, 96, 124, 132, 150, 152, 154, 155, 164
Grieve, Andrew 90
Guggenheim, Benjamin 48
Guggenheim, Peggy 49
Haddock, Captain Herbert 70, 71
Hagan, John (Fireman) 132
Haines, Albert 59, 113
Haisman, David 89, 90
Haisman, Edith 51, 377
Hampton, William M. 212–215
Hancock, Francis (Frank) 30, 32, 33, 46, 61, 62, 64, 66, 76, 168, 178–181, 217
Hancock, Joseph 16, 18, 23, 30
Handy, Cyril (able seaman) 159, 388
Hanley Town Hall memorial 212–216, 220
Hanley, Stoke-on-Trent 16, 38, 206–208, 212–220, 365
Hardy, John (chief steward) 135

Index

Harker, Margaret 'Pattie' 240, 242, 245, 251, 255, 259, 264, 306, 307, 335, 356, 395
Harker, Oswald Allen 'Jasper' (Brigadier) 240, 250, 251, 259, 261, 264, 267, 268, 301, 303, 307, 332, 333, 356
Harrington, James 53, 54, 202, 207, 215, 219, 225
Harrington, Thyrza 22, 28, 207, 225, 362
Harrington, William 23
Harris, Bomber 338
Harris, Frederick (fireman) 159
Harris, René and Henry 99, 135, 136, 384
Harris, Sarah 341, 342
Harrison, Alderman (Lichfield) 224
Harrison, photo artist, Newcastle-under-Lyme 218
Hart, Eva 88, 164, 371, 377
Hart, Henry Martyn 20
Hawke, HMS 59, 60, 61, 62, 64, 79, 83
Hay, John 202
Hayes, Captain Bertram F. 185, 187
Haynes, Alderman (Lichfield) 224
Hays, president of the Grand Trunk Railway 199
Helm, Rev. Francis 302
Hemming, Samuel (lamp trimmer) 121, 138
Hester, Colonel William 65, 196
Heston Aerodrome 315, 316, 318
Hestor, William 208
Hichens, Robert (quartermaster) 108, 117, 121, 124
Hinton Manor 261
Hiorns, John and Wendy 231
Hobson, Valerie 352
Hodder and Stoughton Publishers 34
Hodder Williams, J. E. 34, 201
Hogg, George (able seaman) 156
Holly, F. S. navigator 327, 328
Holt, Richard (Liberal Party politician) 196
Hone, Evie (artist) 340
Horswill, Albert (Able-bodied Seaman) 161
Howell, Sir Walter J. 182
Hoyt, Frederick 73, 150
Hurd, Carlos F. 139, 140, 150, 154
Hurst, Walter (fireman) 155
Imperial Merchant Service Guild 176
Inkpen, Mabel Lucy 37, 224
Inner Temple Gardens 268

Ismay, Joseph Bruce 26, 54, 90, 91, 93, 94, 111, 113, 120, 133, 134, 173, 175
Ismay, Thomas Henry 26
Jenny, the Mascot cat 50
Jerwan, Amin 167
Jessop, Violet 349
Jewell, Archie (lookout) 92
Johnson, Amy 316
Johnson, Ray 230
Johnson, William 'Billy' (sailor) 86, 87, 134
Johnstone, James (first class saloon steward) 115
Jones, Ada 28
Jones, Captain Richard 185
Jones, Councillor (Lichfield) 224
Jones, Edmund 215, 216
Jones, Nora 28
Jones, Thomas 18, 28, 29, 225, 236, 237
Jones, Thomas (able seaman) 128, 129
Jones, William 202
Judd, Charles (fireman) 136
Kamenev, Lev Borisovich 252–259, 271, 302
Kamuda, Edward 354, 355, 361
Kemp, Dr J. F. 140
Kempster, John (Harland & Wolff managing director) 148, 149
Kensington (London) 238, 247, 287, 310, 311, 350, 358
Kenyon, Marion 87, 88, 128, 129
Keynes, John Maynard 247–249, 252, 253, 262, 263, 265, 276, 282, 286, 300–302, 304, 312
King Edward VII 223
King George VI (former Duke of York) 281
King of Spain, Alfonso R. 195
King's Bench Walk, Temple 262, 263, 264, 267, 270, 287, 289, 295, 301, 309, 312, 395, 403
King's College, Cambridge 246, 247, 248
Klein, Luis 98
Krasin, Leonid 254
Krol, Captain (Noordam) 93
Lacey, Pat (author, also Pat McLernon) 15, 237, 359, 362–364, 407
Lanier, Charles 44, 45, 208, 226, 373
Lapland (ship) 168, 169, 178
Latimer, Andrew (Chief Steward) 22, 86
Lawrence, Jack (*Ship News* journalist) 67, 72, 90

Leafield village, Oxfordshire 321, 322, 330, 336, 337, 350, 404
Lee, Dr Paul (author) 348, 385
Lee, Harold H. 142
Leicester Court Hotel (also Strathmore Hotel) 238, 395
Leloup, Commander 83–85
Lemare, Jacques 313
Lengyel, Dr Árpád 139
Lenin, Vladimir 256, 257, 259, 260
Leveson-Gower, Millicent, Duchess of Sutherland 225–227
Liberal party 248, 249, 269, 270, 274–277, 290
Lichfield Council 223, 224, 230, 231
Lichfield, Staffordshire, statue memorial to Captain Smith 221–232, 356, 264
Lightoller, Charles 19, 20, 74, 75, 80, 88, 93, 95, 96, 98, 100, 104, 106, 107, 114, 118, 117, 119, 120, 121, 124–126, 130, 132–134, 155, 164, 167, 168, 330 *Titanic* disaster inquiries 172, 173, 176, 178 autobiography 204, 205
Lightoller, Herbert Brian 331
Lightoller, Sylvia 167, 178, 204, 349
Lindsay, H. 22
Lines, Elizabeth 90, 91, 92
Litvinov, Maxim 259, 263, 302
Longley, Gretchen 142, 143
Longstaff, Councillor (Lichfield) 224
Lopokova, Lydia 262
Lord, Walter (author) 73, 116, 148, 155, 340, 341, 345–347, 360, 361
Lougheed, Mary 338, 351, 355
Lowe, Harold 104, 114, 117, 166, 168, 173, 178, 379
Lusitania, RMS 54, 71, 190
Lycett, Andrew (author) 271, 301
Lyon, Commander Fitzhugh 176
Lyttleton, Christchurch, New Zealand 22
MacGregor, Peter 355
Mackay, Charles (bathroom steward) 116
Mackay-Bennett (ship) 191
MacQuitty, William 347
Madame Tussauds 210, 211
Maioni, Roberta (maid) 130
Mallock, Christian 168, 178
Maltin, Tim (author) 132, 133, 145
Maréchal, Pierre 122
Mariana, Aasaf 145
Marquis of Salisbury 226
Marston, Glenn 67, 68, 69

Martha, Lucy Noël, the Countess of Rothes 129, 130
Martin, John 35
Martin, Rev J. S. 334
Martin, Thomas 37
Master of the Titanic (book) 361–363
Maugé, Paul (restaurant) 116, 121
Maund, Mona 261
Mauretania, RMS 54, 68, 71, 375
Maxwell, John (carpenter) 112
Maynard, Isaac (cook) 152, 154, 163, 164
McElroy, Frankie 92
McElroy, Hugh (Purser) 52, 53, 55, 85, 86, 116, 166, 191
McGann, James (fireman) 137, 151, 158, 159
McGough, George 'Paddy' 156
McKenna, Stephen 264
McLean, Dr William 85
McMicken, Arthur 156
McMillan, D. W. 135, 154
McNeill, Lucy 195
Meissner, Sophie Adelaide Radford de (author) 193
Mellors, William 125, 151
Mersey, Lord Mersey (John Charles Bigham, 1st Viscount Mersey) 176, 178, 181–183, 186
Mesaba (ship) 95
Metropolitan Club, New York 65, 66
MI5, British Security Service 240, 250, 251, 261, 263, 268, 301, 356
Middle Temple 333
Milward, Kevin 38
Minahan, Ida Daisy 99, 100, 379
Monckton, W. T., KC 293
Moody, James 70, 96, 111, 166
More, Kenneth 349
Morgan, Alderman 227
Morgan, Charles (Bellecroft head gardener) and wife Rachel 245, 250, 255
Morgan, J. Pierpont 44, 65, 208, 226
Moscow, Russia 257–259
Moss, Derek and Mary 338, 355
Mullet, J. R., Captain 203, 392
Munsch, Jules 84
Murdoch, Ada 74, 149, 166, 167
Murdoch, William McMaster 19, 50, 55, 74, 75, 79, 80, 83, 84, 93, 95, 100, 106–111, 124, 133, 140, 145, 148, 149, 156, 159, 166, 167, 183

Index

Naismith, Laurence (actor) 347–350
Nash, William A. 208
Nassau Country Club 57
National Maritime Museum 345, 346, 347
National Mutual Life Assurance Society 269, 282, 286, 291, 300, 304
New York near collision 82, 83
Norman, Montagu, Governor of the Bank of England 276
Nye, Elizabeth 161
O.L. Hallenbach (tug) 54
O'Donnell, Mrs 201, 202
O'Loughlin, Dr William 52, 53, 72, 73, 86, 136
Oaksey, Lord 334
Oates, Captain Lawrence 181
Oatley, Joe 285
Olliver, Alfred (quartermaster) 110, 112, 113
Omont, Alfred Fernand 122
On a Sea of Glass (book) 107, 114, 115
Onslow Square 345, 347, 350
Ostby, Helen 93, 115
Oxford University Air Squadron 324
Paddington 11, 240, 284, 299, 309, 311, 340
Paget-Cooke, Oliver 247, 294, 297, 298, 303, 306, 356
Paintin, James Arthur (steward) 64, 84, 151, 169
Pålsson, Alma, Paul, Gösta, Torborg and Stina 162, 163
Parish Church of St Luke, Chelsea 334
Passow, Captain Frederick 185
Patten, Lady Louise 111
Pazio, John 365
Peniz, Dr Willam E. 107
Pennington, Maria Annie 18, 27, 29
Pennington, Sarah 27, 28
Pennington, William 18, 28
Pennyman, Rev. W. O. 266
Perrin, Right Reverend William Wilcox 197, 221, 226
Peuchen, Major Arthur 130, 131
Phillips, Jack (senior wireless operator) 96, 115, 117, 121,136
Philport, Oliver, Flying Officer 328
Phipps, John Arneal Constantine 331–335
Phipps, Nicholas 333, 335
Phipps, Oswald Constantine John 331

Phipps, Sir Edmund 333, 334
Piles, Jonathan (author) 297
Pinewood Studios 347
Pirrie, Lord 153
Pitman, Frederick Archibald Hugo 293, 301
Pitman, Herbert 114, 120, 166, 168, 173, 178
Pitman, Hugo 298, 301
Pladdys, John 16, 34, 338, 339, 351, 358, 359, 404
Podola, Guenther 350
Poingdestre, John (Able Seaman) 122
Polio (poliomyelitis) 334
Portman, Brigadier Guy Maurice Berkeley 332
Post Office Rifles 246, 247, 296
Potter, Alex (author) 250
Potteries Museum & Art Gallery 366
Pratts House, Leafield 321, 323, 330, 337–339, 355, 359, 360
Prince Maurice of Battenberg 269
Princess Beatrice, Henry of Battenberg 241, 243, 269
Priscilla I and *Priscilla II* (yacht) 278–280, 285, 307
Pritchard, Captain John 184, 187
Profumo, John 352
Prowse, Keith 244
Pryal, Peter 191, 192
Pytchley Hunt Ball 280, 282, 292, 351
Queen Alexandra 224, 226
Queens Gate Gardens 238, 262, 264, 267, 309, 310, 395
Raby, Councillor (Lichfield) 223
Radcliffe Infirmary, Oxford 355
RAF 144 Squadron 326, 327, 328
RAF Wick Coastal Command 326–329
Ranson, Captain John 185
Ray, Frederick Dent (saloon steward) 151
Reform Club 260
Reuterdahl, Henry (artist) 158, 160
Reuters 102, 146
Richards, Emily 98
Richards, Jeffrey (author) 348
Rigel, Newfoundland dog 50
Riggs, George 202
Rinder, Captain J. H. 203
Robert, Elizabeth and Georgette 135, 154
Roberts, Captain 186, 187
Robertson, Morgan 24, 372
Robinson, (Chief Officer of the *Euryalus*) 204

Robinson, Annie (stewardess) 115, 116
Rodes, Toby 307
Rolt, David (artist) 320–323, 331, 338–340, 352, 358, 359
Rooke, Mary Jowitt 18
Roskill, Ashton 308
Roskill, John and Sybil 251, 265, 303, 307, 308
Roskill, Stephen 308
Ross, C. L. 199
Roston, Captain Arthur 140
Rostron, Arthur (Captain) 20, 60, 119, 148, 152, 156, 170, 171
Rowe & Pitman 252, 271, 272, 276, 282, 284, 293, 297, 299–301, 303
Rowe, George (Rowe & Pitman) 272
Rowe, Quartermaster George 127, 128, 133–135, 154, 232
Royal Mail postal workers 112, 113
Royal Naval Reserve 20
Rule, Samuel (bathroom steward) 116, 155, 206
Runcorn 28, 236
Runnymede Air Forces Memorial 330
Russell Cooke (née Smith), Helen Melville 28, 76, 306, 307 Alexandra Road 24, 25 Animals 33, 34 Art 275, 282, 339 Birth 14, 24 David Rolt 320 Death 355– 57 Dogs 51, 324, 331 First marriage myth 239, 240 Gardening 275, 312, 313, 338 Hunting 280, 282 Lichfield statue 221, 224, 225, 227 Loss of father 105, 106 Marine Crescent 25, 26, 27 Marriage (Sidney) 262, 298, 395 Name (origin) 15 Pilot 315– 19 Politics 274, 277, 278, 282 Sidney's death 289, 290, 293, 295 *Titanic*'s bridge 73, 74 Yachting 279, 280
Russell Cooke, Margaret Mary (Smith, Dilke) 240–245, 308, 356, 400
Russell Cooke, Priscilla 269, 274, 277, 278, 285, 290, 306, 313, 322, 330–335
Russell Cooke, Sidney 240, 241, 242, 245 Books 270–273, 276 Death 287–304 Education 245, 246 First World War 246, 247, 291 Funeral 302 Keynes 247–249 Marriage (Melville) 262–267, 395 Nervous breakdown 283, 284 Politics 249, 250, 274, 275 Spying 251–261, 268, 271 Stockbroker 241, 268, 269, 273,

289 Will and estate 306 Yachting 278–280, 284, 285, 292
Russell Cooke, Simon 269, 274, 277, 285, 290, 306, 322, 323–330, 332
Russell Cooke, William 240–243, 356, 395
Ryan, Thomas and Patrick (Ryan v. OSNC) 186
Salmond, Captain Robert 149
Sanderson, Harold 65
Sarba, Marek (artist) 365, 407
Sargent, John (artist) 242, 243, 357
Saunders, Rev. S. T. H. 303
Savannah, Georgia 30
Scott, Captain Robert Falcon and Lady Kathleen 224
SeaCity Museum 49, 212
Sealby, Inman (Captain) 65, 167
Seaman Church Institute 208, 209
Seamen's Orphanage for Boys of Southampton 222
Seeds, Sheila 334
Seely, Lady 285
Sefton Council 26, 27
Senate Inquiry into the *Titanic* sinking 171–175
Sengstacke, Frieda 97
Senior, Harry (fireman) 133, 138, 148, 158, 161, 162, 164
Seton, Ernest Thompson 226
Shackleton, Sir Ernest 186
Shaw, George Bernard 188, 189, 260
Shelley, Imanita 96, 172
Sheppard, Jack 300
Sheridan, Clare 251–261, 263, 301
Sherman, George 200, 201
Sherratt, Tim 273
Shirley, Jesse 219
Simpson, First Officer (*Afric*) 204
Sinclair, John J. 196, 208
Skidelsky, Robert 297
Sloan, Mary 128
Sloane, William L. 208
Smith, Donald J. A. 362
Smith, Catherine 22, 28
Smith, Clinch 132
Smith, Donald 344, 345, 361, 362, 364, 407
Smith, Edward John *Adriatic* 42, 43, 48, 51, 52, 53, 341, 373 Bad luck 65 *Baltic* 17, 20, 29–36, 48, 93, 94, 95, 171, 340, 351 Bellecroft 244 Birth 16, 38 Board of Trade certificates

Index

17, 19, 20 *Britannic* 20, 22, 370, 371 *Celtic* 17 Cigars 48, 52, 98, 346, 360 Commodore 44 *Coptic* 17, 22, 377 Cricket 22 *Cufic* 20 Death 150–164 Dogs 48–50 Film footage 57 *Germanic* 28 Insurance/probate 235, 236 *Lizzie Fennell* 17, 32, 33, 202 *Majestic* 14, 23, 25, 28, 32, 36 Marriage 18, 19 Medals 28 Melville birth 14 *Olympic* 47, 53–69 Print collection 45 *Republic* 17, 18, 149 Retirement 62, 64, 70, 71 Salary 44 *Senator Weber* 16, 22, 30 Ship building 43 Stevengraph 28, 29 Suicide rumours 139–150 *Titanic* 60, 61, 62, 64, 70 *Titanic* cabin 78, 79 *Titanic* captain's table 87, 88 *Titanic* coal bunker fire 82 *Titanic* drinking rumours 98, 99 *Titanic* final words 136–139 *Titanic* ice reports 93–97 *Titanic* last dinner 97 *Titanic* lifeboat shortage 67, 68, 69 *Titanic* sinking – inspection 115–117 *Titanic* sinking (first orders) 117–123 *Titanic* sinking, loading lifeboats 123–136 *Titanic* sinking response 110–114 *Titanic* uniform 78 Uneventful life 42, 43 Unsinkable 61, 64, 374, 375 White Star Line 17 Young sailor 16

Smith, Jago (postal clerk) 112
Smith, John (Salt Lake City, Utah) 194
Smith, John E. 239
Smith, Lancelot Hugh ('Lancey') 271, 284, 299
Smith, Lucian and Mary Eloise 131
Smith, Lucian and Mary 98
Smith, Margaret 123
Smith, Robert 311
Smith, Sarah Eleanor 14, 15, 20, 21, 23, 28, 29, 37, 64, 66, 76, 73, 194, 208, 212, 215, 216, 221 Death 309–312, 354 Frank Hancock (letter) 178–181 Grief 234, 235 Lichfield statue 221, 224, 226–228 Marriage 18, 19 Melville's marriage 262–264 St George's Day 206, 311 *Titanic* disaster reaction 102–104, 106, 109, 166 Woodhead 18
Smith, Senator William Alden 171–176
Smith, Ted, Head of Tourism, Stoke 230
Smith, William Henry 343, 344
Smith, William Russell (midshipman) 342–345

Snow, Eustace (trimmer) 138
Somers Place 309, 317, 320, 340
Southampton 36, 212, 235, 311
Southampton City archives 40
Spencer, Carl 231
St Helen's Bishopsgate 303
St Mark's Church, Shelton, Hanley 206
St Mark's, Mayfair 240, 251, 264, 267,
St Michael & All Angels Church 330, 337, 359
St Oswald's Church, Winwick 18, 19
St Paul's Church, Isle of Wight 244, 245, 250, 251, 269
St George's Day Memorial 206
St Martin-in-the-Fields 333
St Mary's Church, Southampton 194
Stalin, Joseph 261, 302
Steele, Captain Benjamin 82, 185
Stengel, Charles 98, 116
Stengel, Henry 172
Stephenson, Martha 132
Stevenson, Francis Seymour 197, 266
Stewart, Captain William 184
Stone, Martha 130
Strathmore Hotel 238, 395
Stuart, Sir Campbell 265, 267
Studley-Herbert, Nina Caroline (Countess of Seafield) 277, 282
Suffragette movement 241
Svensson, Johan Cervin 140, 142
Swalm, Albert W. (American Consul) 234, 235
Swift, Mabel 229
Swift, Margaret 128
Tagus, RMSP 85
Taussig, Tillie 131
Taylor, Elmer 97
Taylor, Thomas Alvin 29
Teacher, R.M. 307
Temple Church 268
Thallon, John 226
Thayer, John 'Jack' 155, 158, 164
Thayer, John and Marian 97, 98, 99
Thayer, Marian 115
The Boy's Own Paper 42, 43
The Man Who Sank the Titanic? (book) 366
Theissinger, Alfred (steward) 116
Thie, Helen 23
Thiriat, Paul (artist) 141, 148
Thompson, J. W. 29
Thompson, Piers Gilchrist (Liberal candidate) 269, 270

Thomson, David 202
Threlfall, Thomas 138
Tilford, Surrey 315, 316
Till, Spencer 216, 218, 238
Titanic (1953 film) 341
Titanic Brewery 38, 365, 407
Titanic Captain: The Life of Edward John Smith (book) 224, 365
Titanic Heritage Trust 231
Titanic Historical Society 354, 358, 359
Titanic Memorial Lighhtouse 209
Titanic Relief Fund 168, 206, 208, 236
Titanic wreck position 119
Törnquist, William (Seaman) 86, 87, 134
Torquay 249, 250, 269, 274, 306
Trestrail, Major (Labour candidate) 249, 250
Trinity House (Corporation) 231
Trotsky, Leon 256, 259, 260, 302
Turner, Captain William T. 190
Turner, Joseph 149, 217, 218
Van Derhoef, Wyckoff 73, 376
Wade, Wyn Craig (author) 139, 171
Wagner, R. V. 17
Waldo, Dr F. J. 293
Walker, George 33
War Office Intelligence Department 247
Ward, William (saloon steward) 133
Warfield, Dr Mactier 192
Warr, Captain 186, 187
Warrington (Winwick) 19, 23, 220
Waterloo, Liverpool 14, 20, 23, 25, 26
Wave Commander, RFA 343
Webb, G. R. 22
Wedgwood, Cecil 218, 219
Weikman, Augustus (ship's barber) 153
Well Street, Hanley 38, 217, 362, 365
Wennerström, August 162
Westerman, Dr A. 294, 295

Westminster Abbey 352
'Whispering Smith' ('Silent Smith') 193
White, Alfred (greaser) 137
Whiteley, Thomas (saloon steward) 98, 160
Whitford, Edith 199
Widener, George and Eleanor 97–99, 151, 152
Wiggin, Kate Douglas (author) 200
Wilcox, Ella Wheeler (author) 234, 235
Wilcox, Mike 230
Wilcox, Reverend Dr Pete (Lichfield Cathedral) 231
Wilde, Henry 19, 67, 74, 75, 77, 80, 113, 114, 120, 126, 132–134, 142, 155, 166, 183, 236
Wilkinson, Norman 80
Williams, Annie Jones 166
Williams, Charles Eugene 159
Williams, Fletcher Lambert 97
Williams, Owen 225
Williams, Richard Norris 144, 145
Willis, Mr. and Mrs. W. P. 69, 149
Winchester College 322, 323, 330, 333
Winn Road (Southampton) 36–39, 105, 392
Winterton, H. J. C., Mayor of Lichfield 221, 222
Woodhead (Southampton) 35–39, 73, 105, 224, 236, 309
Woodman, H. Rea 200
Woolf, Virginia 252, 253, 263
Worthington, A. O. 227
Wright, Andrew 231
Wynn, William (quartermaster) 116, 160
Yeats, Jack Butler (artist) 339
Young, Captain Hugh 184
Young, Marie 122, 128, 139